Common Lands, Common People

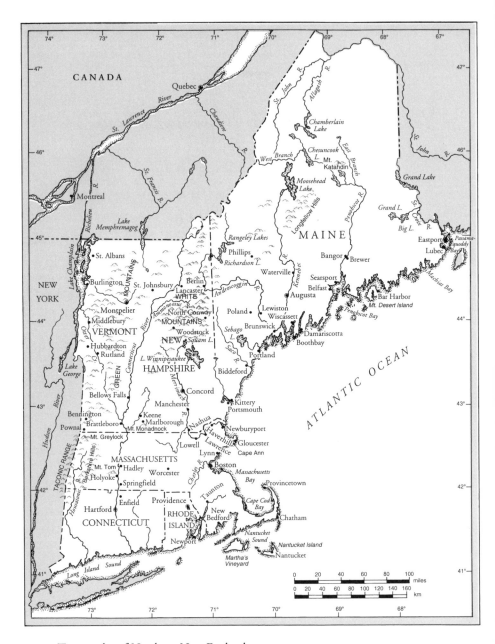

Topography of Northern New England

Richard W. Judd

―――

Common Lands, Common People

THE ORIGINS OF
CONSERVATION IN NORTHERN
NEW ENGLAND

Harvard University Press   Cambridge, Massachusetts   London, England   1997

Library of Congress Cataloging-in-Publication Data

Judd, Richard William.
Common lands, common people : the origin of conservation in northern
New England / Richard W. Judd.
p. cm.
Includes index.
ISBN 0-674-14581-X (alk. paper)
1. Conservation of natural resources—New England—History.
2. Fishery conservation—New England—History.
3. Natural resources, Communal—New England—Management—History.
4. Commons—New England—Management—History.
I. Title.
S932.N44J83 1997
333.7'2'0974—dc21
96-46635
CIP

For Lily,
who reminds me to keep history in perspective

CONTENTS

Preface   xi

Introduction   I

Foundations   13
1 The Northeastern Frontier   15
2 The Commons in Transition   40

Common Lands   57
3 Nature in the New Agrarian Landscape   59
4 Common Stewardship and Private Forests   90

Common Waters   121
5 Conflicting Rights in Fisheries   123
6 The Politics of Interstate Fisheries   146
7 Forging a Conservation Ethic   173

Rural Traditions in the Progressive Era   195
8 The Romantic Landscapes of Tourism   197
9 Tradition and Science in the Coastal Fisheries   229

Conclusion   263

Notes   269

Index   329

ILLUSTRATIONS

Settler's clearing, Norway, Maine	14
The progress of pioneering land-clearing	26
View from West Paris, Maine	33
Deer hunting	48
Pickerel fishing	54
Farmscape perceptions	58
Hunting or timber-cruising party, Rangeley Lakes	113
Goose Creek, Maine	122
Cooperative fishing	126
Camden, Maine	138
Fish ponds	152
Fishway, Lawrence, Massachusetts	162
Fish hatchery, Roxbury, Vermont	171
Rural fishing	179
Cog railway, Mount Washington	196
Sporting party, Rangeley Lakes	207
McKellog family, Vermont	215
Hunter and guide, Rangeley Lakes	221
Small-time fishers, Kennebunkport	232
Seining from a brush weir, Eastport, Maine	242
Boathouses and lobstering gear, Cape Ann, Massachusetts	251

Maps

Topography of Northern New England   *frontispiece*

The Maine coast   134

Buzzards Bay, Massachusetts   235

Growing up in rural northern Michigan in the 1950s, my brother, sister, and I acquired an abiding affection for a familiar landscape that we perceived as unsullied and whole. The arrangement of farms, fields, and villages, the long-abandoned pastures and orchards, carved in random shapes from the woods, seemed to us altogether natural; perches atop lofty sentinel trees revealed a lush forest stretching from horizon to horizon. The land was a trove of childhood curiosities, the hunting of which gave us an intimate knowledge of every corner of our world. This was a land of limitless imaginative possibilities.

It did not occur to me until later that it was also the heart of Michigan's historic cutover. Pioneer logging and farm clearing left northern Michigan a landscape of charred stumps, exhausted soils, and clogged and sedimented waters—the great national object lesson for those who later campaigned to conserve America's remaining forests. Yet to live in an age that had healed over many of these scars was to impute a certain stability—almost immutability—to this very land-scape. This to us was nature—shaped to human needs, but nature nonetheless—and it was the way we wanted the land to be.

Generally, environmental historians posit a different landscape ideal. Primeval nature, if not a "climax" ecology, has become the benchmark against which human impacts on the land are judged. Because this primeval landscape had long since disappeared in the East by the time Americans began discussing conservation policy as a nation, historical interest in this question has gravitated to the West. My own upbring-ing suggests that stable, peopled landscapes commanded loyalties as intense as those that formed the basis of concern for western lands. Focusing on northern New England, this book describes the allegiance these eastern landscapes inspired and the conservation struggles they generated.

My interest in this topic crystallized while I was traveling in rural northern Maine between 1980 and 1985. Time and again I encountered something akin to what Aldo Leopold called a land ethic among people like Irene and Pete Sawyer of Ashland, who considered themselves stewards of the farm they had inherited and would pass on. This sensitivity derived from a lifetime of working the land. My encounter with the Sawyers and others suggested something that should have been obvious: second- or third-generation families, working their own soils, developed powerful attachments to a familiar landscape and to the natural dynamics that sustained it. This popular ethic was neither uniformly conservationist nor anticonservationist, as we define these terms today, but it was indeed a force to be reckoned with. In nineteenth-century New England, this land ethic absorbed a complicated mix of Christian theology, practical wisdom, economic incentive, and secondhand natural history. It inspired a penetrating search for the regularities and harmonies of nature, and it gave local land-use practices a definably moral cast.

This book explores the local cultures of resource use in northern New England. It illustrates the symbolic power of these patterns of use and describes their evolution within changing social and economic parameters. In so doing it aims to provoke a more serious evaluation of land-use philosophies, to explore the grass-roots cultures of American conservation thought, and to lead today's environmental strategists and resource managers to a stronger appreciation for the way land is perceived locally. Though not always in concert with scientific doctrine, this popular consciousness offers a wonderful fund of opportunity and insight for those working with environmental law and policy. To ignore this perception, to wave it aside in the battle to protect the environment, or to expect people living on the land simply to acquiesce in the scientific goals of the national environmental movement, is to court disaster.

Although the language of this book is nontechnical, a few locational terms may warrant some explanation. First, by including rural Massachusetts in this study I have defined "northern" New England rather broadly. For my purposes, however, this grouping makes sense. Vermont, New Hampshire, and Maine were closely linked to Massachusetts by early political events and demographic patterns. More important, the four states share a common natural legacy: similar forests, soils, wildlife, mountain and river systems, and, in the case of Maine and Massachusetts, similar coastlines. Together they form a distinct bioregion. Thus, including Massachusetts among the northern New England states is geographically unbalanced but culturally and biologically accurate.

Second, Maine's coastal axis, which shifts slightly to the eastward between the Kennebec and Penobscot Rivers, gives the state an "eastern" coast and a "southern" coast but no western or northern counterparts. In Maine's complicated geographic vernacular, one ranges "down" the coast by moving northeastward, toward New Brunswick, a reference to a coasting vessel's downwind run from Boston to Maine—with perhaps an allusion to frontier Maine's place in Boston's moral geography.

This book leaves me indebted to many individuals and institutions. Graduate training at the University of California at Irvine two decades ago awakened me to the importance of viewing history from the bottom up. My mentors, Spencer C. Olin and Stanley Aronowitz, encouraged this perspective. My initial immersion in environmental history came while I was working at the Forest History Society under the patient and able guidance of Ron Fahl, Pete Steen, and Mary Beth Johnson. Long discussions with Dick Davis, then compiling his *Encyclopedia of North American Forest and Conservation History*, stimulated my interest in this field. David Smith at the University of Maine introduced me to new ways of thinking about New England. My wife, Pat, has been a constant companion in this intellectual journey.

In connection with research for this book, I am indebted to the staffs of the Massachusetts State Archives, the Maine State Archives, the New Hampshire Records Management and Archives, and the office of the Vermont State Archivist for digging out petitions, remonstrances, and other documents and for their unfailing good humor in indulging my many false leads. Vermont State Archivist Gregory Sanborn, who started me down the trail of legislative records, was especially generous. The staff at the Appalachian Mountain Club provided me access to their library, and those at the Forest History Society combed their ample collections for material essential to the chapter on forestry. People at the state libraries in Montpelier, Augusta, and Concord and the special collections departments at the University of Massachusetts at Amherst, the University of New Hampshire, the University of Vermont, and the University of Maine were equally helpful. Muriel Sanford, Mel Johnson, and Bill Cook were unrelenting in searching out obscure information necessary for a fuller interpretation of events. Dick Hale, emeritus professor of forest management at the University of Maine, and Robert Babcock of the Department of History took an interest in this project over the years and gave me valuable comments on portions of the manuscript. Pete Steen, Tom Cox, and John Reiger labored through other sections, offering insights that improved the analysis. Conversations with Bill TeBrake started me down paths I might otherwise not have noticed. Tom Dunlap gave me several pene-trating and much-valued critical appraisals of the entire manuscript. Michael Fisher at Harvard University Press offered much-needed en-couragement and guidance. I owe them all a great deal. Any errors that remain are, of course, my own.

Earlier versions of material in several chapters were published in the *Journal of Forest History, Business History Review,* and *Environmental History Review* in 1988.

Common Lands, Common People

Introduction

———

On a fall evening in 1835 a farmer in Winslow, Maine, sat down to compose a letter to the editor of the *Maine Farmer.* Having apparently no other purpose in mind than to express an ebullient satisfaction with life in this upper Kennebec River town, he described impressions of a previous afternoon spent boating on the river. The setting, familiar since childhood, seemed particularly poignant on that beautiful fall day as the farmer drifted on the still waters. Extending back from the riverbank into the rolling hills beyond Winslow was a succession of fields and meadows, giving way at the horizon to a mixed forest of spruce, pine, and hardwood, a "perfect picture of rural happiness." Trees along the banks drooped thick foliage into quiet waters; fishermen in light canoes plied their nets, "and every now and then a shoal of herring would come dancing by, throwing their silvery bodies glancing in the sun." As night crept on, the correspondent remembered, "naught interrupted the universal stillness of Nature . . . save the distant roar of the waterfall, and the occasional splash of the fish hawk, as he dove after his finny prey." The moment left an enduring impression: "The clear blue of the sky was reflected so distinctly, that the boat we were in, seemed suspended between two heavens, with clouds above and below it."

Like the small boat, the landscape itself was suspended between two worlds: an aboriginal past belonging to a race "now almost totally disappeared from the face of the earth" and a future, equally mystifying, shaped by the compulsions of distant markets and the quickening pace of commerce. "Will the time come," the writer mused,

> when these beautiful banks will be deformed by wharves, by docks, by mills and by a thousand other means of spoiling Nature

and improving Art, which man is continually inventing? Will these places, which are covered with green fields, with pleasant woods and fertile farms, be usurped by dusty streets and be covered with the abodes of man? These changes may take place, and probably will in this growing country, and Nature, driven from this her most lovely abode, will be compelled to seek places more remote, where she may remain undisturbed.[1]

A half-century later pioneer Vermont conservationist Joseph Battell expressed similar fears that an ordained landscape—farm, village, and nature—would succumb to commercial forces originating outside the region. The source of his concern was a bill before the state legislature giving the Fall Mountain Paper Company rights to alter the White River for log driving. Generations of Vermont farmers had complained that log driving damaged their intervale meadows, but Battell saw the issue in broader perspective. He questioned the company's right to disrupt the landscape by clear-cutting the mountain forests. "This mighty rib of old forests that runs through our State is by far the most beautiful bit of scenery that we have preserved," he argued. The matter was of "deep interest to every citizen of Vermont."[2]

Although popular attitudes toward nature and landscape changed a great deal between 1835 and 1891, the Winslow farmer and Joseph Battell had at least three things in common: a concern for a landscape caught in the throes of change, a moral assumption about the balance of natural and cultural elements in this changing landscape, and a strong pride in place that bonded the people to the land and legitimized their prescriptions for its common stewardship. It would be difficult to say what segment of the broader public shared this moralistic and localistic perspective in 1835, but by 1891 these themes had surfaced in a variety of struggles over land and resources in northern New England.

Assessing the origins and meaning of the conservation movement has been one of the great quests of American historians. In 1957 J. Leonard Bates, influenced by prevailing assumptions about Progressive reformers as middle-class opponents of monopoly power, characterized the era's conservation movement as an attempt to wrest America's natural resources from the hands of rapacious and individualistic vested interests. For Bates, conservation became the crucible in which Progressive-era Americans forged a new concept of democracy based on social justice, national welfare, and a broader sharing of the nation's natural wealth. Two years later Samuel P. Hays opened his now-classic *Conservation and the Gospel of Efficiency* with the assertion that conservation "neither arose from a broad popular outcry, nor centered its fire primarily upon the private corporation."[3] Challenging Bates's claim that the conservation movement was the "fulfillment of American democracy," Hays pointed to the much narrower scientific, professional, and bureaucratic concerns that inspired the movement's leadership. Those who guided America's first great crusade to conserve its natural resources repeatedly set aside democratic goals when they conflicted with concerns for efficiency and scientific wisdom. Interestingly, neither Bates, who highlighted the democratic implications of conservation, nor Hays, who revealed its elitist origins, gave much attention to its popular constituency.

In the nearly four decades since *Conservation and the Gospel of Efficiency* was published, its central thesis—that the conservation movement was essentially elitist in composition—has remained unchallenged. Historians since have explored the intellectual, artistic, recreational, and aesthetic sources of conservation thought, but none has suggested that the movement drew from the wells of popular imagination. Donald Pisani, for instance, has argued persuasively that those who spoke out for conservation after 1864 were intellectual elites and scientists. Similarly, Jim O'Brien has maintained that "the conservation movement . . . was in large part the product of new wealth generated by the growth of American capitalism." Roderick Nash and Max Oelschlaeger have traced the evolving view of nature among America's most articulate groups. Philip Shabecoff, whose popularized account of the conservation movement synthesizes the best of recent literature, asserts that the first calls for nature's protection came from "the scholars, poets, philosophers, scientists, writers, painters, clerics, and even the politicians of the settled, increasingly urbanized East."[4]

During these same years the emerging field of environmental history has enriched research on conservation with new methodological approaches. Probing the natural world and its own history with tools borrowed from ecology, climatology, and other disciplines, environmental historians have uncovered a compelling facet of history heretofore unfathomed: a complex of natural ecosystems organized according to their own laws and principles and operating in dialectical union with human development. Recently William Cronon summarized two decades of method-building in this new field: environmental history is the "story of human beings working with changing tools to transform the resources of the land, struggling over how that land should be owned and understood, and defining their notions of political and cultural community, all within a context of shifting environmental and economic constraints."[5]

Environmental historians have become increasingly sensitive to the natural world. At the same time, however, they have slighted equally significant discoveries in the "new" social history pertaining to inarticulate peoples—in this case, the ordinary rural folk who used and manipulated the natural world that is the stuff of environmental history. A few recent studies have explored facets of this popular consciousness, notably Carolyn Merchant's *Ecological Revolutions,* which describes traditional folk perceptions of nature and its mysteries; and Theodore Steinberg's *Nature Incorporated,* which discusses local responses to industrial use of the Merrimack River.[6] But generally when historians treat the relation between society and environment, they portray the human actors in this landscape as an undifferentiated mass caught between two irresistible forces: ecological changes, with their manifold implications for society; and elite political or intellectual developments aimed at countering certain adverse effects of these changes.[7] This book challenges environmental historians to look more closely at the people who used these resources and, in the second half of the nineteenth century, pondered their conservation.

Understanding the complicated relation between folk thinking, ecological change, and conservation trends is best accomplished through a regional approach, in this instance an area of common culture and landscape comprising the rural sections of Maine, Vermont, New Hampshire, and Massachusetts, where a coherent popular political culture can be discerned and where common patterns in land form and land use can be identified. Here the wellsprings of conservation thought flowed at least as vigorously as they did at the national level, and here we see the sources of rising conservation consciousness in bold relief.

Northern New England is informative because its natural landscape was remade several times over after the European arrival, and because important resources remained in the hands of petty producers.[8] The region also exhibits a strikingly varied resource base. Vast forests on the northern Appalachian plateau, productive inshore fisheries, thousands of miles of coastline, and an immense lake, river, and estuary system generated a full range of conservation issues. This varied landscape, viewed according to a widely held set of cultural expectations, gave nature an interesting standing in regional politics. This book looks at the region as a biologically and culturally cohesive unit and, not incidentally, an area that pioneered a number of conservation ideas for the rest of the nation.

Conserving nature, of course, was far from the minds of the first Euro-Americans in New England. "For the early New England farmers," Hugh M. Raup wrote, "the forested wilderness was an impersonal, physical barrier to be tamed and exploited to the hilt."[9] Students of New England history have been treated to several incisive studies of the manner in which this mentality transfigured the land under the pressures of commercial capitalism and rationalism. But studies like William Cronon's *Changes in the Land,* Merchant's *Ecological Revolutions,* and Steinberg's *Nature Incorporated* see New England primarily as an object lesson in the destruction of nature.[10] If New Englanders led the nation in this regard, they also pioneered the momentous transformations in thinking that laid the basis for sustained-yield management.

This book addresses the local and popular roots of conservation thinking in northern New England. The documents used to trace this line of popular thought include second-generation accounts of pioneering settlement, speeches before local farm clubs, editorial correspondence in the rural press, and petitions and remonstrances sent to state legislators by rural constituents. While these are not always a direct expression of the "inarticulate," they were penned by individuals in intimate contact with friends, neighbors, and kin who made up common classes and groups of rural petty producers.

Current perspectives on these grass-roots ideas are conditioned by our understanding of later Progressive-era conservation debates. In positing a general social context for the conservation movement, historians assume a crude dualism in attitudes toward nature. Roderick Nash expressed this as a love-hate relation to wilderness; others see it as a contest between democracy and monopoly, amateur and professional, utilitarian and aesthete, or conservationist and preservationist.[11] This volume suggests a more complicated set of traditions embedded in the evolving social order of rural New England. Like most folk traditions, it is far more inclusive, eclectic, and contradictory than the carefully refined logic expressed by elite, official, or scientific conservationists. Thus it is difficult to compartmentalize into a single current of thought leading up to the Progressive-era conservation movement. Rather, these traditions should be understood in the context of a dynamic and conflictive rural society, in which the lines between utilitarian and aesthete, amateur and professional, conservationist and preservationist occasionally blur.

Issues relating to land and resources were important to New Englanders because they were central to the region's livelihood. Economic life, Edward C. Kirkland noted in a study of early Vermont, "is a relationship between resources on the one hand and people, including their needs, abilities and social institutions, on the other."[12] But this relationship was moral as well as economic. Debates over natural resources gained their conviction from popular suppositions about properly ordered landscapes and accepted rights of access to nature. To be sure, early conservation was less a movement than a complex of discrete struggles over different resources, but each was grounded in a common set of assumptions—such as those expressed by the Winslow farmer and Joseph Battell. Diffuse and contradictory though they were, these moral concerns were fundamental to the evolving concept of land and resource stewardship. The manner in which they were adapted to various purposes, suppressed, and reinvented is a crucial part of the story of American conservation.

In northern New England these moral assumptions were, broadly stated, a belief in democratic access to, and common stewardship of, the land; an aggressive approach to reshaping nature to serve human needs; and a pietistic, perfectionist vision of the balance of cultural and natural features in the evolving landscape. These beliefs differ in scope and logic from the idea of conservation as it emerged in the Progressive era, but they were the foundation upon which early New Englanders redressed their relation to nature.

Concepts of resource management first entered the American consciousness through colonial town ordinances regulating use of common and undivided fields, meadows, swamps, marshes, and streams. As early as 1641 the Massachusetts Bay Colony established the principle of open access to bodies of fresh water ten acres or more in size. This so-called Great Pond Ordinance guaranteed all citizens the right to fish, fowl, or hunt on lands public or private.[13] Local ordinances echoed this commitment to egalitarian access, but they defined the community of users more selectively and regulated access more carefully. Primitive and localistic as they were, these local common resource regimes established two central principles for the emerging New England conservation tradition: communities bore collective responsibility for managing their resources in a productive fashion, and they were to allocate these resources equitably. In 1993 Donald Worster wrote that conservation thinking at the end of the century expressed an effort to "define and assert . . . some idea of a public interest transcending the wants and desires of a strictly individualistic calculus."[14] In fact this new American commons—this call for common stewardship—has deep roots in northern New England soil.

As the first section of this book makes clear, the moral landscape composed by the New England farmer provided an early foundation for conservation. Chapter 1 describes the essential relation between republican ideology and land use during the initial migration into upland New England. Pioneering New Englanders built their new agrarian republic on the ruins of the natural landscape, but their sons and daughters initiated the nation's first attempts to restore what George Perkins Marsh called the "disturbed harmonies of nature."[15] Chapter 2 describes the numerous experiments with replenishing New England lakes and ponds with fish. To protect their fish, villagers refashioned the doctrine of the commons; their experiments in natural and social law adapted the principles of equitable access and common stewardship to a more individualistic age.

The second section surveys northern New England's common lands. Chapter 3 delineates the moral universe of the midcentury farmer, particularly a faith in common stewardship, an aggressive anthropocentrism, and the concept of an ordained landscape. Forced by economic and environmental changes to reevaluate traditional farm practices, regional agricultural leaders articulated these assumptions as the basis for farmland and forest conservation. Unlike their contemporaries the Romantic naturalists, farm reformers were interested in using nature, not saving it. Primeval nature was an unfinished landscape to be molded to a higher form of utility. Their admonitions were predicated on a view of nature as an infinitely malleable adjunct to the farm economy. In this light, reformers provided a foundation for the strain of conservation ideas later personified by Gifford Pinchot, who argued for a more efficient and rationalized use of natural resources.

Yet like the Romantics, farmers interpreted their reforms as a spiritual quest, a search for the ordained harmony between human and natural forces. In this perfectionist scheme, nature, if not animate, reflected divine purpose. The farmer's endeavor to restore these harmonics helped popularize what Donald Worster has identified as a prescientific model of ecology: an integrated, hierarchical order in which nature was an expression of God's kindness toward humankind. Unlike the Romantics, however, farm reformers remained unabashedly imperialist in their use of nature; their spiritual understanding served their commercial instincts.[16] Indeed, the two conflicting strains in American conservation thought—utilitarian and Romantic—have roots in this popular culture of resource use.

Chapter 4 describes the confluence of this agrarian land stewardship and a newer, urban-based, Romantic strain of nature appreciation. The closing of the frontier, the belief in the uplifting benefits of natural beauty and outdoor life, and the expansion of tourism in upland New England created a Romantic landscape image that blended with traditional moral concerns to lay the basis for forest conservation in northern New England.

The third section surveys popular assumptions about common waters. Chapter 5 describes the democratic, community-based traditions of access to the coastal fisheries in Maine. In the 1830s and 1840s these local cultures of resource use clashed with new social forces requiring open access, individual rather than community use, and industrial control over water resources. Conflicts over dams and fisheries, irresolvable at the local level, gave rise to the New England state fisheries commissions in the 1860s, the first government agencies in the United States specifically devoted to resource conservation. Chapter 6 describes the origins of these fisheries commissions and their changing mission. The agencies failed to implement an ambitious interstate management program for New England's migratory river fisheries, but, as Chapter 7 shows, they did create a biological, legal, and ethical foundation for recreational fishing in inland waters. Struggling to legitimate their new authority, these fledgling agencies created and implemented a modern conservation code, still within the traditional framework of shared community responsibility, aggressive utilitarian use, and democratic access.

The final section focuses on the role of these traditional cultures in the Progressive-era conservation movement. Chapter 8 describes the interplay of agrarian attitudes toward fish and game and newer, urban-based, recreational and Romantic ideals. That these two visions of the landscape were not always compatible was especially apparent in the conflict over deer management. Chapter 9 discusses three turn-of-the-century coastal fisheries. Here science, rather than recreational or Romantic ideals, played the key role in shaping a Progressive conservation message, but again public policy remained in good part committed to traditional, localistic cultures.

It is true that the nation's most notable conservation achievements—the first forest preserves, water conservation projects, and national parks, for instance—occurred in the West. It is also true that these grand crusades were spearheaded by men and women of prominence. Most of them were easterners, a fact that reinforced the conviction that conservation was a theoretical construct imposed by prominent outsiders on local land-users. The more subtle, perhaps more complicated debates over eastern landscapes and resources suggest that local people, struggling to define or redefine their relation to the land, also contributed heavily to America's conservation legacy. The key ideas that guided this movement gained vitality at a grass-roots level, in consonance with the real experiences, desires, and dreams of people and classes in conflict in local situations.

There are elements of both Bates and Hays in this analysis. Progressive-era conservation was indeed guided by urban and scientific authorities. But ordinary rural people were thinking about conservation too, and their republican ideology was an important ingredient in the conservation movement. Whether one views elite voices as the inspiration for popular thought or merely as agents that refined the logic of prevailing popular consciousness, it is important to explore the relation between conservation's grass roots and its leadership.

Appreciation for the harmonies of nature, no less than the reflex to pillage the land, is ingrained in American rural tradition. We need not celebrate this moral vision of landscape, but we must acknowledge it as a reality if public policy is to work. In some regards this tradition carried a logic far removed from that of official policy, but its core ingredient—common stewardship of lands and waters—has been a significant catalyst in conservation thinking. Early on, Americans made their pact with private ownership and use of the nation's resources, but the popular legacy of democratic, common stewardship has been and remains a powerful force in shaping our land-use decisions. Without it the idea of conservation as we know it is simply impossible.

These popular traditions—common stewardship, aggressive anthropocentrism, and reverence for nature—constitute the tangled thicket of social forces that stands between elite, scientific formulations and public conservation policy. As any resource management specialist today knows, there is no simple correlation between pure science and the politics of conservation. Analyzing these local attachments to the land reveals the degree to which they have been incorporated into state-level conservation strategies. In an era of renewed debate over questions of federalism in resource regulation, this insight into local cultures seems particularly important.

Conservation was a social movement. It could hardly be otherwise, New York's forest commissioners reasoned in 1885: "A forest law to effect its purpose must rest on a broad and solid basis of public interest."[17] Beyond the matter of popular political legitimacy, however, these ideas, grounded in the experiences, traditions, and compulsions of nineteenth-century rural America, gave the movement inspiration and direction. Today, when so much of our environmental policy is hammered out by international environmental organizations in legal combat with international corporations, it is important to remember that environmental thought receives its power less from scientific or legal accuracy than from the way it resonates with popular social impulses. Conservation has its origins in the clash of everyday observation and dogged traditionalism on one hand, and wrenching changes in the social and natural landscape on the other. It is a grass-roots phenomenon.

Foundations

A settler's clearing in Norway, Maine, ca. 1830. Debris from the original landscape remained in gardens, pastures, fields, and woodlots. Typically, settlers like the farmer behind the plow (left center) tilled among stumps. (Charles F. Whitman, *A History of Norway, Maine* [Norway, 1924])

CHAPTER ONE

The Northeastern Frontier

As late as 1763, after a century and a half of Euro-American activity along the North Atlantic coast, the vast inland territory north of Massachusetts Bay remained only sparsely settled. Northward migration, circumscribed by poor transportation and by the strength of Native American resistance, began in earnest at the conclusion of the French and Indian War. In the brief interlude between the fall of New France and the beginning of the American Revolution, this frontier advanced rapidly eastward to Maine's Machias River and inland up the major river valleys. Cheap land, productive alluvial soils, thick timber, abundant fish and wildlife, and good water power drew thousands of families northward.[1] By 1800 entire stretches of river bottomlands had been cleared, and fences, pastures, fields, and roads were becoming conspicuous in the southern sections of this region.[2]

Yet even as the frontier drama drew to a close in one locale, it opened farther upriver—in northern New Hampshire and Vermont, western Massachusetts, and last in Maine's remote northern and eastern borderlands.[3] Felling and burning the forest, uprooting stumps, dragging off boulders, leveling the land, eliminating incompatible wildlife species, and introducing new crops and livestock, these third-generation New England pioneers initiated the changes that would transform the region's environment in the nineteenth century.[4]

Distinctive migration paths from sections and towns farther south created a mosaic of microcultures in this frontier region.[5] Migrating in groups, settlers reconstructed the forms of religion, land use, and building styles they brought from their places of origin. Still, as Frederick Jackson Turner pointed out a century ago, the pioneering process blurred these cultural distinctions. A traveler in 1789 generalized about the monotony of life in northern Vermont: "The people [have] nothing to eat, to drink or wear—all work, and yet the women quiet, serene, peaceable, contented . . . Tough are they, brawny their limbs . . . Woods make people . . . kind and obliging and good natured. They set much more by one another than in the old settlements . . . Sleep quietly amid fleas, bedbugs, dirt and rags."[6] But as the impress of earlier generations grew less distinct, local variations based on environmental adaptations emerged. New England is a land of astounding ecological variety, and the emerging cultural mosaic conformed to different economic prospects embedded in this landscape.

Agricultural prospects were brightest in the alluvial bottomlands along the region's larger rivers. The soils of these "intervales," periodically renewed by floods, produced luxuriant crops of grass, grain, or corn. Rising up behind the intervales are large "plains," gently elevated benches and hills composed of loam impregnated with sand, clay, or gravel. In divisions ordered by the contours of the land itself, farms extended back into these rolling terraces or up transverse valleys of glacial till and alluvial silt to the rugged hills several miles back from the river. The extent to which the land was tilled depended on these natural conditions, along with proximity to a market and the optimism that individual families brought to the region. As a rule the soils were poor, but the region offered some surprisingly fertile land, namely the rolling country between the lower Kennebec and Penobscot Rivers, the limestone-rich loams of Maine's northeastern border, the lower slopes of the Green and White Mountains, the Champlain Valley, and the alluvial banks along all the larger rivers.[7]

The dominant constraint on agriculture was the terrain. Early arrivals chose rich intervale lands, but in successive waves newcomers cleared the hilly country farther back from the rivers. Many in fact preferred the ridge and hilltop locations: difficult hauling over hilly country paths did not weigh heavily upon farmers in an era of localized economic activity. Nor did the broken, boulder-strewn fields seem disadvantageous to those who worked mostly with hand tools. The uplands were better drained, and the forests of beech, oak, and maple were considered indicators of rich soil. These hardwoods were in fact easier to clear than the thick lowland stands of spruce, cedar, and tamarack, and they made better fuel, charcoal, and potash. The elevated south slopes warmed quickly in the spring, adding a few crucial days to the growing season.[8] The point at which these receding slopes became mountainous defined the horizon of the settlements; here the rich soils of the valley bottom and the thinner clays of the uplands gave way to rock or hardpan, and croplands gave way to orchards, pastures, and finally forests.

The Green and White Mountains, the Berkshires, and western Maine's submountainous Longfellow Hills thus defined the geographic bounds of profitable agriculture. Along this northern Appalachian plateau, the land is broken and debris-littered; thin soils barely cover the scars left by the advance of the glaciers. It is, as Ira Allen recognized as early as 1798, best suited to serve humankind as "reservoirs of water to supply the adjacent hills and country." New Hampshire's Coos County, north of this mountain system, is a hilly, rolling plateau blanketed with glacial till and dotted with ponds, meadows, and swamps resting in the basins of former drift-dammed lakes. Settlements spawned in the pockets of tillable soil were isolated by expanses of hard, unproductive land.[9] South of the White Mountains a succession of moderate hills gradually gives way to a level, fertile coastal plain. Vermont's Green Mountains extend down the middle of the state, covering a territory ten to twenty miles wide. The gentle lower slopes of this divide offered proportionately more farmland than either New Hampshire or Maine. Still, as one scholar put it, "the people who occupied such a country were destined for the most part to a side-hill life with its attendant material handicaps and spiritual discipline."[10]

Maine's rugged western boundary follows a line of high hills associated with the northern terminus of the Appalachian Mountains. North of Katahdin, the state's highest peak, the plateau inclines gently northward and eastward, drained by the St. John, Allagash, and Aroostook Rivers. Seaward, the western mountains give way to a broad, fertile valley that extends through the central part of the state. This wide basin, some of Maine's best farmland, is separated from the coast by a range of low, noncontiguous hills.[11]

Off this northern Appalachian plateau fall all the great rivers of the region. New England's largest, the Connecticut, begins in a series of small lakes nestled in northern New Hampshire's swampy tablelands. Farther south, the Connecticut Valley's slate and calcareous soils fostered some of the finest agriculture in the region, and at one time the river's drop of some 2,500 feet from headwaters to the sea supplied power to more than two thousand mills.[12] The Merrimack, a "swift and impetuous" river springing from the rocky slopes of the Presidential and Franconia ranges and from Lake Winnipesaukee, powered the looms of Manchester, Lowell, and Lawrence.[13] Other rivers originating in the White Mountains share characteristics with the Merrimack: their numerous feeder streams descend in stepped cataracts through steep mountain canyons and wander across benches of stony glacial drift. Emerging from the lower slopes, they rush down constricted channels flanked by terraced alluvial benches tillable sometimes a mile back on either side.[14] Natural water storage in the glacial gravels, in the granitic soils, in the spongy moss and deep humus of the low areas, and in the numerous ponds, bogs, and lakes on the northern plateau kept even the smaller streams flowing throughout the summer. But early farmers probably considered these saturated soils more a curse than a blessing. Like the stony ridges that bounded them, the damp, cold lowlands afforded risky prospects for agriculture.[15]

Another constituent of the natural mosaic was soil composition. The depth of this mantle changes with elevation and gradient, but there are other variables as well. The bedrock of New England is granitic gneiss, and occasionally limestone that sweetens the soil and encourages a more productive agriculture. Yet much of the region's overburden was laid down by glacial action and bears little relation to the bedrock. Soil patterns were further complicated by deposition of alluvial materials or by sedimentary deposits left in ancient swamp, lake, and stream beds. Even the high valleys occasionally harbor rich soils and level ground, the result of accumulated sediments in post-glacial lakes and ponds.[16] Different locales, as an early geologist explained to a gathering of farmers, were "differently top-dressed as it were, some with a thin layer of soil, some with a deep one, and some with none at all."[17]

Soil quality depends not only on bedrock, glacial deposition, and alluvial action but also on the reinforcing qualities of the vegetation it supports. Cooler, humid microclimates produce a predominantly coniferous forest, which in turn creates acidic soils; warmer areas support deciduous trees and sweeter soils. Under pristine conditions, soils reinforce other aspects of an ecosystem, but this balance is never static, even under virgin conditions.[18]

Pioneer families encountered a forest cover as varied as the soils that nurtured it. In northern and more elevated sections, this consisted primarily of spruce, fir, and northern hardwoods, although pine grew in old clearings, burn paths, and on alluvial benches. South of the Green and White Mountains and through central and southern Maine, white pine and hemlock mixed with oak, elm, butternut, hickory, chestnut, ash, and basswood. These two forest regions were markedly different to the eye. "Those who form their notions of the forests from the Southern portion of New England," a correspondent to the *Yankee Farmer* wrote in 1835, "have but a poor idea of the . . . vast wilderness in the upper part of Maine." Sojourners in this thick northern woods traveled "in perpetual gloom" in damp, mossy, still forests where thick canopy discouraged all but the most shade-tolerant undergrowth.[19] Yet even the thick spruce-fir forests manifested a shifting pattern of openings caused by ice and wind storms, fires, eutrophic lakes, or beaver flowage. Clearings in various stages of recolonization enriched the habitat for wildlife.[20]

This same natural diversity encouraged a wide range of fish species. Confusion over local names and widespread transplanting beginning in the 1820s cloud the natural history of fish, but their abundance is universally attested. Swift, clear brooks, shaded meadow creeks, and small lakes hosted trout; deep, clear lakes harbored trout or pike; and warm, shallow waters, pickerel and horned pout.[21] Springtime brought salmon, shad, alewives, smelt, sturgeon, and striped bass upriver.

The ecological context for upland settlement was not static. In fact changes in this environment could be sudden. An 1832 petition to the New Hampshire legislature conveys the settlers' acquaintance with the terrible energy of the lower Ammonoosuc River: "It sweeps along its channel with irresistible fury & spreads out with a rapid current over large portions of the adjacent intervale lands, carrying along with it whatever may happen to be borne upon its surface." Plunging water, masses of ice and timber, and rolling boulders altered the narrow mountain valleys, uprooting and undermining trees, scouring out earth, and depositing new land where the current abated below.[22] In August 1826 the Wiley family perished in a landslide triggered by a tempest in the White Mountains, leaving behind a legend still powerful in the region. During the same storm the upper Saco River rose twenty-four feet, sweeping the intervales clear of bridges, sawmills, houses, and barns for twenty miles.[23] In such scenes settlers were never the actors; they were spectators, even victims, of the natural landscape. Yet as Jeremy Belknap pointed out, for all their destructive force these floods carried down from the upper region a "fat slime . . . which renews and fertilizes the soil." They also delivered a handy supply of driftwood, "from which the inhabitants of the lower towns . . . are supplied with fuel, and they have learned to be extremely dexterous in towing on shore whole trees with their branches."[24]

The land bore the impress of these forces. Excavators uncovered tangles of trees and logs buried by some earlier cataclysm. "The great depth in which these ancient trees were found buried . . . clearly illustrates the immense changes that have taken place in the valley of the stream."[25] Rivers altered their courses, making and destroying lands; ancient channels became ponds and later were overgrown with weeds, sedges, and trees. Describing the alluvial outwash from Otter Creek, early historian Frederick Hall observed that this "made land" was composed of "different kinds of earth, thrown up, in different places," suggesting to him the wax and wane of currents and the varied flowage patterns of the river.[26] These winding paths could be traced across dry meadows. "Could we know the history of these intervals," another town historian mused, "how they were formed in the course of long ages, the record would be more interesting than anything we can say about its human inhabitants."[27]

Residents in Hubbardton, near Rutland, Vermont, discovered the remains of an entire forest grove buried in a local swamp under several feet of earth. Ira Allen reported that an acquaintance had found a similar bed of logs at a depth of twenty-four feet while digging a well in intervale land. In the logs were about thirty frogs, "so apparently petrified that it was difficult to distinguish them from so many small stones." Exposed to the "vivifying beams of the sun," the frogs "leaped away with as much animation as if they had never lain in their subterraneous prison." From the timber growing near the well, Allen judged the frogs to have been in the earth for six hundred years, buried by "some convulsion of nature." More credulous than most, Allen nevertheless imparts the early settlers' sensitivity to the dynamic natural forces shaping their land.[28]

To early colonizers, these alterations suggested mysterious forces perpetually at work on the land. Fires created "singular appearances" and times of "great obscuration" in the skies. Explorers found evidence of falling rock and earth that swept mountain slopes clear of vegetation, coming to rest at times "so distant from the base, that they could not have rolled thither but in some convulsion of the earth." Jeremy Belknap recorded examples of remarkable weather change—"anomalous instances of inequality and sudden transformation."[29] Settlers' understanding of natural cycles and ecological relations remains ill defined, but clearly they viewed nature as unstable, unsettled, and in need of human domination to make its energies productive.[30]

Early arrivals found other signs of natural change. Throughout the region they struggled against what historian Carolyn Merchant has called the "explosive regenerative power" of New England vegetation. Indeed, the biota of some areas was probably changing appreciably as it rebounded from the influence of periodic fires set earlier by Indians.[31]

Salisbury, New Hampshire, townspeople found rotted stumps of wal-
nut trees in the area when they arrived, but no living specimens. Black
cherry, used for household furniture, disappeared a few decades later,
and carpenters were forced to rely on butternut. Beech and other
nut-bearing species seemed to early settlers to be growing scarce,
affecting the manner in which hogs were foraged.[32]

Settlers discovered a diverse and dynamic natural landscape as they
edged into the northeastern frontier in the 1760s. The energies flowing
through this forest ecosystem diffused and reconcentrated according to
complicated overlapping cycles, disrupted occasionally by some "convulsion of nature."[33] Opportunistic survival strategies molded local
pioneer cultures to this variety and to the natural flux and flow of the
land. Lives were ordered into intervals of sumptuousness and famine,
exhaustive labor and enforced lassitude, as settlers learned to appropriate nature's accumulated sources of energy.

Beaver, for instance, had been eliminated before the settlers arrived,
but their enriching impact on the land was still noticeable. Dead and
decaying trees standing in their impoundments created nesting sites
for birds; the still waters behind the dams offered habitat for fish and
wildfowl, and the new growth in drained ponds and surrounding areas
denuded by beaver provided browse for wildlife and domestic livestock.[34] The highly organic soils of these beaver "meadows," planted
to English grasses, produced luxuriantly. Settlers responded to the
ecological succession in these beaver lands. Some mined thick deposits
of dried pond muck for fuel. The first residents in Lancaster, New
Hampshire, established farms on the "splendid meadow-lands" cleared
by previous generations of beaver. The waters backed behind a beaver
dam powered their first gristmill.[35] In 1795 a pioneer family cut wild
hay in a beaver meadow in Andover, New Hampshire. The soils
sprouted a growth of white pine, and this too was harvested between
1845 and 1860. Shortly afterward millwrights built a dam on the site
of the original beaver dams. The pond, a historian concluded, "now
covers about the same area as in the days of the skillful beaver."[36]

The landscape that settlers encountered was perpetually in transition, shaped by fire, flood, weather, and more mysterious processes. Perceiving themselves as agents in this transformation, the new occupants adapted to the dynamic natural forces about them and at the same time wrenched the land in the direction of their own vision of purpose and beauty. The changes they wrought were more sudden and more sweeping than those already at work, but here, too, land and culture, as historian Donald Worster has noted, were engaged in "an ongoing ecological dialectic."[37]

Forging an Agrarian Republic

In the 1820s the Brigham family moved to Bakersfield, in northwestern Vermont, cleared about twenty acres, and built a comfortable house and a barn. Within a decade they could boast a yearly output of 40 bushels of wheat, 65 bushels of corn, 200 bushels of potatoes, and about 50 pounds of flax—"Enough to support My Family and Some to Sell," according to patriarch Uriah Brigham. "Idlness we are strangers to,—we persevere in industry and the strectest econimy [and] by that means we live well and clear of debt."[38] Uriah Brigham's stark ruminations upon his family, their accomplishments, and their freedoms encapsulate many of the values northern New Englanders held to, and the means by which they hoped to create a new agrarian republic in this wilderness.

If common motives could be ascribed to the thousands of families that traded the exhausted soils of southern New England for the dense forest environment of the north, they would probably cluster around the quest for secure yeoman status: economic independence as small, freehold farmers. Historians have traced the constricting trends operating on older New England towns—diminished crop yields, rising land prices, declining average landholdings—thus illuminating the demographic and ecological pressures working to expand New England's frontier after 1763.[39]

Dread of tenancy and love of autonomy were the givens of New England frontier expansion, but the hunger for large tracts of raw land expressed important communal aspirations as well. Challenging the common assumption that this expansion was driven by individual acquisitiveness, Patricia J. Tracy has argued that frontier landholdings provided only minimal prospects for individual betterment. Most families migrated to ensure a patrimony for the sons; frontier land was a means of keeping families together. The historian of Hubbardton put these motives simply: "Mr. Samuel Churchill, having a large family, wished (as is very natural) to settle them around him. He sold his farm in Sheffield, Mass., estimated at $3,000, and took a deed of 3,000 acres of land in the town of Hubbardton, Rutland County, State of Vermont." Frontier migrants could deed adjacent lands—even if marginal—to their sons. Patriarchal control was assured, families remained intact, and the elder generation kept offspring nearby to care for them in old age.[40]

Migrants brought with them not only family but often also neighbors or coreligionists, thereby perpetuating community bonds and ensuring that the basic components of local society—church, courts, schools, roads—would be quickly reestablished. These overlapping attachments also facilitated the cooperative activity necessary to frontier life.[41] To the north, up the great river valleys, migrants envisioned a more democratic society, where landownership would buttress traditional family and community values. These modest goals—autonomy, family cohesion, community—carried significant ideological weight. "The yeoman farmer," Tamara Plakins Thornton wrote, "was the guarantor of public virtue and, thus, of the continuance of the republic."[42]

For a generation or perhaps two, this agrarian ideal seemed attainable. Much of this northern land fell into the hands of wealthy merchant-speculators, but the undeniable limitations of climate, soils, and labor scarcity and the absence of an obvious export staple dictated small-scale family production. The relative ease with which pioneer families acquired land and appropriated family labor, according to Percy Wells Bidwell, "was one of the principal causes of the prevailing equality in the distribution of wealth" in the region.[43] Still, the land was not free, and credit was dear. The strategies for capital accumulation employed by these colonizers, the ways in which they realized the yeoman ideal, are central to understanding their relation to the land.

In many cases, family endowments or the sale of property in older sections of New England underwrote the pioneering process. Capital demands were further eased by the "make-do" approach of pioneer farming, by cooperative efforts and neighborhood barter, and by the exchange of promissory notes from or to local merchants or lumber operators. Farmers had lumber sawn or grain milled on "halves" at local mills—taking half the product for their own use—and wheat, shingles, and other nonperishables were used as exchange media in the cash-poor region. Farms adjacent to lumbering districts enjoyed a dependable market for winter labor and for produce. Working across the labor-scarce frontier, a young man could acquire the means to buy and clear 100 acres in a new town after one or two years. Early arrivals also profited from selling surplus land to newcomers.[44]

For most families with limited capital, yeoman status also depended on transforming the pristine environment into consumables and commodities on a scale possible only during one dramatic pioneering moment. Land-extensive long-fallow farming, the strategy by which the Brighams and thousands of others eased into modest yeoman status, was a diversified, shifting form of agriculture conducted with primitive tools, little fertilizing, and only the barest of capital improvements. It depended on modest yields from large fields and a rapid cycle of soil exhaustion and forest-fallowing.[45] The process centered upon felling and burning trees and reaping the benefit of virgin soils. Elastic demand for potash, made from the resulting ashes, helped boost families through the difficult early stages of pioneering. On new lands enriched by ashes, they raised a few cattle, planted grains and vegetables among the stumps, roots, and boulders, and thought little about sustaining this modest yield.[46] Although the area cleared by first-generation settlers was relatively small, the process itself, by standards of only a few years later, was wasteful.[47] Liquidating this forest wealth also encouraged population densities higher than those the soil alone could sustain, leaving frontier settlements inherently unstable.[48]

This series, "Four stages in the Life of a Green Mountain Boy," demonstrates the progress of pioneering land-clearing and, in the fourth scene, the cumulative impact of many such small endeavors. (Photos by A. F. Styles, courtesy of Special Collections, University of Vermont)

Wheat, sown in virgin soil, was crucial to this strategy. One of the few crops that could be marketed easily out of the region, wheat stored well and held its value over long trips to market. The crop, however, brought rapid changes in soil chemistry, speeding the process of exhaustion. A light sprinkling of grass seed then transformed the field to pasture, and eventually perhaps it reverted to brush or forest. The fallowed soils regained their fertility, as one account had it, "in the natural way."[49] Meanwhile the family cleared a new patch of forest and planted in the ash-strewn ground. The transition from forest to field to pasture continued until the farm accommodated an optimum number of livestock for subsistence and sale. Promising fields remained in tillage.[50]

Extensive farming was an adaptation to land abundance and labor and capital scarcity, a choice born of necessity in a cash-poor region where the forest seemed so limitless and so intimidating. Nevertheless, it was an uneven foundation for this agrarian republic. In some places the land yielded sufficient returns to permit a slow transition to more sustainable agriculture. In others, extensive farming was the beginning of a long downward spiral that eventually ended in outmigration.

Early New England settlers were forced to come to terms with two seemingly contradictory features of this landscape. Thin soils, broken topography, unpredictable climate, and geographic isolation set narrow parameters for agriculture. At the same time, the natural abundance in the great woods, the waters, and the coastal ecosystems tempted settlers away from the farm into a rich common pool of wild resources. While families like the Brighams struggled to achieve a secure subsistence and a small cash crop, their well-being depended, to a greater or lesser degree, on forage activity, a practice not easily ciphered from account books and census returns, but well represented in local histories and reminiscences.

Even in areas long settled, the arena for forage activity remained extensive. Hugh M. Raup's study of Petersham, Massachusetts, indicates that after forty years of settlement, farmers had cleared only about 10 percent of the land, and forest clearing proceeded at the same slow

28

rate over the next twenty years.[51] Families extended their survival strategies into the great woods beyond the farm to resources that were considered, by common consent or legal right, the property of the community at large.

Settlers were by necessity opportunistic in this rich and changing landscape.[52] They supplemented their few acres of crops, sown amid the debris of the original landscape, "by any means they could invent." When crop yields were poor they foraged as much as they farmed. Even in normal times the sustenance scratched from the soil could be severe—a monotonous round of bean or pea porridge, pumpkin, corn-and-rye bread, and salted or dried meats.[53] But after the obligatory listing of "the privations of the early settlers," local histories commonly point to the wealth of edibles derived from woods and stream. "Meats of all kinds were eaten more freely one hundred years ago than now," one explained. "Wild game such as bears, deer, turkeys and small game was plenty, so that it required but little effort to supply a small family." Janna Churchill eked out his first year in Hubbardton on clams, a mud turtle, woodchucks, "et cetera."[54]

Settlers assumed the right of trespass to this rich provisioning ground. Deeds to coastal lands sometimes specified town rights-of-way for gathering salt hay, muck, seaweed, driftwood, clams, lobster, or fish.[55] Settlers harvested frost grapes on intervale lands to use as a condiment, and native hops growing along streams flavored beer and sometimes served as mattress ticking. Wild plum and chokecherry were "not rejected by any until after the cultivated fruit trees had commenced to bear." Butternuts, hazelnuts, and sweet acorns "helped to beguile and relieve many a long winter evening." Berries of all sorts were dried, jellied, or used for puddings, pies, or flavoring in spirits.[56]

More important were sources of wild meat. Pigeons, grouse, ducks, geese, and shorebirds were hunted for subsistence and market, along with moose, deer, bear, raccoons, squirrels, and in hard times even woodpeckers, gulls, plovers, and porcupines. Hunting was an important seasonal event, coming after the fall harvest when game was full-fleshed and thickly furred. Early snows reflected light in the woods and made tracking easier, and crisp weather insured against spoilage. In some cases hunting was a simple foray into the nearby woods when the family was short on meat or needed cash. For the midwinter "long hunt," farmers loaded provisions and muskets on hand-drawn "moose-sleds" and trekked for weeks in the deep woods.[57]

Women foraged for herbs, flowers, seeds, leaves, or roots to use in medicines, lotions, and dyes. Seeking out these necessary ingredients of family health and comfort required knowledge of various local plants, their habitats, properties, and preparation, and the proper season for gathering them. Witch hazel bark, mixed with alcohol, became an astringent or lotion. Hops cured sleeplessness and relieved toothache; catnip quieted infants; juniper buds and sarsaparilla root were used for lung trouble; burdock helped infants with teething. Women made tonics from sassafras, beer from spruce twigs, dyes from various barks and husks, and vinegar from yellow-birch sap.[58]

Homesteads clustered at constricted points in the rivers, where migratory salmon and shad could be caught. Preserving a barrel of salmon each spring was so common that Connecticut River families who neglected this task were "subject to some degree of condemna-tion or reproach among their more prudent neighbors."[59] Settlers also stocked their larders with pickerel or trout "pitched" from the spawning beds with forks or caught through the ice. Swamps, frequently left undivided as common land, supplied cedar for fencing and shingle stock, oak for lime casks and barrels, and tamarack for bracing. While most building timber came from the farm woodlot, special types of wood for tools, fencing, household items, and handicrafts might be foraged from the unoccupied forests beyond.[60]

In 1761 the town of Andover, New Hampshire, hired Joseph Fellows and his team of oxen to clear a road from the town line to a local pond. Electing to settle there in the woods, Fellows trapped beaver in the town's "Great Meadows" and used the pelts to buy a cow. Draining the beaver pond produced sufficient wild grass to keep both his oxen and his cow through the winter. "The grass on the natural or so-called 'wild' meadows was considered common property until the owners of those tracts arrived to claim their rights," Andover's chronicler explained.[61] The path that led Joseph Fellows from wage work to yeoman status was traveled by many. Taken together, their experiences reflect an important truth: families without much capital or credit could indeed prevail on the northeastern frontier. Common access to undeveloped lands compensated for poor market structures, harsh climate, and capital shortages. These forage rights gave the region's much-lauded republican image a basis in reality—as long as the original ecosystem held out.[62] Using the wild resources torn from this virgin land, migrants found the opportunity to act out, one more time, the founding of the agrarian republic. Yet by the second generation, these resources lay in ruins.

The most dramatic consequence was the decline in wildlife population.[63] Settlers baited deer with salt, hounded them, or ran them down on the crusted snow and cut their throats. Hunting was not a sport but "a grim and deadly necessity, and anything went."[64] Predator destruction, combined with intermittent forest clearing, may have boosted deer populations initially, but by the 1840s they were scarce through most of the region.[65] Moose disappeared except in northern Maine and northern New Hampshire.[66] Settlers netted entire flocks of birds and schools of fish, pillaged nesting and spawning sites, dismantled beaver dams, eliminated predators, and trapped fur-bearing animals to local extinction. Mast-bearing oaks, beech, and butternut were reduced, depleting food supplies for birds and wildlife. Fish were taken on their spawning beds by hook, snare, net, line, or poison. Some were intoxicated by bran soaked in *cocculus indicus*.[67] Vermont prohibited the use of "giant [powder], blasting or gunpowder, or other explosive material" to catch fish, but the law suggests more about the ubiquity of this technique than it does about the lawmakers' resolve to quash it.[68] Pioneer families used their waters as they used their soils, mining the richness until the labor necessary to extract further value outweighed the declining benefits. Then they began anew in a slightly less convenient location.[69]

To a degree seldom recognized, these resources sustained the initial pioneering thrust into the upper Northeast. But the costs to the landscape were enormous. Into an area that had earlier supported perhaps 5,000 Indians, wrote a historian of New Hampshire, "had come 184,000 [Euro-Americans]. At first this rapidly increasing population had lived, with few modifications, in the manner of the original occupants, and so long as game lasted they made use of it."[70]

The loss of virgin-soil fertility proceeded almost as quickly. Wheat production, curtailed by rust, western competition, and soil exhaustion, gave way in the 1830s to pastoralism.[71] In some areas sheep raising was a necessary culmination of long-fallow farming; sheep alone thrived on the coarse, thin grasses of the abandoned grain and hay fields. Pastoralism helped shift the material basis for the agrarian republic. Large flocks crowded out subsistence crops and encouraged market-dependent production. Because sheep raising could be optimized on larger landholdings, even under the confining family labor system, it encouraged land consolidation and altered the distribution of wealth and property.[72] It also further taxed the land, changing the quality of the grasses and the structure of the soils. Farmers grew buckwheat to renew the land, but often the rotations were inadequate. For economic reasons the boom in sheep production ended in 1845, but its legacy was a new sensitivity to market production and a more impoverished agricultural landscape.[73]

The transformation of northern New England had been stunningly rapid. Individual clearings had been small, defined as they were by the limitations of markets, family labor, and available technology, but they had been numerous. Many of the original families had contained ten or a dozen children, and second-generation farms proliferated, particularly in the era before manufacturing drew youth to the cities. By 1850 some 10 percent of the land in Maine had been cleared, 37 percent in Vermont, 45 percent in New Hampshire, and 42 percent in Massachusetts.[74]

Reflecting on this transformation in 1835, the Reverend John Todd, a farmer-preacher from Maine, complained that his neighbors "covet too much land." Farms, he insisted, were from four to ten times too

This view from West Paris, Maine, in 1893 illustrates the vast changes in landscape that farming brought to the northern hill country. Forests were replaced by pastures and fields in much of the region. (Lantern slide by E. C. Belles, courtesy of Jean M. Deighan and Special Collections Department, University of Maine)

large for proper cultivation, a fact he attributed to insatiable land-hunger: "A farmer . . . adds field to field, does not half subdue or manure what he has got, and still wants more." The pattern of extensive farming was not irrational, given the needs of New England's patriarchal society, but as Todd was quick to point out, neither was it sustainable.[75] By 1849 land around Brattleboro, Vermont, a farmer complained, was "so far exhausted, that five acres will not keep an old sheep alive, through the summer."[76] The plight of the New England hill country has been overgeneralized by historians, but innumerable contemporary comments like this suggest at least the limits of wringing further windfall profits from the land as a means of extending the freehold farming population.[77] Northern New Englanders faced a future shorn of the natural richness that had drawn their forebears northward.

Foraging continued to cushion a difficult rural existence, but after 1840 dependence on this activity increasingly served as a demarcation between those who embraced new commercial farming methods and those who lingered in the pioneering phase too long. As agricultural activity became more demanding, differences between foraging families and full-time commercial farmers became more distinct. Lumbering, for instance, continued to provide winter work for farmers, but as the big commercial cuts moved upriver from the settlements, and as livestock and cropping cycles became more complex, the farmer-woodsman pursued husbandry at a disadvantage.[78] In 1867 the *Maine Farmer* discovered a "very poor class of people" making shingles from cedars stolen from the swamps near the Rangeley Lakes. Living in log cabins, they were as "rough, tough, hearty and hawbucking a group of masculines and feminines as you will often see," but they were clearly no longer models for the thrifty pioneer stock that had rived shingles to build equity in a small farm a generation earlier. In the context of modern agriculture, time spent making shingles was time lost to the tasks of managing a farm.[79] As the long cycle of forest to wheat to pasture drew to a close, the focus of energy among this assertive New England stock narrowed and intensified on the more productive valley soils. Farming these select lands, in the face of rising capital costs, stiffer competition, and declining forage possibilities, was an opportunity open to fewer people. The era of free goods in the upper Northeast was over.[80]

Landscape and Order

In the course of fifty years, New England yeoman families had gone far to transform, in cultural geographer Carl Sauer's terms, the natural landscape into a cultural landscape. The familiar image of northern New England was crystallizing: villages of simple buildings, fences, fields, and meadows, nestled in the lush, protected valleys astride meandering rivers, conveyed the essence of rural New England civilization.[81] To these cultural landmarks and the topographical elements that ordered them—intervales, plains, hills, and mountain slopes—the later canticles of northern New England's beauty were directed. To quote one, this was a land of "beautifully intermingling valleys and winding streams [and] . . . smooth and well-tilled fields, relieved by knots of tall and stately trees and clustering shrubbery, which mark the course of unambitious little rivulets and brooks." This late-century icon was indeed a cultivated landscape, accented by outcroppings of nature and rimmed by craggy, forested slopes that gave a touch of the sublime to the picturesque foreground. It was a land where nature was "softened and chastened."[82]

Yet the iconographic forms this landscape achieved in the minds of later town biographers would have seemed foreign to midcentury farmers. The sense of order and balance imposed upon this arrangement of woods, rocks, fields, homesteads, hills, and rivers is nowhere evident in accounts closer to pioneer times. Contemporaries, in fact, noted with evident dismay the difficulty of reducing this landscape to simple prescriptions. However much surveyors and speculators attempted to impose geometric order, farmers could not ignore the natural lay of the land. "Small as New Hampshire is, the variety of her soils is almost endless," Albert G. Comings told the Connecticut River Valley Society in 1853; "our lands incline in every direction and lie in every form."[83] One discouraged reformer alluded enviously to the orderly and convenient arrangement of Pennsylvania fields, each neatly squared and fenced, with smooth, clear surfaces. To this he compared New England's chaotic and asymmetrical farms:

> Looking at the average field with its forest of blackberry bushes and raspberry bushes, with its unaccounted wealth of thorns and brambles, and thistles, that line the entire enclosures, with its huge boulders scattered here and there that rear themselves like sentinels, stone heaps scattered all too thickly, over the entire surface of the ground, and the surface itself lying rough and uneven from the last seeding, I must confess that I do not much wonder at the bewilderment of the traveler [attempting to make sense out of the New England system].[84]

Commentary on this lack of order and symmetry expressed the tension between cultural visions and still-resistant nature. "Every variety of angle that delighted the genius of Euclid, could be matched by the subdividing lines of our farms," a farm reformer mused in 1851. "Our fields present to the eye all the different forms of obtuse and acute angles, and specimens even of the serpentine and the curvilinear, a mighty maze, and all without a plan!"[85] Although nature was "softened and chastened," New Englanders had not yet achieved the feeling, as Carl Sauer put it, "of harmony between the human habitation and the landscape into which it so fittingly blends."[86]

True, the original settlement plots, the divisions over time of small quantities of common lands, and the haphazard consolidations by later generations contributed to this disorder; but more than this, the irregularities of field, meadow, and forest expressed the frustrating persistence of nature in New England. Waste lands were left in common, poorer soils kept for pastures, and richer sections, "in the shape and extent in which they happened to exist," were enclosed for cultivation.[87] Historian Jeremy Belknap noted the difficulty of running boundary lines and laying out roads—imposing order on New Hampshire's convulsed and overgrown terrain.[88] The undeniability of morphology, impressed on the agricultural landscape in varieties of soil quality, topography, stoniness, bedrock features, and other conditions, and coupled with the almost irrepressible regenerative power of the original vegetation, established an enduring impression on the mind of the early farmer.[89]

Northern New England remained a mosaic of land uses, of thrifty farms and villages mixed with ragged and torn lands and interspersed with wild areas seemingly untouched by the wave of civilizing influences that passed over it.[90] Travelers' responses to the local scenery gyrated from the sublime to the squeamish. John C. Baker, who traveled through Vermont and New Hampshire in 1864 and 1865, described the fine intervals of the Mississquoi River in glowing terms, then dismissed the region around North Troy as "rather rusty." The hill country to the south, "wild and picturesque in the extreme," was traversed by a road that dipped into the "deepest gloom of the forest," bounded over ragged hilltops and through "seedy" towns, then again into "deep, dark ravines." In the Connecticut Valley, once again a "glorious view" burst upon the travel-weary party, calling forth the effusive Victorian descriptions reserved for only the most picturesque, if not sublime, panoramas. The erratic quality of Baker's account highlights a landscape variously resistant to human improvement, a dynamic environment that shaped human culture as much as human culture shaped it.[91]

This natural resistance affected the way settlers viewed the dynamics of New England's transition. As the forest yielded before the ax and plow, these "primeval" forces assumed symbolic qualities, conveying both negative and positive moral lessons about how the land was to be changed. The dynamic tension between the primeval past and settlers' aspirations for the future—between nature and culture—shaped attitudes toward the land, the soils, the forests, the waters, and the wildlife. In this dialectic between thought and nature New Englanders carved out a new relation to the land.

Documentary expressions of this emerging landscape vision are sketchy, but they do make three things clear. First, settlers did not view the primordial nature they encountered as immutable; they saw it as a changing mosaic of landforms and resources—an unfinished landscape. Second, they saw themselves as moral agents of this change, working in tandem with momentous and sometimes mysterious natural forces to shape the land according to the ideological principles that had drawn them to northern New England. They assumed a shared responsibility for molding this world into a higher synthesis of human and natural forces.

Third, New Englanders saw this unfolding landscape in terms of epochal struggle, a contest not against nature per se—nature was after all the medium for their farm-and-forage economy—but against the recalcitrant forces that obstructed the proper and ordained balance between farm, village, and wild nature. Farmers waged war on the elements of nature they found incompatible with their own moralistic landscape vision. And a struggle it was: "The forest is lurking at the edges of a settlement or a field ready to bounce back at the slightest signs of a slackening in the maintenance," wrote a Vermont landscape historian.[92] Writing to the Massachusetts Board of Agriculture, Harrison Garfield of Lee, Massachusetts, testified to the dogged persistence of the farmer's vision and to the resistance of his medium. Hardhack in his pastures, Garfield complained,

> gets so strong a hold that no grass will grow at all. It has formed a perfect mat, so that cattle cannot get through, where, ten years ago, there was a good pasture. I have practised mowing it seven or eight years, and cannot kill it in that way. Three years ago I commenced ploughing it up in September and October, pulling it out of the soil and throwing it upon the surface, and when it got dry, gathering it together and burning it; then I manured the land and cultivated it . . . Cutting it down tends to spread the roots and make it grow thicker, so that we have been obliged to tear it out and change the character of the soil.[93]

A pioneer growth, hardhack was itself a result of human disturbance. But it was not a result compatible with the dreams of those who so ardently and relentlessly worked to make their vision of the land a reality. Garfield's struggle with this resistant pest demonstrates as much as anything else the balance of contending natural and human forces that made up the northern New England landscape and keeps it, even today, after two centuries of transformation, in a state of flux.

CHAPTER TWO

The Commons in Transition

In the 1830s New Englanders began reconstructing elements of the natural world that had been lost in the earlier pulse of pioneering activity. These experiments came at a time when farmers were abandoning the forage activities that had sustained their predecessors, yet they demonstrate both the continuing importance of the remembered primeval world and the collective sense of responsibility New Englanders felt for shaping a balance between this older world and the new cultural landscape. The fish-stocking experiments also gave birth to a new interpretation of common lands and common stewardship.

In a seminal essay written in 1968, biologist Garrett Hardin explored the implications of public ownership of natural resources using his now-famous allegory, the "tragedy of the commons." Resources held in common, Hardin suggested, are by nature subject to abuse. Individual rationality dictates that each person use common resources as intensively as possible, since anything saved or conserved might fall to a competitor tomorrow. Others have rephrased this dilemma as a problem of externalities: People "are unlikely to restrain their own behavior when the immediate benefit of their actions are their own, but the costs are passed on to society as a whole."[1]

Hardin's allegory helps clarify the dynamics of resource use, but he has been faulted for ignoring the more nuanced social meaning of "common" property in any given situation. Property—common or private—is a social construct, "thoroughly embedded in historically specific social contexts whose meanings vary."[2] Daniel Bromley, among others, argues that Hardin failed to make a crucial distinction between open access—unrestricted use of "free goods"—and corporate ownership, or cooperative management of common lands. In some historical instances, Bromley points out, community management offered far better prospects for resource conservation than did private property. Unfortunately, in the areas of the nonwestern world where these management systems were prevalent, colonial powers disrupted traditional village authority, and when colonialism gave way, village common lands fell prey to open access—the veritable "free-for-all" that Hardin conflated with common ownership.[3]

Bromley's suggestion that common property be viewed seriously as a management system offers an excellent starting point for understanding New England's earliest conservation policies. In colonial society, the network of rights and duties that bound individuals to family and families to community was the dominant institutional arrangement under which natural resources were managed. Beginning here, we return to the historical roots of Hardin's allegorical "commons": the undivided lands and other natural resources that belonged to the colonial town. Americans responded to Old World forms of privileged access to wild resources by granting all citizens inherent rights to these resources. Yet this egalitarian thrust makes it easy to overlook the ways in which colonial communities restricted and regulated the use of natural resources; in fact free access was qualified by a considerable body of local law.[4]

This social institution—the town commons—was reforged in the great events of the late eighteenth century: the American Revolution, the frontier migrations northeastward and westward, and the new republican ideology that emerged from these two social upheavals. Through it all, townspeople rethought rather than abandoned the idea of common property as corporate ownership.[5] Whether or not these rights and duties effectively sustained the resources they encompassed is a question that cannot be answered in general terms, but understanding ways in which northern New Englanders adjusted common authority systems to the new, post-Revolutionary society provides a key to understanding how wild resources were perceived—and conserved—in early New England.

Forage and the Great Woods

Colonial towns were arranged, Anne Bush MacLear wrote, according to a "curious combination of land held in severalty and lands in common." Even those held privately were "subject to common regulations as to choice of crops, manner of fencing, and reservation of herbage." This mixed system of public and private management was based on the principles of equity and common stewardship. Early arrivals parceled out individual lots with great care to apportion evenly the benefits of soil and terrain, meadowland and forest, and access to transportation.[6] Lands could be held in several widely separated pieces: a home lot; an "acre right," or right of use in the undivided meadows and forests; and other outlying parcels held outright. Large tracts were reserved to use in common, to provide later arrivals with land, or to serve as grants to prospective millwrights.[7]

These remaining undivided lands served a variety of community purposes: forage for livestock, timber for building and fencing, muck for dressing fields, and peat and hardwoods for fuel.[8] Regulating their use was a local affair. State legislatures, according to Michael Zukerman, sanctioned "an almost endless diversity among towns in their conduct of business." This "adamant insularity" left colonial resources almost entirely in local hands. Towns oversaw grazing, timbering, clamming, and harvesting of wild hay; they elected wardens to oversee fishing and to keep the streams free of obstructions; they determined on which days fishing was to be allowed, what methods were to be used, and when the sluiceways in dams were to be opened.[9] Management differed from town to town, but in general land, fish, wood, grass, muck, and other resources were considered common property and allocated carefully to ensure equity.

The priority of community welfare over private rights with regard to land and resources made sense in the region's primitive social climate. Yeomen, David P. Szatmary has noted, "lived in a community-directed culture." They borrowed, traded, and exchanged goods, land, and labor with neighbors and kin, and they cooperated in harvesting the bounty of the natural landscape. Steven Hahn has observed similar foraging practices in antebellum Georgia, where "common hunting and grazing rights took their place beside other 'habits of mutuality' . . . as important features of productive organization." The concept of corporate property was in transition when settlers began carving out homesteads in the northern New England uplands. The periodic divisions of the common lands, the pressures of commercial capitalism, the new interpretations of liberty and individualism, religious fragmentation, and the arrival of new immigrants eroded these community-based management systems.[10] Yet for certain low-yield natural resources like wetlands, berries, marsh and meadow grass, and fish and game, local community responsibility persisted as villagers adapted old management traditions to a new, less cohesive society.

Bounty laws blended this legacy of common stewardship and settlers' aggressively anthropocentric biases in shaping the land. Bounties on predators helped transform New England into a more genial habitat for crops and livestock; they enhanced the cultural landscape by enforcing a dichotomy between "useful" and "noxious" animals.[11] Providing a cash reward for hunting predators raised private incentives for contributing to the common good. A Prospect, Maine, petitioner explained that lynx were "worthless in themselves considered that they are not worth hunting." In 1844 J. P. Haygens and 106 fellow Maine farmers "situated . . . on the borders of the Settlements" petitioned for a wolf bounty that would be adequate "as a remuneration for the labor, risk and skill necessary to destroy those bold and daring animals."[12] These petitions highlight the degree to which farmers expected the state to shoulder collective responsibility for shaping the cultivated landscape. Vermont placed a bounty on wolves and panthers in 1787 and added foxes, bears, lynx, and wildcats to the list in 1831.[13] Definitions of "noxious" animals shifted over time; fox bounties were passed and repealed repeatedly as the animal's pelt value was weighed against the costs of its predation on barnyard fowl. But however wildlife was categorized, it was, as Franklin, New Hampshire, farmers put it, the state's "constitutional duty . . . to provide for the *common welfare*" by altering their presence in the great woods.[14]

Common responsibility for and aggressive interaction with the land blended with a third principle of early resource use: shared access to resources left in a state of nature. Foraging was widespread along the New England frontier, and this form of common use often superseded private landownership rights. Trespassing for game, fish, berries, pasturage, wood, and a variety of other wild resources was premised on the frontier conviction that "vacant" lands were public resources, an idea reinforced by popular resistance to earlier British timber regulations and constraints on using the "Indian lands." Trespassing was also bolstered by the confusion over ownership as town lands were divided. Daniel Ladd's "accommodations" in Salem, New Hampshire, for instance, included four acres "more or less" added to his house lot, five acres "in the plain," nine acres "up the great river," four acres "in the east meadow, more or less," one and a half acres in the "pond meadow, more or less," and another acre in Hawkes Meadow.[15] Since divisions such as these were difficult to farm, land-swapping was rife, and the flurry of exchanging, buying, and selling these vaguely defined holdings kept ownership in constant flux. "Neighbors sued neighbors and settlers sued non-residents for cutting trees and grass," wrote a historian of Pownalborough, Maine. This confusion frustrated attempts to exclude others from private property.[16]

Landownership in the "great woods"—the forests along the settlement fringe or in the back lots of each town—was also in flux. Overlapping claims based on old Indian purchases, on English proprietary estates, and on crown or commonwealth grants left ownership ambiguous. Speculators amassed land they were unable to pay for; desperate refinancing and legislative manipulations kept these ownerships fluid, and new proprietors often changed the informal terms upon which settlers held claim. Conflict between settlers and absentee land speculators in Vermont and Maine, beginning in the 1760s, further weakened private claims; settlers trespassed not only for sanctioned public purposes like hunting, fishing, and trapping, but also for pasturage, fodder, lumber, cordwood, house and barn frames, stave wood, and ship timbers. As Alan Taylor points out, even the most basic definitions of ownership were in dispute along this early national frontier. Squatters dismissed nonresident claims with the understanding that no one was entitled to more land than one family could improve—perhaps two hundred acres. Settlers unsure of their legal title in these grants neglected farm improvements and lived off the land.[17] Frontier attachment to common use-rights, liberalized by these backwoods conflicts, provided an expansive arena for forage activity.

For a variety of reasons northern New Englanders remained sensitive to the social purposes of wild lands. Deer were such an important economic and subsistence resource for early colonizers that legislatures proclaimed closed seasons in Massachusetts in 1694, in New Hampshire in 1741, in Vermont in 1779, and in Maine in 1830.[18] Vesting ownership of wildlife in the community was one means by which thousands of acres of mountain, forest, and marsh lands, privately owned but unsuitable for agriculture, were made useful to the rural economy.[19] In 1828, for instance, citizens from three Vermont towns asked the legislature to oversee hunting in a nearby stretch of mountains in which "no human being has ever made any attempt to Cultivation." On these inhospitable slopes, deer were abundant and "would Multiply and be plenty was it not for the Practice that Sportsmen have got of chasing the Deer with Dogs and Hounds." Sport-hunting in this fashion deprived the untillable mountains of their value to the community.[20] The petitioners assumed common rights to these woods and a public responsibility for preserving their usefulness.

Common pasturing was another form of shared use of unimproved lands. In sparsely populated towns, cattle, swine, and horses foraged in the great woods into the nineteenth century. To protect crops from these animals, farmers were obliged to fence their fields. A Vermonter, recalling his childhood in the early nineteenth century, remembered that his family often had the best corn in the neighborhood. But, he added matter-of-factly, "it would usually be destroyed by the neighbors' cattle before it was time to harvest."[21] Haystacks suffered a similar fate.

As croplands gained importance, laws making farmers liable for their roaming animals were stiffened. Stricter fencing laws, beginning in Massachusetts in the 1830s, suggest the emergence of new attitudes toward forage rights in unoccupied woods: exclusive private use offered a more rational means of commodifying nature in an increasingly commercial age. Progressive farmers demanded that livestock be fenced in.

The closing of this commons suggests a growing cultural distinction between commercial farmers and those who clung to the pioneering farm-and-forage economy. William Bacon, a western Massachusetts farmer vexed by the ragged definition of private domain in his neighborhood, complained to the editor of the *New England Cultivator* that wandering cattle were a "starved, sacrilegious herd of trespassers, sent out to the daily task of highway robbery."[22] That foraging cattle were "unruly" and "ungoverned" was as much a reference to the habits of the owner as to the livestock itself; unfenced livestock suggested a "loose and illiberal state of things," a blur in the vision of the new agrarian landscape.[23] Moses Greenleaf, who surveyed the economic potential of Maine in 1829, surmised that agriculture was languishing in the relatively rich soils of the lower Kennebec and Penobscot valleys because the "vast quantities of valuable timber . . . and the multitudes of fish" diverted settlers from the "slower, though more certain and permanent returns from the . . . cultivation of the soil."[24] As Greenleaf's perspective suggests, closing off this commons heralded a change in attitudes toward those who depended on wild resources.

In Maine, towns retained the right to decide whether pastures or fields would be fenced. One "grower of crops" complained as late as 1876 that he was compelled "to fence out all of the bovine tramps that go to and fro in the earth." Still, townspeople were far from united on the matter, and passage of a general fencing law later in the decade brought little immediate change. Farmers who sought recourse in the law "lost the . . . good will of [their] neighbors" and risked malicious damage to property or livestock.[25] Eventually custom yielded to law, bringing a greater sense of focus to the concept of private claims to unimproved lands; but the pace of change was glacial.[26]

A similar trend in the redefinition of access to uncultivated lands involved the legal enclosure of blueberry and cranberry fields. The rise of Maine's blueberry canning industry in the 1860s triggered a bitter five-year battle between seasonal gatherers and landowners, the latter winning exclusive rights to harvest the eastern blueberry "barrens."[27] Examples like this signaled a growing hegemony of exclusionary property rights pertaining to resources still in a state of nature. Common use of meadows, swamps, and barrens had been components of a larger set of cooperative habits and interdependencies that bound early communities together. The elevation of private title over community custom indicated a legal distancing from these frontier traditions—another episode in the division of the commons.

Reinventing the Commons

Rights of access to fish and game reflected these changing perspectives on wild resources and those who hunted or gathered them. For nearly a century farmers on marginal lands had carved out spheres of autonomy by combining farming with forage in the great woods. But by midcentury, those who persisted in this way of life were looked upon as seminomadic vandals rather than pioneering yeomen.[28] Like farmers who refused to fence their pastures or families who berried in other people's fields, those who depended on foraging for game were relegated to the periphery of the new commercial society.[29] A ditty published in a Vermont gazetteer celebrated the essential role forage resources once played in pioneer life:

> The feathered goose and duck, they make our bed,
> The Beaver, Coon and Fox, they crown our head,
> The harmless Moose and Deer, are food, and clothes to wear,
> Nature could do no more for any land.[30]

By midcentury, foraging for the "harmless Moose and Deer" satisfied symbolic as much as dietary tastes.[31] As the utilitarian links between farm and forest were loosened, the recreational and ritualistic values of wildlife assumed a greater importance, and rights to wildlife changed

A source of provender for pioneering families, deer were later viewed as quarry for sport hunting. This sketch shows the time-worn method of luring game to a salt lick, but the depiction of a doe and fawn suggests the artist's critical view of this practice. (*American Agriculturist*, July 1869)

as well. Early laws had been designed simply to ensure the quality of flesh and fur and the productivity of the forage landscape. Responding to declining stocks of game and to more ritualistic tastes for hunting, game-law advocates sought a more restrictive set of rules that implied the emergence of a more select community of users for this common resource. The historian of Lancaster, New Hampshire, for instance, related the story of one Caswell, a "worthless sort of a hunter," who around 1850 "started in one winter . . . to kill a hundred moose." He came close to meeting his goal, taking the hides and leaving the carcasses behind—a "diabolical waste," according to townspeople.[32] Hunters like Caswell, who squandered game and ignored the new morality of hunting, were increasingly identified as outsiders, excluded from the commons; in fact Caswell was literally driven from the town.

The expulsion of Caswell for his unconscionable overkill is symbolic of new ways of defining community and commons in an era when forage rights were in transition. In 1843 Ruben Gregg and others complained to the Maine legislature of the great destruction of moose and deer by dogs and men, "many of whom are from other States." Petitioners asked for a general law "by which all foreigners may be prohibited from hunting within the limits of this State, on lands not their own." Gregg, and many others who petitioned their legislators for hunting restrictions, superimposed a new ethical identity upon the traditional geographic boundaries of the commons. Vermont petitioners who described hounding as "barbarous" invented an ethical community embracing only those who hunted with musket and ball. The identification of unethical hunting with outsiders built a case for preservation that fused the traditional geographic boundaries of the commons with newer ethical limits defined by ritualized, rather than forage hunting.[33]

This new ethical community was most evident in early fish conservation efforts. The 1820s witnessed the beginnings of a surprisingly widespread campaign to restock New England's depleted inland fisheries. In hundreds of towns throughout the region, fish propagationists attempted to revitalize a public resource that had been part of the fabric of pioneer life. "The little brooks and ponds of the country were once alive with . . . pickerel . . . perch, and . . . trout [which] . . . cost [no] more time to take . . . than they were worth," an editor wrote in 1855, suggesting a traditional utilitarian calculus that equated time expended in appropriating fish with the usefulness of the resulting catch.[34]

The earliest and most elaborate examples of fish conservation involved migratory runs of alewives, a small but abundant herringlike fish that spawned in the headwaters of coastal streams. In 1803 townspeople in the coastal Maine town of Damariscotta stocked a nearby freshwater pond with alewives and constructed a stone fishway through a previously inaccessible section of the stream running to the sea. By the 1860s the stream yielded a harvest of 400,000 to 600,000 alewives yearly, returning between $1,000 and $1,500 to the small town.[35] In 1867 Damariscotta began auctioning the rights to the fishery under the close supervision of the town Fish Committee. In the early twentieth century the Damariscotta River was the largest producer of alewives on the New England coast. Hundreds of coastal streams benefited from similar experiments. Where there was no preexisting fishery, neighbors owning land around a pond or brook sometimes built canals, fish ladders, or other access to the sea, stocked the headwaters, and claimed the right to control the fishery.[36]

Townspeople also experimented with pickerel transplants. Though bony and not particularly succulent, pickerel could be taken in astounding numbers by ice-fishing, and thus served as a welcome supplement to a normally monotonous winter diet. They were also vigorous breeders. Farmers stocked a small pond in Oxford County, Maine, and a few years later reported a yearly haul of seven to eight tons. A similar experiment near Union, Maine, left every pond tributary to the St. George River "rioting" with pickerel. As an afterthought, a local historian added that the trout had been "nearly exterminated."[37]

Experiments like these prompted the region's first inland fish conservation policy, a strictly local body of law that helped reestablish the place of nature in the landscape and redefine the concept of the commons. These experiments are rarely mentioned in local histories, but they are amply documented in legislative petitions, since most required state authority for local protective laws. In 1824, for instance, citizens of Lincoln, Massachusetts, voted at town meeting to petition the legislature for a law "to prevent any person from fishing or tending more than one hook at a time in any of the ponds in said town."[38] Thousands of similar petitions pertaining to individual towns or ponds reveal the mix of motives that prompted the first popular regionwide attempts to restore the natural landscape. Though not a conservation "movement" in the full sense of the term, the fish-propagation experiments of the first half of the century articulated several key transitional attitudes toward common resources.

Like early game laws, these measures harked back to the primeval landscape that fostered the pioneering farm-and-forage economy. S. Dill of Phillips, Maine, stocked a local stream with trout in 1850 and seven years later told the editor of the *Maine Farmer* that he and his neighbors were taking "not less than 2,000 pounds of trout from the waters annually." Explaining this good harvest, Dill drew upon folk memories of the productive virgin soils that had attracted his pioneering forebears to western Maine: virgin waters, like virgin soils, encouraged rapid reproduction; the trout found "a plentiful supply of food among the insects which have been accumulating, doubtless, for ages." By helping the trout along in their migration to this new aquatic frontier, Dill simply assisted "these little fellows in . . . *bettering their condition.*"[39] Residents in Marlborough, New Hampshire, transported a tub of pickerel to Meetinghouse Pond with similar expectations. The rationale—to ensure that "at most times a man might get himself a decent mess of fish with little pains"—expressed a familiar view of wild nature as an object of basic subsistence. Ritually at least, the "mess of fish" so often alluded to reaffirmed the forage landscape that had drawn settlers to the northeastern frontier in the 1760s.[40]

The experiments also harked back to a cohesive community of users willing to sacrifice immediate private gain for future common benefits. Consonant with earlier uses of the commons, fishing would be public, and it would be limited to reasonable, equitable use as defined by the community.[41] "Inhabitants and freemen" of Pownal, Vermont, went to "some offense and trouble in procuring pickerel . . . so that the increase of said fish might be a benefit to the inhabitants of said town"; the community was to reciprocate this act of public virtue by cooperating in conserving the fish.[42] The sanctions the Pownal petitioners and others requested were predicated on traditional formulations of ideal republican behavior: frugality, industry, harmony, and individual sacrifice to the greater needs of the whole community.[43]

The complaints of petitioners like those from Pownal, the necessity of state intervention, and the references to behavior contrary to public virtue all reflect the pressures of a society much less homogeneous than that of earlier times. The Vermont town, Randolph A. Roth writes, found it difficult to maintain the standing order in the 1820s. "Even the relatively mild legal and institutional supports that had been erected in its defense came under attack, and the unity, tolerance, calm, and deference that was vital to its success began to evaporate." Citizens were not yet complete individualists, but they were no longer able to command the range of mutual obligations necessary to protect the fish.[44]

In response, petitioners fashioned a community of users based partly on older community norms and partly on the new realities of more individualistic behavior. Propagationists assumed a stronger proprietary interest in the fish, having gone to "considerable trouble and expense" to restock the waters. As fish stocks became more artificial, restrictive community rights became more distinct. Those who stocked Otter Creek in Vermont, for instance, did so "for the accommodation of the people *in the vicinity of its waters*."[45] Willingness to share this now somewhat artificial resource was usually limited to neighbors or fellow townspeople. The very act of reconstructing nature affirmed exclusive community rights to the resource.

Meetinghouse Pond residents approached the question of excluding outsiders gingerly. Having stocked the pond, locals found that interlopers "from the Neighboring Towns, having more Leisure than generosity," set lines containing ten to fifty hooks each and moved them systematically around the pond, clearing the waters of any pickerel "big enough to take the bait." The Meetinghouse neighbors were careful not to "claim any private property in the Fish" and in fact made their plea for preservation on universal moral grounds: "No person Ought to be allowed to Fish with but one hook at a time." Still, it is clear from the way they phrased their complaint that they felt a vested community interest in the restocked pond.[46] Residents near Musquatamisus Pond in New Hampshire were likewise plagued by "multitudes from the neighboring towns" who used multiple hooks in the winter and torches and spears in the spring to rob their waters of pickerel. They identified these unprincipled foragers as "sundry persons . . . from the state of Massachusetts and other places."[47] That locals might pursue the same means seems to have been unthinkable.

Identifying unethical fishing behavior with outsiders redefined community in beneficial ways. State legislators acted more positively on petitions that seemed to reflect community consensus, and associating nonresidents with the source of antagonism undoubtedly created the illusion of general town support. It also protected the town's own sense of public virtue. The tactic expressed a persisting aspiration to community harmony and homogeneity.

Towns, of course, no longer enjoyed the legal right to exclude outsiders from their ponds. Here again, however, petitioners superimposed an ethical community upon the traditional geographic authority of the town. Neighbors were willing to allow all citizens "of their own and of other towns" free and unrestrained access, but only "for fair and honorable angling." Meetinghouse Pond petitioners pointed out that excessive fishing supported "not a few indolent persons, who prefer sport before honest and reputable employment, misspend their time, and neglect their business." For the "industrious man," on the other hand, occasional fishing "for the expense of a leisure hour" was a legitimate recreational pastime.[48] Experimenters drew a new ethical perimeter around the fish by dictating the methods and moral purposes of fishing.

Petitions for fish conservation, like game laws, reflect the changing

Pickerel, taken with live bait—frogs or minnows—or by "skittering" with a long, flexible rod and a spoon lure, were important elements in the pioneering forage landscape. Villagers frequently stocked lakes and ponds with pickerel and asked for state laws to protect the fish. Their efforts renewed and refashioned colonial concepts of common waters. (*American Agriculturist,* October 1873)

social significance of wild resources as farm families abandoned frontier forage traditions and focused on domestic crops and livestock. Like farmers who refused to fence their pastures or families who berried in other people's fields, those who fished too heavily for subsistence or gain were outcasts in this new agrarian society. Defining the limited, recreational rituals of fishing superimposed a new ethical community of users upon the older egalitarian town-based exclusionary customs: petitioners were groping toward a new demarcation of the commons.[49]

The Musquatamisus petition asked for a ban on torching—the practice of netting fish as they were drawn to the light of a bonfire or a torch. This practice, they argued, endangered buildings near the pond. References to property damage inflicted by trespassing fishers were fairly common in pleas for fish protection; they tied community interest in fish to more established private claims to real estate.[50] The connection between property and conservation suggests that local landowners held a higher moral claim to fish than unpropertied outsiders. But here again Musquatamisus residents linked locality and real estate with an ethical community of users. Torching—presumably by outsiders—presented "to the unsuspecting finny tribes fatal allurements, when they fancy themselves secure under a supposed impenetrable covering" of darkness. Torch fishers "lurk in midnight gloom to decoy by fictitious lights" and then "steal" their prey. It was "too assassin-like to be tolerated."[51]

That not everyone subscribed to the new ethics of fishing was clear from the number of petitions denied by the legislatures and from the number of protective laws subsequently overturned.[52] Joseph Chapman and others in Greensboro, Vermont, argued that a law pertaining to a local pond was "better calculated to disturb the harmony and peace of society than to effect the purposes contemplated by said Act."[53] Chapman apparently saw the law as a threat to the thin veneer of public virtue that still clung to community relations. Citizens in the town of Woodford (Bennington) complained that their attempts to stock the town's great pond had been subverted by a "few men, who love to evade laws, in a clandestine manner." Since those who lived near the pond were "not friendly to said law," it was difficult to obtain proof for prosecution. The petitioners asked that the law be repealed, "in order that those who indevoured to improve the breed of fish, in said pond may legally have their Share for the future." The legislature complied.[54]

Indeed, it is difficult to know how townspeople generally reacted to the laws. But beyond the matter of popular endorsement, the petitions do make clear some important changes in attitudes toward natural resources in the first half of the century. First, the many hundreds of petitions in Maine, Massachusetts, New Hampshire, and Vermont archives demonstrate that a great number of individuals throughout the region were interested, at this early point, in restoring aspects of the primeval landscape that had nurtured their pioneering forebears. New England conservation was rooted in the close of the frontier itself.

Second, experiments with natural processes had a social corollary: once stocked, fish had to be protected in some way. Petitioners experimented with new social laws redefining acceptable means of taking fish; they began the process of rebuilding moral sanctions for regulated entry to the commons. In some cases this meant linking the welfare of the fish to the welfare of private property in the same neighborhood. In other cases it meant identifying a new ethical community exclusive of idlers and outsiders and of behavior inimical to the ethos of Yankee thrift, Puritan exclusionary common weal, and yeoman independence. With mixed success, fish propagationists attempted to bridge the divide between the old community commons and the new social fabric of possessive individualism.

The early New England fish experiments spanned two eras: they were as traditional as the concept of the commons itself, yet they anticipated a future in which the natural landscape would be shaped entirely to human need—the culmination of a long metamorphosis in the New England wilderness. By redefining and reinvigorating an older community ethos, the fish-transplanting experiments also provided a moral groundwork for conservation politics as it emerged in the second half of the nineteenth century.

Common Lands

The New England reform temper influenced farmscape perceptions. The fences prominent in the foreground and background (second sketch) accent the importance of linear design and the articulation of clear boundaries between nature and culture. (*American Agriculturist*, March 1857)

CHAPTER THREE

Nature in the New Agrarian Landscape

In the general scheme of conservation history the American farmer is invariably perceived as a dominant force in the shock wave of environmental devastation that spread west across the continent in the nineteenth century. Although the disruptive impact of the pioneering farmer should not be slighted, this view neglects the changes in thinking that came as the frontier matured and as New England's second-generation farmers came to terms with the alterations wrought by their forebears. In reconciling their views of the agrarian republic with this exhausted land, they became harbingers of a new conservation ethic.

Farm reformers, like fish propagationists, folded into their thinking a mix of traditional and modern views. Their approach was starkly utilitarian; they dichotomized nature into "beneficial" and "noxious" elements on the basis of the efficiency and profitability of the farm itself. Still, they viewed the relation between farms and the natural world in providential terms; farming was a spiritual conduit through which an earlier ethic of resource use was conveyed to the later conservation movement.

In 1873 New Hampshire's Board of Agriculture circulated a questionnaire to selectmen across the state soliciting opinion on a number of disconcerting trends, including soil and forest depletion, market competition, and rising capital requirements. The responses varied: some considered farming remunerative; others, unrewarding; some advocated a return to self-sufficient farming; others felt that to make ends meet in a world of rising expenses, taxes, and wages, farmers would have to devote their attention to a single, profitable commercial crop.[1] These contradictory replies reflect the cross-pressures that drove farmers to rethink the spiritual connection between the farm and the natural world.

In the mid-nineteenth century, the products of northern New England's diversified rural economy were traded through village intermediaries, who served as buffers between local producers and the world of commercial capitalism. A merchant's customers typically included relatives and neighbors, and community norms prevented obvious gouging at the local level. Still, village merchants bought and sold in impersonal markets, traded extensively on credit, and accumulated wealth and commercial resources that set them apart from their neighbors.[2] Their activities altered the nature of economic exchange even at the local level. And farmers extended beyond this local system by making market trips to nearby cities, carrying a varied freight of farm, forest, and handicraft products. Women entered regional markets by weaving, sewing garments, stitching shoes, or fashioning straw hats, corn brooms, and other commodities on consignment. This activity provided rural families with experience in commodity production and exchange at a time when expanding rail networks and the increasing availability of factory goods were tempting them further into the world of commerce.[3]

Yet the impress of commercial capitalism remained relatively light. Most upland farmers operated in a world of poorly developed market structures, unpredictable climate, and thin soils, and they compensated by growing much of their own food and spreading their income and their risks over a number of activities. This diversification was not unusual in American agriculture, but northern New England's distinctiveness lay in the persistence of mixed farming and its sheer multiplicity. Farm work everywhere required a wide range of talents, but New Englanders, who grew no single staple crop with obvious interregional comparative advantage, became legendary for their multiple endeavors.[4]

Demography explains in part the persistence of mixed farming. Because population pressures remained relatively low in northern New England, farmers were not compelled by rising land values to specialize.

Geographic isolation, a condition even the railroads could remedy only partially, further discouraged the shift to specialized market farming. The unevenness of soil quality and terrain left farm communities scattered, and dispersal drove up the costs of transportation. Long winters and unpredictable weather discouraged heavy investments for specialized production.[5] The region's small, irregular fields were ill suited for expensive horse-drawn equipment, and the soils deteriorated rapidly under heavy commercial cropping. New England farmers watched a succession of commodities—wheat, beef, potatoes, wool—succumb to weather and western competition, and this adversity bred caution. "It is not usually safe to venture all in one speciality," a Vermont farmer cautioned. "The owner of the average hill farm . . . should aim to supply his own necessities, as far as practicable . . . and for the surplus raise that which will bring the most for the least expense and not impoverish the farm."[6]

Other features of this environment encouraged mixed farming. Abundant, even rainfall and varied conditions on each farm offered a number of options for crops and livestock. After a few generations, families knew the possibilities of each patch of soil and could deploy fields, orchards, gardens, and grasses across the farm to maximize use of these varied conditions. Experimenting over time, they grew a variety of products neatly suited to the soils and contours of the farm and thus eased carefully into the world of capitalist agriculture.[7]

Farmers operated in the world of commerce, but the multiple market options in the neighborhood, village, and city and the security of raising much of their own sustenance distanced them somewhat from the compulsions of the marketplace. Cash accounts, as one New Hampshire selectman summarized, were largely a matter of "guesswork."[8]

The world of commercial capitalism drew closer to the farm in the second half of the century. The expansion of food-dependent industrial centers and small factory villages throughout the region; the growing tourist trade, with its demand for fresh fruits, dairy products, and vegetables; and railroad extensions into the interior valleys linked upland farms to town and city consumers, challenging old patterns and broadening cultural and economic outlooks.[9]

These developments were widely discussed in the farm press. A farmer inclined to specialize in market production, a newspaper correspondent wrote, must "thoroughly understand it, have a love for it, and be so situated in regard to location, market &c., as to take advantage of every point in his favor." The profits were "sometimes large, are frequently variable and often small, on account of the peculiarities of the season, or the demand of the product."[10] While this was not a step to be taken lightly, remaining on the margins of the market economy was far from enviable. Cash-poor farm families, chained to primitive techniques in the fields, the dooryard, and the home, wasted time cribbing together makeshift equipment, struggling with cumbersome tools, and coaxing crops from poorly prepared soil. The hard labor required in the production of several different crops, each with different sowing, cultivating, and harvesting routines, aged men and women prematurely and drove their sons and daughters from the land. Later generations lauded this heritage of self-reliance, but as Robert Gross has pointed out, farmers' independence was for the most part illusory: they were trapped in a confining web of borrowing, bartering, and "the endless keeping of accounts to ascertain one's standing in the community-wide network of credits and debts."[11]

The paths that individual farm families chose through this welter of considerations were many, but the advice they read in the farm press followed two diverging lines of thought, a schism that reflected the ambivalence of the Yankee farmer in the new commercial age. Modernists, convinced that New England's problems could be laid at the doorstep of traditional thinking, advocated scientific, specialized farming as a solution.[12] These reformers scoffed at the idea that families could get by "having a little patch of corn here, and a few potatoes there; gathering a few tons of hay upon a surface broad enough to produce ten times as much; milking cows that do not pay for what they eat." Carefully calculating costs, yields, and cash returns, the farmer would abandon unprofitable crops and concentrate upon those that paid. Market directives would shape the land to its highest use.[13] An equally vocal group endorsed traditional mixed-farming practices, coupled with better use of manures, compost, muck-beds, ashes, and other "home resources of fertilization."[14] This alternative was not simply unreflective conservatism; traditionalists weighed the benefits and drawbacks of mixed farming carefully. Most recognized that specialized agriculture could be profitable in certain cases, but the average farmer, they felt, isolated and struggling with thin soils, would find mixed farming the safest course. As historian Alan Taylor notes, this strategy also invoked powerful ideological images.[15] Owners of small farms were loath to relinquish their economic independence, despite its costs in family toil. The farmer who "permits himself to be dependent upon the markets for his provender supplies," one editor cautioned, "must submit to the ruling prices of the market."[16]

Most farmers straddled the worlds of commerce and self-sufficiency. Still, they faced a dizzying array of new choices about equipment and techniques and worried that more-intensive farming would sap the richness from their soils.[17] "Each year," a New Hampshire farmer mused, "tens of thousands of cattle and sheep are collected in Vermont and New Hampshire for the *city* consumption . . . In this way, the elements of fertility are transferred, the suburbs of cities are enriched, and remote districts impoverished."[18] As Robert Gross points out, farmers were uneasy about transforming the richness in their soils into cash, treating nature "not as a medium of spiritual growth but merely as a commodity."[19]

Farmers at midcentury entered a world laced with subtle contradictions. Dairy farming, emerging as the region's most important form of specialization, preserved certain elements of traditional mixed husbandry. Manures remained on the farm, and dairying produced a dependable income over most of the year, a source of security not found in other forms of specialized farming in which debts accumulated until harvest time.[20] Still, growth of the "factory system"—dairies, creameries, and cheese factories—brought wrenching changes. It extended the lactation period, increased the number of cows, shifted dairying responsibilities from women to men, subjected farmers to higher standards of quality, and forced them to adopt more exacting accounts. It required off-farm purchases of expensive feeds and machinery, and it was risky. Thus it took a dramatic disjuncture of wool and milk prices to attract farmers into the industry.[21]

Another agent of specialization was vegetable canning, which spread across the region in the 1870s. Here, too, the attempt by canners and their agents to lever farmers out of their secure multicrop strategies was fraught with ambivalence and suspicion. Sweet-corn production, the major canning staple, crowded out subsistence crops and required special care in planting and fertilizing. The flavor of the corn depended upon harvesting at a precise point in the growing cycle. If the corn was not prime, farmers were left with a specialized crop for which there was no alternative market.[22] Sweet corn was remunerative, one farmer admitted, "but more or less uncertain."[23]

In most areas, farmers were optimistic about their new commercial opportunities, but the demands of the new age were unsettling as well, and the debates between traditionalists and modernists in the farm press underscored the weaknesses in New England's rural economy. Cultivation was "not so neat, so thorough, nor so profitable as it ought to be."[24] Conscious of the need for greater efficiency, farmers nevertheless refashioned rather than rejected their traditional view of the spiritual links between farms and nature.

Farm Abandonment and Social Stratification

Next to the debate over mixed husbandry, the most powerful impulse behind New England farm reform was rural outmigration. In the decade after 1850, 33 percent of Massachusetts' towns lost population, along with 39 percent of Maine's towns, 47 percent of those in New Hampshire, and 53 percent of those in Vermont. In the 1860s, partly because of the Civil War, the number of towns losing population rose even higher, then fell below the 1850–1860 figure in the 1870s. Outmigration was heaviest on the slopes of the White and Green Mountains and in the western uplands of Maine and Massachusetts, and almost all of the significant decline came from the smallest towns. Nevertheless, the experience was sufficiently widespread to touch the lives of most northern New Englanders, challenging their sense of the essential rectitude of rural life.[25]

In part the causes of outmigration were national and structural, far beyond the scope of a single regional solution. The downward trends in farm prices, the pull of expanding cities, and the cultivation of the Great Plains disrupted rural lives throughout the country. New England's long winters and stony soils made urban opportunities and western lands seem all the more inviting, but these regional disadvantages merely reinforced the impact of world-shaping trends at work at midcentury.[26]

Classic works like Harold F. Wilson's *Hill Country of Northern New England* portray this period as the "winter" of New England agriculture. As early as 1830, Wilson wrote, "the buoyancy of life on the uplands had worn away." Beginning in 1978 with Paul W. Gates's study of Gilsum, New Hampshire, more recent works have qualified that impression.[27] In his 1984 book on Chelsea, Vermont, Hal S. Barron has argued that outmigrants were mostly poor farmers or their progeny and displaced artisans, whose departure left behind a more solidly integrated community.[28] In some senses, outmigration reflected the vigor as much as the weakness of New England rural life. The abandonment of lands brought into production simply on the strength of their virgin soils and forest resources marked the end of an unstable phase of frontier agriculture. Recently Michael M. Bell has noted a dramatic increase in yields per acre "at the very time when the traditional model posits a rapid fall."[29] Even contemporaries pointed out that New England farmers achieved the highest levels of savings in the nation, and their yields per acre were higher than those in the West; moreover, the prices they received for their produce were twice as high.[30]

Yet few rural New Englanders could dismiss outmigration entirely. At a Vermont farmers' club meeting, Z. E. Jameson complained that many neighborhoods were "so bare of young people, that stillness and dullness and almost a moldiness rests upon the community." Following the reading of his paper, "considerable discussion sprang up, and various opinions as to the best way to prevent the depletion of the State by emigration were expressed." Laments like this punctuate contemporary articles in the farm press.[31]

If indeed the record of rural decline has been overdrawn, why was there so much hand-wringing in the press? Why were signs of a healthy agricultural economy so unconvincing to contemporaries? As H. N. Muller suggests, a turnover approaching one-half a town's population was a social trauma that could not be ignored. Outmigration also disproportionately affected the small, mixed-crop farms that depended on the presence of large families ready to confront the varied tasks of raising several forms of crops and livestock, processing subsistence foods, and preparing items for market—in addition to caring for the vast tracts of land over which this system was thinly spread. Such farms "paid" because family labor costs were literally kept at subsistence levels.[32] Since family and farm were so closely interlinked, the labor crisis precipitated by outmigration was a family crisis as well: it threatened patriarchal succession and implied that rural youth no longer saw farming as their highest ambition. "The instances are far too common where a farmer has reared quite a number of boys, and finds in his old age that not one is willing to remain on the farm, and that in consequence the ancestral home, however dear to the father's heart, must fall into other hands." Descriptions of decimated rural districts, however misconstrued, challenged the Yankee farmer's self-image and self-confidence.[33]

Along with the trend toward commercial farming and outmigration, a third source of uncertainty was a growing awareness of social stratification in rural society. In the second half of the century disparities in wealth became more systemic as latecomers, struggling with marginal lands and poor transportation on the towns' back lots, drew apart socially and culturally.[34] The transition to commercial cropping drew these distinctions more clearly. Farmers with access to markets plied their soils with better fertilizers, seeds, and equipment and watched their yields increase, while those in remote neighborhoods stagnated. Once-prosperous communities, bypassed by railroads, lost population.[35] Hubbardton, northwest of Rutland, was "a small, ragged, poor town . . . [with] no convenient centre—almost all edge and corners," its chronicler explained. He felt compelled to document its existence simply "to keep up the remembrance of it . . . in order to preserve its name and place among the very thriving towns around."[36]

Historians like Christopher Clark have done much to illuminate the unraveling of traditional agrarian economies, but the ways in which rural New Englanders thought about this transformation are not so well documented. What does seem clear, however, is that this troubled generation clung doggedly to a traditional ideology while struggling with the new demands of the marketplace.[37] On public occasions, speakers sang praises to the character of the founding fathers and mothers and to the familiar landscape, and they articulated a commitment to transmit this heritage to the generations to come.[38] Anchored by these values, New Englanders faced the winds of change. Adjusting to a world transformed by commercial capitalism challenged New England farmers, and they responded with a vigorous reform campaign that embraced both tradition and progress.[39]

Farm Betterment and the Reform of Nature

In 1880 the Reverend L. S. Rowland of Lee, Massachusetts, delivered a treatise titled "The Social and Intellectual Life of the Farmer" before the Housatonic Agricultural Society. Rowland's lecture focused on three concerns. First, he worried that isolation and overwork produced a conservative, narrow mind. How could farmers, so indulgent of the old and so suspicious of the new, adjust to the quickening pace of change? Second, Rowland saw New England farmers as wedded to "purely material standards" that led to a "kind of barrenness in the life of many." Even prosperous farmers impoverished their lives in their misguided pursuit of thrift. Third, Rowland worried that farming was too solitary an occupation: men and women suffered from an isolation "often fatal to health, to happiness, and to life itself."[40]

That Rowland questioned the value of self-reliance seems at odds with Yankee self-imagining, but at a time when expanding markets necessitated more formal systems of cooperation, he saw the need for new thinking. His appeal for community interaction also harked back to an older tradition of village mutualism, and his critique of the "grim spirit of utilitarianism" reflected the ambivalence with which farmers viewed the intrusion of market relations into a traditional community-oriented ethos. Rowland went on to pose some remedies, including a "more genial domestic life," greater fellowship, and, of course, spiritual revival. His solutions were naive, but his articulation of the need to reinvigorate old values to meet the challenges of the future characterized the general climate of opinion among local leaders.

Concerns like these paved the way for a broad discussion of rural life. Midcentury, according to Edwin C. Rozwenc, was a "golden age" of county agricultural societies. State boards of agriculture emerged in the 1850s, and fairs were improved to demonstrate and reward exemplary farm products. The arrival of the Patrons of Husbandry (Grange) in the 1870s offered another forum for intercourse among farmers.[41] Much of the discussion in these organizations was technical or economic. In the face of mounting western competition, New Englanders were seeking a new niche in eastern metropolitan markets, adapting their small farms and varied surroundings to efficient, high-yield production. The influence of the new agricultural colleges, fairs, and boards of agriculture; the growing interest in new farm machinery, and the widening impact of rail transportation prompted a lively discussion of all aspects of farm life.[42]

Farmers and reformers reacted to the pressures of change in different ways, but all advice shared three characteristics. First, reformers advocated intensive use of farm resources, either to buttress traditional strategies or to strengthen the competitive position of the single-crop farmer. Second, land-use reform combined a practical response to increased market opportunities with a recognition that the region's more idealistic core values must be preserved.[43] Third, reformers realized that the viability of the farm depended on the viability of the surrounding natural landscape.[44]

Reforms focused most intently on the soils. By midcentury the broad fields cleared by pioneering farm families were "demanding compensation," as one reformer put it, "for the fruits they have so liberally yielded in past time."[45] Farmers were urged to cultivate smaller acreage more intensively, to grub up the weeds from their smaller plots, to plow up the poor meadows, apply more manure, straighten fences, and make their farms more productive.[46] Modernists recommended chemical fertilizers, and traditionalists advised spreading muck from the lowlands and bogs, ashes, bones, waste from watercloses and sink drains, hennery sweepings from the barnyard, and fish or seaweed— "small mines of wealth" that could renew worn soils.[47] Robbing the soils of their fertility was not only unprofitable but iniquitous: "Like all other violations committed against the laws of God," one editor admonished, "land will not be cheated nor cannot be deceived like credulous human beings, as many a man has found who made the attempt." As Carolyn Merchant points out, new intensive farming techniques separated farmers mentally from nature. Still, older transcendental perspectives lingered; reform literature indicates how important this traditional moral landscape was to the reformer's world.[48]

Conscious of the gulf that separated farm from farm, rural people used their club meetings and their press to exchange useful knowledge, and farm journal editors nurtured this practice as a basic function of the agricultural press.[49] According to historian Sally McMurry, they "aimed for an audience of practical farmers rather than for the elite of 'gentlemen farmers' with whom book farming was popularly associated." Hoping to broaden their readership, editors "made the scope of their subject deliberately large, encompassing a wide range of topics affecting rural life."[50]

Among these diverse intellectual pursuits was natural history, a popular pastime with both practical and spiritual significance for farm reform. The study of nature had immense appeal. "In almost every town," a correspondent in the *Burlington Free Press* observed, "there is a farmer or mechanic who has addicted himself to some kind of knowledge very remote from his occupation. Here you will find a shoemaker . . . who has attained celebrity as a botanist. In another village there may be a wheelwright, who would sell his best coat for a rare shell."[51] Editorial correspondents hypothesized about the way dew was formed, why some insects were found in temperate and others in tropical climates, why rocks in their fields were polished, why bottles of liquid wrapped in wet cloth remained cool, and countless other matters of natural intrigue.

This was more than simple intellectual curiosity. The contemplative farmer, deriving a better theoretical understanding of nature, improved the day-to-day applications of his trade, elevated his work, and distinguished his occupation.[52] Farmers worked with nature on a daily basis; their mixed-cropping strategies drew a wide range of natural forces into their intellectual purview. This body of knowledge linked the farm to the natural world and spelled out the arena of common responsibility in reshaping this natural landscape to meet the needs of the modern era.

Farm-journal editors were sensitive to the importance of this popular natural history. While lauding the "great improvements" attributed to academic science, they welcomed the day-to-day observations made by common farmers, and even ventured an opinion or two about the relative advantages of untutored wisdom: at work in the field or woods, one editor thought, farmers enjoyed "greater opportunity to make new discoveries . . . than the professor whose life is spent in the laboratory or academic hall."[53] Such musings confirm our image of the farmer's prejudice against "book learning," but this skepticism expressed more complex rural traditions as well.

Farmers democratized natural history; any person "with right habits of thought and observation," they believed, could participate. They also preferred to judge theories against local empirical evidence.[54] Conditioned by New England's varied growing conditions, they realized that any general scientific premise was subject to local qualification. Work performed in academies was "mainly general"; no such principles could "produce satisfactory results in every place." Understanding would proceed upward, as farmers altered and amended "the faulty parts as practice and experience may suggest."[55] A democratic local dialogue would build knowledge from the bottom up.

Although farmers were suspicious of theory passed down from elites, they were far from closed-minded. Popular natural history was steeped in the everyday details of farm management and charged by the quickening influence of inbred curiosity, new observations, the drive to increase the productivity of the land, and the argumentative bent of the New England mind. One farmer questioned the wisdom of exterminating raccoons, observing that they fed on grubs that ruined local meadows. Such mundane ideas were essential to a better ordering of the landscape: "We must determine the relation between the good and evil before we can strike a balance."[56] Precise knowledge would harmonize the practical use of the land with the moral order of the natural world.

In this flurry of local commentary we find echoes of the contemporaneous Romantic and transcendentalist view of nature, brought to earth and put to work on the farm. It was moral and teleological—a "broad-gauged integrative 'natural history'" that viewed social and natural behavior in the same moral light, as Donald Worster puts it.[57] Precisely how the delicate roots of the plant "gather up the moisture which holds in solution some of the constituents of its own future composition" was not entirely apparent to finite minds, but the spiritual ends of this life-giving principle could be surmised. Natural history revealed the First Great Cause; the principles derived could be applied to the practical management of the farm, the woodlot, or the landscape.[58]

Puritan teleology, whereby the world was understood as a commodious place for Christian work and worship, also lingered in this natural history. Explaining the behavior of dew, for instance, was a striking exhibition of the thinking that bound together the purposes of the farm and the Purpose of Nature. At night, when the surface of the earth cooled, the air, seeking equilibrium, "must cool also." Those substances that cooled first "also attract first and most abundantly the particles of falling dew." Thus providence became manifest. "The grass-plot is wet while the gravel-walk is dry; and the thirsty pasture and every green leaf are drinking in the descending moisture, while the naked land and the barren highway are still unconscious of their fall."[59] Commercial farming had clouded the colonial husbandman's mystical understandings of the natural world, but the revolution in mechanistic thinking, so ably detailed by Carolyn Merchant, remained incomplete: farmers continued to view nature as an instrument of providential design, and farming as an occupation fraught with moral lessons.

Paradoxically, these moral discussions underscore the radical anthropocentrism of the nineteenth-century farmer. Nature "humbled herself" before him: "Her firmest rocks waste away to aid him in his designs. The clouds spread over the earth, and drop fatness, to increase his riches. The thunder roars and the lightnings play, to give purity to the atmosphere whose healthfulness is his strength." Natural forces harmonized to assure the overall success of the farmer's calling. "All nature, from the rolling sun with its planetary escort, to the crawling insect so small as to defy the searching of his vision . . . are his, and operate for weal or woe, in aiding him in his designs."[60] Mountains raked the moisture from the passing clouds and sent it "toward the point it can reach nearest the center of the earth." Rushing to its appointed place, water irrigated the crops, turned the millwheels, and washed the soils of the mountains down to enrich the valley farms. These interwoven natural energies aided the people "in what is greatly essential to their prosperity and happiness."[61] Thus was the farmer's supremely imperialistic relation to nature idealized.

Yet the hubris that put the farmer at the center of this universe also disciplined him: the success of the farm depended on moving in unison with nature's "secret workings." Destiny, written in the environment, was to be carried out by citizens working in conformity with natural law. This moral and practical imperative lent a powerful incentive to observe, explain, and discuss natural processes. It also added a moral component to practical apprehensions about upsetting nature's balance.[62]

When farmers disturbed these laws, nature renewed the soils and regenerated the forests.[63] This redemptive theme, a reflection of liberal Christianity, was coupled with an equally powerful moral sanction against disrupting natural harmonies. "I don't believe *Mother Earth*, if properly treated will ever refuse to remunerate the husbandman for his labor," a Maine farmer thought. But he noted, after a year of unusual drought, that "Nature sometimes forces her lessons with great severity, compelling man to endure hard penalties for his improvidence." Viewing nature as a beneficent female counterpart to the stern patriarchal probity of the Christian God breathed moral meaning into land-use concerns that had lost some of their ethical significance with the privatization of common lands. Abuse of the land brought decisive retribution, not only to the individual farm but to the entire community.[64] This stark but redemptive vision provided a moral framework for natural history and a guide to reasserting common stewardship over the agrarian landscape.

Landscape Reform, 1840–1870

In 1873 Z. E. Jameson of Irasburgh spoke before the Vermont Agricultural Society on the topic of swamp reclamation. Like the naturalists who corresponded through the farm press, Jameson, a reformer, embraced a localistic and experiential understanding of the proper relation between farm improvement and nature. As he pointed out, the soils of Vermont were "so various in their character that almost every farm, however small . . . require[s] the personal attention of the owner to decide how it shall be tilled, how fertilized, and how cropped." The acquaintance of the farmer with the land over the years, "like the friendship of true friends," would become more intimate, and eventually the potential embedded in each configuration would be realized.[65] Farm by farm, Vermont's natural landscape would be transformed to fulfill a larger purpose, a more human end.

The farmer, Jameson thought, would learn over time to appreciate the various ways in which the land could be ordered and made productive. Most farms offered a "swelling, arable soil, that gives the site to the farm buildings, the rich garden, and the fertile fields that surround them." In addition, there was "the high and rocky land," unsuitable for tillage but "crowned by the beautiful trees and bordered by the closely grazed turf." And finally, most farms contained a low section, a wild, dark, tangled quarter resistant to the improving hand. This poorly drained soil—"the last to be cleared, and the most difficult and unprofitable in the clearing"—represented a moral as well as practical challenge. Here nature was threatening rather than beneficent: "The farmer fears for his cattle as they graze over its treacherous, springing turf, and there are traditions of lost cattle buried alive in its depths." This wetlands, stagnant and resistant to the purifying rays of the sun, was a threat to the family's well-being, "poisoning the air by its exhalations, breeding its myriads of mosquitoes, blood-thirsty tormentors, the home of thousands of frogs whose wails and croakings are welcome to the ear in early spring, but soon become anything but heavenly music."[66]

Jameson's farm geography, his aggressively anthropocentric view of nature, expressed in moral terms the New Englander's conviction that every rock and rill of the landscape could be made to "pay" in some way or another. Spurred by market forces and inspired by their own moral view of the land, farmers learned to use their soils more intensively. One commentator enumerated the disordering and obtrusive natural elements that outraged this reform temper: "A parcel of ground is stony and it is in consequence half tilled, if tilled at all . . . Brush is suffered to grow along the fences and around stumps monopolizing too great a share of the field. A little spring of water is suffered to saturate and spoil the land for valuable culture for rods around it."[67] Systematic farming implied a thorough reworking of this landscape, an absolute subjection of wild nature, after weighing each feature's highest potential.

Farmers looked to the land with an improving eye, drawing fine the tension between the natural and the cultural landscapes.[68] In this supremely anthropocentric view of nature, elements either aided or impeded the cultivation of the earth. This thinking brought endless speculation about the "proper ends" of various natural phenomena: "Nature never wastes her energies needlessly."[69] Farmers were urged to excise noxious features and bring order to the uneven natural boundaries of the farm. Ragged, broken surfaces would give way to smooth fields, each assigned its highest purpose.[70]

As Jameson had suggested, the ubiquitous bogs and swamps of the uplands were the most perplexing feature of the morally ordered landscape.[71] Commentators were at some loss to explain the means by which they could enrich the farm and the farmer's pocketbook. "Among the many little obstructions which nature has placed in the way of the practical farmer," J. W. Seely wrote in the New York *Cultivator,* "none appear more repulsive than those little swamps and marshes which are here and there promiscuously seen in the midst of fertile lands."[72] Yet these wetlands filled an important niche in the morally ordered landscape as the "rich receptacles" for the natural flow of organic materials from the untillable hilltops to the more hospitable valleys.[73] This vital intention was hidden beneath the stagnant waters, which, contrary to the rewards inherent in the muck-beds below, harbored worthless plants, "loathsome reptiles, and . . . myriads of annoying insects" and filled the atmosphere with the seeds of human disease. In their unreclaimed state, swamps "disfigure the fair face of nature." Yet draining these foul sinks disclosed "a fertile piece of land, whose beauty shall charm the eye, and whose products shall be wealth."[74]

Contrast between the actual and the possible in this intensely moral landscape made wetlands reclamation a sort of crusade. Thus despite the laboriousness of the project, reformers urged farmers onward: "Go for that swamp, relieve it of stagnant water, smooth its surface, sow the best varieties of low land grasses," Jameson admonished.[75] Farmers met the challenge with incredible energy; they ditched the bogs, burned them, removed the stumps, roots, and fallen trees, and smoothed the surface; they cut off the hard, grassy tussocks, leveled the ground, and carted the matted roots away to the upland to rot. One farmer cut over six hundred wagon loads of tussocks from his hundred-acre meadow in order to mow it with a machine. After years of weathering and working, swamps could be made productive, but this effort, counted in labor time, was often more expensive than the land could recompense. Reclamation illustrated the fact that the farm was a trust and the farmer morally obliged to make manifest its sources of fertility for future generations.

One of the clearest examples of the moral scope of agricultural reform was the emphasis on rural beautification. The farmer, C. H. Joyce told a club gathering in 1870, is "connected by a visible link with those who preceded him [and] . . . those who shall come after him, and to whom he is to transmit a sacred legacy and a home."[76] Though not a conservation theme in the usual sense, farmscape reform illustrates the symbolic nature of the farmer's landscape and the links between the farm and its natural surroundings. It was also a powerful expression of common stewardship over private lands. The cumulative effect of yards and fields blemished by stagnant pools of water, intrusive boulders, odd boards and equipment parts, posts, weeds, toppled stone walls, and cut limbs marred the reputation of the neighborhood and encouraged the belief that the crisis in farming was irreversible. Farm editors and grange leaders launched a vigorous assault on such visual scars, advocating cleaner roads, neater grounds, more shade trees, and straighter walls and fences.[77]

This movement developed partly as a response to metropolitan commentary on rural life. Between 1870 and 1910 the northeastern press carried scores of articles detailing the decline of the New England town. Piqued by these essays, reformers urged their readers to clean up their farms and neighborhoods. Maine farms were not abandoned, one speaker summarized; "they only appeared to be."[78] Rural people grew more conscious of this visual legacy as better rail connections brought travelers, tourists, and summer boarders into their neighborhoods.[79] Rail travel also allowed locals to evaluate landscapes elsewhere. Passing through the suburban estates around Boston, one thoroughly impressed Mainer noted that "the whole region for miles is like a garden."[80] Farm beautification was a community concern: the public had no right to prevent the farmer from "impoverishing himself," an editor lectured, "but it has a right to demand that he shall not make his farm a nuisance to his neighbors."[81]

Attention to farm beautification also reflected a generational change as farms emerged from an era of pioneering land-clearing. Pushing back the wilderness had been an epic achievement, and early farmers' stark views of nature and landscape reflected this legacy of unremitting toil. But as they cleared away the trees, broke the ground, and paid off their mortgages, their perspectives shifted.[82] Regional novelist Rowland Robinson noted this new landscape vision: the ragged desolation of stumps and log-heaps gave way to "broad fields of tilth, meadow land, and pastures . . . dotted with herds and flocks." Wilderness, no longer a tangled barrier to civilization, mingled pleasantly in the mind's eye with the pastoral landscape. "The jangle of the sheep-bell was as frequent as the note of the thrush in the half-wild upland pastures."[83] By midcentury the raw edges of the cleared lands had grown smooth, and farmers were more at ease with their natural surroundings. "These beautiful landscape pictures rarely existed . . . thirty years ago," the *Maine Farmer* observed in 1868.

> Since farmers have cleared out the rocks and stumps from their fields and left them smooth and inviting, and the second growth of trees, such as the maple, the birch and the beech has sprung up, intermingled with the evergreen hemlock, spruce and fir, wherewith to cover up the old logs and rocks, it has wonderfully changed all this, and now almost any place among the older

settled towns has its beautiful views and its pleasant homes, and summer travelers from the cities ramble among them with the greatest pleasure.[84]

Thus while some reformers urged eradicating nature from the farm-scape, others proposed the application of husbandry to the remaining natural features in this domestic scene: farmers should encourage useful vegetation that sprang up voluntarily and take advantage of natural contours, boulders, brooks, and patriarchal trees—features that gave each New England farm its distinctive character.

The "rural art" these reformers advocated was consonant with the traditional view that the well-being of the farm depended on the well-being of the natural world.[85] English country landscapes, centuries in the making, subordinated nature to artifice, but in northern New England landscape ideals depended on a backdrop of forested mountain slopes to accent the domesticity of the cultivated foreground.[86] To some extent, this mix of nature and culture hinged on what farm leaders considered a "proper proportion between forest areas and farming land." A mix of 40 percent forest would ensure a proper balance of nature.[87] Lithographs incorporated this principle in scenes that focused on the farm or village as the font of human culture but extended back to a pattern of evenly fenced pastures and fields, to the woodlot, and finally to the verdant rolling hills that provided the ultimate complement to a broadly articulated country life.[88] This angle of vision, from the valley floor to the distant rim of hills and forests, crystallized an orderly, thematic landscape that extended farm reform into its natural surroundings.

Stretching beyond the tilled field and garden, the farm beautification movement buttressed a subtle conservation ethic predicated, like the farmer's natural history, on the relation between farm and nature. Upon the actual landscape, according to historians William C. Lipke and Philip N. Grime, people superimpose a "mythic, often mental picture." For northern New England, this symbolic landscape was a "harmonious balance" between forest and farm, humans and nature.[89] Landscape stability embodied moral certitude about country living; when its elements were unhinged, rural civilization was threatened.[90] The seeds of a conservation ethic, sown in this landscape, germinated first in farm beautification and woodlot management, then in appeals for protecting the region's forest.

Farm Reform and Bird Protection

Reformers posited an intensely anthropocentric perspective in which the farm stood at the center of a morally ordered natural world. The way in which this perspective affected nature is exemplified by the debate over bird life in the farm press. When the country was new, a Mr. Churchill of Rutland County, Vermont, noted in 1853, "the ear was gratified by a thousand melodious trills and solos, which . . . made the woods an orchestra" and offered moral lessons to the careful observer: "Their gaiety never left them, and their activity was a continual rebuke to the indolent." Robins, thrushes, orioles, wrens, and other species, Churchill lamented, had largely vanished. An important link to the primeval forest—the symbolic natural borderland—had been severed.[91] Spurred by remarks from ornithologists, agricultural reformers, and farmers like old Mr. Churchill, rural people began a prolonged debate over the place of birds in the agrarian landscape. This dialogue set the tone for the bird protection movement at the end of the century.

Some farmers saw birds as beneficial; they eradicated noxious insects, cheered the worker in the field, and delighted the rural family with their song. Now and then they helped themselves "pretty bountifully to fruit," one admitted, but "should they not be paid for their labors, and allowed a dessert after their insect repast?"[92] Others were less generous: "I am in favor of destroying *all* depredators that are proved to be such," a farmer wrote in the *Cultivator* in 1845. "We must take care of our own crops and show no partiality to any intruders or thieves, however handsome their dress or fine their music."[93] Having sculpted the wilderness to their own purposes, farmers were committed to reestablishing nature's symmetry by encouraging only those elements they found useful in the new agrarian landscape.[94]

In its simplest form, the logic of transforming nature to serve agricultural needs determined farmers' attitudes toward birds. At mid-century they began compiling a classification of species that accorded with their impulse to mold the landscape into a more perfect seat of husbandry: some birds were useful, others noxious, and a third group of "doubtful utility."[95] Commentators eschewed sentiment in favor of utilitarian arguments: "Rats are useful—they eat worms, and even one another, when they are very hungry." Yet rats were killed and birds were saved. Partiality and prejudice had to be weeded from this discussion.[96]

In practice, the argument was never so simple. The impulse to weigh the birds' value by their plumage and song was more or less irresistible, and farmers inevitably fell back on aesthetic considerations. Judging the "right to life of the animal races . . . [on the basis of] items of beauty and sweetness" might be unscientific, one claimed, but the sight of robins on the lawn was satisfying: "I will endure far more loss from them than from crows or blackbirds, before I will shoot."[97] Determining the "right to life" for bird species was difficult, moreover, because the study of avian habits was still in its infancy. That birds were an important element in agriculture generally was clear, but at midcentury students of bird life were only beginning to discern the habits and diets of individual species. The attempt to assess the practical effect of birds on crops became, as one farmer put it, "the object of our most familiar intercourse."[98]

A third difficulty with this utilitarian taxonomy was the inevitable tendency to project human qualities onto the subjects under consideration. Birds were viewed in familiar ethical terms, with all the ambiguity that attends moral debates in human society. Although legislative enactments protected robins as songbirds, farmers formed their own judgments, since robins also ate fruits and berries.[99] Friends and foes alike accented the bird's human qualities, some favoring its diligence and its virtue as an "early riser" and others condemning its gluttonous, insolent manner.[100] "I do not know as I voted right," a New Hampshire statesman admitted following a debate over a crow bounty: "I like the skill of crows . . . [They] swoop down [on cornfields], but station one sentinel crow on picket duty, and with the utmost confidence rely upon his skill and faithfulness . . . I heard that crows . . . eat more grubs, worms, and destructive insects than corn, and my mind turned warmly to crows. Then the flank of the [pro-]crow brigade was turned by a statement that crows eat eggs,—eggs of sweet-singing birds,—and I voted for a bounty on crows."[101]

As with human ethics, the ethics of bird life was difficult to map. The debate was further complicated by the futility of viewing any of nature's various parts in isolation. The simple utilitarian categories—beneficial or noxious—captured little of a bird's complex ecological, aesthetic, and even moral significance. The debate, in the end, was an important lesson in the interconnectedness of nature.

Nowhere was this ambiguity more apparent than in discussions of the yellow-bellied sapsucker, which became the focus of a minor verbal tempest in midcentury farm papers. According to John James Audubon, whose word was not considered final by farmers, the food of the sapsucker consisted of "wood-worms and beetles, to which they add small grapes and various berries during autumn and winter." The sapsucker's notable behavior characteristic was its habit of drilling scores of evenly spaced holes in the trunks of trees—and therein lay the debate.[102] It seems ironic that New England farmers, who made a livelihood of drawing sap from a maple tree year after year, would deny a bird the same right, yet the conclusion that the sapsucker indeed sucked sap from orchard trees ranked the creature ethically among those who "live on the products of the farmers' labor."[103] Hence, they were noxious.

But not to everyone. "Of all our woodpeckers," a Boston specialist exclaimed, "none rid the apple-trees of so many vermin as this."[104] There were skeptics: "Is he after worms when he pecks those regular ranks of holes? Nobody has ever proved this, and it is essentially improbable that the larvae of any insect exist beneath the apparently healthy bark of so many different species." The bird, one farmer observed, was "small, but dreadfully destructive."[105] The issue, however, was less the fate of the tree than the moral implications of the holes: was the sapsucker contributing to the weal of the farmer or living off the fruits of his labor?

As was characteristic of popular natural history, the debate focused on practical observation. Defenders noted that the sapsucker avoided those forest trees with the most saccharine or nutritious sap, and claimed they abandoned the orchards precisely when sap began flowing most abundantly. Others observed that many old trees were "completely covered with holes, [yet] . . . their branches were broad, luxuriant, and loaded with fruit." Detractors pointed out that the sapsucker lacked the "peculiar barbed tongue" that true woodpeckers used to draw insects from holes.[106]

Ornithologists, in fact, were not much help in this issue. In 1879 Vermont naturalist Henry Fairbanks, who had sent the Smithsonian its first sapsucker egg specimens only twenty years earlier, admitted that the habits of the bird were still very much in question. Edward A. Samuels compiled conflicting opinions from correspondents in *Our Northern and Eastern Birds,* published in 1883.[107] Seeking to explain the holes, Fairbanks pointed out that he had recently observed a pair of sapsuckers attacking an elm close to his window. After several rows of holes were bored, the sap flowed freely, catching thousands of little flies and ants attracted by the syrup. "Both birds came making a good deal of outcry . . . The whole family remained in the neighborhood a week or more feeding from that tree until the flies were eaten up and the callow birds nearly full grown." Sapsuckers, he felt, were not sucking sap, but instead "setting in this way a fly-trap." Although the holes were no less evident, their moral implications changed. Since then, Fairbanks concluded, "I have not felt much like wantonly destroying them."[108] Close observation and systematic experiments with captured sapsuckers between 1892 and 1911 revealed that the bird did indeed rely on sap for nutrition, but ornithologists continued to defend its habits. Edward Howe Forbush pointed out that "there never are sapsuckers enough here to do much harm." Usually, he felt, they were hunting insects, and their drilling produced only cosmetic defects.[109]

In the 1890s hunting advocates, naturalists, and birdlovers came together in a campaign for nongame bird protection. Key figures in the movement were well-to-do women living, as Robin Doughty has put it, "just beyond the urban fringe" in the new suburban Arcadias.[110] These suburbanites were drawn to the debate over birds for vastly different reasons, but they shared some basic premises with earlier agrarian bird defenders. Their efforts simply refined the farmers' utilitarian bird taxonomy by expanding the list of "beneficial" birds.[111] The avian world, they showed, was essential to the balance of nature.

By the turn of the century agricultural leaders, too, were recommending a general amnesty on birds. In part this perspective reflected a decline in bird populations themselves. Relying on reports from across the state, Massachusetts game commissioners estimated in 1908 that numbers had dropped in some cases to one percent of presettlement figures. In the absence of systematic bird counts, these estimates are unreliable, but they suggest a widely shared perception of loss.[112] The effects of such "biologic blunders" as the bounties on hawks and owls, the slaughter of the heath hen, passenger pigeon, woodcock, and wood duck, and the widespread destruction of nesting spots were becoming apparent.[113] The farmers' reconciliation with birds was also related to a regional shift from grains and orcharding to dairy and vegetables, commodities less vulnerable to avian depredations. The brown-tail moth epidemic at the turn of the century also brought a greater appreciation for insectivorous birds.[114] Finally, campaigns by organizations like the Audubon societies helped reduce the list of birds considered "noxious."

An 1886 letter to Vermont's Grange paper offers a different perspective on the relation between farmers and birds. The granger dismissed the "senseless twaddle about 'sparing the birds'" that cluttered the agricultural press. "After reading half a dozen of these articles one would think that farmers were bent on killing every feathered songster that dared invade their premises." In fact, he maintained, farmers rarely killed birds, not because they did not wish to but because they had no time to waste on birds. Farmers, he concluded, were "thoroughly disgusted with these annual 'bird sermons' preached by those who have more sentiment than common sense."[115] In fact few conservationists would have taken issue with the Vermont granger's observation: concern in the movement had always focused on plumage hunters, careless Sunday shooters, and youthful egg collectors rather than farmers.

The debate over birds in the farm press may have been a tempest in a teapot, but it was important for several reasons. First, it publicized the idea that birds followed a variety of habits. Drawn into the debate on the utility of birds, farmers became intensely interested in the ecological niches that each species filled—and how each affected their crops. The debate had broader implications. Farmers' concerns for the role of each species stirred interest among academics, if we are to judge from their frequent contributions in the agricultural press. Despite the suburban base for bird protection in the 1890s, it is significant that both the Biological Survey and key state ornithological reports originated in departments of agriculture, and that official arguments for bird protection continued to echo the utilitarian taxonomy first formulated by agrarian reformers in the 1870s.[116] The science of ornithology was sharpened on the stone of incessant rural controversy.

The debate also advanced popular perceptions of the balance of nature. Arguments both for and against birds were anthropocentric, but they were set in a larger ecological context. As one protectionist put it in 1873: "The weakening of a single link in the chain of being is productive of dire results." Birds offered lessons in the interconnectedness of nature.[117]

The discussion of the usefulness of birds shifted after 1890 to the women's-club bulletins, academic presses, sporting journals, and conservation publications that we usually associate with bird conservation. Yet the terms of the debate remained remarkably stable. The tension between utilitarian and aesthetic considerations, the anthropocentric premises, and the ecological principles upon which the arguments rested were revealed by farmers long before urban conservationists adopted them. While conservation was becoming a passion among birdlovers and naturalists, farmers were making their own peace with birds.

Farm Improvement and Woodlot Forestry

Both the utilitarian and the spiritual bents of agricultural reform were apparent in the discussion of farm woodlots. As managers of the discrete blocks of land that made up so much of the New England forest, farm families were the first woodland owners in America to confront the problems of forest depletion. Thus they were well situated to pioneer the development of practical forestry.[118] Under the improving eye of the reformer, farmers learned to increase the value of their woodlands by removing unmerchantable species, cutting timber more carefully, protecting the remaining forests, and keeping livestock from the woods.[119] Prescriptions like these carried both practical and moral implications. They were predicated on farm profits, yet they encouraged a general concern for regional uplift and restoration of the "harmonious balance of nature, disturbed by the destruction of former forests."[120]

The woodlot was an important part of the local economy. It was a source of maple sugar, fuelwood, and material for buildings, tools, vehicles, fences, and furniture. It was a bank account of sorts, since trees could be sold occasionally to meet extraordinary expenses. Woodlots also met village needs for construction material and fuel for brickyards and lime kilns.[121]

Despite this importance, woodlots were managed indifferently early in the century. In 1792 the Massachusetts Society for Promoting Agriculture sent out a questionnaire asking, among other things, if the growth of timber in woodlots was keeping pace with cutting. The negative response prompted the society to encourage experiments. Most farmers ignored these early calls, but where urban fuel shortages boosted the value of wooded land or intensive farming left marginal fields fallow, woodlot management drew interest.[122] As they did with other elements of the landscape, farmers learned to categorize trees according to their value to the farm. They enumerated those that should be "profitably cultivated" and condemned others—red cedar, hornbeam, poplar, willow, locust, cherry, red oak, bass, and sycamore, for instance—as noxious. Ongoing discussion of the advantages and disadvantages of each species pioneered the science of practical forestry.[123]

Here, too, the reform impulse was largely experimental. John M. Weeks of Middlebury, Vermont, cleared two acres of dense upland second-growth hardwood in 1814, grew a crop of wheat, then pastured on the land until about 1833, when he discovered small white pines growing thickly through the pasture. In 1839 he thinned and trimmed the stand, leaving about 800 trees to the acre. "Now, on going into this forest, it seems hardly possible that so great a quantity of timber could have grown there in so short a time," he reported in 1850.[124]

Taking their inspiration from experiments like these, reformers developed an impressive store of useful information on woodlot management. Journals printed directions on planting, nurturing, trimming, pruning, and cutting various species.[125] The Massachusetts Board of Agriculture's Committee on the Management of Forest Trees monitored the progress of plantations and woodlots, recording successful seed-gathering and planting methods, growth rates among different species and soils, subsequent increases in land values, and experiments with planting machines. Such organizations consolidated information from practical farmers, gentlemen farmers, and botanists, making it widely available.[126]

Interest in woodlot management was stimulated by several midcentury developments, the most important being improved markets for wood. Railroads permitted long-distance wood shipments and created their own demand for fuelwood and ties. New England's shipbuilding industry and its burgeoning mill towns made serious inroads into native forests, and as the virgin tracts disappeared, woodlots became vital suppliers for fuel and building needs.[127] Concern for woodlots was also sparked by farm abandonment. A well-trimmed stand of trees relieved the gloomy picture of deserted fields and dilapidated houses that so worried New England reformers. Indeed, the remedy for abandoned lands was appearing spontaneously as pine and other trees encroached upon the worn fields. Better woodlots were also central to farmscape reform. As farmers adopted land-intensive techniques, they reforested the outlying acres, planting their gullies, borders, hillsides, and other inaccessible places with valuable trees.[128] "On all old farms there are spots which the plow never reaches, where nothing valuable grows, which, if planted with trees, would reclaim something that is lost."[129]

Woodlot forestry, like agricultural reform, ordered the random acts of nature, transforming the chaotic strife for existence into a harmonious blend of human and natural will. As wood became marketable, farmers extended their impulse for cultivation into a natural realm once considered mostly wild. To serve human ends properly, nature required direction. "Just examine the forest in this State and see how small a portion of the land is actually occupied by valuable, thrifty timber trees," a reformer admonished. Nature was in fact too exuberant; on denuded lands she allowed too many seedlings to start up, too many branches to develop, and too many aged trees to survive.[130] Shaping their woodlots, farmers became agents in a greater landscape evolution: "God's last finishing touch to his newly created earth was to plant . . . trees, and the first work he gave man to do was to 'dress and keep' that park covered with trees planted with his own loving hand."[131] Combining this providential mandate with an eye to profit, reformers advised planting trees at proper distances to achieve the most merchantable shape and height, and in rows, "so that you can run a cultivator through them if necessary."[132] Farmers learned how to "form a beautiful and symmetrical tree, or a grove of such," by careful planting, pruning, and thinning. The "perfect growth" would yield a forest precisely accommodated to market forces; nothing else would encumber the ground.[133]

Although profit was the primary inducement for woodlot management, reformers urged farmers beyond a stark, commercial assessment of their trees. The benefits of tree planting, unlike other forms of cultivation, did not necessarily accrue to the planter; more likely they fell to a later generation. Because trees matured slowly, advocates of better management were inclined to be expansive in discussing the rewards of tree husbandry. Farmers would draw satisfaction from the estimation future generations would bestow upon them and from the practical aesthetics of a vigorous, well-planned woodlot.[134] Not the least of the rewards would be the sight of "naked and barren fields clothed once more in verdure, profitable in itself and serviceable in protecting other things."[135] Forest use, like agriculture, positioned the farmer at the center of the natural universe as an instrument of its law.

The call to forest management blended the commercial urge to bring lands into more profitable use and the moral conviction that farmers were responsible for shaping all of New England's landscape to serve human needs. It ordered the farmscape, economized space, and imparted "picturesqueness to the landscape," linking farm improvement to older norms of community responsibility. It also expressed the divine prescription implicit in the underlying geology and topography of New England: "The Almighty has said to us: 'These hills and mountains . . . are too rough; the rocky formations are set up edgewise, and it is impossible for you to plow these hills . . . You should raise timber.'"[136]

"By the time Gifford Pinchot set out to bring scientific management to the national forests in 1905," historian Thomas R. Cox writes, "he had a body of scientific information to draw on."[137] The discussion of woodlot management, though inchoate, laid the basis for a popular movement for forest protection. It compiled a body of useful information derived from the practical experiences of farmers themselves, it sensitized rural people to the implications of cutting trees, and it legitimized the sense of common stewardship implicit in forest conservation.[138]

Toward the end of the century market pressures narrowed the scope of agricultural reform to the business of farming itself, but while rural people clung to the traditional notion that farming was an occupation rich in sidelines and alternatives, they engaged in a wide-ranging discussion of the commercial and spiritual potential in the natural land-scape.[139] The *Farmer's Monthly Visitor* proclaimed a faith that all of New Hampshire was "valuable for some purpose." Land too rocky for the plow would yield a return on wood, timber, or minerals. Maine's Board of Agriculture urged that the state's "soils, its muck beds, its marine manures, its rocks, its minerals, its fossils, its . . . quarries . . . its forest lands, all need the scrutinizing eye of the mineralogist, the chemist, and the geologist."[140] Prompted by agricultural institutions, states be-gan conducting extensive geological surveys beginning in the 1830s, resulting in some impressive tomes on regional natural history. Philo-sophically, the farm reform movement enveloped the entire land-scape.[141]

The admonitions of farm reformers, aimed at using the land more profitably, were both modern and traditional, utilitarian and spiritual. Concern for farmscape and landscape, bird life, and farm woodlots all dealt with the matter of resource efficiency, yet they carried a heavy moral content. The discussion of the farmers' relation to nature turned on a familiar sense of community responsibility and reverential respect for natural order. This moral foundation animated the politics of conservation at the grass-roots level.

The debate over the place of nature in the agrarian landscape faded somewhat as more aggressive urban elites took up the conservation crusade at the end of the century. But the degree of popular rural support for or antagonism toward this new conservation message depended in good part on how it resonated with an earlier dialogue launched by reform-minded agricultural leaders. The ecological impact of this drive to enhance farms and woodlots and to protect "beneficial" birds is difficult to judge. But it was of inestimable value as a means of preparing common people for the coming battle to protect nature. The principles and attitudes expressed in the rural press helped estab-lish the popular basis for conservation in the 1890s.[142]

CHAPTER FOUR

Common Stewardship and Private Forests

Like farming, forest use had important implications for the region's republican ideology and its popular ecological imagination. Forests protected the region's climate, its watercourses, and, as resort owners later asserted, its health and beauty. These broad practical and aesthetic considerations placed forest destruction in the umbra of public discourse. "We are but tenants of this beautiful earth, not owners in perpetuity," Maine farmers reminded their legislators in 1869 when they called for forestry regulations.[1] Their claim rested on the assumption that the benefits of a healthy forest belonged to the people. When loggers accelerated cutting in the 1870s, farmers, resort owners, and others turned to the states to reassert common stewardship over their landscape.

Although forest conservation has been amply documented as a national movement, we know relatively little about its roots in local politics. Ralph Widner, who surveyed American forestry state by state in 1968, has shown that the rising concern over forest destruction in New England was not unique. Yet each state responded differently, some purchasing forests, for instance, and others embracing private solutions. Forestry brought new forms of common stewardship, but local conditions shaped this impulse in different ways.[2]

Widner's study focused on the state forest commissions themselves, leaving the impression that these agencies, created in the 1890s, spearheaded the conservation movement. The approach misses the broader cultural and political context that gave rise to, and at times challenged, the efforts of these agencies. This attention to official proclamations parallels studies of the national conservation movement. The tendency to glean evidence of rising concern about forests from federal publications, national journals, or writings of prominent thinkers encourages the view that conservation was the domain of a small group of bureau-cratic or professional elites. Yet Harvard botanist Charles S. Sargent, an important conservationist himself, acknowledged in 1885 that "the real progress in sylviculture in Massachusetts has been made by the farmers of Barnstable and Plymouth counties, who have taught us how to plant and raise forests successfully and profitably, under the most unfavorable conditions."[3] Forest conservation is rooted in this gaunt New England soil.

In his perceptive analysis of the Progressive conservation movement, Samuel P. Hays pointed to the disjuncture between popular and pro-fessional attitudes in the 1890s. Creation of a federal forestry bureauc-racy facilitated large-scale corporate use of the forests and weeded from the discourse on forestry those moral issues that gave rise to popular concerns.[4] This phenomenon was apparent at the state level too. As state forestry agencies matured, they adopted the perspective of federal foresters, whose outlook was more cosmopolitan and more attuned to the needs of the larger forest products producers. Still, local political forces molded these overarching forestry principles in a variety of ways, often in tension with official forestry doctrine. In New England, popular conservation blended agrarian pietistic views of nature with newer Romantic, urban-based visions of the forest.

In the 1870s, as America's logging frontier moved inexorably through the virgin forests of the Great Lakes states and the South, New Englanders pondered the use of their own undeniably finite resources.[5] Early settlers focused mainly on transforming forests into fields. But as lumber and fuel-wood prices rose in urban centers, farmers began applying the principles of cultivation to their woodlots.[6] Although botanists too raised the specter of forest depletion early on, it was agrarian concern for woodlot productivity that offered a true bench-mark for popular criticism of logging practices in the second half of the century.[7]

Larger logging operations and railroad extensions into remote forest regions triggered unease throughout eastern America in the 1870s. Destructive fires, resulting from accumulations of logging slash and farmers' field-clearing activity, added to the worry.[8] New Hampshire selectmen, responding to a survey from the state board of agriculture in 1873, estimated a forest cover in their towns ranging from 10 to 65 percent, but much of this, they said, was "brush."[9] Vermont's towns reported a forest cover averaging 30 percent statewide, and the Pine Tree State, according to the *Maine Farmer,* was 46 percent forested in 1879, but most of the valuable timber in the big woods had been cut out, "and every year the spruce that floats down our rivers is growing smaller and smaller, and good pine is hardly known."[10]

Almost everywhere, however, the regenerative power of the forest was evident. In some cases pioneer stands of cherry, poplar, and birch were cut for spool wood, hastening the return to pine, spruce and hemlock, "showing what nature will do when left to herself," a Vermont farmer pointed out with unconscious irony.[11] Rapid reforestation provided a counterpoint to the bleak statements in the New Hampshire survey: North Hampton selectmen claimed that much of the "best timber" had been cut, but a new forest of twenty-year-old hardwood added "to the beauty and value of the town."[12] Others, however, worried that the new forest of dense, low-value hardwoods would not sustain their economy. "Nature is always lavish with her seeds," the *New England Farmer* reminded its readers, but "never considers commercial values." Vermonter William Chapin put the matter bluntly: "We have more bushes than trees." The vast destruction of old-growth timber, it seemed, was a fundamentally disruptive force.[13]

In 1901 J. G. Jack surveyed Vermont's upland timber resources for the U.S. Division of Forestry and took note of this pervasive anxiety. Farmers worried that the region's "most valuable asset" was "fast slipping away from them." The prospect was "generally looked upon as a gloomy one, and yet is taken apathetically because it is imagined that there is no redress or constitutional way of regulating . . . practices almost everywhere recognized as . . . disastrous to the welfare of the community at large."[14] Despite the enormous social implications of forest use, the resource seemed beyond the pale of common stewardship.

Concerns about the second-growth forest marking the aftermath of logging had a practical basis. Upland farmers considered forest destruction inimical to the small industries on which they depended for seasonal wages. Jack found abandoned sawmills everywhere. Granby, a northern Vermont town that had once employed two hundred to three hundred men, had been reduced to one family.[15] "The waning of our forests will bury agriculture and the lumber industry in a common grave," Maine agricultural professor Francis Harvey predicted.[16]

These apprehensions, in the face of a relatively stable forest cover, also reflected a set of moral assumptions about the "primeval" forest— the majestic old-growth stands that connected the farm to the natural energies and forces that sustained it. Despite the vigor of the second-growth forest, Maine farmers worried about the "disturbed harmonies of nature, whose well-balanced influences are so propitious to all her organic offspring."[17] New Englanders perceived these changes in judgmental terms; as the woods around their farms disappeared, then returned in different form, they noted—or imagined—changes in natural cycles flowing through the atmosphere, the soils, and the waters. Forest removal was a moral as well as a practical matter.

Casting their eyes over a forest landscape woven into the fabric of their existence, farmers composed a cosmic view of the importance of trees in the balance of nature. Forests knit together the landscape. They protected the bogs, ponds, and marshes from which issued a steady supply of water to power gristmills and sawmills. Forests shielded the intervale meadows from floods. Fish ponds owed their productiveness to the spawning beds in tree-lined streams deep in remote woods. By the destruction of the forest, "the physical laws of God have been outraged, the harmonious balance of nature interfered with, and disastrous consequences entailed upon mankind, which only centuries of effort can restore."[18]

To the rural mind, the reciprocal influences of forests, streams, soils, and atmosphere revealed the broader designs in nature's plan. Forests kept the air moist and protected fields from desiccating winds. They retained warmth in winter and shielded crops from the heat of summer.

Tree roots penetrated the earth to introduce air into the ground and speed the decomposition of mineral and organic matter. Forests held back the rain and issued it evenly to sustain brooks and springs. Percolating into the soils, these waters carried "more or less ammonia with them, which is a chief agent of rock decomposition." The released minerals moved in sequences of growth and decay through forest vegetation and in season nourished the farmer's crops. Hillside forests laid down a carpet of leaves in fall, and spring rains carried these fertilizing elements to valley farms below.[19] Tracing these numerous cycles was a moral exercise as much as it was natural history. New Englanders grew anxious, despite the evidence of reforestation, because the primeval forest was laden with such powerful cultural symbolism.

Continuing references to Vermonter George Perkins Marsh's conservation message, first delivered before the Rutland County Agricultural Society in 1848, can be attributed to the way Marsh's theories meshed with popular concerns about landscape. Marsh spoke to an audience of farmers keenly aware of the debate over the role of forests in the balance of nature. Ripping the trees from the fabric of this well-appointed landscape was a mistake of cosmic proportions, Marsh argued. Without them, hills became barren, yielding only "noxious weeds" that would "infest, with their scattered seeds, the richer arable grounds below."[20] Quoting this seminal speech nearly four decades later, the *Burlington Free Press* demonstrated its staying power: loss of the primeval forest left a void in the spiritual as well as the economic scheme of rural life:

Every middle-aged man, who revisits his birthplace after a few years absence, looks upon another landscape than that which formed the theatre of his youthful toils and pleasures. The signs of artificial improvement are mingled with the tokens of improvident waste, and the bald and barren hills, the dry beds of the smaller streams, the ravines furrowed out by the torrents of Spring, and the diminished thread of interval[e] that skirts the widened channel of the rivers, seem sad substitutes for the pleasant groves and brooks and broad meadows of his ancient paternal domain.[21]

Marsh's views were significant, but, as Donald Pisani has noted, they were not original; the agricultural press abounded with similar commentary.[22] A tradition of interpreting natural calamities as signs of providential disfavor disposed farmers to worry about deforestation.[23] Sweep the forests from the land, a New Hampshire agricultural leader warned, and the mountains would soon reveal a "desolation as awful as that of the Sahara." Rivers would "forsake their channels" and return as "mountain torrents, bearing inundation and destruction to all they met; going forth in madness, on errands of violence which no human power could restrain." These jeremiads show how radically perceptions of nature had changed: colonial writers viewed the primeval forest as chaotic and amoral; midcentury commentators attributed these same characteristics to a land shorn of trees.[24]

There were several common themes reflected in this popular writing. The relation between forests and climate, noted by farmers everywhere, was especially intriguing in a region where short growing seasons, numbing midwinter colds, and unpredictable frosts left farmers sensitive to vagaries in weather. Some felt that trees, rising perpendicularly from the earth's surface, attracted electricity and hence rain from the clouds. Others thought forests slowed the movement of air and clouds, thus encouraging precipitation. One reasoned that rain-bearing clouds were condensed by the "coolness exhaling" from the forests.[25] Each drought brought a new wave of such speculation.

Forests also fostered the common good as a "vast natural reservoir" retaining rainfall in the soil. Local testimony collected in 1885 by the New Hampshire Forestry Commission showed pervasive distress about diminished stream flow, a concern voiced by conservationists all across the nation. Old farmers blamed the disappearance of water-powered gristmills and sawmills on erratic stream flow, and "boyhood memories" everywhere testified to the loss of these small watercourses.[26] Such assumptions were not without their challengers. Farmers and professional foresters alike debated the effect of forest removal, and gradually it became clear that differences in soil type, slope, vegetation, cultivation, natural storage, wetlands, and overflow lands over hundreds of square miles made any generalization difficult.[27] But concerns about watershed persisted, inspired by local observation and moral interpretations of the landscape, and indeed they were absorbed by prominent American conservationists such as Franklin B. Hough, the physician turned forester who became the first chief of the U.S. Division of Forestry. Ward Shepard, writing in a U.S. Forest Service circular in 1928, noted that "common observations" continued to buttress the watershed theory. "In a forest . . . during even a heavy rain one always has a sense of the dripping of water rather than of a rapid rush."[28]

Influenced by popular discussion of these cultural, economic, and moral implications, conservationists advanced the principle of common stewardship. "W. P. A." argued in the *Maine Farmer* that the lumberman should be allowed "to cut and slash as he pleases in just so far as he himself is concerned," but when aggregate cutting threatened the common weal, "just and wise laws" to restrain him were in order. Although some challenged this public role, concern for the natural balance of forest and farm influenced popular political culture.[29] Still, worried upland farmers saw no way of revitalizing the concept of the commons. New Englanders well understood the contradiction between sanctifying private property and maintaining a properly ordered landscape.

Founding the Forest Commissions

In the 1880s, while Americans marveled at the demolition of the Lake States' vast forests, New England too stood on the cusp of a landscape revolution. As farmers abandoned marginal soils, fields that had once produced corn, potatoes, and grass yielded a vigorous young growth of trees—a new forest that bore striking testament to the regenerative powers of the New England environment. At the same time, rising demand for wood and wood fiber and new logging techniques threatened the verdant periphery of the composed village landscape. Rightly managed, lumbering infused these "useless" lands with new value.[30] Whether this new forest would be composed of increasingly inferior wood or valuable timber capable of sustaining the region's economy and its cultural self-image depended on what forestry procedures were followed.[31]

New England's forestry commissions, created at the turn of the century, reflected growing recognition of the public stake in the forest, a mood apparent nationally in attempts to curb forest destruction on the public domain. Official concern in New England began in 1881, when New Hampshire's legislature created a temporary commission to inquire into the extent of forest destruction. Thinking chiefly about watershed protection, the commission concluded that at least half the state's land area should "remain perpetually devoted to the production of wood and timber."[32] In 1889 New Hampshire established a second temporary board, which continued its investigations until 1891. Two years later the legislature made the commission permanent.[33] Massachusetts forestry owes much to the Massachusetts Forestry Association, formed in 1898. The organization, among other things, agitated for a state forestry commission, which was formed in 1903 with a mandate to survey forest conditions, protect and improve the forests, assist woodland owners, encourage reforestation, and suppress fires.[34]

Vermont's forestry movement began with Joseph Battell, a Middlebury legislator who in 1880 sponsored a bill to create a forestry commission. When this failed, he donated several thousand acres of forest, including Camel's Hump, to the state, as a "sample of the original forests from which Vermont derived her name."[35] In 1882 Battell again introduced his forestry resolution, and the following year Governor John L. Barstow appointed a legislative commission made up of former governor Redfield Proctor, railroad magnate Frederick Billings (whose Vermont estate had become a model of reforestation), and Yale law professor Edward J. Phelps. The committee solicited information from around the world and sent questionnaires to Vermont town officials. Their report, submitted in 1884, had a significant educational impact. In 1888 forestry fell under the purview of the state board of agriculture, and in 1905 the Vermont Forestry Commission was established. In each state, agricultural institutions were instrumental in lobbying for forestry legislation.[36]

The work of these early commissioners was largely educational. Through public addresses, newspaper articles, and correspondence, they cautioned against reckless fires, encouraged tree planting, and advised legislators on new policy.[37] Using a combination of private grants and public funds, Massachusetts, New Hampshire, and Vermont gained possession of scattered tracts of forestland, including some critical watershed. State forests allowed commissioners to experiment with European forestry techniques, showcase the results of good management, and sometimes return a small revenue to the state.[38] By 1916 Vermont claimed 12,000 acres; Massachusetts, 10,000 acres; New Hampshire, 9,100 acres; and Maine, none.[39]

The agencies were also involved in forest-fire suppression. Aware that a small group of strategically placed fire fighters could accomplish a great deal, commissioners organized patrols and emergency fire-fighting crews. They posted warning notices in areas traveled by hunters, anglers, and river-driving crews and encouraged laws against careless burning. In 1909 commissioners in Maine, New York, and New Hampshire, using funds from adjoining landowners, began constructing a system of lookout stations. Town officials and game wardens were commissioned as deputy fire wardens, and towns established patrols during dry seasons.[40]

Funding for even these limited objectives was difficult to obtain. Speaking before a New England audience, U.S. Chief Forester Henry S. Graves noted that many eastern legislators opposed fire-fighting expenditures because the public received no guarantees that the forests they protected would be used wisely by their owners.[41] On the other hand, landowners were slow to invest in proper forestry, given the high incidence of fire. This awkward blend of public and private interest in the eastern forests complicated forest policy.

Without authority to regulate cutting or even to suppress fires effectively, state foresters placed their faith in private solutions. Around the turn of the century a few northeastern companies initiated cutting plans based on minimum stump diameters to allow harvesting on a twenty-year cycle. In New England, International Paper, Berlin Mills, and Great Northern Paper Company hired foresters to survey their timberlands. Other landowners included basic sylvicultural rules in their stumpage contracts, such as specifying the size and types of trees to be cut and the height of stumps and diameters of tops left in the forest.[42] These practices were inspired by nationally known foresters such as Bernhard Fernow and Carl A. Schenck, both German born and trained, and by Gifford Pinchot, head of the U.S. Division of Forestry. Conscious of the sustained-yield ideas circulating among the bigger firms, and aware of their own limited authority, state commissioners shifted away from general questions involving the proper relation between forests and landscape. They narrowed their focus to fire suppression, leaving the matter of sustainable harvests to the industrial foresters. State forestry was progressively shorn of its broader moral appeal.[43] These limited achievements, however, did little to ease popular fears. The continuing debate over forests in the broad scheme of things forced the question: Would conservation reflect popular assumptions about the balance of nature, or the industrial forester's narrow concern for a sustainable cut?[44]

The Campaign for the White Mountains

States responded to this question in various ways, as two examples illustrate. New Hampshire helped pioneer the movement for an eastern national forest between 1899 and 1911, while Maine left the fate of its forests almost exclusively in private hands. In both cases, popular concern for the social implications of forest use initiated a conservation movement, and in both cases proponents of scientific forestry divided this movement after the turn of the century. The results of this tension differed in the two states.

By the end of the century, New Hampshire's small-scale sawmill industry had adapted to New England's second-growth forest. With few continuous tracts of old-growth softwoods left in the hill country, and with a vigorous stand of old-field pine arriving at maturity, mills and woodworking shops dispersed over the countryside cutting second-growth timber as it became merchantable. From this they produced a remarkable array of products, including boards, boxes, pails, doors, sashes, blinds, furniture stock, spools and bobbins, excelsior, tool handles, and pickets. In addition, a number of small water-powered mills continued the tradition of custom sawing for local builders. With few exceptions, these establishments were technologically primitive. About half still used water power, and more than half ran for only two to six months each year. With low overhead expenses and irregular schedules, the small mills and shops used wood conservatively.[45]

After 1880 this small-business economy was eclipsed by large pulp and paper producers. By 1900 the commercial forest was divided almost evenly between farmers, resort proprietors, and owners of small mills on the one hand, and large companies on the other.[46] This new pattern of ownership drew public concern. Earlier logging had been selective, simply because market demand and transport cost discouraged wholesale tree removal. Pulp cutters, on the other hand, could use spruce down to relatively small diameters. "Until the establishment of the great pulp mills along the waterways of . . . New England," J. N. Taylor wrote in the *Boston Globe*, "there was no real alarm concerning the future of the woods . . . But when the pulp mill grinders were put on a diet of four-inch stuff the eyes of the natives who thought their forest invincible, began to bulge with amazement."[47] As a rule, the companies cut their stands conservatively, but they left much of the logging to jobbers operating on thin profit margins and subject to little company scrutiny. The jobbers, working on stumpage lands, took everything merchantable. On the higher slopes, even the larger companies ignored minimum cutting diameters because the remaining timber, growing in thin soil on windswept slopes, was subject to windfall.[48]

At the turn of the century timber purchases by the Diamond Match Company brought another wave of anxiety. Match stock, cut mostly by portable mills operating in central New Hampshire, was shipped out of the state in blocks to manufacturing centers farther west. Asked about company conservation policy, an official explained that Diamond bought land, cut the pine, and resold the "remaining undesirable timber, for what it may bring."[49] Competition for second-growth pine became fierce. Local mills in the Keene area used a total of 30 million board feet yearly. Natural growth in nearby forests met this demand, but Diamond's mills doubled the annual cut, jeopardizing the region's long-term economic stability. Keene's mill owners resented the competition but saw no remedy other than moving "farther back into the mountains for supplies."[50]

Because forests were so important to the region's economy and cultural identity, mountain people saw forest abuse as an explanation for a broad range of problems, including job loss, rising taxes, deteriorating roads and schools, and failing farms.[51] Resort owners, too, grew concerned about the visual impact of forest destruction, and tourists and recreationists from across the region joined the call for regulation as the slopes of the White Mountains, including the Presidential Range itself, were stripped of coniferous growth. The remaining thin hardwood forest had a "bedraggled appearance."[52] Despite the apprehensive mood, appeals for state regulation made little headway in the legislature. Proponents concluded that the only alternative was state ownership.[53]

The most important of these advocates was Joseph B. Walker, considered the father of forest conservation in New Hampshire. Walker first saw the White Mountains in 1838, when he spent several days in the old-growth forests around Franconia Notch. The "work of destruction" began on the Ammonoosuc watershed around 1875, he recalled, and extended eastward toward Mount Washington. The cut and burned lands on the touring route between Bethlehem and the Crawford House inspired "universal regret . . . freely expressed." Walker and others were roused to activity.[54]

Three of Walker's forestry addresses, delivered in 1872, 1891, and

1895, were printed and circulated. Drawing inspiration from Marsh's *Man and Nature*, Walker pointed out the importance of forests as a source of lumber, a moderating influence on climate, an anchor for hillside soils, and a catchment for rainwater.[55] His ideas appealed to three audiences: upland people, worried about wood supplies for local mills; farm leaders, concerned about climate, floods, and watershed protection; and the state's resort owners, threatened by the visual scars spreading up the mountain slopes.[56] Encouraged by Walker's campaign, by the pathbreaking Adirondack Preserve, created in New York in the 1870s and 1880s, and by local agricultural and fish and game organizations, New Hampshire's Forestry Commission began accepting donations of lands and funds for forest preserves.[57]

A wave of land speculation at the end of the century crystallized these apprehensions into a consevation movement. The most notorious example was the New Hampshire Land Company, a Hartford- and Boston-based firm that by 1880 had acquired about 240,000 acres of mountain timberland in northern New Hampshire. The company indicated in its prospectus that it retained an "able corps" of surveyors and lawyers to "watch, protect, and defend the rights and claims of the company." This defensive posture was appropriate to an organization that faced mounting local criticism. The prospectus announced that "in a few years, the timber lands of New England will be held by a few capitalists . . . who will not pursue the almost suicidal policy of overstocking the lumber markets with the products of the forest." Local manufacturers would "gladly contract to purchase given quantities of stumpage annually from the lands of the NHLC"—at monopoly prices. The company proposed to convert the forests to cash on terms that could not have been more unsettling to local forest users.[58] Its speculative activities helped fuse anxieties about outside control to the growing fear of forest destruction.

That this corporate philosophy was at such odds with the up-country's more democratic land ethic explains the popular reaction to a series of attacks penned by an obscure itinerant preacher in 1900. An incendiary pamphlet titled *The Boa Constrictor of the White Mountains, or the Worst "Trust" in the World,* written by the Reverend John E. Johnson, touched off a wave of resentment toward outside speculators and reckless lumber operators. Johnson was an Episcopal missionary to the small communities in the region around Woodstock. In somewhat outlandish prose style, he conveyed the impression that the land company, a "trust of the most concentrated, ruthless and soulless character," was "bent on reducing the entire section to a blackened, hideous, howling wilderness."

An inspired pamphleteer, Johnson shifted the onus for social problems in the upland farm districts to a single outside source. His philosophy made sense of frustrating livelihoods scratched from thin soils, and it politicized the threats posed by a remote power to a value-laden landscape. Sensitive to the ill-defined fears drifting through the valleys, Johnson brought together resentments over reckless logging, outmigration, soil erosion, and destruction of a familiar landscape and focused them with intensity on the company. Mountain farmers, "more lumbermen than agriculturalists," were driven out when the company refused to sell them land or stumpage to pursue their winter work. With the forests wrested from their control, "what wonder that their houses and barns are dilapidated, and their morals also?"[59]

Johnson's tirade was picked up by the agricultural press, which fanned the flames of resentment and drew together the coalition of popular conservationists that emerged after 1900. The *New England Homestead,* published in Springfield, Massachusetts, announced the tract under the banner "An Impending Peril to New England." The entire region, the paper generalized, was "in the grip of the lumbermen and land speculators, and whether or not she will free herself is of vital concern." Forest destruction "on a colossal scale" was about to begin, the editor predicted. A resort proprietor complained in the *New England Homestead* that land speculation threatened to close off access to New Hampshire's scenic gems, placing "an effective veto . . . upon all summer resort extensions."[60] In the midst of this clamor, New Hampshire's governor called for cutting regulations and land acquisitions by eminent domain. Failure to pass these measures brought another whirl-wind of criticism upon the legislature and the timber lobby.[61]

On February 6, 1901, a group of nine prominent New Englanders met at the office of the Board of Agriculture in Concord. Attending were former governor Frank W. Rollins, Joseph T. Walker (son of Joseph B. Walker), Edward Everett Hale, and Ellen M. Mason, repre-senting the New Hampshire Federation of Women's Clubs, and at whose suggestion the resulting organization was called the Society for the Preservation of New Hampshire Forests (SPNHF).[62] Early on, the SPNHF sensed the tensions inherent in the New England forestry situation. Clear-cutting the high slopes, for instance, made sense to private landowners because the stands were almost pure spruce. But it was also a public disaster: it was here that regrowth was most prob-lematic and the public interest most acute.[63] Among its other activi-ties—posting fire-safety notices and lecturing before granges, women's clubs, and teachers' organizations—the organization began lobbying for public forests.[64]

The SPNHF campaign absorbed traditional agrarian views of the forest. Recasting the farmers' jeremiad against forest destruction in more modern terms, SPNHF lecturer John D. Quackenbos argued that deforestation resulted in desiccated lands and silted streams. In a remarkable blend of traditional concern for the balance of nature, newer appeals to the benefits of outdoor life, and sheer medical nonsense, he summarized the vitalizing influences held in equilibrium by the now-disappearing forests:

The rank scenting ozones and balsamic aromas; the volatized oleo-resins of the evergreen trees with their recognized therapeutic value in pulmonary disease; the plant-humidity charged in its passage through the trees to transpiration with antiseptic princi-ples healing to lung and blood and exhausted nerve organs; the exhilarating quality of the forest air at once invigorating, soothing, soporific, and generally inductive of that rapid interchange of tissue that constitutes health first of the body and then of mind—have long made the New Hampshire forest region the Mecca of consumptives, nervous invalids, and sufferers of malarial and other cachexia.[65]

Recounting the benefits that forests provided to all people, SPNHF speakers blended urban concerns for scenery and healthy recreation with traditional arguments about the balance of nature. In so doing, they underscored the tensions between moral stewardship and private ownership.[66]

At a meeting held in 1902 at Intervale, New Hampshire, conservationists from around the region drafted congressional resolutions in support of a "national park or forest reserve" similar to a purchase then being proposed for the southern Appalachian Mountains. Over the next year the U.S. Bureau of Forestry conducted a general survey of the White Mountains similar to a study under way in the South.[67] The bureau, predictably, recommended federal purchases, and the idea spread as people from around New England watched the tide of logging operations converge on the Presidential Range—the supreme image of New England wildness.[68]

The New Hampshire Grange provided strong support for the federal reserve, based on traditional views of the proper relation between forests and agriculture.[69] One conservationist contrasted the enthusiastic SPNHF meetings in rural Lisbon, Bethlehem, North Conway, and Franconia, where farmers drove in "from a distance of ten or more miles . . . on a cold winter's night" and engaged in a "lively and intelligent discussion," with another held before a "genteel audience of city-slickers at Manchester," where the effort to provoke a discussion after the lecture "proved a failure."[70] In addition to the Grange, women's clubs throughout New Hampshire formed forestry committees and sent supporting resolutions to state and federal legislators. The Daughters of New Hampshire headquarters in Boston helped coordinate metropolitan interest in the reservation. Women's delegates attended state legislative and congressional hearings and enlisted members in other states through the General Federation.[71]

As historians John Reiger and Thomas Cox point out, hunters, anglers, and tourists provided another key constituency for forest conservation. The SPNHF gained much of its membership from out-of-state visitors to the region.[72] Hotel proprietors, having published travel descriptions romanticizing the sublime effects of forests "unmarred by the axe," well understood the symbolic importance of the old-growth trees ringing Mount Washington. Although the forests were privately owned, the resort industry considered them essential common resources. The White Mountains were a "kind of continental asset belonging to the people at large," the industry argued; "Public interest . . . is paramount to any private advantage." Ownership of the old-growth forests had been "dormant" for years, as one editor put it, but the pulp companies were changing all that.[73]

Tourism made the mountain forests a regional resource. The Boston press developed an almost proprietary interest in White Mountain scenery. Noting the activity on the northern slope of the Presidentials, the influential *Boston Transcript* complained that the New Hampshire Forestry Commission was fiddling while the "lovers of nature and those interested in the . . . welfare of . . . this section, sorely grieve."[74] Local conservationists sometimes found this outside commentary intrusive, but they could hardly deny the importance of viewing their forests in broader perspective. The call for federal purchases was founded on the argument that "people outside the state, no less, and perhaps more . . . are interested in our magnificent White Mountains."[75]

Concern over erratic river flows, caused by cutting on the upper watersheds, also generated interest among textile mill owners. At times engineers at Lawrence, Massachusetts, on the Merrimack, rationed water power to the point of shutting down some of the city's mills. Company officials from every industrial city in the valley sent petitions to Congress supporting the campaign. In addition, a few larger wood manufacturers joined their voices with that of the SPNHF. Berlin Mills, one of the most important and most progressive paper producers in the area, bore the weight of enormous public concern as it moved its operations onto the northern slopes of the Presidentials. The company remained solicitous about this apprehension. Woods manager Orton B. Brown, who was responsible for the company's purchase of old-growth forests on the Presidential Range, was also a key figure in the founding of the SPNHF.[76]

Large companies like Brown's became less defensive as the SPNHF and the Forestry Commission defined their goals more clearly. As a later account put it, the SPNHF's early criticism of the "lumber barons" had been leveled "in the absence of a general recognition of the true problem." The society had been launched on the principle that a resource serving common interests was under siege by private owners, a theme forcefully presented by the Reverend Johnson in 1901. When attempts to urge this moral stand upon the legislature failed, the society took the advice of Frank Rollins and Orton Brown, subordinating its moralistic appeals to the "more practical and scientific aspects of forestry."[77]

Accenting its shift away from traditional principles of moral stewardship, the society hired Cornell forestry graduate Philip W. Ayres, who insisted that "cussing the lumbermen" was futile. Ayres urged the benefits of sustained-yield management as a blessing to both lumber operators and the people of New Hampshire. But Ayres was equally convinced that the only way to secure scientific forestry was through public ownership; thus his narrower concern for sustained-yield forestry meshed with the broader goals of the popular conservation movement. Influenced by foresters such as Brown and Ayres, the society muted its appeal to the broader ecological implications of forest cutting but retained its focus on public stewardship.[78]

The New Hampshire Forestry Commission, too, moderated its criticism of the big pulp cutters. In 1894 the commissioner had insisted that "with scarcely an exception the owners of pulp mills conduct their business with utter recklessness so far as the future of the forest is concerned." To remedy this, the commission asked the legislature for regulatory powers.[79] Such appeals, as one newspaper editor put it, "hardly received the courtesy of a Christian burial." As the political obstacles to public forestry became apparent, the commissioner cultivated better relations with logging companies, relying on "diplomacy and education" to achieve results. In 1902 the commissioner opined that conditions in the White Mountains were "by no means as bad as certain alarmists would have it appear" and expressed confidence that large owners understood the folly of denuding mountain slopes.[80]

As the SPNHF and the Forestry Commission adopted the mantle of scientific forestry, support for the federal reserve spread into sections of the wood products industry. Professional foresters, however, were less than adamant about the immensely popular issue of watershed protection. Berlin Mills' forester, Austin Cary, cautioned that studies of the relation between forest clearing and runoff "for the most part lack definiteness." Fears expressed in the popular press amounted to "loose talk," he thought, and his own belief was that new growth in the cutover offset the effect of clear-cutting.[81]

The SPNHF, on the other hand, could not afford to pin its hopes on the narrow issue of sustained yield.[82] Not only were appeals to the broader implications of forest cutting popular, but the federal-funding proposal required recognition of the White Mountain forests as a landscape of regional importance, a point driven home by the watershed theory. The organization thus became a repository for the confused mixture of impulses that went into turn-of-the-century forest conservation. Some saw the federal reserve as a vehicle for holding together a landscape they understood vaguely as an expression of providential design. Others were interested mainly in sustaining the small-scale, timber-based economies of the upland towns. For some, the reserve idea offered protection for a scenic ideal, ensconced more in the mind of the metropolitan traveler than in the actual lay of the land. Still others saw it as a means of enforcing a common standard of scientific, sustainable forest use. The SPNHF, to its credit, proclaimed a message sufficiently general to pull these tangents together into a movement.[83]

At the insistence of the SPNHF, the state legislature sent to Congress in 1903 a joint resolution in favor of a national forest reserve. The spring of 1903, which brought a dramatic expansion in lumbering activity, a series of forest fires, and several violent floods, was a propitious time to launch the campaign.[84] The question before Congress, as the *New York Times* put it, was "whether the federal government should do for New Hampshire what it did for Wyoming, or whether New Hampshire should do it herself, as New York is doing in the Adirondacks." The proposal was indeed difficult to argue: Westerners were still not reconciled to federal reservations in their region, and unlike the western forests, the White Mountains were privately owned.[85] Opponents of the reservation pointed to the preserves in New York and elsewhere, acquired through state funding. New Hampshire's lackluster public conservation record fell short as a gesture of good-faith effort at forest preservation. Acknowledging this, conservationists argued the critical watershed and recreational benefits for all of New England.[86] The logic of the campaign forced proponents back to popular arguments about moral stewardship and the balance of nature.

Despite letters of support from all over the United States, the bill initially failed in Congress. Concerns about cost dampened enthusiasm, as did a number of complex issues involving proprietors' rights, federal jurisdiction over watersheds remote from navigable streams, and skepticism about the watershed theory.[87] In April 1908 the House Judiciary Committee ruled that the Appalachia bill was unconstitutional unless it was limited strictly to protecting watershed for navigable rivers.[88] As the watershed controversy mounted in New England and elsewhere, Congress directed the U.S. Corps of Engineers to investigate a navigable river in each district and furnish data on watershed behavior.[89] Using textile company records dating back to the 1840s, the Corps surveyed the Merrimack watershed, on which forest conditions had changed several times, and found no support for the "general popular belief that deforestation has exerted a harmful . . . effect upon stream flow." Rather than laying the issue to rest, the presentation of this massive collection of statistical data precipitated a vigorous interagency debate between the Corps and the Forest Service. The study moved the debate in the direction of factual evidence, but it failed to resolve the issue—testament to the popular appeal of viewing forests in terms of broader natural forces.[90]

In 1909 Representative John W. Weeks of Massachusetts, who had grown up in Lancaster, New Hampshire, in the shadow of the White Mountains, introduced a bill calling for federal funds to purchase forest lands on the watersheds of navigable streams. Weeks, a member of the House Committee on Agriculture, took charge of the bill not because he had an abiding interest in forestry but, as he explained to Gifford Pinchot, because he had been "born and brought up in the country." His bill was based solely on the watershed argument, since protecting navigable rivers was clearly within the federal government's constitutional purview. This was also Weeks's most powerful argument for the national preserve, since fears that the rivers were shrinking and floods becoming more destructive were widespread. Purchases were to be certified by the U.S. Geological Survey to be of "such character that the maintenance on them of a forest cover would contribute to the navigability of the stream."[91] The bill also authorized matching funds for state forestry and creation of a National Forest Reservation Commission to consider acquisitions.[92] Supported by advocates of the southern Appalachian and White Mountain purchases, it passed in March 1911. The most significant forestry legislation to occur in the region in the century, it accelerated the trend toward public forestry and public ownership already under way in the states. After a delay to survey, purchase, and pass title on selected private lands, the White Mountain National Forest was established in 1918.[93] The purchase included large tracts in Woodstock, where the Reverend Johnson had made his valiant stand against the "Boa Constrictor of the White Mountains" eighteen years earlier.

The White Mountain National Forest was a product of several trends in popular conservation thinking, not the least of which was the moral vision of an agrarian republic predicated upon the flow of natural energies from forest to farm. The roles of the watershed issue and the SPNHF demonstrate the persistence of these older moralistic, common-welfare claims; New Hampshire conservationists fused the old economy of nature and the new economy of sustained-yield forestry. Things were different in Maine.

Maine and the Private Alternative

Ralph R. Widner's *Forests and Forestry in the American States* concluded a brief chapter on Maine with the statement that "fire control was just about the be-all and end-all of Maine forestry" until the 1920s. This weak record of public forestry was ironic, he pointed out, since Maine, alone among the northeastern states, "retained an economy heavily dependent upon the forest resource." There were in fact some important developments in private forestry, and a small portion of the White Mountain National Forest—around 30,000 acres out of a total of 434,000—extended over the border into Maine. But as Widner pointed out, public stewardship was attenuated in the Pine Tree State.[94] Compared with New Hampshire in its crusade for a national forest, Maine stood curiously silent in the public defense of its forests.

Although the popular impulses fueling a conservation movement were regionwide, the differences between Maine and New Hampshire highlight the importance of local political and environmental conditions. First, the smaller size of New Hampshire's forests generated concern about sustaining the big cuts. More important, the intermixture of New Hampshire's commercial forest lands with settled areas visibly linked the fate of the forests with the fate of nearby communities. In Maine, the key lumbering districts were isolated on the headwaters of the big rivers, and thus were buffered from public scrutiny. Third, New Hampshire's rugged topography accentuated the impact of logging activity. Both states had a public stake in forests, but Maine's gently rolling hills and broad valleys were less subject to flooding, erosion, and landslides. Fourth, forest landownerships in New Hampshire were smaller; those in Maine ranged into the tens and hundreds of thousands of acres. Maine's family and corporate landowners were more entrenched and less willing to abdicate their prerogatives to the state or federal government. Fifth, New Hampshire's investments in tourism and manufacturing made its forests more valuable as scenery and watershed than as wood products. And finally, credit must be given to the inspired leadership of the SPNHF and its ability to blend traditional concerns with newer industrial forestry principles.[95]

In Maine as in New Hampshire, farmers attributed their agricultural woes to those who denuded the land, and they showed an early interest in forest conservation.[96] Here as well they gained allies among resort proprietors and industrial water users. But in Maine the calls for common stewardship were turned aside by a vigorous campaign to narrow the public's control over forestry decisions. These environmental and economic constraints prescribed a different mix of public and private forestry.

As in New Hampshire, the shift to pulpwood logging brought widespread apprehension. Company officials argued that the millions of dollars invested in plant, equipment, dams, reservoirs, and timber stands gave mill owners incentive to cut nearby forests conservatively. Since the mills needed a constant supply of water for log transportation, power, and processing, the argument went, the watersheds the companies were cutting were essential to operating the mills themselves. The companies were simply too comprehensive in their use of the landscape to risk the regional problems of forest destruction.[97]

Despite these assurances, warnings of an impending timber famine appeared in the state's presses in the 1880s. The *Maine Farmer* considered paper companies' optimistic declarations "idle talk," and the tourist-oriented Portland *Board of Trade Journal* noted that it normally welcomed new industries into the state, "excepting in our heart pulp companies, for while recognizing fully the amount of money they bring . . . we know also the terrible destruction [they] . . . mean to our beautiful forests that now make Maine the playground of the nation." The *Maine Woods,* organ of the Rangeley Lakes tourist industry, and the *Maine Sportsman* ran articles with a similar thrust.[98] Farmers and resort-industry leaders campaigned for public regulation but lacked a counterpart to the dynamic SPNHF.[99]

An unidentified hunting or timber-cruising party in the Rangeley Lakes area. The thick spruce stand in this view, typical of the upland New England forest, served a variety of public purposes. Forests thus became a focus of common concern in the late nineteenth century. (Courtesy of James B. Vickery)

In 1891, under pressure from the Grange, Maine created a forest commissioner's office by simply renaming the old State Land Office, which had become irrelevant in the 1870s after the state sold the last of its timberlands.[100] Conflict between the public concerns that gave rise to the agency and the private rights that dictated forest use was apparent in the early forestry reports. Maine's first commissioner, Cyrus A. Packard, predicted that suppressing fires and encouraging the practices then in use by larger companies could sustain the cut. But his report also included a sample of the conservation message circulating in Maine's civic clubs and Grange halls, and here opinion was less optimistic. George F. Talbot, a lumber manufacturer from eastern Maine, surveyed the history of Maine's forests and concluded that "to expect of men whose prudent judgment has led them to fortune, to make investments in enterprises, from which no substantial return is to be expected until after the lapse of a century, is making too large a demand upon the disinterestedness of human nature." Private ownership was incompatible with sound forestry.[101]

Packard was replaced after only one year by timberland owner Charles E. Oak. Like Talbot, Oak regarded pulp-cutting as a threat to the woods; Maine's timber supply would last no more than twenty years, he thought. To verify this claim, Oak hired Austin Cary, a brash young native of Brunswick, Maine, who had previously worked for Berlin Mills as America's first company forester.[102] Cary proposed an extensive survey of the state's upper watersheds to "settle these questions" about the timber supply. A rigorous advocate of the new science of forestry, Cary ignored concerns about the broader landscape and focused on efficient forest use.[103] Like the SPNHF's Philip Ayres, he narrowed the conservation question to sustained yield. His consuming interest was annual spruce growth under varying natural and harvesting conditions—the "growing power of the land," as he often called it.

Cary began his "long cruise" through the upper Kennebec watershed in the spring of 1895.[104] His report, published by the commissioner the following year, was optimistic. His summer in the woods had revealed a vigorous spruce-fir forest. Yet his answer to the great question of the day—the sustainability of the forest—was ambiguous, wrapped in technical contingencies and qualified by the forester's vast appreciation for the complexities of land form and growing conditions in the region. Cary surmised that across the state spruce was not being over-cut. But what would the future bring? The "growing power" of the land was the key: "Some count it, some ignore growth, some inflate it." Noting the different methods in use, he calculated that "the yearly cut of spruce lumber on the river must soon shrink."[105]

His conclusions, rendered in technical terms as cold as the winters he endured on the northern Appalachian plateau, helped shift the debate away from matters of broad public concern.[106] Rather than defending his views publicly, Cary explained that they could be substantiated "by reference to facts that only those familiar with . . . lumbering would . . . understand." The public should find solace, he

COMMON STEWARDSHIP AND PRIVATE FORESTS

thought, simply in the fact that companies had too much at stake to cut timber unwisely.[107] Cary avoided judgments about climate, watershed, health, and scenery and expressed disdain for popular conservation theories. In the Presidential Range he had once encountered a group of prominent tourist-conservationists, none of whom, he remarked pointedly, could tell the difference between "primeval" forests and those recently cut over. "For scenic purposes," he declared, young hardwood, "which in this climate quickly covers almost every stripped or burnt piece of ground," served as well as old-growth spruce. One tree was as good as another for those who had no technical appreciation for what they were looking at. "This White mountain problem," he declared, was being "made too much of."[108]

If Cary offered little to endear him to the popular conservationist, his scathing descriptions of cutting practices were no more welcome to pulp operators. "The hardest cutting ever seen by the writer outside of a wood lot," he remarked in passing through a section near Berlin, New Hampshire. On the Kennebec, the waste of timber was "needless and glaring." Cary, like Talbot, believed that the forest destroyer was doing "what every other business man would do in the same circumstances if he were as strong in his purposes and as sharp in his calculations." Yet where others would have suggested state appropriation of forests or state-mandated forestry, Cary drew back. After "considerable thinking," he was "not entirely clear on that point." The complexity of the forest and the risks of ownership left him reluctant to submit these matters to political solutions.[109]

Cary's pioneering spruce-fir inventory techniques laid a strong foundation for scientific conservation in the Northeast, but his public stand typifies the gap between scientific and popular conservation. Focused on the complicated technical problem of sustained yields, Cary refused to commit himself on the pressing questions of how forests should be used and who should administer them. In the woods, Cary was a forester's forester, but he understood the complex world of conservation politics as poorly as he believed the popular conservationists understood his trees.[110]

When Charles Oak resigned as forest commissioner in 1901 Cary applied for the opening, as did Edgar E. Ring, a timberland owner connected to the Republican party's powerful Penobscot lumber lobby. The contest was "spirited," and the outcome—Ring's selection—was a political victory for the lumber lobby. Possibly Ring was as competent as Cary, one editor concluded, "but it was the political endorsements of the former that won for him the appointment."[111] Ring was far less ambivalent about the direction forestry should take: under his guidance, the office became devoted to the private use of Maine's forest.[112]

In conjunction with the Great Northern Paper Company, Ring hired Ralph Hosmer, a Yale forestry graduate attached to the Bureau of Forestry, to survey a single woodland township and draw conclusions about sustaining the timber supply. Hosmer's report glossed over Cary's acerbic but sophisticated analysis and focused on a few modest recommendations that, he predicted, could maintain cutting at even higher levels.[113] The report, like Cary's, signaled a new departure in state forestry publications. Scientifically derived statistics on growth, reproduction, and reseeding under various conditions eclipsed earlier speculations about the role of forests in the broader landscape.

With Hosmer's evidence in hand, Ring shifted his focus to fire prevention, a topic far removed from the politicized questions of timber famine and the social impacts of forest abuse. In January 1903 the legislature appropriated $10,000 for fire suppression, but in the face of huge fires that summer Ring called for even larger funding.[114] Reacting to the commissioner's narrowed vision of forestry as a science dedicated to private profit, legislators pointed out that fire-fighting appropriations protected an investment that simply lined the pockets of speculators in Boston and New York City.[115]

While landowners sought to narrow the issue of public forestry to fire suppression, popular pressures for state regulation mounted. Farmers grew concerned about the effects of forest cutting on climate following a series of dry years after the turn of the century. Maine's women's clubs, like their counterparts in New Hampshire, established forestry committees and issued public proclamations on the need for conservation. In 1907 manufacturers interested in protecting watershed for central Maine's textile industry asked the legislature to prohibit cutting spruce and pine below a twelve-inch diameter, a plan endorsed, as in New Hampshire, by the Grange, women's clubs, and the tourist industry.[116] The campaign culminated in two scathing essays on Maine timberlands: Frank Putnam's "Maine: A Study in Land-Grabbing, Tax Dodging, and Isolation," in *New England Magazine;* and Liberty B. Dennett's "Maine's Wildlands and Wildlanders," which ran serially in *Pine Tree Magazine* in 1907 and 1908.[117] Dennett, a lawyer and gentleman farmer from Gorham, won a seat in the state legislature and carried the crusade for regulations and higher "wildland" (timberland) taxes to Augusta.

When lawmakers raised constitutional questions about a state-imposed minimum cutting diameter, the legislature sent the measure to the state Supreme Judicial Court for an opinion. To the surprise of everyone, on March 10, 1908, the court deemed state regulations within the scope of government as a means of preventing drought, protecting soils, and preserving the natural water supply. Assuming that Maine would act upon this judgment, President Theodore Roosevelt singled out the state for its "wisdom and foresight" at the May 1908 Conference of Governors called to promote conservation of natural resources.[118] The 1908 decision did serve as a precedent for other states, but Maine virtually ignored the ruling. This inaction largely reflected Edgar Ring's success in keeping Maine's conservation debate focused on fire suppression and away from the issue of public stewardship.

By 1908 conservation thought in Maine had split into two camps. Popular conservationists—those concerned about forests from the point of view of agricultural stability, health, scenery, watershed, and the balance of nature—insisted on mandated cutting limits or state land acquisitions. Industry and state officials, on the other hand, saw conservation simply in terms of efficient production of wood and timber.[119] In New Hampshire the SPNHF meshed popular concerns for landscape integrity with the goals of scientific forestry; in Maine these two positions could not be reconciled.

As the call for a stronger state role in forestry mounted, another smoldering controversy ignited. Farmers, manufacturers, and urban citizens had long contended that Maine timberland owners were not contributing their share of taxes. The argument was compelling, given the widespread conviction that lumbermen had "stolen" the forests from the state in the first place.[120] Liberty Dennett complained that the state's wildlands, a territory larger than Massachusetts and Connecticut combined, returned only $27,700 in taxes. The Grange pointed out that the treasurer of International Paper Company's timberland purchasing division was also chairman of the state board of assessors. In 1903 Dennett introduced a measure that would have boosted wildlands valuations 300 percent. The bill failed, but in the following sessions legislators funded a township-by-township survey of timberlands that resulted in substantial increases in revenues.[121]

Landowners raced to stem the tide of reform. In 1905 they revived the Maine Lumbermen and Landowners Association, formed in 1896 to articulate the views of the industry. In 1907 it became the Maine Forestry Association.[122] Its arguments, given prominent airing in the Bangor papers, hinged on two points. First, the state, by withholding funds for fire prevention, limited the owners' return on the taxes they paid; therefore, valuations should remain low. Second, the public used these commercial timberlands for hunting and fishing—a legacy of the colonial Great Pond Ordinance, which vested ownership of fish and game in the people as a whole.[123] This state-sanctioned trespass underwrote an elaborate system of sporting camps, guide services, and hotels.[124] Like New Hampshire's conservationists, Maine forest owners stressed the multiple uses of their forests, a concept then taking form in the U.S. Forest Service. Landowners pointed to these broader public purposes not to encourage public stewardship but rather to demonstrate how much the state owed them in terms of tax consideration and dollars allocated for fire suppression.[125]

In the legislative session of 1909, proponents of state-mandated regulations tried to push the supreme court's earlier decision to its logical conclusion. Others, including Austin Cary, spoke in favor of state forest acquisitions in critical watershed areas.[126] Legislators sought a compromise that would leave forestry decisions in private hands, maintain the rights of recreationists, and settle the issue of state services rendered for taxes paid on wildlands. In 1906 the *Bangor Commercial*— the "official organ of the tax dodgers," as a rival paper put it—had announced an "ultimatum on the wild land tax proposition": Land-owners would agree to a higher tax, "provided that the amount so raised shall all be expended [exclusively] in fire protection for forests."[127] Three years later several prominent industry officials fashioned such a bill, and it was passed by the legislature. The law added a surtax on forest lands in the unorganized townships specifically to subsidize a new Maine Forestry District. The commissioner's office was thus given funds to launch large-scale fire-fighting efforts, and legal authority to compel all landowners to support it.

In his inaugural address in 1913, Governor William T. Haines, himself a wildlands owner, capped the long debate over common stewardship in Maine. The state might have erred in selling off its public lands to speculators, Haines admitted, but it was "much better to leave all our wild lands as they are today, in the hands of private owners, with the right reserved . . . to everybody to go upon them for hunting and fishing, recreation and pleasure, which makes of them a great natural park, in which all of the people have great benefits and great interests."[128] With this implicit common right—a minimal con-cession, in light of New Hampshire's achievement—leaders in Maine forestry shunted aside other considerations in defining Maine's forest commons.

As head of the new Maine Forestry District with a mandate nar-rowed to fire suppression, Edgar Ring came into his element. An experienced lumber operator in close communication with the legisla-ture and with all branches of manufacturing, he quickly organized what Gifford Pinchot considered the best forest-fire patrol in the country. The system included some of the first lookout stations in the nation, stringent fire-control measures, fire wardens, and plans for an imme-diate call to arms in the event of a large fire. Ring received a $50,000 appropriation, including $20,000 for building and operating expenses and $30,000 in emergency funds for fire fighting.[129]

As in New Hampshire, Maine's farmers, manufacturers, women's clubs, resort owners, and recreationists, concerned about the integrity of the forest for a broad spectrum of reasons, launched a conservation movement that challenged the industrial monopoly on forest use. In both states, this impulse revived and refashioned a traditional concept of forests as common property and of forest use as a common moral responsibility. In New Hampshire, this popular conservation sentiment was crucial to the concept of a national forest serving regionwide interests; in Maine, arguments for popular stewardship met firm resistance from scientific foresters, forestland owners, and the state's forestry agency. Control over forest utilization remained securely in the hands of landowners.

Popular concerns like watershed, scenery, health, climate, and soil protection left a vastly deeper impress on the White Mountain National Forest than they did on the Maine woods. The national forest, Sherman Adams once wrote, was a "people's proposition." It derived from a "public recognition that all forest land, even that in private ownership, contributed to the public good."[130] New Hampshire's forest became a part of the new "American commons": a system, in Donald Worster's words, of public lands "where individuals may go to find natural resources but which no one can take into his or her exclusive possession."[131] Yet even in Maine, where common rights to nature were excised from the conservation debate, public assertions of the new American commons remained just below the surface—close enough to circumscribe, politically if not legally, the private dominion over nature. Maine and New Hampshire met the public call to protect their forest commons in different ways, but popular concerns left their mark on both.

Common Waters

Goose Creek, Penobscot Bay, Maine. Villages along this isolated coast developed
community-based strategies for protecting and enhancing fisheries resources. Expanding markets threatened these localistic fishing cultures, necessitating state
intervention. (*Harper's New Monthly Magazine,* August 1877)

CHAPTER FIVE

Conflicting Rights in Fisheries

On January 7, 1840, citizens of Gouldsborough, in eastern Maine, petitioned their representative for a law making the nearby Harbor Stream fishery a "town Privilege." The town would elect a fish committee at the annual meeting in March and confer upon it discretionary powers to remove dams or other obstructions and "to take such Steps & measures as will in their judgment best promote [fish] . . . passage up [Harbor Stream] . . . and into Forbes Pond." Eleven days later the legislature granted the request, forging one more link in a chain of local jurisdictions that defined access to coastal fisheries in New England.[1]

The community codes that governed the taking of fish in towns like Gouldsborough were formulated in the late colonial period as part of a larger town-based common-resource management regime. These local networks were not unique to the New England coast. Fishers and other rural petty producers, in both modern and historical times, learned to manage their resources in a variety of local contexts to preserve stability and equity. The regulatory mechanisms varied from internalized norms and subtle social pressures to elaborate written codes. In the Gouldsborough law, there is only a faint echo of the wider community sanctions that guided fishing behavior, but the republican basis for this localized system is clear in this and other Maine petitions regarding fish and fishing.[2] Like the early protections devised for ponds stocked with pickerel, these coastal common-management systems preserved a commitment to local management and egalitarian access.

As market expansion, new industrial river uses, and a competing ideology of possessive individualism strained these local systems, citizens and their legislative representatives struggled to find new institutional arrangements by which resources could be allocated in a democratic and sustainable manner. Yet the boundary between common rights and individual rights was no more clear in New England's waters than in its forests. Disputes over fish and dams, fueled by the wrenching social transformations of the age, resulted in a new external form of management—state laws—for these common waters.

Nowhere was this conflict more apparent than in the coastal and river fisheries of Maine. The issues that emerged here laid the political groundwork for the state's first resource management agency. Fish commissions like Maine's, established in the 1860s, accommodated a vastly expanded scale of fishing activity and river use. Still, they operated within the ethical framework established by communities like Gouldsborough in the 1840s. The republican vision of the commons, implicit in the Gouldsborough petition, lingered in the minds of those who shaped New England fisheries policy during the heyday of the conservation movement.

Preoccupied with the herculean tasks of carving settlements from the virgin land, pioneering families relied heavily upon a harvest of wild plants, game, and fish for sustenance. Of these forage resources, fish were the most important and the most severely overexploited.[3] Still, local fishing was relatively limited. Farm families introduced a variety of destructive fishing methods, but the families were few in number, fished only when other duties allowed, and limited their catch to local necessity. While upland regions remained commercially isolated, the fish "were not materially diminished," as a farmer near Maine's Bryant Pond explained. But once the railroad reached the area the fish soon disappeared. Commercial fishers were "money-makers, who worked every day and all the day," catching fish not only for themselves but also to sell to strangers.[4]

Expanding commercial networks also threatened the anadromous fisheries—the spring runs of Atlantic salmon, shad, and alewives. Traditionally, each village was assured access by the migratory event itself, which dispersed the catch with relative consistency through each river basin. Migratory runs yielded each village a quota for local use, under the terms of local management, and allowed a portion of the run to continue on to the spawning beds. As one petitioner explained, fisheries were "located & distributed" through an entire watershed "for the benefit of those residing near & about said waters."[5] Contrary to this diffused fishing system, commercial fishing concentrated the catching effort at a vulnerable point in the river, usually near the mouth. This practice not only jeopardized the entire run; it separated fishing from the moral and natural constraints of the dispersed village system.

At the beginning of the century, river weirs usually extended out into the shoal water along the banks. As these flats were overflowed by the tide, the fish ran into the nets. Low tide exposed the flats, shutting down the fishery for a portion of the day. As market forces intensified, owners extended their weirs into the deeper channels.[6] At times, weirs and nets running out from opposite shores interlinked so tightly as to make passage almost impossible. "Whenever these wares are erected and maintained for two or three years in succession," one observer claimed, "it has diminished & nearly destroyed the run of fish so as to render the maintenance of such wares unproductive." Owners abandoned them until the runs recovered sufficiently for commercial use. Like fisheries everywhere, the runs on each river followed a downward spiral of exploitation, depletion, partial recovery, and renewed exploitation.[7]

As these commercial pressures increased, townspeople invented new legislative measures to replace village custom and the laws of nature. Those on the upper Connecticut petitioned the New Hampshire legislature in 1788 to halt the destructive commercial fisheries at Bellows Falls, explaining that families upriver were "settling and Cultivating the New lands & at great Distance from the Sea Coast, [and] must be Deprived of what the Alwise being has in his Wisdom Provided for us." Their argument touched on the importance of the resource to the line of frontier settlements moving up the watershed and on the rectitude of this natural system of distribution for subsistence use. Similar protests resulted in state-level regulations protecting shad and salmon on the Connecticut and Merrimack in the 1790s.[8]

The cooperative spirit evident in this coastal Maine scene buttressed a communitarian claim to the inshore fisheries. Villagers used state conservation codes to protect their waters from outsiders. (Courtesy of Kennebunkport Historical Society)

A half-century later, villagers along the Androscoggin River in Maine asked for laws "prohibiting the taking of fish, whether by nets or wares, from sunrise on Friday morning until sunrise on Monday morning of each week." On these days a gate in the pocket of the weir would be opened, freeing the fish. Like the upper Connecticut villagers, they demanded a legislative means of dispersing a harvest that had been traditionally apportioned by village custom and the progress of the migratory event itself. The law required each town to choose a fish committee to enforce the law.[9]

Such legislation was laden with ideological significance. For generations, townspeople had integrated migratory fish runs into their community livelihood, investing this activity with values linked to common identity and yeoman ideology. Fishers were held accountable for the number of fish they took, the manner in which they used them, and the price they asked for the catch. New laws were necessary, villagers argued, to preserve this system: deep-water weirs monopolized the fish to the "Benefit of the few, [and] to the great Annoyance and infringement of Equal Rights to the many." Commercial fishers claimed that these corporatist laws violated individual rights and disrupted the bond between producer and consumer—those "who buy the fish of us and with whom we traffic and trade in [this] . . . branch of home and industrial industry humble and laborious [as] it is."[10] Historian Ruth Bogin views commercially oriented classes like these fishers as "working to transform the traditional 'moral economy' into a defense of personal independence and moderate opportunity." The definition of liberty implicit in their petitions freed them not only from "those [elites] who held the political reins" but also from the older community sanctions that circumscribed their economic activity.[11] The question of how "equal rights" were to be assured in this changing ideological universe was fraught with ambiguity. As older forms of resource distribution crumbled under new market pressures, the conservation debate moved from the towns to the state. Lawmakers forged compromises between traditional community-use customs and new liberal ideologies of open access.

Localism and Coastal Fisheries

Early in the nineteenth century southern New England lobster dealers developed a technique for transporting live lobster in seawater holding wells aboard small sailing vessels. When they began buying lobster on the Maine coast in the 1840s, Harpswell's local catchers moved their traps to the more productive fishing grounds off the nearby islands. Those living on the islands defended their local claims by destroying the new traps or selling "privileges" at five dollars a season to the mainlanders. Denouncing this "arbitrary power" over the island waters, the Harpswell fishers asked the Maine legislature to declare the lobster an open-access resource, "giving to each and every person an equal right and privilege to Sett . . . traps and netts . . . either within or without the limits of Said town." Professing a concern for the resource,

the legislature upheld the islanders' claims, and lobster catching remained—as it is largely today—a jurisdiction of local fishing "gangs."
The incident demonstrates the link between commercial expansion and
new ideologies of resource use.[12] Regionalization of markets was a
powerful catalyst in the debate over community control and open
access to natural resources.

Competing claims to the fisheries raised the issue of conservation.
Eastern Maine herring bait-fishers, for example, protested the presence
of large nonresident schooners using purse seines in their bays. "In this
barren and unproductive region," they reasoned, fishing was their "chief
means of support"—their moral claim by right of occupancy. Yet they
also argued that weirs and dip nets, their own traditional techniques,
were less destructive than the seines.[13] Grand Banks schooner owners,
seeking access to these eastern bays, argued that bans on purse seines
deprived "one part of our fellow citizens of their Rights" while giving
"Exclusive privileges to an other." They, too, blended ideological arguments for open access with conservation principles: weir fishing was
"fare more destructive to the Herring."[14] The legislature removed the
ban on seining in 1844 but replaced it over the next decade with a
town-based system of oversight. Jonesport, for instance, was allowed
to dictate mesh size, net placement, and hours of use, and seining was
restricted to Maine citizens. The midcoast towns of Friendship and
Cushing used similar appeals to obtain a law prohibiting "inhabitants
of other States" from seining for shad in local bays.[15]

Alewives, too, were guarded by traditions that harked back to the
colonial town commons. During the 1830s weir fishers at the mouth
of the Eastern (Orland) River, a tributary of the lower Penobscot,
extended their nets out beyond the shoal water in the river. The protests
mounted by upriver towns disclosed the moral basis for community
management: "We are willing that those of our fellow citizens, who
reside on the tide waters below us, should have their full share of the
fish," villagers argued, but "those who evidently look more to their
own personal gain and present emoluments, than to the present comfort, or future benefit of the public" deserved no part of the fishery.

The legislature granted Orland the right to oversee passage of migratory fish in the river below them. Villagers all along the coast responded to growing commercial pressure by writing republican community ideals into local ordinances and state laws.[16]

The alewife fishery on the central coast demonstrates the complexities of these competing ideological claims. In the late eighteenth century farmers in Newcastle and Nobleboro on the Damariscotta River transplanted alewives into a freshwater lake at the river's headwaters, previously inaccessible to the migratory fish. They built fishways around the falls and began harvesting the resulting run of fish. As was customary, the state granted the two towns exclusive rights to oversee the catch and distribute the fish locally.

In 1844 landowners below Damariscotta Mills, where the town fishery was located, built weirs out into the river. The resource, so carefully husbanded by upriver towns, declined precipitously. At town meetings in Nobleboro and Newcastle on January 18, 1845, residents endorsed a petition to the legislature asking for a law prohibiting weirs, pounds, nets, and seines along the entire sixteen-mile length of the Damariscotta River—including sections below the towns' jurisdiction. Residents claimed rights to a resource they had *"growed, and matured"* through their own efforts, but their defense hinged on a more basic issue: the fish should benefit "not only . . . the Towns, but the public at large."[17] The downriver weir owners exacted a price more than double that allowed by the town fishery, "and probably more for those which they packed, and sent out of the State, as they generally denied selling to the [local] people." The weir owners deprived "many poor and destitute families . . . of their benefit."[18] Commercial fishing was less democratic and less responsive to community needs.

Denying these community claims, weir owners drew upon common-law rights giving riparian property owners control over their own sections of the river—"rights . . . we claim have existed since the earliest settlement of the Country." In reality these "private ancient rights" were more philosophic than historical, since towns had always managed fisheries as a common resource. This legal tactic, however, reflects the complicated political upwelling that gave birth to early conservation thinking. "Farmers and artisans alike found it possible to support an unfettered market economy when this served their needs," notes Ruth Bogin, "and to plead for protection [from economic liberalism] when they felt jeopardized." In this "tangle of ideological strands," a new synthesis of republican values was emerging.[19]

Indeed, the rights that weir owners sought to protect were radically different from the corporatist ideals espoused by the towns, a product of the growing separation between public and private enterprise in Jacksonian America and of the legal conception of property adhering to individual, as opposed to common weal. John Glidden, a riparian farmer living downstream from the town fishery, calculated that his flats were valuable as staging for weirs, but neither he nor his neighbors received just compensation for the public appropriation of this resource. Nobleboro and Newcastle enjoyed an artificial monopoly, Glidden argued, a special legislative privilege "odious to the great majority." Glidden and other farmers drew support from the Jacksonian antimonopoly crusades that had swept frontier areas like Maine during the previous decade. Was it proper, they asked, "to protect the property of . . . a corporation, by legislating away the property of another?"[20]

Downriver weir owners lost their bid to fish the river, but they advanced claims that would be urged more insistently over the next few decades. Local government, they argued, was not a reciprocal bond of obligation among neighbors, but a mere contrivance predicated solely on the need to secure individual rights to property appropriated from a natural fund. Regionalized markets and new doctrines of access upset the traditional balance between community and individual and led to a new articulation of the concept of resource use. The erosion of community common-property regimes moved the debate over conservation upward to the state legislature.

While local battles took shape around contending groups of fishers, dams built across the major river stems in the early decades of the century precipitated another crisis. Colonial statutes required fishways on most dams, but like many such laws, they were poorly enforced.

As sawmills and factories appeared on the larger rivers, fishers began a sustained battle to restrict or reverse industrial river development.

Mill owners challenged the static agrarian conception of property that entitled the towns to undisturbed enjoyment of their river monopolies, pleading for a more dynamic and instrumental view of resource rights based on what legal historian Morton Horwitz has called "the newly paramount virtues of productive use and development."[21] The dams, mill owners pointed out, were of greater benefit to the towns than the fish. The mills they powered offered a more intensive use of the waters, added more value to the products of the region, and attracted more capital than fishing. Still, older community fishing rights were surprisingly persistent.

In 1852 Portland resident Jonathan Morgan decided that the nearby Presumpscot River was a public resource unjustly monopolized by owners of several large mills. These waters, he surmised, could be put to better use if the salmon, shad, and alewife fisheries, long since destroyed by the dams, could be revived. Morgan petitioned the legislature, explaining that "it would be of great public utility" to have fishways over the dams. He proposed a law requiring fishways on the Presumpscot dams and asked that he and his heirs and assigns be granted the "exclusive right . . . of building, upraising, and keeping fish ways open in the waters of said . . . river, & tributaries."[22]

This novel bid for self-employment was promptly squashed by owners of the mills, but it illuminates the thinking of those who supported fish protection in the face of more productive uses of the waters.[23] Morgan's self-promoting distinction between "private" use of the river by mill owners and "public" use as a fishery typifies the growing separation between village life and the big export-oriented merchant mills appearing on the rivers at midcentury. Commercial fishers, even though they served regional markets and often chafed at village mutualistic traditions, were still enmeshed in village culture. The movement of local farmers and other small-scale producers in and out of the fishery cemented this relation and gave fishing a moral edge as a form of river use. The fisheries also gained community standing by virtue of prior use and by the conviction that fish were an integral feature of the existing natural order. "In times past," Brooksville, Maine, farmers wrote in a typical prelude to a fishway petition, villagers had been "accustomed to take Alewives from the Stream leading from Gray's Pond."[24] It was difficult for legislators to decree the destruction of this ancient form of river use. Fishing was also important to the community in another sense. Residents considered access to the fisheries—an aspect of the forage landscape—crucial to extending the frontier of agriculture along the eastern coast and up the great river valleys. Baring, Maine, settlers urged that protecting fisheries would promote settlement of the "wild lands in this vicinity."[25]

As John Cumbler notes in a study of the Connecticut River fishery, the decline of alternative employment for farmers also accented the importance of fishing. The decades after 1820 were uncertain times for coastal agriculture, handicraft production, and lumbering. Citizens from Woolwich on the lower Kennebec, for instance, endorsed a mill owner's right to build a "tight dam" across Nequasset Falls in 1830, but when the river's shipbuilding and lumber port activities were captured by more vigorous river cities, they reconsidered the relative importance of the fishery, petitioning to open a passageway through the dam.[26] On Ducktrap Stream in western Penobscot Bay, sawmills blocked upriver migration as early as the 1780s. Around 1815 the Massachusetts legislature gave Ducktrap leave to remove the obstructions, but as in Woolwich, settlers chose to ignore this option, "not wishing to sacrifice too much of the interest of Mill owners."[27] Only in 1844 did they ask that the fishways be reopened. Although the loss of this fishery had seemed of little consequence when the 1815 law was passed, petitioner Joseph Miller explained, "the case is now presented in a different aspect; Lumber has become scarce in the vicinity of the Stream and the Mills are mostly in a decayed state, and probably will never be rebuilt." The petition was accompanied by numerous testimonials to the importance of the fishery to the area's first white inhabitants. Martin Tower remembered having caught alewives by "heaving them out of the stream with [his] hands" when the fish warden opened the dam briefly in 1833. Conditioned by a regional tradition of opportunistic resource use, Miller and his fellow petitioners turned to the fisheries as a convenient supplemental livelihood.[28]

Mill owners objected, and the Ducktrap dams remained in place, without fishways, but the incident illustrates the reasoning pursued by those who sought to buttress traditional forms of local resource use with state law. As the coastal economy began to decline in towns like Ducktrap and Woolwich, farmers turned again to the fisheries, and they became more critical of merchant-mill owners.[29] The big mills undoubtedly produced more value than the fisheries, but the benefits were largely external. Local producers and resource users still commanded a higher moral standing with regard to Maine's common waters.[30]

The Penobscot Fisheries

These disputes were a mere prelude to the acrimony over Maine's major rivers, where both fisheries and merchant manufacturing concentrated. Maine's early "fish laws" authorized towns to appoint wardens and provide penalties for mill owners who refused to keep their dams open to migrating fish.[31] These laws, grounded in older community-based mutualistic sanctions, were predicated on democratic principles of access. The fisheries eventually succumbed to the combined power and prestige of the mill owners, but the legislative commitment to these traditional principles remained surprisingly strong, infusing the politics of resource use with a moral fervor that helped shape conservation thinking in the second half of the century.

The Penobscot River proved to be the Maine fisher's Armageddon. The battle began in 1825, when the legislature directed the owners of a dam at the head of tide in Bangor to provide passage for fish. The owners complied, but the resulting sluiceway was passable only at high tide, when the current was slack through the falls, and the fish competed with boats, gondolas, and lumber rafts during this brief period.

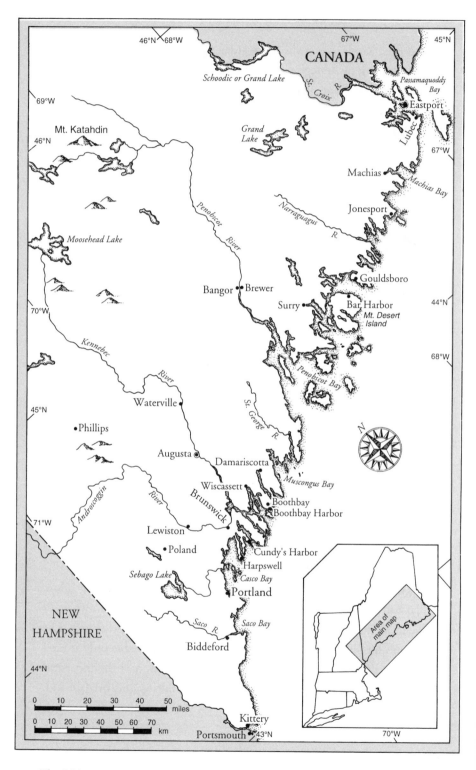

The Maine coast

The increasing commercial traffic crowded out the fish, and the annual migrations diminished. Aware of the obstruction at the head of tide, owners of new dams upriver refused to build fishways.[32]

The legislature experimented with a more permanent and comprehensive authority over the river. In 1828 the Penobscot fish law was revised, creating a new board of fish wardens and deputies for each of the three counties ringing Penobscot Bay. These officials were to meet annually, examine all dams deemed eligible for fishways, and enforce the fish laws in their respective counties. The law regulated the placement of weirs and established weekly "closed times" for the fishery, when gates in the weirs would be kept open, freeing the fish.[33]

The law exempted several tributary streams where dam owners convinced the legislature that fish were naturally scarce, the topography resistant to fishway construction, or, more important, the dams benefited the immediate community more than the fish did. Owners of small, custom mills found a ready audience in the legislature, particularly when their pleas were backed by petitions from their neighbors. Those in Orrington, Brewer, and Bradley successfully argued that fishways would be "ruinous to the interests of . . . a great proportion of the inhabitants of the vicinity" whose needs were served by the mills.[34] In Enfield, Cold Stream powered three custom sawmills, a grist mill, a carding machine, and two shingle machines, mainly serving neighboring farms. Here, too, dams were calculated a greater community benefit than the fish.[35]

By the late 1830s the owners of the merchant mills had appropriated the argument for community benefit. The Penobscot lumber boom was in full swing, with Bangor one of the world's most important lumber ports. Faced with staggering horsepower needs, mill owners extended several large dams across the main body of the river. Income from the fishery dropped from $160,000 yearly in the 1830s to around $10,000 by 1843.[36]

In 1837 John B. Smith circulated a petition among Penobscot mill owners and workers to exempt the entire river above tidewater from the fishways provision. He objected to the "extraordinary powers" conferred upon the fish wardens to dictate construction of fishways, "thereby prostrating enterprise . . . on which is founded not only individual interest of great magnitude, but the best hopes of the County and . . . the very basis of its advancement & prosperity." Convinced that manufacturing was destined to replace agriculture and forage practices like fishing in the frontier region, dam owners dismissed all competing claims to the river. Civilizing influences—dams, steamboats, mill wheels, forest clearing—ordained the destruction of the fishery. That the "interprise and resources of the valley of the Penobscot" should be "forgone for the sole . . . privilege of taking for a few days or weeks in the season a small supply of paltry fish" was inconceivable.[37] Fish, another petitioner argued, did not "half pay for the troubel and expense of taking and curing them to say nothing of the great waste of time by our citizens in congregating and waiting about the fish ways." Destruction of this primitive form of appropriating nature would benefit the county and its citizens.[38]

At the crux of this debate were two fundamentally different opinions about creation of economic value. To men like Smith, fishing was a residue of backcountry indolence dragging down the valley's vigorous industrial economy. Rather than adding value to the resources of the region, fishing "occupied the Husbandmen about all of that Season which should have been devoted to . . . Harvest."[39] Penobscot fishers clung to a traditional agrarian concept of labor as the source of economic value. They contrasted mill owners' profits, based on speculative capital, with value created by the shad and alewife fishery, which was "more than *four fifths* . . . the product of labour." Dams were an exercise of class prerogative, perpetrated by "gentlemen lawyers" in league with the mill owners.[40]

In 1839, during a panic following a spectacular wave of forestland speculation in Maine, local courts found owners of the mills above Bangor guilty of neglecting their fishways. Mill agents pleaded that the indictment would "render the property comparatively valueless." Bangor's Democratic paper opined that such an event would give "more to rejoice than to mourn." Mill owners, "not content with their exclusive corporation rights, must . . . to the great injury of the public, almost totally ruin the fishing business in the Penobscot waters . . . Will the time ever arrive when the wealthy and influential *few* will not be permitted to recklessly trample on the rights of the hard working and obscure many?"[41] To the editor's Democratic audience, the big dams were a profoundly unsettling manifestation of alien monopoly power. "At least in this State," one petitioner announced, corporations would be "henceforward . . . watched and guarded with a jealouse eye." Fisheries, on the other hand, were a "means of which the poor have been supplied and the hungry fed, a blessing provided by nature" to the people of the region.[42]

In the teeth of the surging Penobscot lumber trade, fishers continued the battle to keep the fishways open. They invoked the region's pioneer heritage—"This section of the State could not have been settled and brought forward as it has, had it not been for the primitive blessing of taking fish in Penobscot Bay, river and tributary waters"—and they assured legislators that there was ample water for the mills and the fish. The salmon, shad, and alewives deserved protection "as long as 'Old Penobscot rolls his current on.'" Petitioners in the Kennebec and St. Croix river valleys likewise denounced the "sacrifice [of] the rights and privileges of a large number of the inhabitants . . . for the benefit of a few individuals."[43] Monopolizing river privileges violated moral and natural, if not civil law.

Dam owners could do little to counter the moral authority of fishways petitioners, but they enjoyed an advantaged position in arguing historic inevitability: dams had already "so diminished" the fisheries that there was little left to protect. It was inconceivable that lumber operations would be suspended, "or even restricted," to accommodate a "lesser interest." With lumbering operations at full tide on the river, "all the Laws in the world will not bring [the fish] back unless the greater interest is absorbed in the less."[44] The argument had economic merit, but the Whig party philosophy of industrial development that inspired it was at odds with a statewide political culture that was largely Democratic.

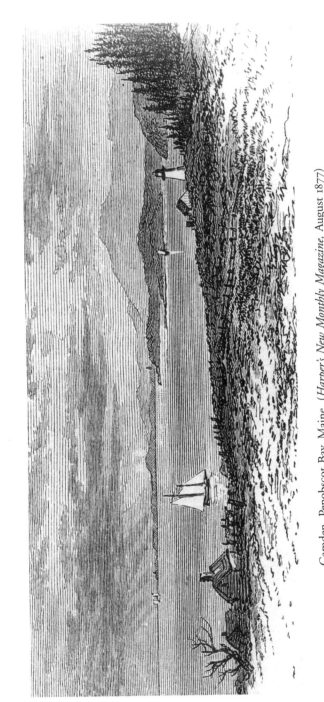

Camden, Penobscot Bay, Maine. (*Harper's New Monthly Magazine*, August 1877)

Those interested in the upper river fisheries might have made their case more effectively had they spoken with a united voice, but they faced a second challenge from fellow fishers along the shores of Penobscot Bay. In 1839 petitioners from Lincolnville, Camden, and Penobscot asked the legislature to exempt the waters of the bay from the weir restrictions in the fish laws. On the river itself, "the waters are narrow and obstructed by Mills & dams"; regulation was necessary because the fish were vulnerable. But shore weirs had little overall impact in the broad, deep bay, they argued, and the structures were frequently rendered ineffective by strong winds that forced the fish into deeper waters. The additional burden of closing the bay fisheries two days a week rendered them useless.[45] In order to protect the legitimacy of the laws pertaining to the river itself, the legislature exempted the bay. Mill owners also discovered allies along the lower river, who watched the fish saved from their nets by a closed time fall prey to competitors upstream. Two downriver towns petitioned for repeal because, among other things, the fish law created "a hord of useless ofices which are filled by men who swell up large bills against their respective counties."[46]

By the late 1830s the legislature's attempts to appease competing river users had produced a large body of confusing and contradictory special laws pertaining to the river and bay. Not a session went by, one legislator complained, "without passage of [another] '. . . act, in addition to the several acts for the preservation of Fish in the Penobscot River and Bay, and the several streams emptying into the same.'"[47] Because the laws were so particularistic, they were difficult to enforce, and the legislative debates on fisheries appeared endless.

Balancing Rights

Overwhelmed by the conflicting demands coming from the Penobscot region, the Maine legislature commissioned a study of the fish laws. In 1839 a Joint Select Committee inquired into the "expediency of repealing all laws in relation to fish" and passing a standardized code to replace them. Their report was the first of three important documents that highlight the weaknesses in the fish laws and presage the coming of more comprehensive and flexible institutionalized arrangements.

The report of the Joint Committee, which took into account both coastal and inland fisheries, reflected the frustration with contending claims to Maine's water resources. The report criticized the community focus of the fish laws. The system was confusing and contradictory; fishing that was legal in one pond might be illegal in the next, "though the circumstances are in their own nature the same." Laws, the committee argued, should be made uniform for all waters. "Why should McCurdey's pond and Cochnewagan pond be surrounded with the terrors of pains and penalties, and other ponds, with names equally euphonious, be left to the eel-pots and spears of the destroyer?" More than a hundred such special laws crowded the statute books, and debates were taking up valuable time in the legislature. The committee attributed this situation to the tendency to vest regulatory rights in the towns. Laws, members felt, should rest with the "people in general."[48]

The committee's solution was draconian: abolish *all* laws relating to fish. Dismissing the community rights that were becoming so confusing to the legislature, the committee also ignored the matter of how these vulnerable resources were to be regulated by the "people in general." It waved aside the threats posed by new types of fishing gear—"It has generally been considered that labor saving machines should be encouraged, not prohibited"—and reduced the complex realities of competition for finite resources to a simple principle: "Every one has a right to fish in his own land, and by the earliest usage in this country all have a prescriptive right of a common . . . fishery." Common management would yield to open access.[49] Their solution, however unrealistic, underscores the dilemma state legislators faced as they accepted the burden of jurisdiction from the towns: conscious of the broad scope of resource use in an expanding commercial world, they viewed local waters simply as open-access resources. The standardized solutions they applied ignored the informal, particularistic sanctions that held exploitation in check locally, and they created no effective overarching authority to replace them.[50]

Despite the 1839 report, the resulting 1840 act was not remarkably different from previous general fish laws, reflecting the poverty of state-level strategies in this era of localism and limited government. The Joint Committee's hearty endorsement of economic liberalism clearly ignored the threats to the industry, and because the committee offered no workable alternative to local regulation, the legislature left the special enactments in place. The report did, however, highlight the need for comprehensive laws guiding resource protection.

In 1843 the legislature, acting on petition, again revised the fish law, authorizing the governor and his council to appoint three "suitable persons" each from Penobscot, Waldo, and Hancock counties to watch over the dams. Towns were to appoint wardens to inspect fishways and mill-dams. After the fish had ascended the streams, wardens would close the fishways "safe & tight" for the rest of the year. They were also directed to license weirs and nets, prevent them from reaching more than halfway across the streams, specify closed times, and keep records on each weir. Although the new law was designed for comprehensive application, villagers quickly asked for—and received—special exemptions and exceptions.[51] Nevertheless, the 1843 law became a prototype for the state fish commission established two decades later.

Events elsewhere demonstrated the need for comprehensive state agencies empowered to manage resources and the contentious people who harvested them. The shad and alewife fisheries on the Taunton Great River in southern Massachusetts generated disputes that had become legendary by the 1830s.[52] In 1832, for instance, fishers in Berkley and Bristol complained that those across the river in Dighton were entitled to set seines five days each week, whereas they were allowed only four. Fishers on the upper river complained that those below them blocked off the runs, and downriver fishers countered that their upstream rivals threatened the spawning beds. Squabbles like this were the source of "much heartburning, bickering, and contention."[53]

The delicate balance of rights to Taunton River resources was disturbed repeatedly by the rising commercial value of the fish and by the industrialization of the area. New dams destroyed fisheries, forcing locals to encroach on other towns' privileges. Elsewhere, fish ladders redirected the migratory flow, benefiting some fisheries and impoverishing others. The perception of equity, so essential to compliance in any common-pool resource regime, was impossible to maintain given this shifting set of advantages. When Bridgewater lost its fishery to a dam, citizens petitioned the legislature for rights to set weirs on the Newmasket, a nearby tributary. Those living upriver remonstrated: if Bridgewater's fishers and manufacturers could not exist together, Middleboro residents argued, the people of Bridgewater should "decide which shall be retained, and which shall be abandoned."[54] Middleboro petitioners summarized feelings along the river in 1843: the fish law was "inconsistent and absurd in its provisions and cannot be enforced."[55]

In 1854 the Massachusetts legislature appointed a committee of three to inquire into local conditions and recommend changes.[56] By this time conflicts between dam owners and fishers had subsumed all other controversy. Mill workers blocked attempts to inspect the fishways, and sabotage was prevalent. The ill-regarded job of fish warden attracted only those so desperate for work that they could be forced by circumstances to "endure certain abuse and injury for the sake of large pay." The committee's report, submitted in April 1855, began with a cautionary note hinting at some of the frustration the members experienced in dealing with the people along the river: "That the wishes of every individual contained in nine towns situated on the banks of a river of thirty miles in extent will be fully gratified, your Committee do not anticipate."[57]

Having carefully scrutinized the divisive opinion along the river, the committee drafted a lengthy bill they considered the best possible compromise among all interested parties. They closed their report with an important admonition: effective regulation would "require that such legislation should remain intact for many years to come." The committee anticipated the inevitable local requests for amendments to the bill, which would "disturb its harmony"—that is, disrupt the new balance of rights the committee sought to establish on the river.[58]

The committee's bill passed into law, but the forebodings that concluded the report were borne out within days. Virtually the same people who had petitioned for a general law now argued for its abolition. As on the Penobscot, legislators were frustrated in their search for the illusive combination of rights that would ensure equal access for all parties along the river and at the same time safeguard the fishery.[59] The issues of equity and community rights could not be put to rest by ad hoc committees or by universal laws. Contrary to the hopes of the Fisheries Committee, no static balance of rights could prevail in the dynamic society of coastal New England.

Legislative reports on the Penobscot and Taunton Rivers suggest the persistence of community claims in the age of regionalized river use, as well as the need for a comprehensive yet flexible institutional arrangement for adjusting these claims. A third report offered an opinion on the important matter of republican values—a legacy of the community commons—as a foundation for these new state-level regulations. In 1849 Benjamin Shaw wrote to a state legislator summarizing his three years as a Penobscot County fish warden. Shaw's lengthy correspondence reveals again the flaws in the local management system that were driving the people of New England to create the nation's first permanent conservation commissions.

Shaw in fact remained optimistic. There were still sufficient shad and salmon on the spawning grounds to generate an "old fashioned run," he thought. People in the fishing industry were ready to support the laws, and everyone agreed that fish would return to the river with proper management. Still, there were two overriding problems. First, the inequities in the fish law encouraged conflict. Penobscot Bay and several tributaries had been exempted, and uneven enforcement left fishers disinclined to observe the laws. "Permit me heare to say that Laws suitable to command the respect of New England . . . Yankees or Penobscot Fishermen must be tinctured a little with Justice and Equality to command quiet and ready . . . submission." Local fishers remained unshaken in their conviction that equal rights pertained in a republican society, and, being fiercely competitive, they demanded regulatory laws based on this principle. They were ready to conserve the fish if the moral authority of the commons could be reestablished. Give the law "that principle of justice and equality that every American Admires"—and the river would "again Swarm with fish of old." Fishers would "chearfully combine in respecting the Law," and not incidentally "treat the authority of the Fish Wardens with more Respect." Without equity, the fish were doomed.[60]

Shaw pointed to a second problem: the assumption among mill owners that manufacturing lumber and catching fish were incompatible. Shaw felt that construction of numerous log-driving dams in the upper basin and a recent water diversion from the Allagash River had improved flowage on the Penobscot. Dam owners could well afford spilling enough water to fill the fishways. Nor were the lumber mills entitled to monopoly rights. Farming, Shaw believed, was the Penobscot Valley's true source of wealth, and fisheries were essential to spreading agriculture into the wilderness regions north of Bangor. "The Fish and actual Settlers have always gone together." Lumbering, farming, and fishing moved in tandem along the settlement frontier; each required its own protections. Shaw closed his correspondence with a brief allusion to the real business of the majority of local inhabitants: "All well. Good growing weather but little news here."[61]

At midcentury conservation initiatives still rested largely with citizens acting locally. Nevertheless, as the reports on the Penobscot and Taunton Rivers made clear, the system was increasingly impractical. Petitions from across Maine reinforce the point. After a half-century of neglect, fisheries in the town of Machias were rebounding under patient care, "but our Fish Law being only applicable to this town, it left us exposed to the avariciousness of the adjoining towns."[62] Citizens living along the St. Croix River complained that county wardens were too remote to enforce the laws, and asked that town officials be given jurisdiction; those on the nearby Pleasant River complained that town officials were too negligent, and asked that county wardens be given jurisdiction.[63] When a statute pertaining to the Narraguagus River failed to prevent poachers from "sweeping in the usuall lurking places of said fish," locals asked for a new set of laws.[64] In Warren, on the St. George River, conflicts over individual and community rights had "become a bone of contention among the people and a prolific source of Litigation," generating "heart-burnings, strife and lawsuits."[65] Fish laws changed constantly as petitioners searched, on a town-by-town basis, for a new ethic to assure a growing number of local interests equal rights to the water and its resources.

Between 1830 and 1850 the system of community jurisdiction collapsed under the weighty problem of allocating fish and water among the various classes interested in these finite resources. By the time Massachusetts passed its first comprehensive "Act to Encourage the Cultivation of Useful Fishes" in 1869, nearly four hundred laws relating to fisheries were on the books in the state. Fishers everywhere complained that such laws were, in the words of one, "partial, incidental, and spasmodic."[66]

In the mid-1860s northern New England became the first region in the United States to create permanent statewide fisheries-management agencies. The establishment of the agencies amounted to official recognition, as Arthur McEvoy puts it, "that the North American frontier was not, after all, boundless."[67] Yet the commissioners were not the first to recognize that fish resources were finite. The traditional community regulations they replaced were more than simple anachronisms; these local arrangements transmitted a set of republican values that would become the *sine qua non* of any popular commitment to conserving fisheries in the formative era of the conservation movement. The long ideological dispute that preceded the founding of the New England fish commissions conditioned America's first official conservationists to treat these republican values with some sensitivity. Warden Shaw's admonition about the need for equity among river users was prescient. State agencies inherited a quest for cultural and natural harmonies that began with the fish-transplanting experiments of the 1820s and 1830s.

CHAPTER SIX

The Politics of Interstate Fisheries

At a special meeting of the American Fish Culturists' Association held on the Centennial Exhibition grounds in Philadelphia in 1876, association president Robert B. Roosevelt, whose nephew would become America's best-known conservationist president, summarized a quarter-century of fish conservation. He began by listing the abuses of the nation's natural resources. "Our first farmers chopped down the forest and shade trees, took crop after crop of the same kind from the land, exhausted the soil and made bare the country." Then, Roosevelt told his audience, "came the restorers": farmers who manured and fallowed their land, rotated their crops, planted trees, protected useful birds, "and [who] will, I predict, ere long, restock the streams, rivers, and ponds with the best fish that once inhabited them." Roosevelt's assessment of the need for fish conservation was accurate. Migratory fish were already extinct in many northeastern rivers, and several freshwater varieties were perilously reduced. This alarming situation had already triggered numerous experiments in fish conservation, a trend that paralleled, as Roosevelt noted, interest in farm improvement.[1]

As befitting the national centennial celebration, Roosevelt's speech ended on an optimistic note: "In America are to be found the largest lakes . . . the longest rivers . . . and the most remarkable variety of water in the world." Fish of almost any type could be grown in these waters, under infinitely varied conditions: clear water, confined water, turbulent or stagnant water, "from the hot springs of the West, to the mountain trout-stream . . .—even underground ponds and streams inhabited by eyeless fish." Science could turn these reservoirs into teeming sources of protein for the poor and hungry, or into sporting havens for the more discriminating angler. "A new science was being born into the world . . . an endless vista lies before us, [if] we are enabled to tread it with firm and intelligent steps."[2]

By 1876 nineteen states had created fish commissions, as had the U.S. government. These pioneering conservation agencies were founded on the hope of transcending the piecemeal, town-by-town system of conservation that choked the statute books with conflicting legislation. More positively, they would use the new science of pisciculture to enhance the fertility of the waters and the lives of the people. New England's commissions, the nation's first, did much to consolidate popular support for conservation. They encouraged the conceptual affiliation of various discrete grass-roots conservation efforts by providing an institutional focus with an overarching ideal. They brought meaning to the numerous local experiments with propagating fish and to the ad-hoc laws passed to appease local interests. Given an official nucleus, these efforts began to resonate as a movement.[3]

These early commissioners drew inspiration from the contemporaneous farm reform movement. Like farm reformers, they saw no limit to the anthropocentric transformation of nature—to their vision of natural abundance coaxed to fruition by the hand of science. Their faith in a detached, scientific path to a more productive future encouraged a view of nature as a commodity to be manipulated and dominated in the interest of greater material wealth. They were, in this sense, progenitors of the utilitarian, scientific wing of the Progressive conservation movement. Yet fisheries managers also drew inspiration from the agrarian quest for a moral balance between nature and culture. Farm reformers who exhorted their peers to cultivate less acreage and grow more crops, to fertilize, and to make better use of wetlands and hillsides placed these endeavors in the context of a purposive universe in which natural forces were created to serve human needs. This teleological point of view was central to the emerging science of pisciculture.[4] Finally, the commissioners were inspired by an agrarian vision of the democratic commons. In time, access to fish would be universal; pisciculture would become so exact that fish managers would need only to ascertain the level of demand in a river, to allow for fish mortality, and to stock the appropriate number of eggs.[5]

Yet by the end of the century this magnificent democratic vision had been replaced by a much narrower goal of supplying elite anglers with a source of spring and summer recreation. Like forestry, fish conservation shed much of its popular moral content and its democratic grounding as the New England fish commissions entered the Progressive era.

The philosophy of fish propagation was heavily influenced by pioneer fish culturist Seth Green. Born near Rochester, New York, in 1817, Green made several fishing trips to Canada as a youth, where in 1838 he watched salmon spawn and began thinking about artificial propagation. Later he conducted hatching experiments, and in 1864 he erected a hatchery at Caledonia Springs, near Rochester, the first such commercial facility in the country.[6] Green's comments on fish culture were widely reproduced in the agricultural press and compiled in 1888 in a tract called *Home Fishing and Home Waters*.

Green linked fish culture directly to farm reform: "No class of people should be more interested in fish culture than the farmers . . . Their homes are among the lakes and streams . . . and they, above all others, should be interested in keeping them stocked, so that when they wish a change of food from the regular farm diet . . . they can get them for the taking." Appealing to the farmer's instincts for cultivation, Green explained that nature "carried out her design in the apparent over-production of the millions of seeds of plants and trees, and the millions of eggs fish are made to produce." As farmers had known for millennia, a careful husbanding of this overabundance increased the yield—of plants or fish. This was the essence of agriculture and the logic that placed the farmer at the apex of nature's design.[7] Thus Green integrated fish culture into the teleological thinking of the farmer.

Green's agrarian analogy was a powerful inspiration for fish culturists. Strike a scythe in a field of timothy in blossom, a Massachusetts farmer once declared: "There is a perfect cloud of fertilizing or dust pollen . . . an amount of material which passes all conception, coming from the male organs of the plant."[8] This superabundance represented a tremendous natural reserve, available for human manipulation. Like farmers who took "the earth from nature's hand . . . so to manage and dispose it artificially," fish culturists would redirect these forces of procreation to meet human needs.[9] The farmers' radically anthropocentric view of nature was a perfect backdrop for the philosophy of fish culture.

Taking their lead from the rising productivity of the farms, most fish culturists, like Roosevelt and Green, were lavishly optimistic. In a region blessed with a generous supply of water, Malthusian arguments paled before this vibrant positivist faith in the fusion of natural and scientific forces. Waters were capable of meeting almost any demand, they argued; only human obstructions—improper fishing, unscientific attitudes—limited their productivity. Fish culturists would meet the needs of a growing population by the "application of science to the cultivation of water resources."[10]

Origins of Fish Culture

Two experimental traditions, one amateur and the other academic, converged to produce the discipline of pisciculture. Within the latter was Harvard naturalist Louis Agassiz. In 1840, in a washbasin in his bedroom, Agassiz conducted what he considered the earliest attempt at artificial propagation in the country. In subsequent years he devoted considerable attention to the subject, visiting fishways in Ireland and hatching ponds in France. In a well-publicized paper read before a Massachusetts Board of Agriculture gathering in 1869, Agassiz articulated the emerging view of fish culture, explaining its significance in terms similar to those used by Green.[11]

If Agassiz's washbasin was the first American hatchery, the first experiment to be widely reported was made by Theodatus Garlick and H. A. Ackley near Cleveland. Garlick had read an account of successful incubation by two French fishers and saw in this "one of the most important discoveries of modern times." Garlick and Ackley placed several brook trout in gravel-lined wooden boxes in a small pond in

June 1854. Later they stripped and fecundated the eggs and left them to mature. The first fish hatched early the following March, Garlick recalled: "There lay . . . on his gravelly bed the first baby fish artificially propagated on this continent." Soon the boxes were alive with young trout.[12] One year later E. C. Kellogg, also inspired by experiments in Europe, built a hatching house on a spring-fed brook in Simsbury, Connecticut. Kellogg published his results in the Connecticut State Agricultural Society transactions, hoping that some "enterprising Yankee . . . would venture an investment, sufficient to carry on a fish-breeding establishment successfully."[13]

At the same time New England's agrarian reform movement was yielding a variety of improvised fish-hatching experiments. The most ambitious was conducted by Upham S. Treat, an inquisitive fish dealer and farmer from Eastport, Maine. Treat conducted the nation's first successful experiments with canning juvenile herring as sardines and developed processes for extracting fertilizer, fish oil, and nitrates for explosives from his fish wastes.[14] Learning of Kellogg's experiments, he obtained rights to three large ponds draining into the St. Croix River and in 1857 began breeding striped bass, salmon, alewives, and shad. As his progeny matured, he released them into the river. In 1862 he reported his findings to the editor of the *Maine Farmer*. Salmon, he observed, matured at sea in four years and returned to their home waters. "The instinct of these fishes is very remarkable: they know their homes and will not mix with neighboring streams not more than two miles apart, although the fish are of the same species." The *Maine Farmer* followed Treat's subsequent experiments closely. In 1866 the Eastport farmer and fish processor concluded that the waters of Maine could be "made as productive as the land," a premise the state fisheries commissioners would echo often in the coming years.[15]

Another ambitious fish cultivator was David C. Pottle of Alna, Maine, who began experimenting with trout in 1862 purely, he said, out of a "love for the finny tribe." Reading of attempts at artificial propagation, Pottle blocked off a nearby stream and built a hatching house. His "trout farm" was divided into eight pools: as the fish gained size, they passed into larger pools. The final pond contained some 2,000 three-year-old trout averaging ten to thirteen inches. Not yet content with the productivity of his stream, Pottle used the runoff to drive a millstone, lathe, churn, and other light machinery. Pottle, too, communicated his expertise with the "wants of his *finny flocks*" to readers of the *Maine Farmer*, giving minute descriptions of pond maintenance, optimum water temperatures, problems with fungus, feeding experiments, and procedures for hatching.[16]

These farm projects were part of a broader Jeffersonian interest in natural history, a wide-ranging curiosity about the natural world not unexpected among people whose livelihood depended upon the play of natural forces across their land. From experimenters like Green, Treat, and Pottle, agricultural editors derived a wealth of detail about converting ponds and wetlands into productive units of the farm.[17] European pisciculture, though well established, served Americans in only general ways; each New World species required, as the *New England Farmer* put it, a "life which is suited to them."[18] When the new state fish commissions launched the conservation movement officially in the 1860s, a fund of information on fish propagation was already at their disposal.

The direct occasion for the founding of fish commissions in Massachusetts, Vermont, and New Hampshire was a plea from citizens to reopen the upper Merrimack and Connecticut Rivers to salmon and shad runs. Salmon had disappeared from the upper Connecticut River after construction of a dam near the Connecticut-Massachusetts border in 1798, and shad had been stopped by a higher dam built in South Hadley in 1849. On the Merrimack, the Lowell dam, built in 1826 was passable, but a structure thirty feet high at Lawrence, built in 1847, had brought an end to fish runs in the upper river.[19]

In response to a petition from "sundry citizens" of Merrimack County in 1856, the New Hampshire House of Representatives created a special committee to urge Massachusetts and Connecticut to mitigate these obstructions. Vermont's legislature passed a similar resolve the same year. At the same time, Ambrose Lawrence of Lowell gathered

Farmers stocked fish ponds to add another facet to their diversified cropping strategies. Farm journals published the results of these experiments, providing useful information for New England's state fish commissioners in the 1860s. (*American Agriculturist*, February 1873)

petitions from hundreds of Massachusetts citizens living along the Merrimack. Printed and mass produced, the petitions pointed to the Essex Company's charter, which called for a fishway on the Lawrence dam. The "heavy spout" installed at one end of the dam was woefully inadequate. Adding to the injustice, the company sold exclusive rights to catch those fish still schooling at the foot of the dam, "thereby actually deriving a revenue from that what should subject them to heavy damages." Citizens in Massachusetts, Vermont, and New Hampshire urged their legislators to action.[20]

The legislative studies of dams, fishways, and artificial propagation that resulted from these petitions excited further interest.[21] Vermont's widely disseminated report, compiled by the venerable George Perkins Marsh, was a compendium of facts gathered from foreign and American publications. It contained a philosophical rationale for fish propagation, a history of fish extinction and reintroduction from Roman times onward, and a more complete study of the waters of Vermont, including speculations on the effect of forest clearing on stream flow and spawning beds. Appended were Kellogg's address to the Connecticut State Agricultural Society and excerpts from various European studies of fish breeding.[22]

The Massachusetts committee focused on the 1847 charter for the Lawrence dam. As petitioners had pointed out, the charter called for a fishway, and the resulting structure, even though certified by the Essex County fish commissioners in 1847, was indeed ineffective. The ineptitude of the design, the legislative committee concluded, was "a most singular, unjust, not to say unprincipled prescription, for which the company might have been or might not have been, to some extent responsible." Yet the question remained: Could the company be required to do more? Here the commissioners delved into legal, as opposed to moral issues. Despite a confessed bias in favor of the petitioners, the committee advanced the opinion that the state had no right to require improvements. The contract, such as it was, had been consummated "to the very letter."[23]

The commissioners had other misgivings about the fishway—similar, perhaps, to those that had compelled the Essex County fish commissioners to take their responsibilities less than seriously back in 1847. An effective fishway would cost up to $40,000, and yet no one was certain that fish would ascend "so long and so high an artificial water-course." Even if the state had solid legal footing, the commissioners wondered, would it be "just to require said company to make such an expenditure, the result of which might prove an entire failure?" Given the pollution and industrial activity near the dam, the project appeared too uncertain.[24] This tension between moral and legal considerations highlights the ambiguity surrounding dams and fishways. Morally, the case for restoring the fisheries was easy to make, yet the uncertain legal grounds, the lingering doubts about experimental fishways over high dams, the reflexive deference to the needs of manufacturers, and the argument that fisheries and civilization were incompatible plagued the movement through the rest of the century.

Despite the committee's negative report, the legislature, prodded by testimony from New Hampshire, voted to remind the Essex Company of its obligation to "make and forever after maintain . . . a suitable and sufficient fishway."[25] The company appealed the resolve to the Supreme Judicial Court, which found for the company on the basis of its having paid for the fishing rights immediately above the dam. The issue died in 1857 as Massachusetts and the nation became embroiled in more pressing issues leading up to the Civil War.[26]

In 1864 legislators in all three states picked up literally where they had left off in 1857. Responding once again to resolutions from New Hampshire and Vermont, the Massachusetts General Court formed a joint legislative committee in March 1865 to hear testimony on the fisheries. Selectmen from Chelmsford, New Hampshire, explained that before the dams had been built, townspeople had "derived about one third of their animal food from the Merrimack river."[27] On the basis of the committee's finding that fish restoration was "practicable at a comparatively small expense," the state set aside $7,000 for a more detailed study of dams and pollution. Theodore Lyman of Brookline and Alfred Reed of Boston were appointed as commissioners.[28]

While Lyman and Reed were gathering information, Governor Frederick Smyth of New Hampshire signed into law on June 30, 1865, an executive order appointing the nation's first permanent fish commission. Commissioners Henry A. Bellows and Winborn A. Sanborn were to consider ways of restoring sea- and freshwater fish to New Hampshire waters, "provided the expense does not exceed the sum of one hundred dollars." Their understandably brief report of 1865 described the new science of "aquae-culture" and called attention to developments in Massachusetts. In 1866 the legislature increased their budget to $3,000.[29]

The following January Lyman and Reed presented to the Massachusetts legislature a lengthy summary of the obstructions in both rivers. The report explained the legal implications of the issue and provided models for fishways over the high dams at Lawrence and South Hadley. Using tables supplied by the dam owners, Lyman and Reed concluded that flowage was sufficient for both power and fish. The report was optimistic, but already they understood that the issue was much broader than fishways. Since migratory fish had been extirpated from the river, successful reintroduction would require a stocking program. Moreover, the best fishways and the most extensive breeding programs would avail little without laws protecting the fish. Protection in turn would require a staff of commissioners, agents, and wardens, as well as cooperation between the various states bordering the rivers. There were traditions of local regulation, Lyman and Reed pointed out, but they had been abandoned when dams had blocked off the fish migrations. Restoring these rules under state auspices would be difficult.[30]

Responding to the petitions, the hearings, and the report by Lyman and Reed, the Massachusetts legislature in 1866 authorized the governor to appoint two permanent commissioners to design and inspect fishways and consult with their counterparts in adjacent states.[31] Vermont had founded a fish commission under Albert D. Hager and Charles Barrett the previous year, and in 1866 Connecticut appointed F. W. Russell and Henry C. Robinson. Maine's commission was established in 1867 under Nathan W. Foster and Charles G. Atkins, and New York's in 1868 under Horatio Seymour, Robert B. Roosevelt, and Seth Green. In 1867 commissioners formed the New England Commission of River Fisheries, meeting yearly thereafter to discuss common problems. Massachusetts established the nation's first public hatching station at South Hadley Falls on the Connecticut in 1867, in conjunction with Seth Green. In 1871 Congress formed the U.S. Fish and Fisheries Commission under Spencer F. Baird of the Smithsonian Institution.[32]

In Maine official interest in fish culture began in 1863, when Ezekiel Holmes added a study of Maine's fish resources to the Board of Agriculture's report on the natural history and geology of the state. The following year the board's annual report included an article by Holmes on "aquaeculture." Holmes, editor of the *Maine Farmer,* was by 1864 an agricultural reformer and naturalist of national recognition. Born in Kingston, Massachusetts, in 1801, he received a medical degree from Bowdoin College in 1824. Instead of practicing medicine, he became president of the Lyceum in Gardiner, Maine, and in 1832 he started the *Farmers' and Mechanics' Journal.* Later renamed the *Maine Farmer,* the journal reigned for nearly a century as one of New England's most influential farm publications. Holmes was also the Maine state naturalist, the first secretary of both the Kennebec Agricultural Society and the Maine Board of Agriculture, a professor of chemistry at Waterville (Colby) College, and a member of the state legislature. Having dedicated his career to uplifting Maine agriculture, Holmes was well suited as Maine's premier fish conservationist. Like Seth Green, he viewed the landscape as a providential natural setting for both agriculture and pisciculture.[33]

In 1865 agriculturalist Samuel L. Boardman completed a survey of Kennebec County for the Board of Agriculture. Devoting much of the study to fish culture, he repeated Holmes's observations, described the history of fish transplanting in Maine, and ended with this interjection about the Kennebec Valley:

Look at the facilities for the propagation and culture of fish in this county! The Kennebec running through the centre of it . . .

by its tributary streams connecting the numerous ponds on both sides of the river, affords opportunities that but few sections of this extent are possessed of . . . With a little capital and energy they might be made to produce an almost unlimited amount of the choicest sorts of edible fish, and return a profit far greater than that of any one branch of husbandry carried on by our farmers. Shall such opportunities for industry and wealth remain much longer unimproved?[34]

Holmes and Boardman brought to the movement the farmer's conviction that an obedient nature expressed order and purpose by providing for countrypeople's needs—in this case, dispersing fish along interconnected waters throughout the countryside. Working with nature's laws, farmers and fish conservationists could extend this bounty endlessly.[35]

Like Holmes and Boardman, Maine's new commissioners saw fish culture as supplemental to agriculture. Fish was a staple, they pointed out, "as much as . . . our domestic animals, our poultry, or the grains and root products of our fields."[36] They shared the agricultural reformer's vision of an ordained landscape accessible to the people as a whole. The runs of sea fish were nature's gift to farmers: a "most wonderful system of commissary, by which the fish, when loaded with fat, fresh from the ocean, penetrated far up into the interior of the state and supplied the settlers with a store of . . . food." It had been a crime against nature to allow dams to block the "river highways by which these ocean visitors traversed" to the "very doors" of the inland people.[37] Responding to the early experiments by farmers and academics and to the growing interest in fish as a resource, New England's commissioners pioneered the institutional basis for conservation in America.

Fishways

While Maine's first commissioners concentrated largely on salmon, those to the south turned to the shad in the Connecticut and Merrimack. In New England the shad migrations come in early May. The fry leave the rivers the following fall, then return in two or three years, averaging three pounds for males and five for females. Shad follow well-defined paths along the shores and up the rivers, permitting knowledgeable fishers to stop large portions of the run. They are easily propagated, but few fishways, even those used by salmon and alewives, were successful in attracting them over dams. Migration patterns could be altered by changing temperature, wind, or current conditions, and yearly variations were often confused with human-caused changes, generating endless disputes among fishers. This legacy of contention made regulation difficult. Another problem was the interstate nature of the shad fisheries. Except the Kennebec, each of the East Coast's great shad rivers traversed more than one state.[38] The New England shad fisheries provided the most glaring example of the obstacles before the propagationist's vision of unlimited abundance.

The commissioners' first challenge was popular skepticism. Fishways and hatching were experimental, and expecting fish to return regularly to a specific river and climb ladders around dams seemed to many visionary, if not absurd. In the popular perception, fish declines were connected to a whole complex of developments—bridges, steamboats, waterwheels, pollution, noise, forest clearing, and constant movement along the banks. Thus many were skeptical of restoring migrations. To allay this mood, in 1867 Seth Green built a shad hatchery at South Hadley, in concert with commissioners from the four states sharing the Connecticut drainage. Green's improvised hatching box produced 15 million shad eggs in two weeks. Over the next two years he placed more than 100 million young shad in the Connecticut, predicting they would begin returning in 1870.[39]

Shad fishers were not quick to embrace Green's ideas. When he arrived at South Hadley, as he later recalled, "they thought I was crazy and treated me accordingly." His hatching boxes were vandalized repeatedly.[40] Fish culturists attributed this response to ignorance and skepticism, but it also expressed the commercial fishers' fears that manipulating nature would disrupt their markets. As conservationist Fred Mather reminisced in 1896, fishers "rebelled at the first efforts at shad hatching . . . because [Green] said that he could 'make shad cheap.' He meant that they would be made plenty, and merely used the wrong word to the fishermen." Semantics aside, Green did indeed drive down the price of shad to a point where fishers "were unable to get fair pay for the labor of taking them."[41] They also feared, realistically, that experiments would alter legal constructions of property in fish, undermining their rights to the river. Despite these tribulations, as Green called them, in May 1870 sea captains reported immense shoals of shad in Long Island Sound, "all making for the mouth of the Connecticut River."[42]

Early trials with salmon were equally promising. As their first official act in 1865, New Hampshire Fish Commissioners Bellows and Sanborn sent W. W. Fletcher of Concord to New Brunswick to obtain salmon eggs. Fletcher hatched and planted some 15,000 fry in New Hampshire waters. In 1871 Maine Commissioner Charles G. Atkins, working with his counterparts in Massachusetts and Connecticut, established a hatchery at Craig's Pond, in the lower Penobscot Valley. The facility became the major source for salmon eggs in New England and later the first federal hatching facility in the nation, producing by the 1880s about 700,000 fry a year.[43] On the basis of these stocking experiments and a gathering of information about local waters throughout the region, commissioners devised a comprehensive, four-state plan to restore New England's waters: Massachusetts was to compel companies to build fishways and reduce pollution; Connecticut was to control the use of weirs and gill-nets at the river's mouth; and New Hampshire and Vermont were to breed salmon and shad in the upper waters and protect the young fish.[44]

The first step in this ambitious project was passage over the dams. At the time, most American fishways were simple trenches dug around dams and checked at intervals by large stones. At Lawrence and South Hadley, commissioners faced the daunting task of building the nation's first high-dam fishways, virtually on an experimental basis and in the face of skepticism from manufacturers. Moreover, these structures had to carry more than one species of fish. Commissioners were aware of

European designs based on a trough divided by partitions and hoped to adapt these to the higher dams.[45] In the late 1860s Maine's Nathan Foster produced a plan similar to those in Europe but patterned after a small alewife fishway at East Machias. With some misgivings and much good faith, the Lawrence manufacturers built the fishway, but whirlpools in the bays confused and exhausted the fish. A second plan, completed in 1872 by Massachusetts Commissioner E. A. Brackett, proved more successful. By changing the angle of the crosspieces, Brackett eliminated the whirlpools; water fell at an even, gentle flow from the top to the outlet. His design, used on both sides of the Atlantic, opened up thousands of miles of river formerly blocked by dams.[46]

By 1870 the technological problems of fishway construction had been largely surmounted, but the political obstacles in the fishes' path proved more formidable. A brief controversy on the Taunton River is exemplary. In 1873 villagers in Norton, on a tributary of the Taunton, protested construction of a new high dam on Mill River below them. A subsequent hearing before the Senate Committee on Fisheries in Taunton offers a thorough record of feelings for and against fishways and explains why dam owners were so resistant to the propagationists' vision of fish abundance.[47]

Mill River manufacturers, like those on the Penobscot, complained that fishway requirements obstructed a higher form of use for the waters of the basin. The river could be "worked to its full power" only by supplying energy to manufacturers, who gave "employment to hundreds and thousands of men, women and children." Arguing the importance of manufacturing, they reinforced a corollary impression that fishers were idlers. "It is well known," they argued, "that a man . . . will spend a whole day worth two dollars to catch a dozen fish worth twenty five cents, and feel as if he had done well at that."[48]

During the 1860s dam owners everywhere were learning to economize water use by making dams tighter and improving the efficiency of waterwheels and turbines. As mills and factories increased in size, reaching the limits of local hydromechanical potential, these water conservation measures assumed great importance. The extension of industrial control over New England's rivers, according to historian Theodore Steinberg, expressed a "subtle anxiety over the limits of nature, [an] alarm that production might exceed the river's ability to provide water."[49] These matters weighed heavily on the minds of dam owners, who fought to retain absolute control over the waters. Having utilized "every drop of water" in Mill River, as they repeatedly said, dam owners calculated the diversion to the fishways—a stream two feet wide and six inches deep during migration—to the last penny. "Every particle you take from us is lost to us." The fisheries, by comparison, were "nothing—a mere bagatelle, in importance."[50]

If Norton wanted fish, dam owners advised, the town should "stock their ponds with bass and pickerel," which would "give the people a hundred times as many fish as they will have of [migratory] herring." The legislature concurred, exempting the dam for twenty years, provided the manufacturers paid the town of Norton $1,000, "or if requested by [the] town . . . stock the ponds at the headwaters." Ultimately the commissioners throughout New England would be forced to the same strategy: when intransigent dam owners or other political obstacles closed off options for restoring migratory fish, commissioners turned to saving nonmigratory freshwater varieties stocked in remote ponds and lakes isolated from industrial influences.[51]

Restoration on the Great Rivers

The story of New England's larger rivers, the Connecticut, Merrimack, Kennebec, and Penobscot, was the Mill River tale writ large. With some variation, the rivers all suffered the same fate: the optimistic vision projected by Robert B. Roosevelt in 1876 was obscured by a combination of politically powerful dam owners, contentious commercial fishers, and interstate rivalry.

On the Merrimack the fishery fell prey to legislative inertia in the face of intense industrial use of the river. The Lawrence fishway, completed in 1866, surmounted a dam twenty-eight feet high, one of the most difficult passes in the country. Although salmon, shad, and

This view of the Lawrence fishway, cornerstone of the effort to restore migratory fish to the Merrimack River, shows some of the difficulties fish encountered on their way to the spawning beds in New Hampshire. Access to the fishway was difficult from the base of the huge dam, and the shallow waters below the dam were heavily polluted. (Massachusetts, *Report of the Commissioners of Inland Fish and Game* [Boston, 1918])

alewives labored over the dam in limited numbers in 1867, New Hampshire commissioners deemed the Bay State's efforts insufficient and suspended their own stocking operations.[52] The two states renewed their cooperative efforts in the mid-1870s, restocking the river and replacing the fishways at Lawrence, Lowell, and Manchester. In 1877 commissioners found both salmon and shad "disporting, in ever-increasing crowds" in the Pemigewasset.[53] According to one estimate, around a thousand salmon passed over the dam yearly. In 1887 Massachusetts commissioners announced a limited season for salmon fishing with hook and line.[54]

Political obstacles clouded this success. A hatchery at North Andover revived shad and salmon runs, but the bait fishers who plied the brackish waters off Newburyport for menhadens objected to restrictions on mesh size designed to protect the hatchlings.[55] In 1877 the commissioners agreed to permit small-mesh nets under the fishers' "personal promise" that they would release any shad or salmon they caught. The accord held until 1881, when the menhadens failed to appear in the bays, and the Newburyport fishers sold juvenile shad and salmon as bait to the banks schooners. After a protracted discussion in the legislature, the mesh size limit was reimposed, and in 1885 the shad runs revived. Large numbers passed over the Lawrence fishway that year, an accomplishment unmatched at any other fishway in New England.[56]

Still, the project never received the sustained commitment that would have ensured success. In the 1890s New Hampshire dropped its guard on fishways maintenance and poaching in the upper river, and in 1895 the Massachusetts legislature, bending to pressures from commercial fishers, repealed laws protecting shad and alewives in the river below Haverhill. A new dam built near Concord, New Hampshire, contained no fishway whatever, and in 1896 a flood swept away portions of the Lawrence fishway, lynchpin of the restoration project. Commissioners rebuilt the fishway on the opposite shore, but when the new location proved unsuccessful they again allowed the fishway to deteriorate. According to one source, 1898 was the last year salmon were seen in the upper waters of the river.[57] Restoration efforts continued into the early twentieth century but remained unsuccessful.

The Connecticut River story accents similar weaknesses in the interstate compact. Again, despite the successful fishway technology, states could not muster the political resolve to save the fish. In 1868 Massachusetts brought suit to compel the Holyoke Water Power Company to build a fishway over its South Hadley dam. While the courts decided who would pay for the construction, commissioners and company engineers began work. In 1872 Connecticut legislators, impatient with delays at South Hadley and convinced that shad protected in their portion of the river would simply die in the waters below the dam, removed restrictions on the fishery. The shad run so carefully nurtured by Seth Green was stopped at the mouth of the river.[58] In that year the U.S. Supreme Court forced the Holyoke company to pay for the fishway, and the 440-foot-long structure was completed in 1873—one of the largest and most expensive ever constructed. Shad, however, initially refused to enter the structure, and observers both above and below Massachusetts blamed the state for faulty construction. Bitter feelings doomed the fishery.[59]

Connecticut River salmon fared no better. When the stocked fish returned in the late 1870s, fishermen at the mouth of the river clamored to repeal the laws protecting them. The Connecticut legislature complied, to the astonishment of those upriver. Vermont's commissioners called the repeal an act of "unspeakable greed and rapacity," and those from Massachusetts and New Hampshire inserted similar maledictions in their annual reports.[60] Connecticut commissioners explained that the increase in fish generated a corresponding increase in fishers, making it difficult to enforce the laws, particularly where "the public sentiment . . . was in sympathy with the fishermen." The few salmon that passed the gauntlet of seines and gill-nets in Connecticut were stopped at South Hadley, where poaching was rampant.[61] In the midst of this impasse, commissioners discovered that shad would spawn successfully below South Hadley. After 1875 efforts to urge the fish over the dam diminished as the two states devoted their attention to sustaining the runs in the lower river. Disappointed but convinced that nothing more could be done, Vermont and New Hampshire turned to propagating nonmigratory fish in their own waters.[62]

Even with renewed stocking efforts below South Hadley, the 1877 catch plummeted to one-fourth the previous average, touching off another legislative war between Connecticut and Massachusetts. When Connecticut proved unresponsive, the Bay State abolished fishing regulations in its own share of the river. The Massachusetts catch jumped from 12,425 in 1880 to 57,028 in 1881 as fishers raked in the juvenile fish. A short-term victory in the game of one-upmanship, the act sealed the fate of the South Hadley fishery.[63] By 1883 the catch in the Connecticut section of the river was 177,308, and in Massachusetts, 3,591. Effectively, the last shot in this war between the states was the construction of a high dam at Enfield, just below the Massachusetts state line, in 1885. Connecticut continued stocking the river below the Enfield dam, but from 1886 through 1889 the catch fell from 118,000 to 42,000. In 1894 the Holyoke Water Power Company appeared before the Massachusetts legislature and asked for an exemption to the fishway law. The company was given leave to allow the fishway to deteriorate.[64]

Fish restoration on the Kennebec and Penobscot Rivers, although their waters were entirely within one state, brought similar frustrations. The key obstacle to restoration of the Kennebec fisheries was the Augusta dam, built in 1835.[65] Like most, the charter called for a "good and sufficient passage-way" for fish, and when the dam was built it included a structure designed by local fish wardens. This proved ineffective, and because it threatened to undermine the dam, it was removed.[66]

In 1869 a flood destroyed a section of the dam, and salmon returned to the upriver spawning beds in impressive numbers.[67] Their reappearance stirred popular interest, and the commissioners renewed their demand for a fishway. Violation of the charter, they announced, was a "robbery of the public on the whole length of the Kennebec River, for the benefit of Augusta."[68] Besieged by dam corporation lawyers, the legislature exempted the company from its charter provisions for another decade; finally in 1879 the company commenced construction.[69] When the fishway was opened in the summer of 1880, some five hundred celebrants assembled as Governor Daniel F. Davis heralded a new era in fish conservation. But by this time, native Kennebec-spawning salmon were nearly extinct, and the few that passed over the fishway in 1881 succumbed to poachers upriver. The drawn-out battle over the Augusta dam demoralized the commission and exhausted its budget, and each new dam built upriver promised a fight as difficult as the first. In 1884, only four years after completion of the fishway, the commissioners abandoned restocking efforts on the river.[70]

The Penobscot story was somewhat more encouraging in the short run. Through the first quarter of the century this magnificent salmon river had remained open to the headwaters, and even after the lumber boom of the 1830s the dams had contained gates and aprons for running lumber rafts. At midcentury the Penobscot was the only major river in New England still supporting salmon.[71] Still, increased commercial traffic over the aprons threatened the migration, and in the late 1860s the state commissioners received several petitions from upriver towns demanding "just rights" for those interested in the fisheries. With some prompting, dam owners installed fishways, and by 1877 salmon were migrating deep into the Penobscot headwaters.[72]

As on the Kennebec, however, industrial development outpaced the commissioners' efforts. Between 1882 and 1900 the Penobscot Valley gained sixteen pulp and paper mills. The fishways for each of these giant developments added to the expense of guarding the run against poachers.[73] In 1887 the commissioners described the demoralizing scene below a new impassable dam built above Bangor: the pooling salmon, "breathing the poisoned waters from the pulp mill, trying to penetrate the current of running water flowing beneath the mills, looking in vain for some means to ascend to the waters above the dam," succumbed to spears, gaffs, nets, and pollution.[74] By the 1890s the Penobscot salmon run, the "pride and glory of the state," was sustained only by a yearly planting of young fry, and even this artificial population was rapidly diminishing.[75]

In 1920 fishways again opened the Penobscot to the East Branch, and a new fishway built in Bangor in 1924 was reported to be among the most effective in New England. By this time, however, commissioners in Maine and elsewhere faced an even more obdurate problem. As early as the 1890s they were beginning to notice lines of dead fish drifting in the fouled waters below the pulp mills. In Maine, commissioners warned that the "admission of pulp mills upon our streams, more especially upon the Penobscot River . . . was and is a most fatal error." Industrial development, they admitted for the first time, was indeed incompatible with sustaining the fisheries.[76]

In 1920 Massachusetts rebuilt the Lawrence fishway at the urging of local fish and game clubs; alewives and freshwater fish braved the polluted waters to ascend it, but no shad or salmon were so inclined. In Maine, the Kennebec above Augusta looked more like a neglected woodyard than a river.[77] Mill waste matted the river bottoms and smothered spawning beds. Tanneries choked streams with offal, carrion, bark, and foul-smelling liquors. Pollution, with its multiple sources, was a problem far more complex than dams. Although commissioners were critical, there was little they could do: they harbored no illusion that their concerns would override the states' commitment to industrial growth.[78]

Commissioners made headway against one form of pollution, however, and their successes here helped reshape the fish conservation movement at the end of the century. Unlike large manufacturers, owners of small upland sawmills were vulnerable to political pressures from conservationists. The mills were usually located on lesser tributary streams, and their sawdust typically affected the habitat of trout—a "higher order of fish" that garnered sympathy from wealthy constituents. In a matter of weeks a portable mill could destroy a pristine local stream to which there was enormous sentimental attachment, and the single cause was apparent to everyone.[79] "Equity," a farmer and part-time lumberman himself, enumerated the many inconveniences caused by sawdust pollution, which "invariably finds its way through our villages, contaminates the water, drifts on the intervales, and fills up the mill ponds and bulkheads situated below."[80] Commissioners received scores of similar complaints, particularly when mills affected waters previously stocked with game fish. Encouraged by riparian farmers, recreational fishers, and a population increasingly concerned about forest abuse, fish commissioners mounted a campaign against sawdust pollution. Although large lumbering and manufacturing interests blocked passage of general antipollution bills, commissioners sometimes prevailed against smaller mills in the upper river basins.[81]

Despite their disappointments, commissioners still hoped to restore the smaller upper-basin waters to nearly pristine conditions. They abandoned the big rivers, with their potential for massive migratory fish runs; here the balance of nature had been undone, and a new industrial equilibrium established.[82] Headwater streams, remote from the scourges of industrial development and commercial fishing, offered firmer moral ground: appeals to the sporting instincts of the genteel angler were far more effective than brandishing laws before downriver market fishers.[83] With this shift they turned further from the broad, democratic vision of fish as an unlimited source of food for the masses and as a central element in the ordained agrarian landscape.

The Changing Constituency for Conservation

Vermont commissioners noted in 1908 that "no country on the Globe has reached the efficiency of the United States in the artificial propagation of fishes, and no country on the Globe has assumed a more reckless waste of her natural resources."[84] This ironic blend of superlatives encapsulated the historic struggle to restore New England's migratory fishes. Reviewing this frustrating history in their annual report for 1888, the Massachusetts commissioners detailed the 1856 petitions from New Hampshire and Vermont, the pioneering work by Seth Green at South Hadley, the interstate agreements made "in a spirit of comity," the fishways, and the Holyoke lawsuit carried to the U.S. Supreme Court. Each seemed in retrospect an expensive lesson in the futility of interstate fisheries management. Not only did the states fail to reach agreement on a vital common concern, but the fishing interests themselves were hopelessly divided. The "bitter feeling among the seiners, gill-net men, and pound men, each accusing the other of overfishing and interfering with their rights," precluded an interstate solution to the problem of the migratory fish.[85] The region that had pioneered statewide fisheries management techniques, assembled the science of fish propagation, and mastered high-dam fishways technology found it impossible to steer to a political objective that encompassed needs beyond state or even local boundaries.

Just as debilitating was the feeling that poaching was almost unstoppable. Commissioners were given only tenuous authority to protect the hundreds of thousands of fry they placed in the rivers and lakes yearly. The prospect of guarding each spawning bed and fishway in New England seemed overwhelming.[86] The great democratic crusade to restore the rivers and provide food for the masses collapsed under a formidable combination of weak political resolve, bitter interstate rivalries, rampant poaching, and more-intensive industrial use of the rivers.

In the last decades of the century the constituency for protecting the fisheries changed, adding impetus to the commissioners' reevaluation of conservation philosophy. On one hand, salmon and trout fishing were coming into vogue among wealthy metropolitan anglers. On the other, farmers committed to commercial production were achieving rapprochement with manufacturers—and with the dams and pollution that industry seemed to require. As woolen and cotton textile mills, shoe factories, and papermaking complexes spread through the river basins, the benefits of dam building, previously realized by the larger downriver communities, diffused into the countryside. And as farmers began to see themselves as business managers rather than as stewards of the landscape, they began to accept their traditional rivals as allies. Upland manufacturing centers served as important "home" markets, better insulated against western production than the large eastern cities with through-rail transport and interregional wholesaling facilities. Although farm journals still supported the fish commissions in the 1880s, editors warmed to industrial river development.[87] The political implications of river use were shifting, albeit subtly at first.

Forced to retreat into the upper watersheds, fisheries managers attracted a new, more genteel constituency: wealthy anglers, tourists, and those who depended upon tourism for income. Still holding to a populist rationale, Massachusetts commissioners articulated this basic shift in the political economy of conservation: "The real practical consequence of fish in the waters may be justly based upon the amount of money put into circulation by sportsmen, by the increase of demand for farmers' products, by the employment of labor, by enhancement of value of real estate . . . and by the money that unavoidably flows through many other avenues to benefit local residents." Noting the forest and soil depletion in upland Massachusetts, commissioners argued that the region's "chief natural asset . . . is found in the brooks."[88]

This changing rationale created new divisions in the struggle over

New England's water. Aggressive enforcement of the sawdust abatement laws in Massachusetts brought a reaction from the owners of small upland mills—and from the farming communities that now seemed to support them. Opponents of the laws argued that they had been "enacted solely in the interest of the idle or rich and against the interests of those struggling to earn their bread by the sweat of their brow." Fisheries managers claimed that their actions promoted the "greatest good for the greatest number," but the argument was less convincing in the farm districts as a rationale for tourism than it had been as a means of restoring the forage landscape.[89]

The commissioners' narrowing focus on upland streams was accompanied by an expanding interest in restricting access to the fish. Frustrations with dams, overfishing, and pollution made two things clear. First, the survival of salmon, shad, or trout in New England would depend on artificial maintenance. Farming and logging destroyed the cool, mossy stream banks where fish spawned and their larval and insect food bred; never again would trout breed naturally in such great numbers. As an artificial resource, maintained in a habitat no longer capable of spontaneous growth, they became a property of the state rather than an element of the providential natural landscape.[90] Before artificial stocking, a Bangor trade paper observed, "everybody caught fish when and where they pleased." Hatchery stock, on the other hand, were "the commission's spawn—theirs, not nature's bounty."[91]

Second, fish were not replaceable at virtually any level of demand, as commissioners had originally thought. Increasingly, they came to realize that fish could be accessible to farmers, commercial fishers, and anglers only according to strict conservation rules determined through expert knowledge by those who, in effect, produced the resource in the first place. The emphasis on restricting access to an artificial, state-generated resource helped fuse the interests of fisheries managers and elite anglers, who endorsed a more restricted and more ritualized form of fishing.

The positivist vision linking science and nature had assumed a cant

When the attempts to restore migratory fish to New England's great rivers failed, fisheries managers like those at the Vermont State Fish Hatchery at Roxbury narrowed their vision to restocking upland lakes and streams. An artificial resource maintained in a habitat no longer capable of spontaneous growth, fish became a property of the state rather than an element of the providential natural landscape. (Courtesy of Vermont Historical Society)

of certainty in the early years of the fish conservation movement. Science would come "to the relief of outraged nature," as A. N. Chaney of the American Fish Culturists' Association put it.[92] When these hugely optimistic predictions were not borne out, commissioners blamed those who refused to bend to the dictates of science. They came to view commercial fishers and rural foragers as political adversaries, a class "accustomed to dealing with things in a solely practical way," immune to the logic of science.[93] The popular politics that left the compact between New Hampshire, Vermont, Massachusetts, and Connecticut so friable drove fisheries managers to a more rarefied conception of the science of fish conservation, further removed from its roots in the countryside. Frustrated with the confused motives and the intransigence of a broadly defined conservation movement, they steadily moved the science of fish culture toward an intellectually exclusive conceptualization.

By the end of the century the sweeping vision of providing unlimited sources of food for the masses through scientific manipulation of nature's own abundance had narrowed considerably. The commissioners initiated their programs in the 1860s confident that, like farmers tending their fields, they could keep rivers and streams stocked at full carrying capacity despite virtually any demand, simply by hatching and releasing a scientifically derived number of fry. As the limitations of this democratic vision became clear, the agrarian analogy that inspired its first practitioners turned full circle: conservationists began with the premise that fisheries managers could manipulate the superfecundity of nature just as farmers did; they ended the century by assuming that they, like farmers, should control the harvest of the resulting "crop."

The growing affinity between fisheries managers and genteel anglers shifted the conservation movement away from its roots in the small communities that first developed concern for the resource in the 1830s. It also considerably narrowed the vision of New England's common waters. The result was a complex and shifting struggle among three classes of water users: rural people following traditional forage practices; tourist promoters striving to reshape the landscape to appeal to wealthy out-of-state sports enthusiasts; and industrial developers, who saw rivers in terms of water power and waste disposal and dismissed all other uses as subordinate to the challenge of industrializing New England's landscape. Fisheries managers struggled to reorder a landscape torn by conflict, to accommodate a traditional concept of husbandry and nature with a newer, more instrumental vision of river use. The campaign to restore the great rivers of New England failed, but fisheries managers gained a better appreciation for their shifting and sometimes conflicting constituency. This served them well even as they retreated to the region's upper rivers and streams.

CHAPTER SEVEN

Forging a Conservation Ethic

By the 1870s state fish commissioners were turning their attention from the great rivers to the upland lakes and streams, where they could conduct the science of fisheries management free of the oppressive hand of commerce and industry.[1] Yet even in this more limited context they found the shift from local to state fisheries management daunting. Restocking would have to proceed hand in hand with regulating access to the fish, and this undertaking required immersion in the popular political discourse that commissioners found so frustrating.[2] Compelled to justify an unprecedented level of state control over a common resource, they carefully articulated their powers to accommodate as much as possible the local traditions on which their science rested.

As rural society became more mobile, more fragmented, and more commercially expansive, traditional community sanctions proved inadequate to prevent overfishing. Yet state fisheries managers had not achieved their own legitimacy. Conservation laws, it seemed to the *Burlington Free Press*, were passed merely "to amuse the Legislature."[3] Notwithstanding these obstacles, the commissioners clarified their mandate, gradually tightened the laws regarding access, and gave these sanctions sufficient moral standing to become the law of the land.

This was a crucial phase in the conservation movement. "The developing rationale of the conservationists is of the utmost importance in explaining their conduct and influence," J. Leonard Bates argued some time ago.[4] These critical years reveal the mix of idealism, pragmatism, and class and group reconciliation that conservationists used to gain popular support for their efforts. In the case of northern New England, they also show how commissioners redefined local democratic traditions and rural principles concerning the balance of nature. Relying on the farm analogy—increasing the productivity of the waters as farmers increased the productivity of the land—commissioners gave institutional support to popular common-waters doctrines.

Early Resistance to Fish Conservation

Sensitive to democratic traditions of access, commissioners trod lightly on old forage rights.[5] Still, restrictions on fishing were not long in coming. The core of this regulatory strategy was to ban fishing during spawning times. Vermont's 1867 code was typical: it established closed seasons for various species, banned or regulated certain forms of fishing equipment, prohibited stocking public waters with pickerel, and gave commissioners authority to close stocked ponds for up to three years. It also gave towns the right to close local waters they had stocked.[6]

Despite this relatively liberal access, commissioners found the problem of enforcement a grave one. Vermont's trout law, the *Burlington Free Press* noted, was "broken . . . in every town where there is a trout stream." The *Maine Farmer* likewise complained that laws were rarely enforced, "for the reason that with many, they have been regarded as encroachments upon their inalienable rights, and no one has cared to make complaint."[7] Commissioners also encountered resistance in the legislature. As late as 1896 New Hampshire gave its commission only a $250 annual appropriation. Such paltry sums reflected an undercurrent of skepticism about fish culture and a powerful antibureaucratic bias among legislators. Many Vermonters, the commissioners grumbled, were "very fearful that somebody will make money out of the office of Fish Commissioner."[8]

This resistance highlights the discordant social thinking embodied in the change from local common management to state-sponsored conservation ethics. Vermont's commissioners noted an "inborn . . . dislike of game laws . . . inherited from many of our fathers and grandfathers, who, in England, Ireland and Scotland, have felt the full severity of the English game laws."[9] Since colonial times, local ordinances and community mores had mitigated against this free-spirited attitude, but state authority was still too remote to excite a comparable ethical awareness. One Vermonter complained that after ten years of conservation controversy, fish, other than salt cod, still formed "no very prominent article of food." If the fishing was not to be improved, he insisted, "let us have less talk in the legislature, less law, less posting of notices against trespassers, less jealousy of spears, nets, pounds and other devices to capture fish." Access to nature was a matter between neighbors, not to be left to the impersonal whims of state legislators.[10]

Fishing rights were an ambiguous form of liberty, racked by the contradictions in a system embracing both private landownership and public waters. States proclaimed the right of inhabitants to trespass across unenclosed private lands to hunt and fish, as embodied in the Massachusetts Great Pond Ordinance of 1641. Farmers, with little recourse against this practice, viewed laws protecting fish as an inducement to anglers to destroy fences, trample crops and grasses, cut limbs for firewood, leave campfires burning, and disturb livestock.[11]

Commissioners were aware of the controversial implications of the laws they recommended. Successful enforcement would depend on laws that conserved fish with the least possible intrusion on private property rights and existing forms of commercial, recreational, and subsistence access. Thus early on, regulations were enacted sparingly, with the understanding that if the natural supply failed, the first recourse would be to restocking.[12] Given the fragile nature of state authority and the long tradition of local management, the commissioners also invested the towns with as much responsibility as possible. Townspeople interested in fish protection, New Hampshire commissioners cautioned, "must attend to this matter themselves." They were to appoint wardens, provide for their compensation, stock local streams with fry provided by the commissioners, and try violators before local justices of the peace.[13] Commissioners urged local officials to bring fishing regulations before their town meetings, to "insure a public sentiment in favor of protecting all streams after they are closed."[14] They hoped to meld the science of fish conservation with local consensus on democratic, equitable access.

Deference to local authority undoubtedly encouraged respect for the law, but it also left enforcement uneven. A Vermont editor predicted that too many local functionaries—a "superfluity of cooks"—would "spoil the broth"; and indeed the system did prove unwieldy. Compliance depended on the part-time efforts of sheriffs or constables and the occasional warden appointed by select boards or town councils.[15] These officials were put in the uncomfortable position of prosecuting their neighbors for violating laws that few people took seriously. Citizens who brought complaints sometimes faced retaliation, and commissioners noted a widespread feeling that it was a disgrace to inform on violators. Local justices, moreover, were frequently predisposed against convictions in fish and game cases, particularly in those in which violators were too poor to pay fines. One official complained that it took "more direct evidence to convict a poacher than it does to convict a man for murder."[16]

Local pressures continued to produce a blizzard of special legislation in the 1870s. Vermont legislators introduced around a hundred new fish and game laws each session. Although few passed, those that did added to a body of law bristling with inconsistencies, local applications, and discriminations against nonresident anglers. The result was a general misunderstanding of laws that in most cases were publicized only in obscure sources. People, one warden suggested, needed laws they could understand "without having to consult a lawyer."[17] In their counsel to legislators, commissioners asked for a body of law that was equitable and enforceable in each town, yet consistent across local and state boundaries. They maneuvered between those who favored unrestricted trespass for fishing and those who championed exclusive property rights in land and water.[18] Forging an acceptable code of fishing out of these complicated cross-pressures was one of the great achievements of the early conservation movement.

Game and Food Fish

Early commissioners justified conservation in practical, democratic terms, citing its benefits for small-scale farmer-landowners and its potential for supplying cheap, nutritious food for the masses.[19] Properly cultivated waters offered a "dish fit for the gods," the *Burlington Free*

Press pointed out, but more important, they offered a dish fit for the poor—"the cheapest food in the world for the people."[20]

The implications of this democratic philosophy were summarized by Samuel L. Boardman, editor of the *Maine Farmer,* in 1865. The "great desideratum," Boardman wrote, was to "obtain such fish as will propagate rapidly, and which can be taken in large quantities." With this vision of fish for the masses before him, Boardman cautioned against trout, a "gentleman's fish" that required pampering. Boardman, like his predecessor Ezekiel Holmes, favored perch, smelt, or Great Lakes white fish as the people's choice: each propagated freely, adapted to a wide variety of habitat, and could be caught in great numbers by recreational or commercial fishers without fear of depletion. They would sustain almost any demand without special care from the state, they took bait readily, and they afforded "rare sport to those who love to catch a great many fish in a short time, without any special outlay of skill or labor." Perch fishing required no "peculiar tact in the management of fly and rod," he admitted. Rather it was "a plain old-fashioned democratic fish, and makes a business of seizing the bait without any *palaver* about it, and a worm on a well bearded hook, suspended from a spruce pole, is as good an apparatus as any for catching as many as you want."[21]

Others shared Boardman's misgivings about trout. "I do not believe the trout appreciate what is done for them, and they will not replenish the waters of the state," a disgruntled farmer wrote. "Less aristocratic fish," on the other hand, seemed to thrive. Although his neighbors spoke eloquently of the sport of trout-fishing, when it came to sup-plying the table, he opined, they were far less discriminating: "As the shades of evening give obscurity the fisherman hies away to the dark, turbid waters of some cove or mill-pond and successfully angles for the sucker, horn pout, mullet, eel and pickerel, and he has fish for breakfast."[22]

Genteel ritualized sport was at the other end of this spectrum of fishing philosophies. Anticipating the enthusiasm for outdoor life that marked the turn of the century, George Perkins Marsh proposed recreational fishing as a health restorative in his lengthy report made in 1857 to the Vermont legislature. The people of New England suffered from an "absorbing attention to pecuniary interests, and occupations of mere routine." Having tamed the wilderness, they found their contacts with nature less rigorous, less physical. Hunting could hone their instincts, but in this regard the New England landscape was "shorn and crippled." Only the "watery kingdom" could provide a taste of the primitive contest with nature.[23]

Boardman, too, acknowledged the recreational value of fishing, but whereas Marsh drew upon English genteel sporting traditions as a rationale, Boardman saw recreation as part of a range of democratic uses of nature grounded in country culture. The artisan, "watch[ing] for the pickerel among the lilies . . . rejoices over his rare entertainment, and regains the vigor he had lost in the city." Poor youth—both rural and urban—could "go to these homes of the perch, pickerel and trout, and catch enough to satisfy the immediate wants of the family."[24]

The rising popularity of genteel recreational fishing after 1870 complicated the commissioners' task.[25] Highly ritualized and symbolic, fly-casting and other forms of genteel angling rationalized more restrictive forms of access to the resource. Concern for the art and ethics of fishing quickly set the cultivated angler apart from those interested primarily in sustenance or casual recreation. Conservation strategies thus took on class overtones. Rural traditionalists denounced any new restriction on fishing practices as a "'nabob' law, calculated to protect the rich in their idle sport, and to deprive the poor fishermen of their means of livelihood."[26] Commissioners wrestled with the political implications of their work, caught between older forage traditions and newer sporting ethics.

Fish stocking brought these tensions to the surface. Trout and salmon were the fish of choice among the sporting set, but the species could never sustain the widespread forage fishing necessary to ensure popular endorsement of conservation programs. Suitable habitat was restricted, and the catch had to be strictly monitored. Stocking trout implied conservation for the few at the expense of the many.[27] Coarser

Titled "John Nichols fishing," this view of the Connecticut River near Putney, Vermont, captures the essence of rural fishing: a casual pastime yielding a traditional forage resource. Although rural people were not always opposed to the angling rituals of the upper-crust fly-fisher, class differences made fish conservation an arena of political conflict. (Courtesy of Putney Historical Society)

species could be maintained with less disruption of traditional forage practices. Seeking a balance, New Hampshire officials took pains to explain that they introduced fish that could "come within easy reach of our citizens, with as little expense to them as possible, and not those varieties which are shy of the hook and difficult to capture."[28]

The most controversial "food fish" was pickerel. Among the first to benefit from farmers' experiments in transplanting, pickerel fulfilled the requirements for good forage: they transported well, adapted readily to new habitat, reproduced prodigiously, and survived a veritable onslaught of fishing both on and off the spawning beds.[29] A pond in Oxford County, Maine, stocked in 1858, yielded between seven and eight tons of pickerel each winter after only eight years. Catching a "mess" of pickerel, as it was termed, was forage fishing in its most elemental form. Yet as an aggressive predator, pickerel was the nemesis of the better game fish. Stocked trout became, all too often, a "free banquet for the voracious pickerel."[30] Accordingly, most prominent fish culturists deplored the earlier stocking programs. Seth Green considered pickerel a "dangerous fish to put anywhere." Fred Mather opined that they were "the weeds, so to speak, of fish culture." Transplanting pickerel, Theodore Lyman expostulated, converted "thousands of the finest fishes into their own soft, muddy-tasting flesh!" States should bounty rather than protect them.[31] Some were more accommodating. E. Lewis Sturtevant of Framingham told the Massachusetts commissioners that he despised pickerel, but it was the "best fish for waters liable to be fished by the public in season and out," since many people were "not educated as sportsmen."[32] The commissioners themselves equivocated. Vermont's Albert Hager and Charles Barrett acknowledged the pickerel's predatory habits but noted that they rarely entered swift water where young salmon bred. Still, by the 1870s commissioners were taking pains to separate themselves from earlier stocking policies.[33]

As a compromise, commissioners turned to black bass. Like pickerel, bass adapted easily to new habitat and required little management after stocking. Moreover, they competed well with, and in some cases even eradicated, pickerel.[34] At the beginning of the century there were no black bass in any interior waters except those connected to the Great Lakes–St. Lawrence system. After construction of the Erie Canal, they spread through the Hudson River watershed, and they were introduced into New England from an initial plant in East Wareham, Massachusetts, by Samuel Tisdale in 1850. In 1872 New York commissioners stocked sixty adult black bass in Raquette Lake, from which they spread through the Adirondack region, and about 1875 they were introduced into southern Maine by George Sheppard Page. New Hampshire commissioners were the most vigorous proponents of bass, since the clear waters and gravel bottoms of New Hampshire's lakes were well suited for their propagation. Bass were first introduced in the state in 1864 or 1865, and by 1876 commissioners had stocked about forty lakes and ponds.[35] Carried easily from one body of water to another, bass also spread quickly through natural migration, especially as small upland mills and dams began to disappear. As the bass advanced, brook and lake trout disappeared.

Bass provide a certain amount of sport and, when properly prepared, good eating. Thus they initially seemed a good compromise between pickerel and trout. Before bass were introduced, the Massachusetts commissioner pointed out, "we had but little to offer that would induce sportsmen to travel any considerable distance."[36] Yet not everyone was convinced of the virtues of bass. Since they were best taken with minnows, plugs, and other "unsporting" devices, elite anglers found them disappointing. On the other hand, some forage fishers found bass too aristocratic. Vermont's Grange paper printed an article by W. C Prime denouncing the "mania" for bass. Avid forage fishers—"the boys in the country," as he called them—did not have the necessary tackle for bass fishing, and by mid-September the fish stopped biting. Available only during the high tourist season, when farmers were preoccupied with cultivating, bass were "of small value to the local inhabitants."[37] Like pickerel, they betrayed the divisions in the fish conservation movement.

Much of the debate about bass, as with pickerel, involved their predatory habits. Seth Green cautioned that black bass stocked in small ponds would "eat the young of all kinds of fish, bite the old fish, and before starving, would eat themselves if possible." They had a "bull dog disposition." Sensitive to popular pressures, New Hampshire commissioners suspended bass plantings in 1880. By 1891 Maine's bass program was in disrepute. Commissioners rationalized that bass ate crayfish, minnows, larvae, and frogs, rather than small trout, but the argument was not entirely convincing.[38] The greatest outcry resulted from the displacement of brook and lake trout in the Adirondacks. The bass-stocking experiments of the 1870s meant, as one belatedly outraged New York commissioner put it, that "we have to-day hundreds of ponds that offer no fishing worthy of the name." Resigned to the situation by the 1890s, New York commissioners began stocking crayfish to raise the quality of the bass.[39]

A much more successful transplant was landlocked salmon. The beautiful *Salmo Sebago* were found originally in Sebago Lake on the Presumpscot River and in Schoodic Lake on the St. Croix. The first extensive transplants took place in 1866 in New Hampshire's Newfound Lake and Lake Cardigan. Others were subsequently placed in Winnipesaukee, Sunapee, and Squam lakes. Later a hatching station was established at Grand Lake Stream in Maine to supply eggs for larger lakes throughout New England.[40] Fish propagators also experimented with a variety of species exotic to the region. New England commissioners shipped Atlantic salmon to the West Coast and shad to the Great Lakes and Mississippi basins, accepting in return Pacific salmon and western brook trout. Carp were also transplanted in New England in the 1880s, but the region's waters and climate proved too cool, and the experiment was dropped. Most exotic transplanting projects were later abandoned.[41]

Legitimizing Recreational Fishing

Tensions between those who favored democratic species and those who insisted on select sporting varieties were sometimes subsumed in a broader controversy over the image of recreational fishing generally. One of the more pressing constraints on conserving fish was the association of fishing with indolence. The impression that those who spent time with hook and line were idlers emerged as farmers abandoned semisubsistence activities for specialized commercial farming. Early families had settled along the great rivers in good part to supplement their diet with fish.[42] In those pioneering times the springtime return of salmon, shad, alewives, or smelt combined work, socialization, and recreation into a community celebration. Sylvester Judd, the historian of Hadley, Massachusetts, described the "industrious farmers" who arrived at the falls from all points of the compass to catch or buy shad. The gatherers "indulged in plays and trials of skill," accompanied by noise, bustle, confusion, and friendly rivalry among people from different towns. "They bantered and joked abundantly . . . not from ill-nature, but from a propensity for fun and sport." Judd also commented upon another class at the falls, "composed of the idle, the intemperate and the dissipated," who came to "drink and frolic, and some to buy shad if their money held out."[43]

Judd's distinction between the industrious and the idle, probably somewhat artificial, reflected changing attitudes toward forage practices. Fishing fitted alongside other productive activities in the mixed-occupational strategies of first- and second-generation farm families, but over time the region's soils and pastures yielded a more reliable, and indeed more profitable harvest. Foraging—for recreation or necessity—came to be viewed as frivolous.[44] In agriculture, as in most industries, work and recreation were separated as categories of activity late in the century: The "industrious farmer" and "idle fisher" became two discrete types, just as farming and foraging were two discrete livelihoods. According to one farmer, fish protection benefited only the "idle men and boys . . . who ought to be at work."[45]

In an oft-quoted rhyme that seems to impose later values on earlier forage practices, local poet William Stark denigrated the Derryfield (Manchester) Scots settlers' dependency on fishing at Amoskeag Falls:

> From the eels they formed their food in chief,
> And eels were called the Derryfield beef;
> It was often said that their only care,
> And their only wish, and their only prayer,
> For the present world, and the world to come,
> Was a string of eels and a jug of rum.[46]

Commercial fishing, of course, was a serious pastime, but as fish stocks declined the business grew more tenuous and the fishers more penurious. Farmers, by contrast, husbanded and nurtured their resources. Thus even commercial fishing was likely to be regarded, as a conservationist admitted, "a mere temptation to waste time." How, then, could fishing be rendered worthy of conservation efforts by the state?[47]

As they accepted control over the fisheries from the towns, fish commissioners approached the problem in two ways. First, they defended sport fishing by emphasizing the constructive aspects of ritualized recreation. Fishing according to a strict sporting code—obeying the game laws—was a serious and necessary endeavor. Engaged in "the chase," as Marsh put it, recreationists were building character, quickening the eye and the hand, developing self-reliance, and sharpening the spirit that undergirded the national character. Ritualized fishing was thus distinguished from the simple act of drawing food out of the waters. And as the commissioners elevated the ethics of recreational fishing, forage activity became a receptacle for the negative judgments leveled at fishing. Sport built character; foraging promoted indolence and moral lassitude. In every village, New Hampshire commissioners complained, could be found a "class of worthless 'ne'er-do-weels,' with few wants and no responsibilities, content if they can secure their rum and tobacco, who infest our forests and streams, killing every living thing they can, provided it will fetch a price in the market."[48] Over time, commissioners blurred the distinctions between forage fishing and lawlessness, thus elevating both the character of the recreational angler and the legal codes that set them apart from the forage fisher.[49] Conservation was rationalized around the image of fishing as a sporting ritual free of the negative associations attached to simple forage fishing.

Commissioners also hoped to deflect criticism by encouraging private property in fisheries. Private ownership would elevate the fisher to the status of farmer. As commercial fishers learned to cultivate and husband their own resources, they would become more temperate, and by producing more fish they would appear less idle.[50] Shifting ownership to individuals also resolved the thorny problem of enforcement. Early commissioners were not sanguine about instilling their conservation ethic. Lacking the necessary moral or legal authority to ensure compliance, their choices seemed stark: unbridled access, or division of the waters into private ownerships. Given the dispersed nature of the resource and the commissioners' rather Hobbesian view of public behavior, private approaches seemed the more realistic solution.[51]

To some extent, all commissioners expressed interest in redefining property in waters. The farmer who troubled himself to stock and feed fish, the *New England Farmer* pointed out, was all too likely to look out one morning and find "half-a-dozen men fishing at the mouth of his brook, each one with a basket full of his trout."[52] There was some precedent for exclusionary rights to these waters. Since colonial times, fishing stations on the Connecticut and Merrimack had been allotted to individuals according to an elaborate system of private rights. State laws secured these rights and rendered them transferable, and eventually water power companies were compelled to buy them when their dams destroyed the runs of fish. States also gave individuals and associations control over various ponds and streams to encourage propagation.[53] In 1863, for example, the East Falmouth Herring River Company was empowered to "open a brook or ditch through their own land from Ashumet Pond to Bourne's Pond, so called, and from thence to the Vineyard Sound, with full powers to regulate the same so far as is necessary for an alewife fishery." Towns, too, were allowed to control, sell, or lease exclusive fishing rights within their bounds.[54]

The logic of dividing common resources, as Steven Hahn has pointed out in a discussion of southern game restrictions, "melded easily with the dominant bourgeois currents of postwar America."[55] In New England, conservationists derived further rationale from the farm analogy: "It has been the habit to cultivate the land and neglect the water; the one has been reduced to a private ownership and constitutes a large part of individual wealth, while the other is a sort of common property . . . abandoned . . . to yield what it may without care to the few chance persons who make a living out of it." The analogy was raised repeatedly by those who sought a division of the waters.[56]

In his 1857 report Marsh proposed that the state merely sanction private experiments with fish propagation and provide information to interested parties, on the model of the Board of Agriculture. Once private initiatives had perfected the science of fish culture, the state might attempt to restore public waters.[57] Working out the inconsistencies in this facile logic was left to Commissioner Middleton Goldsmith, Marsh's successor. To justify the novel idea that riparian owners enjoyed exclusive rights to the fish in "their" waters, Goldsmith argued that any use of the water that did not interfere with right-of-way was attached to the soil. He anticipated, correctly, that this opinion would not be popular. Customary rights of trespass were both enduring and ambiguous, he acknowledged, but the legislature could, in time, "take such measures as are necessary to determine . . . the exact limits of public proprietorship in lakes and ponds."[58]

Goldsmith buttressed his argument by pointing to the greater pleasure derived from fishing privately stocked waters. Where fish were free to all, inaccessibility was the only form of restraint; brooks near towns were quickly depleted, and tramping through brush and woods to more remote locations was not conducive to agreeable recreation. But "suppose you could hire north Britton brook and have it all to yourself, to fish and husband at your own good will, wouldn't it give right good sport . . . Wouldn't it be cheaper?"[59] Goldsmith's argument that fisheries should "belong exclusively to the owner of the land under the water" rested on the assumption of near-universal landownership in Vermont.[60] Similar laws in England excluded an entire class of landless individuals from the bounty of forest and stream, but in a democratic society such exclusions would not be oppressive, since "wealth with us is the guerdon of insight, pluck and thrift—not the gift of primogeniture." In Vermont, exclusive laws could secure to the landowner "the full earnings of his land."[61]

Most states defined "great ponds" as common property—those over twenty acres in extent in Massachusetts and ten in Maine, for instance. Goldsmith advocated a criterion based on use: waters that were traditionally "places of general resort" and large enough to "add materially to the food of the people living in the neighborhood" should be regarded as public waters. The rest should belong to abutting owners. Yet fish populations, he acknowledged, "cannot be sundered." Pike from Lake Champlain spawned in private streams, and trout from these same streams received their food from Lake Champlain. Thus the political economy of the fisheries would always be somewhat arbitrary. Moreover, all fisheries were public in the sense that their conservation added to the general wealth of the region. This common interest suggested a public mandate for protection. Goldsmith's challenge was to define the waters of the state as sufficiently private to encourage individual investment, yet sufficiently public to admit state protection for the free movement of fish up and down the water courses. Defending these ambiguous rights, in a context of powerful trespass traditions, was a complicated task. Fisheries could not be divided up like pastures. In this sense, the farm analogy was a difficult match.[62]

All New England fish commissioners expressed some confidence that the invisible hand could regulate fish-taking as it regulated other aspects of the farm economy. A Massachusetts report encouraged farmers to stock streams on their property and lease them to wealthy urbanites. Vermont commissioners proposed leasing rights to build fishways; individuals would hold exclusive claim to the resulting fish migration. The venture would "cost the state nothing," and if it failed the losses would be borne by private parties.[63]

Some attempts to shift the problem of conservation to private concerns were effective. Special enactments in Massachusetts allowed associations or individuals to lease ponds, screen the outlets, and stock the waters with fry supplied by the state. Managed as private or quasi-public local resources, these projects achieved scattered success. Yet they were not the general solution that commissioners hoped for. Private ownership, as historian Theodore Steinberg points out, offered no guarantees that waters would not be depleted.[64] Moreover, the nature of the resource itself mitigated against such divisions, since fish moved from "property" to "property." And finally, this strategy underestimated the popular attachment to trespassing rights. Private solutions failed to resolve the tragedy of the commons.[65]

Vermont commissioners, so limited in funds to promote conservation, wrestled more than others with the implications of private access to fish. Their failures illustrate the difficulties of separating fish into private enclaves. Vermont law defined waters as private in a variety of ways. An 1844 law banned fishing in artificial water bodies without the owner's consent, and another in 1867 outlawed unauthorized fishing in waters "belonging to any other person or corporation . . . stocked with fish."[66] On the other hand, the state's constitution specifically conferred upon all citizens the right to hunt upon unenclosed lands and to fish in "boatable or other waters, (not private property)." By 1874 court decisions had determined that all natural ponds and lakes were public fisheries, as were streams extending back as far as the water level rose and fell in the lakes or ponds. This meant, Goldsmith complained, that the only use Vermont could make of its fisheries was sport and recreation.[67]

Attempting to clarify the ambiguities in Vermont law, in November 1876 the legislature passed a comprehensive fish law that sanctioned public fishing on "boatable" waters—bodies subject to commercial transportation—but prohibited public fishing from private lands or on unnavigable waters. An uproar ensued. Protesters argued that the law robbed the landless poor of hunting and fishing privileges. Some feared monopolization by a rich sporting elite; others saw the law as unconstitutional, and indeed the right of public access to all "boatable or other waters, (not private property)," was ambiguous, applying either to *all* boatable waters, and others "not private property," or only to waters that were "not private property." Goldsmith reasserted the yeoman premises of the law: "Our . . . farmers, mechanics, artisans and laborers, are not a set of beggars eternally seeking private or public help." The law was opposed, he insisted, only by "that class which would rather fish than work."[68]

A test case in 1886 sustained the constitutionality of the 1876 act, but it was challenged again in 1890. This time the court decided that the public had rights of access across private lands to fish any "boatable" waters, but the definition of boatable remained in question.[69] In May 1895 the state supreme court gave the New England Trout and Salmon Club exclusive rights to a seventy-five-acre pond in the town of Marlboro, declaring that the waters were incapable of conveying products to market and hence were not boatable. Another judge in June 1897 ruled that excluding the public from *any* waters—even for conservation purposes—was unconstitutional. Anticipating a "general scramble to get some fishing on the posted brooks," commissioners advised local parties that they would be liable to prosecution in the future. Another test case in 1898 vindicated the commissioners—partially. The decision recognized the state's right to control fishing, but it broadened the concept of public access to include waters flowing across private lands. In so doing it challenged the commissioners with the task of regulating these waters as a commons.[70]

This troublesome episode illustrates the difficulties state commissioners encountered as they accepted responsibility from the towns and sought, once again, to redefine the commons. When their authority proved too fragile to protect the resource, they invoked the legitimizing powers of private property. The effort became stalled in legal and political ambiguity, and in the 1890s commissioners returned to the fundamental premise that New England's waters were a common resource.

The failure of the private alternative left commissioners with a final prospect for instilling an ethic of recreational fishing. As the enormous difficulties of policing this commons became clear, they resolved to supplement their puny enforcement arm with educational campaigns designed to highlight the science and the morality of their task.[71] Vermont's pioneer conservation publicist was Commissioner Frank W. Titcomb, who held office from 1891 through 1902, left to become chief of the Division of Fish Culture in the U.S. Bureau of Fisheries, then returned to Vermont's commission from 1910 through 1916. Titcomb attended state legislative sessions regularly, lectured widely, wrote numerous articles in popular journals and newspapers, organized Vermont's Fish and Game League, and was instrumental in funding a state fish hatchery and a game refuge, both of which served important educational purposes. By the end of the century commissioners considered educational activities such as these the key to enforcement.[72] Unlike the attempt to shift the burden of conservation into private hands, this approach took for granted common rights to inland waters and cultivated an ingrained conservation sensitivity among rural and urban people.

The Broader Impact of Fish Conservation

In 1914, nearly forty years after Robert B. Roosevelt had predicted an era of almost unlimited abundance issuing from the waters of America, the Massachusetts commissioners of inland fish and game wrote that the goals of the movement—reconciling public and private access to the fisheries, creating a local enforcement structure, and spreading the gospel of conservation—remained elusive.[73] Fish commissioners progressively narrowed the scope of their activity to the headwater regions, where chosen species could flourish in relative security, far from the recalcitrant medium of commercial civilization. But although the democratic goal of unlimited abundance remained beyond the commissioners' grasp, the movement did achieve some important objectives.

During these years fish commissioners and other groups interested in fishing initiated ambitious transplanting projects that changed the character of New England's inland waters. These programs expanded in the 1870s from pickerel, shad, salmon, and trout to exotics like black bass, Great Lakes whitefish, and landlocked salmon. Commissioners spent considerable time compiling local information, surveying inland waters, and experimenting with fish species to find the most suitable varieties each body of water would sustain.[74] Not all attempts were successful. Some stocked fish were dwarfed by food shortages; others found so much natural food on hand that they refused to rise to the bait. And in all too many cases, exotics drove out or precluded restocking with native fish.[75] Generally speaking, however, the inland waters of New England gained as recreational resources from these programs, yielding at least some form of sport and protein in waters previously depleted of any but the coarsest fish.

The movement also pioneered new attitudes toward nature. Among the important conceptual developments of the nationwide conservation movement was the understanding that natural-resource issues were interrelated. Early fish transplants proceeded without this realization, but at midcentury propagationists began to absorb the broader, integrated-landscape visions of New England's farm reformers. Before a gathering sponsored by the Vermont Board of Agriculture in 1883, George H. Perkins illustrated the role that informed rural observers played in the development of this new science of conservation. Perkins urged farmers to be more diligent in the study of their surroundings. It was the farmer's responsibility, he felt, to contribute to the accumulated knowledge about birds, forests, and fish and their relation to agriculture. Natural science was a common commitment: the solitary scholar was liable to mistakes, "and needs the help of other workers that he may have his errors pointed out." Extolling a Thoreauvian curiosity about the natural world, Perkins wrote compellingly of "intricate and wonderful structures, singularly beautiful adaptation of part to part, and many other interesting facts . . . continually appearing where least expected." The toad, unloved by "those ignorant of its habits," was a "most valiant destroyer of insects"—and extremely interesting. Perkins emphasized the multiple interactions that ultimately affected the farm family, benefiting or obstructing their work in the fields. The general lesson was that "it is often better not to meddle at all with nature's arrangements, than to interfere without sure knowledge of what should be done."[76]

Perkins was not encouraging an end to the manipulation of nature, but rather a more sophisticated understanding of how human activity could affect these natural processes to achieve proper ends. Farmers should understand the interconnections between predator and prey, between forest and field, or between farming and fishing, before they eradicated presumably "noxious" elements of creation. "Only as one knows the whole history of an animal is he competent to decide as to its character, and he must know this in more than one place."[77] This wisdom was incorporated into early conservation codes. Farmers speculating about their woods and fields, fisheries managers observing the impediments to migration, and private fish culturists experimenting with various species in small ponds found themselves discussing similar issues. Assessing the play of forces across this interlinked landscape revealed a grand equilibrium in which human activity, for good or ill, played an important role.

Not only was this understanding an important practical tool for resource management, but it gave the movement a cohesiveness that earlier debates over specific resource-related issues had lacked. The concept of interrelatedness was not fully articulated until much later, but in simpler ways early conservationists formulated, as historian Donald Pisani has pointed out, the "idea that nature operated according to clearly defined, predictable natural laws." This notion "served as the intellectual foundation for the dictum that the various uses of each resource be carefully integrated and coordinated."[78]

George Perkins Marsh, whose 1857 report to the Vermont legislature set the tone for much of the early discussion of fish conservation, noted that fish stocks were affected by changes associated with land clearing. And when fish disappeared, the otter, mink, muskrat, and waterfowl that fed upon them were impoverished.[79] It was the rural press that first aired Marsh's observations, amplifying, testing, and eventually passing these views on to the state fish commissioners. A correspondent to the Concord, New Hampshire, *Mirror and Farmer* speculated about high waters that destroyed trout eggs planted by fish culturists. When the country was new, he surmised, the primeval forests had filtered rainwater through a thick canopy of leaves. Now, "every smart shower washes more or less of the mud into streams, and in less than one hour they are running torrents of mud."[80] Agricultural journals were filled with similar speculations. Farmers who carefully watched the turning of the seasons and the changing fertility of their soils were quick to note the relation between fluctuating fish populations, the state of the nearby forests, and the changing quality of the waters. Sensitive to these interactions, farm reformers and fish conservationists, like Marsh, learned to associate fish declines with changes in the land.

At the end of the century the body of knowledge generated by fish culturists, curious farmers, and agricultural reformers was absorbed, via the fish commissioners, into the new science of conservation. Commissioners received letters "almost daily throughout the year" complaining about the destructive effects of sawdust in trout streams or the depletion of adjacent forests.[81] These correspondents offered no

practical solutions, but their pleas undoubtedly influenced the commissioners' thinking. And as Frank Titcomb's path from the Vermont
commission to the U.S. Bureau of Fisheries suggests, they were carried
upward to the federal agencies.

In 1900 Frank H. Carleton, a former Vermonter residing in Minnesota, wrote a long letter to the Vermont game commissioner on "why
forest preservation should interest fishermen." After propounding the
value of both fish and the waters in which they thrived, Carleton
offered the observation that forest preservation was essential to the
protection of fish. Forests regulated the flow of water in rivers, prevented floods, and increased the rainfall. "More than any other factor,"
forest clearing was responsible for the decline in fish in New England.
Reflecting on his experience in Minnesota, Carleton drew lessons for
Vermonters. As a consequence of forest destruction, "the great system
of lakes, marshes, springs, rivers, and giant forests, which went to make
up and protect the sources of the great Mississippi," had been damaged
irreparably. When the forests were felled, the soils washed into the
streams. Lake bottoms, once clear, were covered with silt. The waters
were made shallow, the vegetation destroyed, the crustacea killed, and
the muddy bottoms leveled to a "uniform, monotonous depth." When
the deep holes were filled, fish froze in winter or were asphyxiated in
the heat of summer. The treeless shorelines, once a "great feeding
ground for all fish at different seasons of the year," became muddy
banks. Rivers were flooded each spring by a "resistless current sweeping
spawn and young fish away from its habitats."[82]

Carleton's description of this ecological nightmare is a classic Progressive-era document, typical of those that inspired the great conservation crusades during the first years of the new century. But the
elements that gave it force and dynamism—the connection between
fish and forests, soils and water, human greed in one area and its
manifestation in another—were not theoretical constructs based on the
science of resource management. They were principles Carleton had
absorbed from Vermont's rural political culture. Forged in the give-
and-take of a changing northern New England society, they were ap-

plied to the devastated midwestern landscape. In a small way, Carleton's letter epitomized the political geography of the conservation movement, which was so eastern in its formulation and so western in its application.

Northern New Englanders in the nineteenth century changed the face of the land in ways that would have been incomprehensible to the first settlers. For some, the lessons of this great transformation were revealing. The founding of the fish commissions, followed by similar agencies in charge of game and forest preservation, and the growth of a large corpus of conservation law expressed a growing interest in the relationships between natural landscape and human welfare. Advancing a law to protect song- and insectivorous birds, the Massachusetts commissioners argued that "scarcely a crop of any kind can be raised without spraying with poison to kill the insects which were formerly kept in check by the birds." The penalty for destroying the balance of nature, they admonished, was "everywhere apparent."[83]

Drawing together these various strands of nature was a political insight rather than a new ecological paradigm. Viewing natural processes as interrelated linked a number of constituencies into a broader conservation coalition, including those interested in farming, sporting, tourism, and other resource-related pastimes.[84] But this strategy also drew upon and reinvigorated a moral view of nature to which farmers had been bound for generations. This human-centered rural perspective helped lay the political groundwork for a vigorous conservation movement in the 1890s.

Rural Traditions in the Progressive Era

Mount Washington' Cog Railway ran from this base station to the summit of New England's highest mountain. This and a variety of other natural and cultural attractions drew vacationers to New England in the second half of the nineteenth century. The influx altered the symbolic meaning of farmlands, forests, wildlife, and waters. (*Harper's New Monthly Magazine,* August 1877)

CHAPTER EIGHT

The Romantic Landscapes of Tourism

In 1899 O. H. Leavitt vented his frustrations over a new political mood sweeping New England, as he sensed it from the vantage of his New Hampshire farm. Writing to the *Maine Farmer,* he complained of the many constrictions he faced as a result of a new body of conservation law passed at the insistence of urban hunters and anglers: "You are not permitted to kill game on your own land nor catch fish in your own streams . . . Your forests are ruined by fires set by these roving hunters, and you are blamed for not caring for your woodland, and threatened with restrictive laws to define what you shall cut when you want a set of sled stakes." Under this growing complex of conservation laws, he asked, "how much better off are the farmers of New England than the peasant tenantry of Europe?"[1]

This tirade confirms current impressions of the Progressive-era conservation movement, which cast urban, elite champions of preservation against resistant petty resource users like Leavitt. "Farmers and ranchers made poor nature lovers," historian John Reiger writes.[2] Rural people were closely involved in shaping fish, forest, and landscape conservation for practical, class-specific reasons. Yet Leavitt's complaints were indeed typical at the turn of the century, and historians have extrapolated from these views the understanding that rural people were innately resistant to protecting the resources that made up their livelihoods.

In fact Leavitt's tirade marks a turning point in rural attitudes toward conservation. The emphasis on wildlife in the 1890s was part of a powerful new thrust in the American conservation movement, coming not from the farm districts but from the city. It was predicated on recreational rather than utilitarian concepts of land use, and on Romantic visions of the wilderness. Unlike rural traditions, this ideal projected nature as immutable and separate from human activity. It represented the urban, Romantic influences historians see as a foundation for the conservation movement in its classic, Progressive form.

Farmers did turn their back on this formulation of wildlife and nature, but their changing attitudes deserve a more nuanced understanding if we are to appreciate how conservation ideas were forged in this critical period. Why farmers refused to endorse urban impulses for wildlife conservation, much less to take the initiative in a matter that played such a central role in the landscape they inhabited, is an important question best viewed in terms of broader social changes and conflicts. Landowners like Leavitt were reacting to a shift in control over the symbolic and legal constructs that ordered the rural landscape in the 1890s. This shift was part of a new era in which rural people no longer spearheaded the conservation movement. Yet the gap between urban and rural views in this contested landscape were not unbridgeable. Wildlife conservation represented a compromise between urban and rural ideologies that produced a richer and more diversified multiple-use pattern for these symbol-laden common lands. And, as a confrontation over industrial water use in Maine's Rangeley Lakes suggests, the united interests of rural and urban people could be a powerful catalyst for conservation. Rural traditions continued to be an important component of the Progressive-era conservation movement.

Tourism in New England

Wildlife conservation gained a new constituency in the last quarter of the century when urban travelers redefined landscape values in the Northeast. At a time when spas like Saratoga, Long Branch, Bar Harbor, and Newport set new leisure standards for the American elite, an emulating class of clergy, artists, journalists, professors, small-business owners, and others of modest wealth spread the impact of summer recreational travel to resorts throughout northern New England. Between 1870 and 1900 this "summer trade" evolved from an aggregation of makeshift hotels and summer boardinghouses into a major industry with powerful political advocates.[3] Those interested in this lucrative trade established a set of land-use needs not only different from agrarian traditions but at odds with newer industrial developments. The compromises worked out among tourists, farmers, and industrialists helped legitimize a new concept of multiple use for the region.

Tourism grew in response to forces unleashed by northeastern urban-industrial development and to the self-conscious creation, as John Sears has it, of a national culture and an American landscape as the basis of that culture.[4] At a time when the problems associated with rapid urban growth put a premium on health and open space, improved rail and steamship service aided summer egress from the cities. Better travel opportunities spurred construction of elaborate hotel and cottage complexes in New England's coastal, lake, and mountain resort areas.[5] Between 1879 and 1909 investments in Maine summer resorts increased from $500,000 to $138 million, and tourist-industry income rose from $250,000 yearly to $20 million.[6]

New Hampshire's burgeoning tourist industry offered mountain settings that triggered the sublime emotions so well appreciated by late-Victorian travelers.[7] The region's earliest tourist facilities were constructed by the legendary Abel Crawford, who, with his son, Ethan Allen Crawford, began in 1819 cutting trails and bridle paths up the mountains, providing boarding and livery service, and guiding visitors to the area's famed peaks. The Summit House, atop Mount Washington, was built in 1852, and a carriage road to the summit completed in 1861. Eight years later the first train arrived at the summit via the new cog railway. The 1880s brought a boom in hotel, highway, railroad, and bridle-path construction throughout the mountain region.[8]

In Vermont tourism developed at a more modest pace. The state seemed to lack the central defining feature that set off the industry elsewhere—the rock-bound coast in Maine or New Hampshire's Mount Washington. Vermont's tilled fields, grazing livestock, and modest hills were "too familiar to vacationers who were often one generation or less 'off the farm' themselves."[9] Nevertheless, the state participated in the intense tourist promotions that swept northern New England, and it ultimately defined its own landscape ideal: partially wooded hills, verdant fields, and quiet brooks that epitomized time-honored values like simplicity, honesty, and a life lived close to nature.[10]

In the last quarter of the century New England's tourist industry attracted an army of promoters bent on refashioning the image of the region. Summer hotels represented a powerful voice for publicizing New England travel, and scores of speculative land syndicates, each spawned in the expectation of realizing yet another "less expensive Bar Harbor," issued loud boasts about local scenery and culture, hoping to attract rail or steamship service that would raise the value of surrounding property.[11] Even more vocal were the region's common carriers. The Maine Central Railroad, serving a rural territory with relatively few important exports, shifted its focus from freight to passenger service in the 1880s. The company circulated a monthly travel magazine along with thousands of other pieces of descriptive literature, sponsored promotional trips to resorts, and compiled statistics on country real estate and boardinghouses. Other railroads advanced similar campaigns.[12]

Equally interested in the development of a tourist landscape were urban merchant associations. During the 1890s Portland's hinterland industries—shipbuilding, fishing, farming, and lumbering—stagnated, while Boston, New York, and Saint John, New Brunswick, encroached on its seaport functions. Local leaders responded by publicizing the Forest City as a debarkation point for the stream of tourists heading down the coast or to the Maine interior. They encouraged rural markets for farm real estate, truck gardening, guide and livery services, hotels, and boat building, hoping to reawaken outlying farm districts and revive the city's hinterland trade.[13]

Resort owners commodified local natural and cultural features by casting them according to the expectations of the metropolitan clientele who patronized their resorts. The new landscape mosaic that emerged in the 1890s was a dialogue between the locality and the desires and inventions of the urban tourists who apprehended it.[14] For a generation, northern New Englanders had complained that their countryside lacked aggressive development—that it was "simply a sort of grindstone for the rest of the Union, on which Yankees were sharpened for cutting and carving out success and fortune where there was a chance for enterprise." In the 1890s this arrested frontier assumed new commercial meaning. Informed by the Colonial Revival movement, urban publicists embraced these "unchanging and static elements of the landscape" and transformed them into a positive preindustrial vision for the region. Responding to the ills of the industrial city, writers invested the Yankee village with new symbolic importance as the antidote to the traditionlessness, the nervousness, the heat, and the heterogeneity of the urban setting. The very lack of industrialism became northern New England's comparative advantage.[15]

At a time when city dwellers confronted a multitude of sanitary problems associated with overcrowding and industrial growth, tourist promoters cultivated rural New England's reputation for hearty, healthy, vigorous people and bracing sea breezes or mountain air. Publicists reminded America that boyhood trips to the north Maine woods transformed Theodore Roosevelt from a "frail youth" into a "man of energy and power." Scores of spring-water bottling plants captured and exported this reputation for health.[16]

The elaboration of an appealing "Yankee" stereotype also served urban needs. Middle-class Victorians, so uneasy with the heterogeneity of their urban environments, associated the New England village with ethnic purity and spontaneous communalism. Innocent of the harsh realities of competitive capitalism, Monhegan Islanders, for instance, lived "like one large family or clan, with no aristocracy, no middle class, no poor . . . 'Share even' seems to be the ruling motto in all business deals." A traveling elite, eager to romanticize rural life, found fishing, farming, and lumbering ennobled by the "wholesome lessons [of] communing with nature."[17]

In a series of articles on abandoned farms, *Century Illustrated* writer William Henry Bishop noted the impact of these new urban values on the New England village, then emerging as an icon of the Colonial Revival movement:

Time has been when all these white country meeting-houses alike seemed to freeze the imagination with their coldness; but times change, and we with them. The charming grace and lightness of design that many of them possess have been recognized . . . In short, they are coming back into favor again, with the many other nice old-fashioned things of the period, and the invasion of Gothic [that is, Catholic] chapels that succeeded them had better look well to the security of its domination.[18]

Here city folk, unsettled by the shifting ethnic and cultural complexion of their own world, found affirmation of the Anglo-Saxon foundations of American society and the virtues with which these founders had wrought a civilization.[19]

Although northern New England banked on this wealth of preindustrial images, developers were also sensitive to the needs of a well-heeled clientele familiar with the East's most opulent watering holes. Promoters tuned this rustic landscape to the sensitivities of America's traveling elite. Hundreds of miles deep in the interior Maine woods, visitors to the rambling Kineo House on Moosehead Lake feasted on roast lamb, wild strawberry preserves, and cream in the largest dining hall in the state. They delighted in the hotel's comfortable beds, steam heat, gas lights, open fireplaces, and in-room bathrooms before disembarking by canoe into the "freedom of the forests." Reporters dispelled the "popular delusion about the black fly," which allegedly had been driven from the area by the onset of civilization. Promoters altered the essence of nature in the interest of the "touristic experience," as historian Martha Norkunas notes.[20]

In 1901 William Bishop went "hunting an abandoned farm in upper New England" and published the results in *Century Magazine*. The homestead he selected was located on the summit of a ridge, with pastures and fields falling away to a wooded valley carpeted with "cool, delicate ferns." The view beyond this "miniature glen" included the obligatory distant mountain on the horizon. Bishop's farm "happily contained within itself nearly all the most desirable forms of rural charm": an artful scattering of old pear, apple, quince, and nut trees; a fragrant pine grove; fields bounded by natural hedges and old stone walls, scattered clumps of wild roses, raspberry, grape, strawberries; and a brook stocked generously with trout. In a similar article Minnie L. Randall subjected a worthy New Hampshire homestead to the full power of the late-Victorian descriptive imagination. It offered "acre upon acre of grass-land, orchards, groves, pastures, and woodland," lorded over by an old white farmhouse—"large, cool, and roomy." Its capacious fireplace, central chimney, crane, hooks, and iron pots were "an inspiration, calling up visions of old Thanksgiving days, children and grandchildren gathering for . . . dinner." Across the valley stood "the picturesque ruins of an old mill, . . . the moss-covered boards of the now empty milldam, and . . . a sedgy brook."[21]

Like the original farmers, Bishop and Randall proposed an ideal blend of nature and culture. They demanded a landscape as varied as the primeval forest had been, but they desired a complexity that expressed the various overlays of land use imposed by several generations of Yankee farmers, each veiled slightly by time and decay and by the healing hand of spontaneous regrowth. It was an appealing synthesis of human history and natural resurgence—each farm a physical encapsulation of New England's mythical origins and development. "It would be difficult," Bishop concluded, "to find a greater variety of scenery than we have in so small a number of acres."[22] This immutable preindustrial vision—a working landscape frozen in time—offered a solid anchor for those adrift in the confusing world of urban-industrial development.

The latent profitability of this landscape encouraged a campaign to recast rural New England, accenting its charm. "In all the older parts of the country the acres and acres of abandoned farms . . . might be made small gold mines to their owners," the Portland Board of Trade urged. Wild berry bushes and apple trees growing along the country road could be trimmed and cultivated and "left for the city person to gather with delight." Rich urbanites, stirring to their "old-English nature," would refurbish these homesteads as country estates. Abandoned farms would be reoccupied, the value of adjoining property enhanced, and the "spirit of the active communities from whence they come" would be impressed upon the quiet rural neighborhoods.[23]

Animated by this compelling urban imagination, farm leaders and tourist promoters urged rural folk to rejuvenate their farms, erect cottages, trim their lawns, paint road signs and fences, plant vegetable and flower gardens, and learn to cook what city travelers expected country people to eat. George W. Perry of Chester, Vermont, provided exact instructions on attracting boarders to the farm: the house must be comfortable and tidy but studiously "old"; hand-loomed rugs, windows that opened wide to the night air, and beds furnished with "very old-fashioned bedsteads" set the proper ambience. The old apple orchard, put to grass and mown short, would offer a charming place for lounging. Hen yards and pigsties, Perry cautioned, were to be set well back from the home. "There are senses besides that of sight that you must provide for."[24]

Tourism promised a new, multiple use for the seemingly exhausted northern New England landscape. "You can get any class of summer boarders you please," George Perry admonished, "if you use the right bait and tackle for them." This forthright appeal expressed the essential dialectic of the tourist landscape: promoters recognized the importance of dialogue between local culture and urban imagination. The Poland Spring Hotel's *Hill-Top* magazine admonished rural people to thank summer travelers for "awakening us to the significance of our home." The suggestion, though somewhat unrealistic, was not an idle one. The campaign to convince rural folk that tourism was in their best interest was crucial to the New England image; summer visitors, willing to pay large sums of money "for the very air we breathed so freely," came north expecting to see peopled as well as natural landscapes.[25]

How seriously rural people took all this advice is difficult to say, but in important ways the new tourist landscape reinforced their own perceptions of the world. Rural leaders, like tourist promoters, had for generations contrasted the simple virtues of country life with the jaded values of the city, and indeed they generally spoke well of the opportunity for another source of income in the countryside. Abandoned farms were a moral blight, and the chance to fill them with food-dependent urban families was too good to ignore. The farm press regularly listed "desirable farms" available for boarding or sale to summer people. Always adaptable, rural families embraced the opportunity to market their land, their lakes, and their untillable mountains. Those who grew weary of the long, one-sided combat with cold climate, unyielding soils, and western competition looked for a margin of profit from the tourist landscape, warming to its visions of the region as both scenic and bountiful.[26]

Others seemed less enthusiastic about this flood of cash-bearing visitors. "As a whole, the disposition to provide especially for the needs or desires of visitors is not strong," wrote a correspondent for *The Nation* after visiting Maine. "The assumption seems to be, rather, that the visitors are sure to come anyway, and that the less there is expended for their gratification, the greater will be the profit from despoiling them." William Bishop noted that his "fellow-villagers" seemed to lack his sensitivity to the "quaint and old-fashioned" in their surroundings. Harold Fisher Wilson concluded in his classic study of the northern hill country that tourism received "mixed reviews" among the locals. Some touted the enlivening effect of this influx and the social leveling encouraged by summer boarding, while others complained that summer people distracted families from their work, drove up farm wages, and set dangerous examples of extravagance.[27]

In the artfully chaotic landscape constructed by the summer visitor could be found the nexus of a growing tension between urbanite and native. The former's infatuation with "rustic" scenery incorporated exactly what the farmer saw as scarcity and decay. Romanticized descriptions of ruined mills, sedimented streams, overgrown orchards, and played-out fields yielding blackberries and quail were radically at odds with the sense of order and progress rural generations had imposed upon the land.[28] The veneration of rural ruins, the elevation of nature over culture, and the picturesque representation of local decay created a schism between tourists and farmers.

Farmers, Fish, and Tourism

This clash of images laid the basis for a sharp debate over game and fish management in the 1890s. American sportsmen, as John Reiger points out, rated hunting and fishing grounds in terms of their picturesque qualities, thus diffusing conservation concern beyond the narrow issue of game and fish. Although both rural people and summer tourists viewed the landscape as an ordained balance of culture and nature, they interpreted this balance in different ways. Landscape features that farmers considered waste—overgrown fields, tangled woods, brooks, bogs, alder thickets—became valuable recreational resources as game cover, habitat, or scenery. Promoters tried to bridge this gap by reducing conservation to a practical question: "how to sell the most game for the most money."[29] Farmers could well appreciate the economic logic of more intensive and comprehensive land use, but the ideological implications of this new tourist landscape were unsettling.

Fishing represented one area of conflict that had to be reconciled before farmers and tourists could share this land. Well into the 1870s fish commissioners, like most rural people, thought of fishing either in subsistence or commercial terms or as a form of recreation unburdened by special "sporting" skills. Maine commissioners noted the essential injustice of local people's bearing the expense of fish and game protection while "men from abroad come into our woods, and . . . hunt our deer . . . [and] feed on our fish." As early as 1874 they pondered the economic impact of this influx of genteel anglers, but their primary responsibility was guarding commercial fisheries. These biases in favor of rural fishing traditions were evident in early controversies over ice-fishing. Responding to petitions from summer resort proprietors in the 1870s, the Maine legislature outlawed ice-fishing on several lakes, since it placed demands on the resources when no tourists were in the area. Commissioners denounced the laws as a "monopoly" granted to the hotel owners: farmers were "cut off . . . from their share

A sporting party on the Rangeley Lakes. Urban recreationists offered a new source of income for upland New England and a new economic rationale for fish and wildlife conservation. The philosophic premises of this recreational landscape challenged traditional ways of thinking. (*Scenic Gems of Maine* [Portland, 1898])

of a sport [for which] they pay their full portion in fostering and protecting."[30]

During these years, however, the constituency for fish conservation changed. Farmers experienced relatively good times following the recession of the mid-1880s, and as they focused on the business of farming, their interest in fish propagation waned. Fish commissioners, on the other hand, drew support from urban elites and resort interests. The pressure behind this shift to a recreational constituency came largely from state and county fish and game clubs. Between 1865 and 1900 scores of these organizations appeared throughout New England, typically lead by prominent locals and wealthy out-of-state sporting enthusiasts.[31] The clubs linked arms with state fish and game commis-

sions and helped turn the conservation movement toward urban formulations of common-resource use.

This new urban conservation vision excluded certain entrenched
rural practices, such as bait-fishing for trout or salmon. In a letter to
Maine Fish Commissioner Leroy Carleton, Philadelphian Jay Cooke
Jr. punctuated his conservation message with a blunt reference to the
economic power exerted by recreationists of his class:

> As you know I have a very expensive home in Maine, my place
> there having cost me up to this time at least $10,000 . . . and in
> addition to this my yearly expenditures in Maine for wages,
> supplies, etc., amount to several thousand dollars . . . If there is
> to be a constant falling off in fish and game it cannot be expected
> that . . . a class of people will visit the State who, drawn by the
> sport to be found there, employ guides and spend large sums for
> supplies which go to the farmers and artisans of the State.[32]

Game clubs and elites like Cooke, backed by an expanding resort industry able to muster powerful economic arguments for ritualized recreational fishing, narrowed the range of uses for these common waters.[33]

The growth of this urban conservation constituency renewed the
debate over inland fishing. Typical was a dispute over Maine's Rangeley
Lakes. For generations local inhabitants had come down to the shores
during the late summer to take fish, which provided an important food
supplement during the busy harvest season. When branch railroads
reached the lakes in the 1880s, city anglers began crowding these locals
at the good fishing spots.[34]

In 1891 the Bangor *Industrial Journal* noted a "warm discussion"
taking place regarding the respective virtues of bait-fishing and fly-casting around the lakes. "Some pretty rough titles are given to the [local]
bait fishermen," the editor noted, by those who had recourse only to
the fly. Anglers followed an elaborate sporting ritual that emphasized
practiced skills; locals tolled the waters with chum and, using a "jib-
boom," as an unsympathetic observer described it, "derricked" the trout
to land. The journalist recorded the following exchange:

"Play him! Play him!" screamed the excited sportsmen from the city.

"Play your grandmother!" bellowed back the [local] cook. "I ain't here to play, I'm here to fish." And as he spoke he boosted over his head a fifteen pound laker. Any man in the Boston crowd would have given ten dollars to have played him an hour at the end of an eight-once rod. 'Twas too much for their nerves. They came away.[35]

As commissioners warmed to these "Boston men," locals grew disaffected with fishing codes. A Bangor newspaper correspondent complained that entire lakes were being "monopolized by the wealthy," and farm leaders launched a campaign to limit funds for restocking programs.[36]

In 1905 the exclusive Oquossoc Angling Association petitioned for a ban on plug fishing—using a lure as opposed to a fly—as a means of saving the Rangeley Lakes from abuse by locals. Locals complained that the ban discriminated against "scores of men, women, and children who enjoy fishing, but had no idea of handling a fly." The legislature compromised by lowering the twenty-five-pound day limit on trout and salmon to four fish per day, acknowledging the multiple uses of these inland water resources. Sensitivity to local fishing traditions helped ease tensions over new conservation regulations, while public familiarity with stocking programs encouraged a stronger commitment to preserving fish resources. Commissioners preached the economic benefits of tourism at Grange meetings and lauded the spiritual rewards of angling before city audiences. Maine's common waters, they urged, offered something for everyone.[37]

Wildlife and the Tourist Landscape
Game protection again added a new overlay of uses to the traditional agrarian landscape, but as with fishing, it tested the commissioners' ability to spread the conservation message across class lines. As James Tober suggests, the rising value of game triggered political and judicial

debates over access to farmlands and to the game upon them.[38] Small-game conservation, however, achieved relative consensus, since protection was largely in the interest of local hunters. The edges between field and forest, growing flora traditionally considered the bane of the "thrifty" farmscape—bayberry, sumac, alder, cedar, sprout wood—provided cover and forage for grouse, woodcock, quail, rabbits, squirrels, and other game. "Abandoned by the farmer," these lands could be "made populous and productive . . . by a proper . . . system of protective law." Ruffed grouse, woodcocks, geese, and ducks were protected in the 1870s, and after the turn of the century commissioners introduced pheasants and quail in lowland and southern sections of New England.[39] Measures like this encouraged new uses for farm fields, enhancing their value as common lands.

Big-game conservation was more imperative and more divisive. Disappearance of New England's woodland caribou around 1900 sensitized sport hunters to the need for better laws. Since caribou were migratory and New England provided only marginal habitat, they had wandered out of the region several times in the nineteenth century, but the last were seen in Maine in 1902. The region's moose herd weathered a devastating assault by hide-hunters and lumber-camp provisioners at midcentury but persisted in more remote areas of Maine and New Hampshire. In 1897 Maine restricted the hunting season, and a four-year moratorium on moose hunting, beginning in 1916, began the process of rebuilding the herd.[40]

New England's deer herds had been nearly destroyed by relentless hunting and forest clearing early in the century. Vermont banned deer hunting in 1865, with few, if any left in the southern part of the state, and New Hampshire closed nine of its ten counties to hunting in 1878. Remnant herds survived in northern Vermont, New Hampshire, and Maine, despite poor brouse in the spruce-fir forests, and a "few wild-eyed and apprehensive deer" haunted the pine woods of lower Cape Cod.[41]

Deer herds recovered in the 1870s. Their vigor can be attributed to new protective laws operating in combination with vegetational changes in the region. The most significant trend was field abandonment in the hill districts. That reforestation was uneven, depending on soil and topographical features and land-use history, was important, since deer sample a wide variety of foods daily. Small, scattered logging cutovers, adjacent to old-growth forests, offered an excellent combination of fodder and cover. Fires, which often followed logging operations, prepared the way for cherry, aspen, and birch. The emerging landscape of fields interspaced with abandoned lands, patch-cut forests, remnant old-growth stands, dense conifer swamps, and neglected orchards created prime habitat. Crops gone wild—parsnips, grasses, berries, roses, grapes, apples—combined with vigorous revegetation, offered a veritable feast for deer and other game species. A reflection of economic change in the Northeast, the deer herd was as dynamic as the landscape itself.[42]

In the spring of 1878 a group of Vermont sportsmen acquired seventeen deer from New York and Pennsylvania and released them in Rutland and Bennington counties. Enjoying state protection and encountering no natural predators, the herd thrived. By the 1890s Vermont farmers were beginning to complain about damage to orchard crops, and in October 1897 the legislature opened a hunting season for antlered deer. The event attracted a flood of nonresident hunters, causing concern that the deer, innocent of the gun, would be wiped out. But if the deer lacked caution, the hunters lacked experience: only about 150 deer were killed, and the herd continued to increase. New Hampshire's herd proved equally prolific under fire. Massachusetts opened a hunting season in the western counties in 1910.[43]

Managing the new deer herds added a significant burden to the state fish and game commissions. Trolley extensions, better rail service, new logging roads, automobiles, and motorized boats spread hunting activities through the backcountry, and cheap breech-loading and repeating rifles and automatic pump-guns boosted the kill. Speculation about the state of the herds became rife. With little substantiation, newspapers reported unsettling declines, while tourist publications touted the expansion of the herds.[44] Fish and game commissions entered an era of intensely politicized conservation policy.

Deer conservation was most divisive in Maine, which possessed the largest game herds and the greatest annual influx of recreational hunters. Elsewhere, traditional subsistence hunting had been abandoned when deer were eradicated early in the century. Rural people proved more willing to protect the herds when they returned. In Maine the attempt to curb practices dating back to the colonial period brought a difficult period of adjustment.[45]

Heavy nonresident sport hunting, combined with Maine's continuing tradition of market and subsistence hunting, gave the state a particular reputation for brutality. Each night in the fall, the lakes north and east of Bangor came alive with jack-lights, and during the day hunters used dogs to run deer into the water, where they could be shot at close quarters or even clubbed from a canoe. Commissioner Elias Stilwell characterized these northern waters as "slaughter-houses." A Boston correspondent noted in 1897 that even in England, where the killing instinct was strong, shooting female deer was condemned by public opinion. But in Maine it was "shoot, shoot, shoot, at anything moving, male or female, big or little, good or bad." Reports of hunters' taking up to ten deer a day were not uncommon. In 1882 the Maine legislature passed a series of laws—"war measures," as the commissioners termed them—to save the state's remaining herd. Exporting carcasses was banned, a closed season imposed, and hunters were limited to three deer each. Despite modest appropriations, the commissioners resolved to enforce these laws "to the bitter end."[46]

Among rural folk, it is possible to identify a core of practical sympathy with these measures. Some saw game laws as a constraint on frivolous recreational killing of wildlife valued as important to the balance of nature. Others appreciated restrictive laws simply as a means of keeping city hunters in check. Without them, a Granger from Oxford County wrote, "every loafer, every gentleman-of-leisure sport will be shooting at all seasons, regardless whether his target be cow or deer, man or moose."[47] Initially, however, commentary published in the rural press was negative.

Why rural spokespeople, who had helped define the basic concepts of land, forest, and fish conservation a half-century before, responded in this manner is an important question. We know a great deal about how new, positive images of wildlife were articulated by prominent American writers and thinkers, but much less about how these views were received by those who confronted wildlife on a day-to-day basis.[48] The agrarian response to urban-based pressures for game laws illustrates both the deeper ideological issues at stake in wildlife use and the intensely anthropocentric terms upon which rural people accepted these laws. Confident that some elements of the natural landscape, like forests and fish, abetted the spread of agriculture, farmers pioneered conservation thinking in these matters; convinced that other elements, such as wetlands, "noxious" birds, and deer, were at odds with this agrarian design, they could be remarkably resistant to protection.

Game laws required a profound shift in thinking about access to wild nature. The Vermont commissioners noted a lingering conviction that the right to bear arms implied "the right to use [them], and the right to use, the right to shoot whatever animals there are." Undoubtedly rural people were resistant to abandoning these ancient forage rights, particularly at the insistence of outsiders, but their biases express a more complex relation to urban demands for conservation.[49] The flood of recreational hunters into the upland game districts in the 1890s created a volatile mix of old and new attitudes toward wildlife that commissioners found almost impossible to reconcile. Opinion polarized around three points: hunting techniques, crop damage, and more basic questions about the nature of the New England landscape.

The ethics of hunting, which involved techniques that dated from pre-European times, were in flux at the end of the century. Dogging, for instance, had been popular with urban hunters at midcentury as an "exciting and not laborious" method suited to a more casual knowledge of the woods and gun. Typically, local guides "started" the deer from their feeding places, and the dogs drove them to a body of water, where hunters waited on foot, on horseback, or in a canoe. Upland farmers, on the other hand, sometimes complained that using dogs made deer too reclusive. Jock Darling, who built some of northern Maine's first sporting camps, remembered locals who shot city hunters' dogs because they were "not willing for a rich man to come and drive the deer off."[50]

A gathering of public opinion about hunting techniques compiled by New York game commissioners in 1895 reflects the fluid state of hunting ethics in the Northeast. In the Adirondacks, locals preferred jacking, setting a light in the bow of a canoe or boat and moving quietly along a stream or lakeshore at night. City hunters here, too, preferred hounding, although the report suggests that it was falling out of favor. Stalking and still-hunting were "deemed the most . . . credible method because the deer were given a sporting chance." Still, several writers cautioned against total bans on hounding and jacking, since these were the only practical means available to the unskilled hunter— the "true and legitimate sporting man that takes his vacation annually from the cities." Dogging was finally outlawed in New York in 1901.[51]

While both urban and rural hunters seemed ambivalent about hunting techniques, the 1890s brought a change in attitudes among elite sports hunters. Stirred by literary naturalists and nature writers who insisted on a moral standing for wild animals, by the example of prominent hunters like Theodore Roosevelt and his prestigious Boone and Crockett Club, and by editors of journals like *American Sportsman* and *Field and Stream,* elite urban hunters began to define a new sporting code and to communicate this ideal to state game commissioners. As commissioners responded to genteel prescriptions against dogging, backlot farmers took up the defense of traditional techniques—including dogging. Bangor fur dealer Manly Hardy insisted that bans on dogging were based on "class distinctions," sanctioning the practices of the "rich who come to waste, and berating those of our State who kill to eat." Differences obviously ran deeper than the presumed effect on the herd itself.[52]

Darling's viewpoint sheds light on the ideological issues behind the

The McKellog family of southern Vermont. Rural hunters were deeply immersed in a local culture of forage and resource use. Progressive-era game commissioners superimposed new elite hunting ethics on these older traditions. (Photo by H. L. Chapman, courtesy of Historical Society of Windham County)

conservation debate. Viewed in class terms, game laws violated rural prescriptions for egalitarian access to common resources. Those who "toil much for a small return and have no pleasures, are alive to the fact that upon their own soil they should have something like equal rights with the wealthy, pleasure loving citizen of Boston or of New York." Rural commentators denounced the demand for a shorter hunting season coinciding with the busy fall harvest routine. After the city hunters left the state, they feared, the game would be locked away. Manly Hardy claimed that "the rich have, for reasons best known to wardens, been allowed to kill, to waste, while poor men who have killed to feed their families have been arrested." Nor did Hardy agree on the significance of the hunt: gentlemen emphasized the invigorating benefits of the chase; farmers, the forage or commercial value of the kill. Hardy objected to "calling the men who . . . kill our game in summer and waste it, 'true sportsmen,' and calling other . . . good men 'thieves and poachers,' if later they kill what they need to eat." Debates over hunting codes were part of the contentious process of accommodating rural attitudes to the new tourist landscape. Just as rural folk were ambivalent about transforming their villages into Colonial Revival parks, they resented the fact that upland New England was becoming "a rich man's game preserve."[53]

Uneven law enforcement sharpened these class antagonisms. To be effective, laws had to be enforced impartially—particularly across class lines—but also with a certain amount of flexibility. To meet this subtle but important requirement, states relied on locally appointed wardens reimbursed by a portion of the fines collected upon their complaint. The combination of local indifference and the "half-fine" system of payment discouraged uniform high conduct. Local hunters often found the wardens "bitter and vindictive," and even the *Maine Sportsman,* organ of the Sportsman's Fish and Game Association, considered them "low-class political appointees." Those in eastern Maine were held in particularly ill repute, partly because of a campaign to poison dogs suspected of running deer. Persistent rumors about poisoned heifers, colts, or even children suggest the animosity between locals and wardens. In his masterly study of down-east "game wars," folklorist Edward D. Ives demonstrates clearly where local sympathies lay.[54]

While these complaints left the backcountry hostile to game laws, challenges to traditional property rights spread this resistance among more established farmers. Wildlife conservation added to the multiple uses of New England farmlands, but protecting the game implied new rules for rural landownership. Farmers were constrained from killing game on their own land, yet "nonresident prowlers" were permitted to hunt and fish on these same lands. An editorial warned against the state's stepping in "to make public what the law of the state has made private property." In 1903 Commissioner Leroy Carleton wrote an open letter to the *Maine Farmer* defending common-law provisions that gave the people as a whole jurisdiction over fish and game—a concept that justified public trespass on unenclosed private lands. Earlier, rural people might have understood this argument for common use, but responsibility for game in earlier days had been vested in the town, not the state, and farmers had viewed these resources as complementary to their endeavors on the farm. The surge in deer populations and the new state hunting codes altered the meaning of wildlife for farmers, who viewed deer as a threat to their crops and the protective laws as a threat to their property rights. By the turn of the century, both the locus of conservation authority and the meaning of wildlife had changed: seemingly aloof state agents managed deer in the interest of nonresident recreationists. The law of the commons no longer resonated with the morality of the farm. As the state asserted control over nature, farmers insisted on the sanctity of their own boundaries.[55]

Farmers complained that deer rubbed bark off fruit trees, nibbled back new growth, broke down young trees, and ravaged grain fields and gardens. In Vermont and New Hampshire, where deer had been recently reintroduced, these disturbances were confined mainly to marginal farm districts, and commissioners, despite initial misgivings, responded to complaints with reimbursements for crop damage and hunting to cull the herd. Deer became more wary, and complaints about crop damage declined.[56]

In Maine, commissioners were less accommodating, and, if the vigor of complaints is an indication, the crop damage was more burdensome. In 1900 the *Maine Farmer* began systematically publishing opinions on deer damage from "representative men" around the state. Considering the wording of earlier bounty petitions, which suggest farmers' implacable opposition to anything they perceived as a threat to their crops, resentment over deer protection ran deep. Oxford County orchardist C. H. Abbott predicted that farmers would "some day . . . rise in a body and demand the repeal of these injurious laws, which benefit the few at the expense of the many." Maine farmers viewed the wildlife question in stark contrasts: lands could sustain deer or crops— not both.[57]

Again, the vigor of these complaints suggests a sentiment that ran deeper than the deer themselves. Wildlife protection challenged a basic agrarian assumption that civilization was to supersede the wilderness. Farmers recognized nature as a crucial element in their landscape composition, but always at the periphery. The notion of protecting wildlife suggested, as a Grange publication put it, that northern lands were "good for nothing else but to be a hunting ground for the rest of the nation." This clash of images—the productive farm and the recreational wilderness—was powerful. The Grange held wildlife laws responsible for the abandoned fields and resurgent forests in the hill country, an extremely sensitive issue that pierced the core of New England identity. The "home, the church, the schoolhouse, the factory and the grange hall represents all that is noblest and sweetest in our civilization, and they must be permitted to advance."[58]

Like other forms of urban leisure culture intruding into the agrarian world, sport hunting also violated a rural producers' ideology that elevated work as the moral and material basis of civilization. One farmer associated hunting with "drink, ribald jests, vile songs . . . gambling [and] . . . seducing and ruining girls and women." Another suggested that deer should be annihilated precisely to rid the state of "young sporting rakes from the cities." In a variety of ways, the game-law controversy brought to the fore agrarian resentments of urban values. "Off Hoss," a frequent contributor to the *Maine Farmer*, proposed that the "money received from the city spendthrifts who term themselves sporting men, is a greater curse than blessing to the State of Maine. Down with the game laws!"[59]

Tensions escalated into political war in Maine as the Grange took up the fight against deer protection. The legislature provided payment for deer damages but left the delicate question of calculating the losses in the hands of Game Commissioner Leroy Carleton, a professed advocate of tourism who publicly dismissed the farmers' complaints as groundless. In any case, the Grange rejected the principle of reimbursement and argued instead for repeal of the game laws. Wildlife conservation, Grangers felt, should be restricted to the uninhabited lumbering districts in the northern interior. In the settled areas, farmers should have the right to protect their crops from deer, just as they protected poultry from foxes.[60]

In 1905 farmers won the right to shoot deer found doing "substantial damage" to crops and to consume the offending animal, but the new law, passed on a trial basis, appeased no one. Resort proprietors and guides raised strenuous objections, and Commissioner Carleton insisted that farmers took advantage of the law to fill their larders. Grangers saw the 1905 law as a "sop" that required farmers to catch the deer red-handed in their fields. Hoping to starve the commission financially, the Grange organized meetings across the state to influence legislative budget decisions. The situation, according to one farmer, resembled that in Ireland, "where a rabbit is worth more than a man's life."[61]

Farmers in New Hampshire, Massachusetts, and Vermont likewise urged a "decisive test" of laws that made their districts "a game preserve at the expense of the farmers," but here, where tourism was less vital as a political force, commissioners proved more flexible. Massachusetts officials admitted that "in certain counties the logic of the case is that the deer must either be exterminated or so reduced as to no longer be a menace to the fruit-growing industry." On this premise, the three states allowed farmers to cull herds, confident that there were still "thousands of acres of land" available to the sport hunter.[62] Commissioners, legislators, game experts, and farmers continued to disagree about the role wildlife played in the larger scheme of things, but the debate, which had once challenged the most basic premises of wildlife conservation, was narrowed to determining the optimal herd size to protect farm property, keep deer healthy, and provide maximum opportunity for hunting. Excess deer were to be "eliminated in such a manner as to give no special privileges, but yield a public revenue." These considerations established the foundation upon which state and federal officials began constructing a science of game management.[63]

In Maine, tensions abated after 1910, when Leroy Carleton was joined on the commission by J. W. Brackett, who better understood the political imperatives of the position. Brackett and other advocates of conservation put their message before the Grange and farm press, arguing that nonresident hunters and anglers left millions of dollars yearly in the ring of villages that bordered the great gamelands of New England—the very regions farmers complained were most oppressed by game laws. Railroad officials reminded farmers that continued local passenger service depended on a heavy tourist traffic. These arguments helped turn the tide of rural opinion. In 1913 the commission implemented a general revision of fish and game laws that left the regulations more uniform, more understandable, and more equitable.[64]

Nonresident license fees, levied in New Hampshire and Vermont in 1903 and in Maine in 1904, also helped smooth the way for wider acceptance by funding a more efficient, professional warden service and by shifting the financial burden of conservation to the "outside hunter." Crop-damage reimbursements also became more generous. Within a few years commissioners began arguing for a small resident license as well. "From practically a bankrupt condition two years ago," the New Hampshire commission announced in 1918, "the department enjoys the distinction of being financially healthy, and for the first time in its history is in a position to do effective work."[65]

Warden service improved as well, as commissioners molded a miscellaneous band of local part-time appointments into a more unified game-protection force. In Vermont, for instance, wardens gained sheriff's powers in 1882, and in 1888 the legislature gave the state commissioner discretion to choose temporary wardens directly. By the 1890s town officials were routinely passing applications through to the state agency, although commissioners continued to defer to local authority regarding an applicant's good standing and woods lore. Better salaries, abolition of the notorious half-fee system, and year-round employment provided the commissions with a staff of dedicated wardens who created a better image for the agency and its mission.[66] In 1897 Maine began licensing hunting and fishing guides. State Licensing, along with development of professional guiding associations, molded guides into a new force in the fight to conserve game and fish.[67]

Over the years, it would be safe to say, farmers accommodated to

A Rangeley Lakes guide maneuvers a client closer to his quarry, probably a moose. Guides served as a bridge between the urban, genteel hunters they ushered into the backcountry and the rural communities in which the guides lived. Thus they were an important means of reconciling two conflicting views of wildlife. (Courtesy of James B. Vickery)

urban values and acquiesced in "sportsmanlike" codes of recreational hunting and fishing. Encouraged to view the new tourist landscape in economic terms, they learned to accept its premises. The economic and ideological compromises wrought in the period 1890–1910 were important because they redefined the place of wildlife and wildness in the rural landscape. As John Reiger points out, conservation codes imposed during these years reflected a new recreational vision of nature that was largely urban and upper-class in origin. Yet the resistance to this vision was not as one-dimensional as it appeared from the vantage of these well-known historical actors. The battles over deer in New England pale before the later clashes between wildlife preservationists and livestock owners out west, but the stormy transitional period in New England suggests the importance of addressing deeper ideological issues to achieve an effective wildlife conservation policy.[68]

Beginning in 1870, as James Tober notes, the ideology of game protection moved from the Northeast to the West and gradually into the South. In each state "it confronted local custom, existing statute and common law, state legislatures, the courts, sportsmen, market hunters, farmers, and the U.S. Constitution."[69] The diversity in the resulting laws reflects a play of local forces as varied as American regional culture itself. Conservation was molded to this mosaic of land and culture. Reconciling old and new land-use ideals was a complicated process, best understood, as Tober suggests, at the regional level. What we gain from the New England example is an appreciation for the ground that had to be covered before urban and agrarian ideals could be blended into a new form of multiple uses for New England's common lands.

Tourism and the Industrial Landscape

Game commissioners and legislators protected wildlife not because they subscribed to the morality of the gentleman hunter, but because these wealthy recreationists supported an important segment of state economies. The impact of tourism on this conflicted landscape is equally apparent in a struggle over dams and scenery on Maine's Rangeley Lakes. In 1907 industrialists on the Androscoggin River asked the Maine legislature for permission to lower the water levels on the lakes by about six feet to facilitate water storage. The debate over this proposal was couched in familiar terms: "conservationists" argued for dams as a more efficient use of the water; "preservationists" countered that the aesthetic integrity of the Rangeley Lakes was paramount. This clash of principles, similar to the Hetch Hetchy controversy taking shape in California at that moment, was apparent throughout northern New England in promotional literature that described lakes and waterfalls as compelling industrial resources and at the same time highlighted these waters as part of an undeveloped paradise for hunters, anglers, and tourists.[70] Vigorous assertion of the latter vision helped cut another facet of New England's common landscape.

In the mid-nineteenth century, industrial development of New England's water power was a given in political debate, and the Rangeley

Lakes, like all sizable water bodies in New England, were harnessed to the task of storing energy for mills situated on the fall line below them. The Androscoggin River offered some of the best water power in New England. In 1885 the Union Water Power Company, a corporation controlled by owners of the valley's textile and paper mills, gained the right to backflow the lakes. The resulting dam system raised the water levels some fifteen feet, and for about twenty years a tangle of unsightly dead trees and stumps ringed the lakes. This alteration, completed before the onset of large-scale resort development, was acceptable to local inhabitants. In fact the dams helped regulate water levels for the lakes' new steamboat fleet.[71]

In the twenty years after the Union Water Power Company gained control of the flowage, the Rangeley Lakes became a mecca for northeastern fishing enthusiasts. By 1907 the local tourist industry, backed by the area's two prestigious private fish and game clubs, the Oquossoc Angling Association and the Megantic Fish and Game Corporation, wielded considerable political clout. During these years industry in the valley was growing, too. By 1907 the Androscoggin served manufacturing establishments employing around 15,000 people.[72]

The proposal for drawing down the water met unexpected resistance in Augusta. Although deference to the wishes of water power companies was a long-standing tradition in Maine, the Rangeley proposal was the first to affect the state's large lake reservoirs since the development of the tourist industry. Other proposals affecting Brassua Lake on the Kennebec, Chesuncook on the Penobscot, and Sebago Lake near Portland made the event seem portentous. In the legislative committee hearings, officials from the valley's large textile and pulp mills faced off against civic leaders from Portland and small-business owners from towns around the lakes. Industrial users argued that water languishing in the lakes was "wasted" on nonresident anglers—the "forty-dollar man with a hundred dollar rod striving to kill a twenty-five cent fish." The draw-down would ensure more efficient use, with industrial benefits spread widely through the valley. Every cubic yard of water, the rains and snows that delivered it, and the lakes that held it, would be turned to dollars and cents to ensure the greatest good for the greatest number.[73]

Behind the fight to save the lakes was Edward P. Ricker, who had done more than anyone else in Maine to shape the emerging tourist landscape. Ricker's grandfather, Wentworth Ricker, had established a tavern at Poland Spring in 1797 on the stage route between Montreal and Portland. The hotel gained fame as the family promoted the curative properties of a nearby mineral spring. In 1876, during the early years of the inland tourist boom, Hiram Ricker, Wentworth's son, transformed the tavern into a magnificent resort. By the turn of the century the Poland Spring Hotel, boasting golf links, tennis courts, a library, a music and art hall, a botanical conservatory, and a small geological museum, was among the East's most lavish resort complexes.[74]

Having spent thousands of dollars promoting tourism through the hotel's advertisements, brochures, periodicals, and information bureau, the Rickers were willing to spend freely to defend the industry politically. Hiram and his sons helped form a progressive faction within the ruling Republican party to promote issues like pollution control, forest regulation, and game management. The family's hand-picked governor, Bert M. Fernald, championed these conservation issues during his brief 1909–10 tenure.[75] In 1907 Edward Ricker understood the threat the draw-down proposal presented to resorts in western Maine, and his promotional successes with Poland Spring water gave him a keen instinct for publicizing his attack on the Union Water Power Company. Ricker staked his considerable reputation on the issue. Passage of the bill would indicate legislative indifference to the needs of Maine's resort business; henceforth he would "dare [not] to expend another dollar" on its development.[76]

In a series of front-page newspaper editorials, Ricker contrasted the devastation caused by manufacturers with his own industry's vision of a landscape antithetical to industrialism: industrial development despoiled the forests and lakes and left "nothing but the mere wreck and ruin of what was once a prosperous summer resort state." The infusion of Ricker money and organizational talent into the campaign, the spreading fame of the lakes, the pressures brought to bear by well-positioned metropolitan anglers, and publicity in papers across New England sensitized Maine legislators to the importance of this classic conservation issue.[77]

People in the farm communities around the lakes aligned with the preservationists in this case. A *Maine Farmer* editor worried that the draw-down would lower the water table around the lakes and disrupt agriculture. Rural people adapted the antimonopoly rhetoric in national conservation campaigns to their own heritage of democratic access to the land. If they at times resented the outside interference from resort interests, they were also sensitive to the fact that profits from industrial degradation went "into the pockets of men residing out of this State."[78] Several traditional resource-based industries, notably deep-water fishing, ice harvesting, shipbuilding, lumbering, and granite quarrying, had succumbed to monopoly control shortly before the turn of the century. The connection between financial concentration and economic decline in these staples industries encouraged an anticorporate mood that colored the Rangeley debate. Opponents of the draw-down reminded Maine people that they had not benefited from the "illimitable wealth" of their rivers and forests, resources that had "slipped away" to benefit those "from which the state gathers no toll."[79]

The explosive issue of resource monopoly helped bridge the ideological gap between rural people and tourist promoters like Ricker. An Oxford County senator testified to the widespread feeling that the "sparse livelihood" his constituents eked out of the land would be "destroyed" by extending the power of the mill owners. Industrial domination over the lakes threatened not only the fishing but also the economic prospects for guiding, livery service, handicraft production, domestic work, rod- and flymaking, and myriad other small tourist-related trades that buttressed the livelihoods of rural Franklin and Oxford county families. Opponents of the bill contrasted the vision of Maine as a vacationland peopled by democratic and independent farmers against a landscape devoted to single industrial use. The campaign fused the modern tourist vision of the lakes with traditional concerns over local sovereignty, economic independence, and agricultural stability.[80]

In a dramatic climax to the legislative hearings in Augusta, Edward Ricker strode to the speakers' desk and, "punctuating his remarks with vigorous thumps of his clenched fist upon that piece of furniture," declared that if the bill became law he would "deed to any member of this committee or any other man our cottage up there on the lakes for fifty per cent of its value." Despite this pyrogenic conclusion, the committee gave the company bill an "ought to pass" recommendation. The Senate, however, voted to substitute the minority report, and the bill was defeated.[81]

During the debate, compromisers raised the possibility of an alternate dam site at Magalloway Lake, upriver from the Rangeleys in a region still untouched by tourist development. There, a dam would backflow land thought to be of little value to farmers or resorters, allowing the mills to run at full capacity all year. In 1909 the Union Water Power Company asked for a charter to dam the Magalloway and met no resistance in the state legislature.[82]

As a preservationist victory, the Save-the-Lakes campaign was unusual; expressions of popular preservationist sentiment this strong would not be heard again in Maine until the 1960s. But the debate did help establish new guidelines for land and water use in Maine. It was Wallace White, attorney for the water-power company, who best enunciated the dramatic change in public mood that swept through Maine in 1907:

> Until Mr. Ricker arrived on the scene no one ever doubted the power of the legislature to regulate and control the use of the waters of these and similar lakes as it saw fit . . . But now all is changed . . . No future legislation shall grant to the manufacturing industries in this State any of those rights and privileges. The waters of our streams and great rivers must hereafter flow idly to

the sea, unvexed by the whirring wheels of industry, unpolluted by the hand of honest labor.[83]

Although the point was overmade, Ricker and other preservationists did establish the collateral rights of the recreation industry, and they reinvigorated the agrarian concept of democratic responsibility for an ordered landscape.

The debate indeed signaled a new mood in Maine. In a long article in the *Lewiston Journal* in 1914, Mrs. Edward M. Lawrence noted that for generations Maine had been perceived as "crude and undeveloped" by its neighbors. Like most Mainers, she harbored a passion for industrial growth to overcome this image: "Let us compel three [industrial] plants to grow where one now grows. Let us harness every babbling brook and compel it to serve us. Let us get the most from our fisheries and the best from our forests." Lawrence interjected a new theme into this age-old rallying cry, however. Recently, she noted, the state had developed its own "atmosphere"—a character "so vivid as to distinguish it from every other state in the Union." The people of Maine were coming to terms with their arrested frontier—forging their own distinctive reconciliation of nature and culture. Industry was essential to human welfare, but developers should guard Maine's "present proud distinction as a State": its naturalness, cleanliness, moral integrity, and wholesomeness.[84] Lawrence's heartfelt plea for tempering industrial development with landscape conservation undoubtedly drew inspiration from the acrimonious debate over lake development seven years earlier—a debate shaped by the interface of conservation and preservation ideas.

Yet the story is not so simple. Beginning with the pioneering works of Samuel Hays and Roderick Nash, historians have interpreted the conservation movement as divided between aesthetic "preservationists" and utilitarian "conservationists." This distinction may seem clear in the Olympian battles waged at the national level between giants like John Muir and Gifford Pinchot, but for those whose lives centered upon everyday tasks of getting a living from nature, the distinction between utilitarian and aesthete blurs.[85] Regionally, the conservation movement embraced a broader and perhaps more complex set of assumptions, rich in ideas derived from local attachments to the land. These land-centered traditions encouraged ordinary people to take up the conservation banner—to appropriate and reshape its ideals. They gave the movement popular standing.

The Save-the-Lakes campaign was a conservation benchmark for Maine. In 1907 people using or living near the Rangeley Lakes determined that no single industrial agent should be given power that precluded others from using the same resource. Speaking before the legislative committee, Rangeley steamboat captain Fred C. Barker placed the issue within a broader framework of conflicting land uses. The lakes, he contended, would not recharge sufficiently from the proposed draw-down because the forests around them had been abused. When the forest cover was destroyed, "the early spring sun and wind thaws and wastes the snow so by day and the cold night freezes it so that it makes but little water." Without proper watershed management, the lakes would serve neither resort owners nor industrialists properly.[86] The interactions between conflicting forms of land use could no longer be ignored; legislators groped for a multiple-use principle to serve these various needs.

About a decade after Ricker's victory, Arthur Staples of the *Lewiston Journal* retold the story of the Save-the-Lakes campaign, concluding with a summary that suggests the fragile and somewhat momentary victory over industrial might: "No one will ever again try to drain a lake for commercial purposes to the damage of its scenic beauty," Staples announced, "*unless it is absolutely essential* [my emphasis]." Tentative though it was, this victory over rampant industrialism was an important assertion of the rights of nature—or at least the rights of common people to use it. The result of the Magalloway compromise, the Lewiston editor noted, was that the waters of the Androscoggin Valley had been transformed into a "perfect supply," shaped to the conflicting needs of industrial, agricultural, and recreational users. No river in America, he reasoned, had been better "conserved."[87]

CHAPTER NINE

Tradition and Science in the Coastal Fisheries

During the Progressive era the coastal fisheries of Maine and Massachusetts were threatened by rising levels of exploitation. Here, as elsewhere in an age of advancing conservation consciousness, local cultures of resource use were eclipsed by state management policies inspired by explicit scientific theory. The shift from traditional community fishing ethics to a science of fisheries management, so typical of Progressive-era resource management, marked a difficult transition. Policymakers were most successful when, as political scientist Elinor Ostrom puts it, they "codified into law the fishing rules devised in local settings."[1]

Few historians have systematically dealt with the question of conserving marine resources. Edward A. Ackerman's classic 1941 study of the New England fishery briefly alludes to the matter. The fisheries, he suggested, evolved through stages of low prices and underutilization, market expansion and increasing exploitation, and finally depletion. Waning resource availability triggered a series of "serious and studied measures of conservation." Arthur F. McEvoy, in his highly regarded study of the West Coast fisheries, has further explored the implications of this tragic cycle. Although fish resources were initially guarded by extralegal ethnic territorial claims, these conservative fishing cultures were disrupted by market pressures and state management policies, and fisheries declined precipitously under the full weight of market exploitation.[2] Attempts to remedy this "tragedy of the commons" were fraught with difficulty. Every faction in the contentious debate over who gets the fish, Richard Cooley concluded in his history of the Alaska salmon fishery, "tends to rationalize his own actions and to find a scapegoat for the outcome of the actions of all. The result is a fantasy

229

in which the truth becomes lost in a sea of meaningless jargon. Everyone is for restriction—on the other fellow."[3]

Such was the apprehension of those who sought to save the fishers from themselves. According to a pattern Samuel P. Hays discovered in the broader Progressive-era conservation movement, they hoped to apply an overarching criterion—the greatest good for the greatest number in the long run—to solve resource problems through applied science and centralized authority. Anything less than dispassionate decisionmaking, based on testable theories and precise data gathering, would immerse resource managers in a morass of particularistic concerns and local politics. Science would extract resource use from this web of local and particularistic politics and place it under the umbra of an objective, high-level government administration.[4]

Yet the transition from local systems of access to broader scientific policy was never that neat. Applied science, no less than local politics, is a product of a particular social and political milieu. Moreover, not even the most detached expert can point to a single, definitive "scientific" solution. The multiple policy options available—quotas, size limits, closed seasons, moratoriums, or restricted entry—force experts to weigh costs and benefits to particular groups, considerations that immerse them in politics.[5] Awash in this sea of half-truth, local received wisdom, and self-interested observation, fisheries commissioners struggled to project their ideal of dispassionate observation and analysis. Legislators accepted this scientific opinion as only one part of a broad mix of considerations. Scientists did not shape the conservation movement in the coastal fisheries. The question is, who did?

Ironically, it was the fishers themselves who first took up the legislative battle for conservation. Individualistic, tradition-bound petty resource users like the New England coastal fishers are not generally included in the pantheon of American conservation champions, yet the Progressive-era debates over the fisheries illustrate the important role they played in initiating this movement and in shaping its policy considerations.[6] They did this for their own reasons: typically to protect local control over resources and to ensure equitable allocation.

Coastal fisheries in New England—and elsewhere, scholarship suggests—were subject to a range of community sanctions. As commercial pressures mounted, fishers petitioned the states for laws that would perpetuate these local fishing cultures. Conflicts over marine resources, as Bonnie McCay astutely points out, were also "conflicts about cultural meanings and social relationships." The body of marine conservation law that guarded the shore fisheries by 1910 reflected the emerging science of fisheries management, but it also mirrored the ethical precepts behind older local systems. Coastal marine conservation was a complicated blend of Progressivism and traditionalism. Science played a role in striking this balance, but it was never the decisive factor.[7]

Through most of the nineteenth century, New England inshore fishing remained technologically conservative. Although New Englanders sold their catch in metropolitan markets, their relation to these modernizing institutions remained casual. A wide array of income choices buffered them from the stark compulsions of the marketplace. Combining trades in order to make the most of limited resources and capital, inshore fishers were also part-time farmers, woodcutters, boat builders, and sailors, using their small fishing vessels to "smack" lobsters, wood, or produce to ports to the south. Pursuing a seasonal round of hand-lining, lobstering, clamming, and tending weirs or nets, they participated in a form of occupational pluralism characteristic of coastal villages on both sides of the North Atlantic basin, an adaptation to environmental conditions, the cyclical habits of various marine species, and the limited capital available to small coastal outports.

These complex patterns of seasonal work gave a cluttered appearance to the coastal villages, where fishing flakes, smokehouses, drying nets, boats in all stages of repair, clam hods, and lobster traps were scattered among small gardens, grazing livestock, farm implements, and woodworking equipment.[8] Although the shore fishers were linked to regional markets, modernizing forces remained relatively weak, since few fishers were totally dependent on any one source of income.

The uncertainties of this existence cast coastal villagers in a peculiar light. "Each new day brought its fascinating possibilities of sudden

Harry and Fred Hamilton and Benjamin Watson and his daughter Maud contemplate a catch of mackerel in Kennebunkport. Versatile small-time fishers like these adapted to the overlapping cycles of fish migrations, weather, and growing season. With multiple sources of income, they remained independent from urban fish dealers—and maintained their control over local fishing waters. (Courtesy of Kennebunkport Historical Society)

profit," wrote a visitor to the Maine islands, who summarized this way of life as a matter of "living in perfect contentment on a hundred dollars, cash, per year." Such observers delighted in examples of opportunistic and carefree lives patched together by baiting trawl lines, digging clams, tending a few lobster traps, and hand-lining—all "just enough to keep from starving." George Brown Goode's exhaustive 1887 study of Atlantic fishing communities suggests that this pattern of work was far from a reflection of indolence, but it was indeed situated on the margin of the nation's market economy. Natural cycles of season, tide, weather, fish migration, and crop yields conditioned this way of life far more than did market forces. Coastal inhabitants' varied activities required continual evaluation of markets, weather, and species availability but also provided a wide range of personal choice and independence. These hyphenated fishers grew much of their own food, built their own homes, barns, and boats, harvested their own firewood, and butchered their own meat. Each household need that could be met locally, as David Thelen pointed out in a different context, helped to dissociate rural inhabitants from the compulsions of an urban-based market.[9]

Facing no compelling outside competitive pressures, each locality cultivated its own economic rationality and its own ethical approach to fishing.[10] At the end of the century expanding commercial and transportation structures, new fishing technologies, and community fragmentation eroded these local fishing cultures, and participants turned to the state for reconciliation. The degree to which commissioners and legislators succeeded in implementing new conservation policies depended on how well they accommodated established community concerns and preserved traditional patterns of resource use.

As early as 1872 it had become clear that New England's coastal fisheries were declining. In that year a worried Commissioner Elias M. Stilwell of Maine wrote to U.S. Fish Commissioner Spencer F. Baird asking for scientific information on the "probable cause of the rapid diminution of the supply of food-fishes on the coast of New England." Borrowing a thesis first suggested by Maine's pioneer fish propagationist Upham S. Treat, Baird linked the decline to destruction of the river fisheries.[11] The annual migrations of anadromous fish—shad and alewives—attracted feeding pollock, cod, haddock, and hake to shore, making them available to the small-boat fishers. As dams and pollution destroyed these river fisheries, the coastal line fisheries were diminished as well.

Baird's belief that the disappearance of cod and other ocean species resulted from changing feeding habits rather than overfishing reflected current scientific thinking. No method then in use, Baird felt, could seriously diminish the overall supply of ocean fish. Aside from the vastness of the sea, scientists like Baird pointed to the fact that females deposited countless millions of eggs each year, and since they spawned in the open sea, there was "no possibility of any human interference with the process."[12] This analysis meshed nicely with the needs of the new, more intensive commercial fisheries developing along the coast. The heavily capitalized vessels that occasionally swept the bays, Baird implied, need not concern local fishers who for generations had controlled these resources: the fish would return. Baird's science buttressed an emerging view of the coastal fisheries as a regional rather than local concern.

Pitted against this Olympian analysis were those whose life experiences in the local fisheries told a different tale. Bigger nets and larger hauls unsettled traditional fishers, who perceived that local stocks were diminishing and reflexively blamed those from away. State commissioners, drawn into the fray, brought with them a positivist vision of impartial scientific arbitration between the competing factions, but the riddle of the inshore fisheries eluded them. Perhaps, the Massachusetts commissioners mused, one day when the fisheries had been saved from the fishers themselves, "the honorable guild of fishmongers will erect a monument of their gratitude, and will inscribe on its tablets the names of scientific men who have, in our time, labored to create a new industry." In 1884 this must have seemed a distant era indeed.[13]

Localism, Science, and the Buzzards Bay Line Fishery

Controversies over weir fishing in Buzzards Bay, in southern Massachusetts, demonstrate the degree to which the science of fisheries management was enmeshed in local fishing cultures. Disputes between small-boat line fishers and owners of weirs—fixed nets extending out from the shoreline that stopped migrating schools of fish—can be traced to the 1840s on Cape Cod. Primarily, weir owners sold alewives and menhadens as bait to Georges Bank schooners, but they occasionally entered fresh-fish markets controlled by the line fishers. Disputes over the weirs in Buzzards Bay initially involved this by-catch. Scup, tautog, and striped bass, along with the menhadens and alewives, appear in the bay in seasonal cycles complicated by changes in air and sea temperature, currents, and available prey species. When the fish

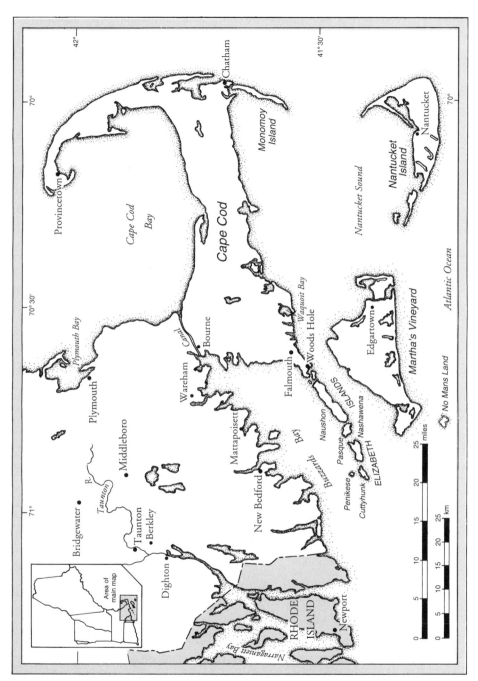

Buzzards Bay, Massachusetts

failed to appear, line-fishers blamed weir owners, who, like Spencer Baird, insisted that the fishery was too vast to succumb to changes in fishing techniques.[14]

Weirs also aggravated the upstream trap-fishers. Like the migrations of salmon and shad up the great rivers, longshore migrations of bait-fish distributed the catch naturally to each seaside and streamside village. This migratory behavior and the limitations of primitive fishing equipment ensured equitable distribution to towns along the coast. Weirs were controversial because they interrupted these longshore migrations, transcending local authority. "Not a fish can be taken . . . in the weirs and pounds of Mattapoisett . . . that does not injure the fisheries of Marion, Wareham, Bourne, Fairhaven, and New Bedford," a petitioner explained, asking for a ban on weirs.[15]

In 1870 citizens of towns on Buzzards Bay presented the Massachusetts legislature with a petition containing 3,023 signatures praying for a law restricting weir and offshore seine fishing, both of which circumvented village common-access arrangements.[16] Remonstrants, totaling 7,958 signatures, came from a broader geographic area, representing those who saw the bay as an open-access property of the Commonwealth at large. Gloucester schooner operators considered the bay's net fisheries a critical source of bait-fish, access to which was an "inalienable right" of all citizens. Fertilizer manufacturers from Weymouth and Woods Hole, and farm representatives from as far away as Deerfield also objected.[17]

Hearings on the petition began on February 15 and continued through eighteen sessions, often running into the evening. Following this "tedious and costly" debate, the Committee on Fisheries recommended against the ban. Chairman N. E. Atwood declared the bay a regional rather than local resource and dismissed the declining catch as the result of a natural flux in fish migrations. Still, his endorsement of the seines and weirs was not absolute. Opposed to a general prohibition, he nevertheless favored "any local legislation that might prove needful" to prevent localized overfishing.[18] This qualification reflected the ambiguity in official opinion about the ocean fisheries: commissioners were unwilling to accept local testimony at face value, yet they could not entirely dismiss the widespread impression that the coastal fisheries were declining.

Anticipating further controversy, in 1871 the fisheries commissioners rented a weir at Waquoit Bay and kept careful daily records of the catch, the wind, the weather, and the air and sea temperature. Future discussion, they resolved, would be limited to "the exact observation of unprejudiced persons." Their report for 1872 confirmed the impression left by Spencer Baird in his letter that year to Maine's Elias Stilwell: the ocean "is a vast, teeming workshop, crowded with fabrics torn in pieces ere they are half finished, to be converted into other fabrics, which in turn are as rapidly destroyed." Reasons for the perplexing cycles of scarcity and abundance lay hidden in the depths of the sea. Yet the many controversies along the South Shore left them, like Atwood, ambivalent. They, too, felt that the "equilibrium of reproduction and destruction" could be fragile in a given place. "A very small thing may disturb it, or may not."[19]

As the commissioners groped for a scientific solution to the problem, they sensed that regulating the weirs would, if nothing else, provide order in a chaotic political situation. Unrestrained, the weir owners were "mere marine squatters." Proper laws would give them legal footing, defining their rights and obligations. Regulation was a political if not a biological necessity: "Each pound should be viewed in two ways: first, as an engine to be encouraged, because it furnishes large supplies of food; and secondly, as an engine to be wisely limited, whenever it becomes a monopoly, or is destructive."[20]

Bending to local political pressure, the commissioners reformulated their thinking on weirs and seines. Although they valued Baird's "careful scientific training," they arrived at a different interpretation: "When so many fish are annually taken from the waters that the remainder are not numerous enough to produce a new crop equal in numbers to the old one, there must be a progressive decrease in the yield." When fish schooled in the open sea, matters might be different, but in the bays and coves, under the scrutinizing eye of science and the persuasive powers of local politics, the fish appeared vulnerable.[21]

Thus commissioners and legislators were not unresponsive as over the next decade coalitions of line-fishers, sport fishers, and upstream fish-trap owners applied pressure on a town-by-town basis to restrict weirs and nets. After 1870 local bans were extended from Mattapoisett, on the western shore of Buzzards Bay, to Wareham and Bourne at the head of the bay. Despite warnings that banning weirs would give a "special monopoly" to the bay towns and a "few sporting characters" who visited during the summer, in 1886 the legislature gave towns in Buzzards Bay the prescriptive right to close their shores to seines and weirs. Prohibitions extended eastward along the lower Cape. Traditional concerns remained at the core of the debate: weirs disrupted natural village-by-village distributions, allowing "a half-dozen men [to] . . . scoop up the most of the fishes that come in to the shore" and depriving the majority of access.[22]

In 1893, after more than twenty years of local skirmishes, opponents of the weirs and seines mounted another massive petition drive, asking for a general ban throughout Buzzards Bay. The bill was directed against the few towns that still permitted weir operations. The legislative Committee on Fisheries and Game reviewed the history of the debate and discovered that over the years the conflict had narrowed; resistance to the ban now came almost exclusively from the weir owners and the banks fishers whom they supplied. Both insisted that only weir-caught alewives were suitable for bait, since those taken in the upstream fish-traps were "so charged by fresh water that they will not keep." River trap owners countered that their alewives were taken within hours of leaving the ocean.[23]

The conflict dissolved into a matter of whether fish should be taken in the shore weirs, "directly at the mouth of the herring-streams," or in the traps, set only a mile or so upstream. A one-mile difference blocked resolution of the decades-old controversy. The ban would not diminish the supply of bait available to the schooners; alewives not caught in the shore weirs would surely enter the herring streams. "So many of them therefore, as are not taken by the pounds or nets in the Bay, will go to the fish-ways."[24] At issue was not a scientific formulation of conservation measures, but a question of who should control the catch.

Although there was no scientific evidence that the ban would protect the fish, it was clear that it would protect a particular way of fishing. As the bait-fish swept along the shore in their annual spring migrations, they returned to their natal streams, giving nearby villages a special claim to their share of the fishery. Cognizant of the moral commitment to these village rights and the rising authority of sport fishers, the legislature endorsed the general ban. The remaining leases expired in 1897, and Buzzards Bay became a haven for hand-liners and village bait-fishers who trapped in the rivers as they had since the 1600s.[25]

The new law also banned offshore purse seines in Buzzards Bay. Since this move seemed to violate the open-access nature of offshore fishing, purse seiners boldly challenged the ban. Seining vessels from Rhode Island and New York hovered at the entrance of the bay, waiting for a "chance to dodge in and catch a school." In Congress, seiners lobbied to extend federal jurisdiction to the coastal waters as a way of circumventing state and local control, and they challenged the ban in several court cases. Neither recourse was successful. Federal judges established the jurisdictional limits of the state at one marine league from the shore and extended the boundaries of coastal municipalities to the outermost jurisdiction of the Commonwealth.[26]

The conservation victory rested on the convergent interests of line-fishers and sport fishers and on the commissioners' own inability to define a general scientific thesis regarding the ocean fisheries. The controversy secured the states' right to regulate the coastal fisheries and thus gave standing to appeals from the towns. In assuming control over the fisheries, Massachusetts commissioners took on the burden of mediating the dictates of science, local fishing cultures, and transregional commercial interests. The charge was not easily executed, but sensitivity to local concerns brought an acceptable blend of policies that preserved an element of democratic control over the inshore fisheries.

The Moral Economy of Maine's Herring Fishery

In eastern Maine, the balance of local rights and transregional interests tipped again to the coastal communities as state legislators debated the wisdom of laws protecting the herring fishery. This Progressive-era battle in a remote corner of Maine provides another example of the compromises between those who saw conservation as a means of exploiting resources more efficiently under expert guidance and those who perceived it as a way of preserving traditions in the face of an expanding scale of extraction and exchange. Debates over herring stocks rested on certain abstract scientific principles, but again science was subordinate to the villagers' drive to protect a traditional fishery. The controversy shows how effective local conservation initiatives could be against the combined interests of scientific experts and corporate capitalists.

Herring are wanderers, traveling in dense schools along the continental shelf on both sides of the Atlantic. In the western North Atlantic, their distribution is limited by the Labrador Current to the north and the Gulf Stream to the south. Juvenile feeding schools enter shallow coastal waters during the warmer months and move offshore during the winter. Their tendency to school in large aggregations makes them a cheap and important resource commercially but also leaves them vulnerable to overfishing.[27]

Traditionally herring were caught in weirs in eastern Maine. They were sold as bait or smoked for regional markets. In the early 1870s seafood packers began canning juvenile herring as a domestic substitute for French sardines. The new "sardine" canneries fronted mostly on Passamaquoddy Bay, in eastern Maine and Canada, a region well suited for the fishery by its nutrient-rich waters stirred by twenty-foot tides and by its heavily indented shoreline. As Maine herring replaced the more expensive and duty-burdened French product, sardines changed from a luxury item into a staple seafood, and the industry grew rapidly.

By 1900 herring had become the eastern coast's most important marine resource, providing livelihood for about 1,800 fishers.[28]

Between 1886 and 1900 the number of canneries grew from forty-five to seventy-five, and a case of 100 cans, which had sold for twelve dollars in the early 1880s, brought less than three dollars a decade later. In 1888 and again in the early 1890s local canners attempted unsuccessfully to keep prices high through marketing agreements. In 1897 a few large New York and Chicago packinghouses consolidated the industry. Working with the state legislature, they established legal standards for quality and shortened the packing season by about forty days. Despite an increase in the pack, the syndicates expected to create higher profits by reducing "the whole great industry to a perfect system, with uniform prices for fish, supplies and labor and a uniform price for the goods when packed." But notwithstanding the promise of economic expansion, corporate consolidation left the coastal communities uneasy.[29]

The new, technologically advanced canning operations stood in marked contrast to eastern Maine's traditional weir fishery, which provided most of the region's herring. The roughly 240 weirs in eastern Maine were constructed simply by driving stakes into the soft mud bottoms and intertwining brush between them. At low tide fish were seined or dipped into a skiff and transferred into a waiting sardine boat. The weirs were "perhaps the most primitive form of apparatus in use at the present time in the fisheries of the United States."[30]

Despite flush times in the sardine industry, weir fishing was an uncertain proposition. The weirs' stationary placement exaggerated the element of risk inherent in fishing operations: "Like the frog in the fable, which waited with its mouth open for a fly to drop in, the weir . . . waits for the herring to come to it." Herring migrations were affected by bottom contour, the amplitude and direction of tidal currents, wind, water temperature, and the amount of phosphorescence in the water, which "fired" the nets at night and made them conspicuous to the fish. Weir placement was always experimental, and catches ranged from 100,000 pounds in a single night to a few dozen fish all

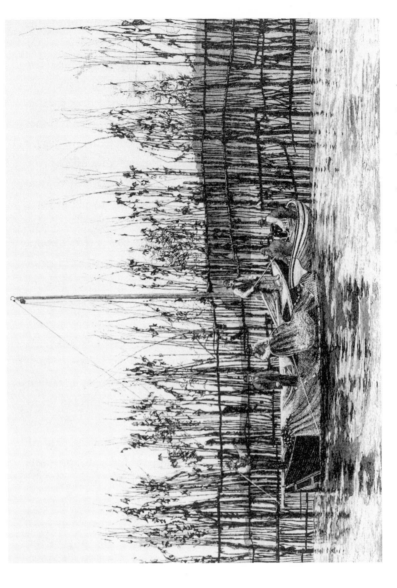

The sardine industry in the 1880s. Fishers seine juvenile herring from a brush weir at low tide near Eastport, Maine. (George Brown Goode, *The Fisheries and Fisheries Industries of the United States*, vol. 5 [Washington, D.C., 1887])

season. The eastern coast was "marked by the remains of weirs that have proved unprofitable ventures."[31] But weir fishing was only one among many activities that occupied their owners. Like other New England outports, eastern Maine villages preserved a multioccupational way of life adapted to the natural rhythms of the coastal ecology. If the weirs remained empty, their owners were fortified with other options.

These diversified work patterns suited the fishers' cultural and economic needs but not those of the packers. Whereas the canneries were forced to operate in competitive national markets, weir owners enjoyed a rare independence based on their varied income and subsistence options. Their casual relation to the market dampened enthusiasm for technological improvements, and their primitive system was a bottleneck in the syndicates' attempts to rationalize the industry. Moreover, this independence was buttressed by a legal system that gave local fishers virtually exclusive rights to the inshore herring fishery. A series of laws dating from the 1840s limited use of purse seines in Washington County waters.[32]

Differences in these two political economies were apparent in the marketing structures for herring. Weir owners bargained with independent dealers who plied the coast in small, gaff-rigged vessels. Prices were determined by "auction" and depended on the size of the overall catch and the going price for canned sardines. A correspondent to a regional trade journal described the spirited haggling: "On the one side are the factory boatmen, loud, blustering, important, and always rampant 'bears' of the market. On the other, the quiet, canny fishers, who have a way of knowing just what the 'catches' have been from Machiasport to St. Andrews, and they are always stubborn 'bulls.'" Prices varied radically. When the first factory opened in 1875, sardine-sized herring brought one dollar a hogshead (1,000 pounds); by 1887 excited bidding over light hauls ran them as high as fifty dollars. In such times the weir owners made fabulous profits, "for the competition [among buyers] is always brisk and the factories must be kept running." The pricing system was as primitive as weir fishing itself, and the packers, working within a broader market economy, found these traditional methods decidedly cumbersome.[33]

As part of the plan to rationalize the industry, the syndicates bought up the sardine boats that collected herring from the weir operators and established new purchasing agreements, shifting some of the burden of falling profits to the fishers. Rather than depend entirely upon the weir operators, the canneries also encouraged the development of a fleet of offshore purse seiners, which could take in herring on a more regular basis. The purse seiners, with heavy investments in vessels and huge, 600-to-900-foot nets, were tied to the same market system that drove the canners.[34]

In 1901 and 1905 the canning syndicates petitioned the legislature for a law allowing free seining up to within 600 yards of any weir. The bill reopened the debate over conservation and control of the fishery. Weir owners complained that when the herring struck the bays, seining vessels appeared by the dozens; they were helpless to prevent the interlopers from "scoop[ing] the entire body of fish from the bay." Purse seining, they felt, smothered a portion of the catch, which, when left to decompose, spoiled the coves for other schools. Cannery officials stressed the need for more fish and less regulation. Conservation was best served by maximizing economic returns from the resource through heavy capitalization, spreading benefits to cannery workers, fishers, and the state generally.[35]

To arbitrate the controversy, the legislature turned to A. R. Nickerson of Maine's Sea and Shore Fisheries Commission. An offshoot of the original Fish Commission established in 1867, the agency reflected the state's interest in realizing broad public benefits through scientific resource management. Impressed with the outside capital flowing into eastern Maine, the commissioner sided with the syndicates, arguing that herring was a state rather than a local responsibility. Existing laws, written at the insistence of "certain localities," were "often drawn with great looseness." Reiterating Spencer Baird's proposition that no technique could deplete an oceanic resource, Nickerson insisted that the herring should be taken "wherever and whenever they are found."[36]

At town meetings along the coast, weir owners drafted petitions to state representatives defending their community waters. Their objections were rooted in traditional values that ascribed ethical catch limits based on a modest fishing technology. The weirs, they insisted, provided fish "in sufficient quantities to satisfy reasonable men." The apparatuses were indeed linked to a more democratic culture; they were usually owned in shares by several local families, and each was given a specific name—Yankee Doodle, Wild Man, Long Stakes, Dyder Ali, Grasper, Democrat, Jeff Davis, Uncle Sam—that memorialized a "habit, trait of character, circumstance, personal history, [or] incident" in local lore. Each community hosted a small cannery, "dependent on its local weirs for their supply of fish, and in that respect [gaining] a slight advantage [over] its larger rivals." Like other traditional fisheries, weir operation was bound up with a sense of community identity.[37] Steeped in democratic values, citizens defended the weirs as an ethical as well as biologically sound alternative.

The debate in the 1905 legislature was spirited. On one side, free-seining proponents portrayed the herring as an important export commodity crucial to reviving the depressed coastal economy. Other legislators, representing the coastal towns, conveyed the ethical judgments, republican rhetoric, and concerns for the herring's resiliency expressed by their constituents. Ultimately, a representative from Surry carried the argument for conservation. This small midcoast town, he pointed out, had once reaped a $30,000 yearly harvest in menhadens, "and it didn't take but a little money to go into the business." The fish disappeared when "people from Rhode Island, New York, Connecticut, and the western states . . . [came] in here." Melding concerns over resource exploitation with populist and localistic resistance to large, nonresident corporations, the Surry representative closed his argument: consider the fate of the menhadens, he asked, "and vote for the people."[38]

The defeat of the syndicates was cause for great celebration in the down-east villages. The *Machias Union* reported victory balls in the towns along the coast, with suppers and "gala nights at the opera house, thronged with people from all parts of the country." Dance tunes inspired by the triumph of localism included the "Weirmen's March to Victory," "The Defeat of Monopoly," a march for the "Protection of Our Fisheries," and "When Money Didn't Count."[39]

Six years later the weir operators consolidated their victory by forcing a ban on the use of "fake weirs"—traps made of twine floated in a bay temporarily and then moved by large fishing boats. This time fishers from southern coastal Maine joined the debate, asking that seining be prohibited along the entire coast. In late March the legislative counsel for the packers reached an agreement with the weir owners. A revised bill outlawed the fake weirs but committed weir fishers to seek no further restrictions on seining and to build only weirs they actually intended to use, since weir placement established the local boundaries of the purse-seine ban. Licenses for weir building would be granted by town selectmen after an open hearing. Both sides claimed victory, and in 1913 the fisheries commissioner noted less friction along the coast than he had seen for two decades.[40]

The local herring fishery ultimately fell victim to larger offshore operations. Laws regarding purse seining were liberalized in the 1940s, and a deepwater purse-seine fishery began during the Second World War in the Bay of Fundy and the eastern Gulf of Maine. The purse seiners were more efficient but also more destructive. Herring catches peaked in 1950 and began declining on the eastern coast late in the decade. The size of the catch, of course, is influenced by economic as well as natural conditions and therefore is not entirely reliable as a measure of the abundance of the fish.[41] Yet in the mid-1970s correlations between fishing intensity and declining stocks were close enough to trigger concern about overexploitation. Catch limits of increasing severity were imposed, and in 1977 federal agencies began rebuilding fish stocks in the grounds that fell within the new U.S. 200-mile limit.

Although the 1911 accord was not final, the weir fishers, whose democratic approach to resource use became law as the shadow of the metropolitan economy fell across their remote villages, helped define coastal marine conservation for Maine. During this Progressive-era shift from local fishing cultures to large-scale industrial resource use, herring conservation reflected scientific principles far less than it did traditional, locally derived solutions. The tenor of this debate was evident in other coastal fisheries as well. In 1911 Maine's fish commissioner observed that until recently citizens had considered the fisheries inexhaustible, "and laws regulating them were looked upon . . . as restrictive and burdensome." He noted a new mood in the second decade of the century.[42] The ghost of Spencer Baird, if not exorcised, at least moved farther offshore.

Lobster Conservation and the Problem of Credibility

The Progressive era brought a difficult period of adjustment in the lobster fishery, as fisheries commissioners in Massachusetts and Maine responded to increased exploitation and new management policies. Here, too, the fishery had been a prerogative of the towns, and local politics played a key role in the transition to state management. Credible enforcement remained elusive until state officials achieved a balance between local traditions and new, scientific management policies. Their policies were justified on the basis of scientific research, but as the history of this fishery shows, there was no simple correlation between science and conservation.[43]

Commercial lobstering began on Cape Cod in the late 1700s. Around 1840 shippers developed techniques for holding live lobsters in the wells of small, specially designed sloops, or "smacks," and the Cape fishery began to feel the pressure of markets in Rhode Island, Connecticut, and New York. Over the next decade the industry spread eastward into Maine. New entrants, attracted by higher prices, violated established territorial claims and found their buoys cut free or their pots ransacked—signals that the grounds had been spoken for.[44] Still, it was clear by 1880 from the growing number of traps that this localized system of controlling access was under siege.

Commercial expansion was driven by two distribution networks: seafood canners and fresh-fish dealers. New England's seafood-canning business began in Eastport, Maine, in the 1840s. By 1854 Upham S.

Treat, who patented the technique for canning lobsters, was shipping his product as far west as California. Canners like Treat pioneered transregional handling procedures and helped diversify the coastal economy at a time when other staple marine products like mackerel and salt cod were declining in value.[45] Live-lobster dealers offered a second marketing structure, serving restaurants, hotels, and fish marts from Maine to New York.

Rivalry between these two expanding sectors initiated the debate over conservation in the lobster industry. In Maine, canners successfully petitioned the legislature in 1874 to close the fishery between August 1 and October 15—peak season for the live-lobster dealers, but months when the canneries were not processing lobster. The Massachusetts fishery, oriented to nearby urban fish marts and to the summer resorts on the Cape, followed a conservation strategy that favored the fresh-fish dealers. Canneries generally purchased juvenile lobsters, too small for fresh-fish markets, sometimes using a score of these tiny crustacea to fill a single one-pound can. Acting on pleas to halt this destructive practice, Massachusetts legislators in 1874 established a minimum size limit for lobsters at ten and a half inches. Maine fresh-fish dealers followed suit with a similar law in 1883.[46]

This initiative demonstrates the growing economic power of the live-lobster dealers. Taking advantage of improved railroad systems, they extended shipments throughout the eastern and central states. The expanding distribution system and the growing "summer trade" crowding New England's huge coastal hotels put a premium on live lobsters and increased the political power of the fresh-fish dealers. Seafood canneries, unable to compete for the premium-priced ten-and-a-half-inch lobsters, abandoned the fishery, some of them relocating in the Maritime Provinces. The size limit saved the juvenile lobsters from the voracious canneries, but it committed the two states to a management system that was difficult to enforce.[47]

Not surprisingly, given the politicized nature of the laws, few fishers took them seriously. Despite the disappearance of the canneries, demand for undersized lobsters remained strong. Fishing smacks from

New York, where the shorter lobsters could be marketed legally, migrated into New England waters each summer, and the spread of tourist facilities along the coast created local incentives to violate the law. Catchers broke off the tails and scalded them in cauldrons aboard their boats, then peddled the meat to hotel owners and tourists along the beach. Fishers sometimes used their unsold undersized lobster as hen food, trap bait, or even fertilizer for their gardens. Enforcement was pitifully inadequate against such abuse, and haphazard and sometimes vindictive implementation by local wardens undermined the credibility of the commission. Uneven application of the law demoralized otherwise honest fishers, who perceived that returning short lobsters to the sea was a noble but futile gesture.[48]

During the 1880s the Massachusetts legislature responded to local pleas for better enforcement by deeming mutilation of any lobster *prima facie* evidence that it was undersized, by giving wardens police powers and the right of search and seizure, and by requiring identification on all contrivances for catching and keeping lobsters. The state increased funds for patrols, prohibited the possession of egg-bearing lobsters, and regulated the distance between the slats in the sides of the pots. These measures left the commissioners hopeful about effecting a stronger respect for the law.[49]

Nevertheless, enforcing the size limit remained difficult. The vast extent and complexity of the coast gave enormous advantage to violators. Fishers on the islands and peninsulas could spot approaching officials at great distances and used flags or the steam whistles on seafood canneries to warn others. Smacks passed information about wardens from cove to cove. In addition, the lobster fishery faced mounting commercial pressures in the 1880s. Higher market prices drew more catchers into the business, and the traditional eight-month lobstering season gave way to year-round fishing. Power boats enabled fishers to double the number of traps they tended. Yearly per-trap yields in Massachusetts dropped between 1888 and 1900 from eighty-one to forty-six.[50] Though alarmed by these trends, coastal inhabitants "hardly [knew] . . . what to suggest," fearful that any change in the law would make their immediate situation even worse. The question of whose interests were to be served by conservation vexed the industry, and the constant political skirmishing eroded credibility. The lobster problem, an official mused, "is difficult to solve in view of the fact that those engaged in the business differ so materially in regard to it."[51]

Between 1881 and 1888 Massachusetts commissioners campaigned to replace the unworkable size limit with a summer closed season, when lobsters were molting and considered less marketable. The closed season appealed to lobster fishers because it could be enforced more equitably than the seemingly random raids in search of undersized lobster. Also, it would close the fishery to summer cottagers and New York smack owners, outsiders whose encroachments were particularly galling to local fishers. Responding to appeals from those who depended on summer fishing, the legislature rejected the closed season, but it recognized the popular sentiment behind the proposal by prohibiting lobster fishing by nonresidents, thus driving the New York smacks from the coast.[52]

Commissioners continued to apply the size limit, but they operated under two disadvantages: the law lacked credibility among fishers, and uneven enforcement undermined the sense of equity in its disposition. "The compliance of each," as resource specialists recognize today, "depends on the compliance of the others." A South Duxbury fisher who chose to abandon the trade explained the crisis in more concrete terms: "It seemed hard for me to heave overboard twelve and fifteen short lobsters out of every pot, and the next one put them into his boat. I could not stand it any longer." Until the fishers and dealers could agree on a law that would "meet all requirements of trade and at the same time prove efficient in protecting the lobster," conservation would inspire no widespread allegiance. Worse yet, local pressure for lowering the minimum size limit seemed to be growing.[53]

In 1904 Charles E. Davis, a state representative from Waltham, wrote a long missive to the Committee on Fisheries identifying what he saw as the key threats to the fishery: illegal catches and dogfish, a small shark that seemed to thrive on juvenile lobster. The size limit was not

Close-ranked boathouses and lobstering gear on Cape Ann, Massachusetts. The composition illustrates the small-scale investments typical of lobster fishing and the community context out of which territorial claims to the fishery developed. (George Brown Goode, *The Fisheries and Fisheries Industries of the United States*, vol. 5 [Washington, D.C., 1887])

only unenforceable, but it gave "the sand-sharks a practical . . . monopoly of the Short Lobster Industry." Davis asked that the size limit be replaced by three countermeasures: a federal bounty on dogfish; a summer closed season; and a law specifying that trap entrances be constructed to prevent lobsters *above* a certain size from entering. The trap design would protect the larger, more vigorous breeders, and during the closed time fishers could occupy themselves earning the bounty on dogfish, thereby saving the smaller lobster from predation. Change the trap design, destroy the illegal pots, fine the dogfish rather than the lobster catcher, and the problem of credibility vanishes, Davis concluded: "It has always been easier to catch a Lobster-Trap . . . than it has been to catch a Lobster Fisherman." The lobster would "increase in number and . . . the Lobster Fishermen will earn a better living provided the Federal Bounty on Dogfish be passed."[54] Davis' intriguing idea was turned down by the Committee on Fisheries, but it received support from Massachusetts fisheries officials.

The notion of protecting the largest rather than the smallest lobster had been gaining currency since the 1880s, as federal and academic researchers compiled a body of scientific literature on *Homarus americanus.* In a series of reports written for the U.S. Fish Commission, Francis H. Herrick of Western Reserve University compiled an exhaustive survey of the lobster's life cycle.[55] In light of Herrick's work, in 1902 George W. Field of the Massachusetts Institute of Technology reviewed conservation options available for the New England states. Closed seasons, he argued, had no overall effect on yield. They burdened those with investments in gear and withheld the resource from public markets. When bans were lifted, fishermen recouped losses by returning to the sea with "redoubled energy," bringing glutted markets, economic waste, and a "rapid return to the former conditions which made a close season necessary." Field offered an alternative: relying on Herrick's discovery that reproductive value increases rapidly after lobsters reach nine to ten inches, he recommended both minimum *and* maximum size limits. The law would protect larger, sexually mature adults and allow exploitation of immature lobsters down to a reasonable market minimum. The "double-gauge" law not only would increase the sustainable yield but also would be more enforceable: the scientific basis of the law would commend it "to fishermen and others who know . . . the lobster in a practical way." Field saw the double-gauge law as the key to achieving consensus throughout the region.[56]

Borrowing from Herrick and Field and from Davis' ingenious trap design, in 1907 the Massachusetts commissioners proposed a law limiting trap entrances to three and a quarter inches in diameter and requiring slats in the sides at least one and a half inches apart. The small entrances would keep out the largest lobsters, and the openings between the slats would allow smaller prey to escape through the sides.

The measure conformed to new scientific opinion, and, more important, it could be "readily and economically enforced."[57]

Along with the commissioners' pot design, three other proposals came before the Massachusetts legislature from 1904 through 1907: a reduction in the minimum size limit, a ban on lobsters *greater than* eleven inches, and Field's double-gauge law. Apparently confused by the array of technical choices before them, legislators passed the nine-inch-minimum provision but failed to add the eleven-inch maximum. In 1907 lobster landings, which had been steadily declining, jumped from 487,332 to 1,035,123 as catchers hauled in the windfall of previously illegal nine-inch crustaceans. By 1913 the catch had again fallen to 543,129 lobsters.[58]

In the face of this perceived legislative disaster, it is instructive that the years after 1907 saw the beginnings of effective lobster conservation in Massachusetts. Commissioners achieved greater credibility in part through experiments in artificial propagation, an area in which there was widespread consensus. Beginning with the first federal attempts at lobster planting in 1888, Massachusetts, Rhode Island, and later Maine began working with the U.S. Fish Commission to develop hatching techniques. By 1909 the federal hatcheries at Woods Hole and Boothbay Harbor were returning over 100 million fry to the coastal waters yearly. Given low survival rates among released fry, the program probably did little to boost the yield, but the federal activity lent the entire conservation effort a sense of scientific purpose.[59]

The more promising changes came not at the state or federal level but from the fishing villages themselves. An important development was the enactment of a lobster-license law, at the urging of lobster fishers, dealers, and others interested in the business. Licensing symbolized, at least, individual acknowledgment of commissioners' authority and opened communication between fishers and the agency. Fishers also lobbied for better enforcement. Using a combination of automobiles and boats, wardens began working in teams, or "flying squadrons," raiding along the coast in sections infested with violators.[60]

More-uniform enforcement promoted a sense of equity and assurance that individual compliance would not be futile.

The formation of several local lobsterers' associations, beginning in 1894, helped restore a sense of community control over the Massachusetts fishery. The movement began spontaneously along the South Shore in response to declining yields. Lobster catchers pledged to return short or egg-bearing lobsters to the sea and to report violators to the wardens. They were comfortable with the nine-inch law, and with out-of-state smacks banned from Massachusetts waters and local territorial rights still widely respected, their mutual sanctions gave credibility to the law. The commissioners encouraged the movement, and by 1918 the local associations embraced about 500 members—a number exceeding that of licensed fishers in the state.[61]

Finally, commissioners stepped up their confiscations of short and egg-bearing lobsterers entering Massachusetts from the Maritime Provinces. The interceptions were both object lessons in equitable law enforcement and a means of restoring the Massachusetts lobster grounds: commissioners liberated thousands of contraband "seed" lobsters in waters where Massachusetts catchers were "living up to the laws." Threats to the industry remained, but by 1918, for the first time in decades—barring the windfall of 1907—the catch increased. Inquiries along the coast showed that compliance was becoming the norm.[62]

Another important aid to conservation, to which the commissioners did not allude, was the impact of large supplies of lobsters reaching Massachusetts markets from Maine and the Maritime Provinces. Fisheries to the east of Massachusetts were more productive, the coastline being more extensive and the waters colder. Imports of cheap lobster equalized prices in Massachusetts at a relatively low level, a development that in turn discouraged more intensive fishing. The influence of the local associations, the licenses, and the credibility achieved through better enforcement brought good results in the years after 1907.[63] Brought to the brink of commercial ruin as jurisdiction shifted from the towns to the state, the Massachusetts lobster fishery stabilized at a relatively low level of exploitation in competition with cheaper lobsters from Maine and the Maritime Provinces.

Unlike Massachusetts, Maine clung to the ten-and-a-half-inch limit, but here, too, consensus remained elusive. In 1905, for instance, the legislature deliberated a bill prohibiting the export of live lobster from the state during the summer season. A Penobscot County senator framed the antiexport argument in a manner that was all but self-evident to his audience: "I say if we are going to spend a thousand dollars for the protection of lobsters, there should be some restrictions against shipping them ad lib all over this country, against the interests of this State." The "interests of the state," more precisely, referred to the growing tourist industry, which competed with out-of-state dealers for a finite supply of fresh lobster. The antiexport bill had less to do with lobster protection than with lobster protectionism—keeping "State of Maine lobsters in State of Maine waters for the State of Maine representatives and their families," as one legislator later put it. The bill failed passage, but it announced the concerns of the tourist industry, which added to the mix of conflicting commercial interests in lobster legislation.[64]

After 1907 southern Maine tourist promoters became more insistent about lowering the size limit. With the Massachusetts nine-inch law in place and a similar one in New Hampshire, legislators suspected that illegal Maine lobsters were appearing on tables in Boston and elsewhere as legal fare.[65] Making passing reference to Maine's notorious temperance law—another sore point among the state's resort proprietors—a York County senator explained how the ten-and-a-half-inch law "works out in practice."

About every afternoon in the summer when the automobiling is good . . . in all those [southern Maine] cities and towns where the merry dietists . . . have their habitat, the frequent invitation is, "Let us go up to Portsmouth [New Hampshire] and have a lobster supper at Hamm's." Of course, in our part of the State, there are those evil minded individuals who say that there is another commodity at Hamm's dispensed which cheers the human system quite as much as nine-inch lobsters do but your knowledge of the culture and refinement of those people who go there of course will dispel any such unworthy thoughts.[66]

Restaurateurs in Maine paid premium prices for legal lobsters, while smack men spirited away cheap undersized catches to restaurants elsewhere. Maine hotels could compete more effectively if they too could serve nine-inch lobster.

Legislators from York and Cumberland counties, where much of Maine's coastal resort business was concentrated, clearly understood that the nine-inch minimum—a retreat on the conservation front— would not be acceptable in eastern Maine, where large, premium-priced lobster were still abundant. Accordingly, they offered a solution that would equalize Maine's minimum length with that of neighboring states but at the same time produce a "biologically sound" conservation measure. In an interesting legislative ploy, they advanced the double-gauge law proposed more than a decade earlier by George Field and Francis Herrick. Outnumbered by eastern fishers, they raised the issue to a matter of scientific principle: reproduction studies indicated an exponential increase in egg production *after* lobster reached eight to twelve inches; therefore, Maine was protecting the wrong lobster. However appealing the double-gauge law appeared as a scientific measure, it failed to meet the commercial needs of eastern Maine. Despite the invocation of America's preeminent lobster authority, the Maine Senate turned the measure down, voting largely along sectional lines. In Maine, as in Massachusetts, local and commercial conflicts prevented a compromise that could be perceived as equitable by all parties. And here, too, the impasse produced a crisis of compliance. Without proper enforcement, a Cundy's Harbor fisher wrote to Fisheries Commissioner Horatio D. Crie, "we are licked."[67] Maine's conservation ethic was fragile indeed: Those who complied with the law depended upon the wardens to keep in check those who did not.

At the local level, the appeal for uniform compliance was frequently mixed with a territorial defense of local waters. As anthropologist James M. Acheson discovered, lobsterers in Maine created informal territorial divisions along the coast and limited access to local kinship or community groups. This tradition of closed community access provided a local basis for compliance with the conservation codes. A correspondent to the fisheries commission explained this basis for enforcement: "We fishermen always has thrown our shorts away for a good many years . . . Others has cleaned up there side of the Bay and now they have come over on our grounds to clean ours up . . . Are you going to help us or let them go? Mr. Crie I am beginning to wonder if this lobster law is a real honest to goodness law or a fake. If it is no good I am beginning to feel I might as well have my share."[68] Catchers used the state laws to secure their territorial claims.

The economic crisis of the early 1930s changed the dynamics of lobster conservation in Maine. The Depression hit the industry with devastating force. Since lobster was a luxury, markets disappeared quickly enough, but the trend was exacerbated by a flood of Canadian imports. Maine traditionally dominated the New England restaurant market for larger lobsters, but during the Depression restaurants shifted their orders to the less expensive smaller fare, legally harvested in Canada but not in Maine. During these hard times, wardens used greater discretion in interpreting the laws. Conditions, one warden reported, were "awful hard . . . down here and I hardley go around among the men for I fear that I might catch them with a mess of shorts and if I did the rest would want to kill me." As Elinor Ostrom points out, tolerance for infractions under such circumstances does not damage the credibility of a code so long as it appears temporary and does not threaten the survival of the resource.[69]

The Depression, however, encouraged lobsterers to use the conservation codes to bolster their territorial divisions. Unemployment forced many people back to the coast to take up clam digging or lobstering as an occupation of last resort. Those willing to condone the legal transgressions of townsfolk or kinsfolk in difficult times were quick to inform the commissioner when "outsiders" intruded. Thus a warden explained a flurry of complaints about violators from Haycocks Harbor, in eastern Maine: "Seth Jones and William Ramsdell and Walter Ramsdell thinks they had ought to have from Moose River point to Bog Brook all to themselves and nobody else . . . Moores' men belong in Moose River and were born their and the[re] is nothing else to do down here and they have gone to fishing lobsters and Ramsdells has made all the trouble they could for the Moores' men."[70] By invoking the state codes, catchers buttressed their traditional community exclusions in a period of declining local authority. In Maine as in Massachusetts, commercial rivalries precluded a widely accepted and enforceable resource policy. Yet in both states local initiatives built a case for compliance from the bottom up. Local self-regulation, ultimately the only effective enforcement for an industry as remote and scattered as the lobster fishery, was an important ingredient in protecting the lobster.

By 1933 catchers faced a difficult situation. "I owe the dealers here for every trap I set in the water in the year 1932," one told the commissioner. "Nearly every fisherman that I know is situated the same as I am. If there is not something done for the poor fisherman, they are totally ruined." Using the slogan "Let's Remember the Fishermen and Have Two Lobster Days Each Week," Crie alerted the public to "bargain" prices at the local lobster pound. The commissioner traveled to the other New England states arguing for a regionwide ten-and-a-half-inch law, which would drive small Canadian lobster out of the area. None agreed to Maine's conservative measure. In Congress, Maine's senators pleaded unsuccessfully for a tariff on short Canadian lobster.[71]

Rebuffed in other New England states and in Washington, Commissioner Crie turned to Maine's own fishing regulations for industry relief. In January 1933 he released a lengthy statement to newspapers all along the coast announcing a change in his point of view on the lobster code. The industry had been making progress since the turn of the century, he thought, as a result of Maine's ten-and-a-half-inch law, but with fishers becoming desperate, the question assumed a new perspective. Something had to be done to save the lobsterers as well as their catches.[72]

Crie sent agents out with fishers to measure, count, and weigh all trapped lobsters to determine, as precisely as possible, the biological effects of various legal limits. A scientifically derived formula, he felt, was the "key to the whole situation." Using Herrick's earlier findings and his own calculations, he predicted that a nine-to-thirteen-inch double-gauge limit would increase the value of the lobster catch and protect the same number of eggs.

Catching more lobster and at the same time preserving more lobster would, Crie thought, appeal to the catchers. Throwing more product on the market was not a prospect that dealers would endorse, but there was another angle to the double-gauge solution: the lower limit would allow Maine dealers to handle small lobster, giving them a full range of shellfish—from Maine or Canada—for sale throughout New England. Finally, the new measure would give Maine restaurants access to smaller lobsters.[73] The double-gauge law had something for everyone.

Along the coast feelings were sharply divided. York County residents lauded the double-gauge proposal, but eastern and central coast fishers viewed it as a dealers' ploy for importing more Canadian lobsters. Warden C. S. Beal informed the commissioner that he had carried a petition for the double-gauge law around "until it is almost wore out but could not seem to get the men to sign it." Beal reported a widespread impression in eastern Maine that Crie had "sold out to the nine inch fellows" and added a plea for his own safety: "I hope Mr. Crie that you wont let my name be brought into this as . . . they are a funny lot of people down here."[74]

Compelled to find new markets for dealers and new hope for hard-pressed lobsterers, Crie pointed to the scientific basis for his proposal. "Actual tests" showed that the minimum and maximum lengths would produce more marketable lobster by the pound and more fry. The deepening economic crisis drove home the logic of Crie's solution; his appeals to science, protectionism, and commercial good sense broke down resistance on the coast and in the legislature.[75] In 1934, without much fanfare amid the grave issues of the day, the state mandated the only double-gauge lobster measure in the world. The law bridged, as much as possible, the gulf between dealers and catchers and between towns south of the Penobscot and those to the east. The emphasis on science cemented over remaining schisms, while local territorial attachments provided the legitimacy without which such laws would be self-defeating, given the problems of enforcement on the coast.

A product of special Depression-era conditions, the double-gauge law remains the basic conservation premise for Maine's vitally important lobster fishery. It was supplemented in 1977 by laws mandating escape vents on traps to reduce mortality among undersize lobster, and in 1974–1977 by new measures to mark and protect egg-bearing lobsters. Size limits have been altered over the years, but the double-gauge principle remains inviolate, even though the scientific understanding that informed the law has changed somewhat. Although some have questioned the scientific theory behind the double-gauge law, there have been no successful efforts to overturn it, in good part because fishers have persistently supported the code.[76] The permanency of the double-gauge law tells us less about biological effectiveness than it does about its ability to accommodate shifting forces within the industry.

The appearance of weirs and purse seines in Buzzards Bay, the emergence of packers' monopolies in eastern Maine, and the evolution of regionalized lobster markets on the New England coast were complex phenomena, but they share common themes. Burgeoning demand for marine resources and disintegrating local systems of allocation created sectional and intra-industry rivalries that required new, state-level regulatory agendas. Conservation policy was born in this tug-of-war between traditional local cultures of resource use and new, large-scale systems of exploitation and exchange. Gradually the law assumed the trappings of scientific, sustained-yield management, but only after accommodating these conflicting social and political forces. Conservation policy in the coastal marine fisheries was not initiated by concerned experts and bureaucrats; it emerged out of the attempts by petty producers to protect a local culture of resource use that extended back generations.

Ultimately the small-scale line and net fisheries succumbed to the forces of large-scale capitalism. The lobster industry, still pursued in traditional fashion, is a guarded success, partly as a result of the codes put in place from 1907 through 1933. A nonmigratory species, lobster reacts well to local and state efforts to regulate harvesting and to traditional cultures of exclusion. And for many reasons the crustacean has been the focus of intense statewide concern: Maine's coastal tourist industry is almost inconceivable without this famous garnish.

The outcome of these Progressive-era struggles differs from the scenario advanced in the standard account of conservation in America, which maintains that political decisions about resources have been shaped by the needs of modernizing corporate users. Richard Cooley, for instance, documented the tight control large packing companies enjoyed over the Alaskan salmon industry and the utter disregard for local fishing rights on the part of the U.S. Bureau of Fisheries, which supervised the catch. Arthur McEvoy has noted the fragmentation of ethnic fishing cultures that had provided some control over the California fisheries during these same years. State or federal resource laws speeded the destruction of traditional fishing cultures.[77] In this light, the persistence of community rights and small-scale fishing in New England seems extraordinary.

Traditional fisheries remained vital in New England for three reasons. First, although the fishers were marginalized economically, they were far from apolitical. This coastal region had responded enthusiastically to the nation's bid for independence in 1776 and to the cause of the Union in 1861, and folk memories of these intensely political and patriotic actions remained strong; having paid the awful price of liberty, citizens felt no reservations about exercising it. They became remarkably adept at using state conservation politics to achieve community goals. Republican values, resting on patriotic traditions and democratic economic structures, buttressed an abiding sense of anti-monopoly—and to a degree antimodern—feeling.

Second, unlike Cooley's Alaskan fishers, who were forced to plead their case in far-off Washington, the coastal villages petitioned their state governments through representatives who knew their needs intimately. The U.S. Bureau of Fisheries confined its judgments to matters of efficient use and expert management, which, as Samuel Hays astutely pointed out in *Conservation and the Gospel of Efficiency,* favored large resource users. The New England fisheries commissions adhered to the same scientific philosophy of efficient use, but they were weak agencies, and state legislators, who controlled resource policy, were as sensitive to local politics as they were to issues of economic efficiency.[78] Finally, science appeared more problematic in the context of local politics than it did in Washington offices. Enmeshed in these bitter sectional and commercial rivalries, experts lost their posture of impartiality. Any single pronouncement on the fisheries was bound to favor or condemn at least one segment of the industry. Experts could persuade, but only within politically defined parameters.

Still, these local cultures are perhaps more representative than historians have realized. Anthropologists, resource economists, and others interested in common-use resource regimes have discovered a fascinating array of viable local management systems across the nation and around the world. Economic change is everywhere destabilizing, but traditional norms can show a remarkable persistence and vitality even in the face of a fully developed commercial economy.[79] Viewing the conservation movement in the light of these evolving popular cultures seems as rewarding as perceiving it in terms of scientific measurements of a declining resource base. Sorting out the changing commercial interests, the scientific impulses, and the popular concerns behind the movement to conserve the nation's resources is a complex task, but it promises a sharper focus on the origins of one of the most important reforms in American history.

Conclusion

━━━━━

In the early 1980s the environmental movement faced a crisis. A popular president, interpreting his electoral victory as a mandate to roll back environmental regulations, staffed key federal resource management offices with administrators who seemed at odds with the mandates of their own agencies. Environmental organizations went on the defensive, and when the smoke cleared, it was the administrators who were gone rather than the regulations. For environmentalists, things seemed brighter at the end of the Reagan and Bush years, but by 1994 the movement faced an assault far more ominous than that of the early 1980s. The situation seemed all the more grim because, despite continued popular support for environmental regulation, those who controlled Congress appeared convinced that these laws were elitist.

This charge has a familiar ring. Generally, historians have argued that the conservation movement began among America's elites—federal scientists and bureaucrats, elite hunters and anglers, prominent writers and naturalists, or others at the upper reaches of society. This prevailing approach feeds the contemporary impression that the conservation movement has been an "elitist conspiracy," as historian Stephen Fox puts it.[1] Focusing on the momentous changes in thinking that presaged the Progressive-era conservation movement in a single region, this study, in contrast, reveals that grass-roots concerns about nature and its uses left a deep imprint on official policy, contributing to some impressive accomplishments that were part and parcel of the American conservation movement. At the turn of the century New England states created pioneering resource management agencies with jurisdiction over wildlife, timber, and sea and shore fisheries and, with mixed success, defined basic common rights to the heavily utilized forests and rivers of the region. These achievements helped define what Donald

Worster has called the "American commons": a fundamental awareness of public rights to, and responsibility for, the nation's resources.

Northern New England, a region of farms, villages, and small cities anchored to an agrarian past by strong family ties, well earned its reputation for traditionalism in the nineteenth century. Yet people immersed in this traditional culture participated enthusiastically in early efforts to protect and sustain their natural resources. Traditionalism, in fact, encouraged this participation. The region's petty resource-based economy required democratic access to forests, lakes, streams, and fisheries, and rural people defined their commons accordingly. Biographical storyteller C. A. Stephens described the local tradition of wading into the spawning pools on the upper Kennebec in springtime with a four-pronged fork to "pitch" salmon into a bushel basket. The practice was condemned, for good reasons, by fisheries managers, but this generations-old way of getting sustenance from the land also inspired the first attempts to restore inland and migratory fisheries in America.[2] Rural people guarded their traditional forms of access closely; their commons provided a means of living less expensively and more democratically; it fostered independence, and it cushioned them against growing corporate control over New England's staples economy. Democratic patterns of resource use allowed petty production to thrive alongside some of the nation's largest land and resource monopolies.[3]

New England rural life, shaped by a harsh environment and by generations of interaction with soils, water, woods, and wildlife, conditioned people to respect what John R. Stilgoe calls "a fragile equilibrium between natural and human force."[4] Lura Beam, in a fascinating study of downeast Maine at the end of the nineteenth century, explored the impress of this fragile equilibrium upon third- and fourth-generation farm families. The thick evergreen forest bordering the upland pastures and crowding the banks of the river, she wrote, circumscribed all human effort. "The river and trees were the themes, running through the history and the lives," eternal, yet constantly changing in color, mood, mass, and form.[5] Shaped by centuries of use into familiar forms, this half wild, half cultivated landscape generated an aesthetic and moral outlook that found its way into decisions about conservation policy. Fields cleared from a forested background evoked independence, self-sufficiency, and democracy; a run of herring into a brush weir renewed faith in the perfect dynamics of nature.

At midcentury rural people confronted a series of changes in the ways their landscape and resources were used. They responded by reasserting their claims to the commons, rebuilding traditional justifications, and adapting, finally, to the new authority systems that were necessary to accommodate the broader scope of resource use and distribution. Their response, animated by a moral vision of democratic access to common lands and by a perfectionist drive to complete this natural landscape, blended, albeit uneasily, with urban Romantic visions and scientific expertise to give New England its basic resource-management policy.

Even though conservation ideals changed as authority systems shifted from the towns to the state and federal governments, it is important to give recognition to the movement's popular origins. This vital component of the American commons should be reevaluated, not just as a matter of historical justice, but because it reveals an important reservoir of local support for improved environmental policy. The potential in this local perspective is most evident in recent studies of local common-resource management regimes, such as Elinor Ostrom's pathbreaking *Governing the Commons*.[6] Although the examples Ostrom and others raise may be atypical in their firmly established boundaries, their specific communal rights, and their clearly defined behavioral formulations, they do suggest the variety of mechanisms ordinary people have used to ensure responsible use of natural resources. They prove that people acting in concert can build worlds in which nature and culture interact more harmoniously.

Pioneering New Englanders, as historians have pointed out, devastated the "virgin" landscape they encountered as they pushed out from the heartlands of central New England. Yet those who remained on the land after this wave of pioneering plunder passed on to the West began reconstituting an equilibrium between nature and culture. Their work is ongoing, but this beginning should be recognized for what it was: an important commitment among common people to protect and preserve a familiar landscape in the face of unsettling social and ecological change.

Searching out the seeds sown in these local cultures of resource use reveals the spiritual source of the American commons: the love of place, the faith in common stewardship, the commitment to democratic access, and the reverential respect for a fragile equilibrium between culture and nature. This is the legacy that made the American people so receptive to conservation at the turn of the century, and the source of their abiding concern for protecting and sustaining the natural world today.

NOTES

INDEX

NOTES

—————

ABBREVIATIONS

MAINE

MeBA   *Annual Report of the Secretary of the Maine Board of Agriculture* (Augusta, 1856–1901); *Annual Report of the Commissioner of Agriculture* (Augusta, 1902–1914)

MeBLIS   *Annual Report of the Bureau of Labor and Industrial Statistics* (Augusta, 1887–1907)

MeF&G   *Report of the Commissioner of Fisheries* (Augusta, 1867–1879); *Report of the Commissioner of Fisheries and Game;* (Augusta, 1880–1894); *Report of the Commissioners of Inland Fisheries and Game* (Augusta, 1895–1924)

MeFoC   *Annual Report of the Forest Commissioner* (Augusta, 1891–1911)

MeSA   Maine State Archives, Augusta

MeSSF   *Report of the Commissioner of Sea and Shore Fisheries of the State of Maine* (Augusta, 1898–1924)

MASSACHUSETTS

MAG   *Annual Report on the Agriculture of Massachusetts* (Boston, 1837–1845); *Abstract from the Returns of the Agricultural Societies* (Boston, 1846–1849); *Transactions of the Agricultural Societies in the Commonwealth of Massachusetts* (Boston, 1850–1852); *Annual Report of the Secretary of the Massachusetts Board of Agriculture* (Boston, 1853–1889)

MF&G   *Annual Report of the Commissioners on Inland Fisheries* (Boston, 1867–1885); *Annual Report of the Fish and Game Commissioners* (Boston, 1886); *Annual Report of the Commissioners of Inland Fish and Game* (Boston, 1887–1901); *Annual Report of the Commissioners of Fish and Game* (1902–1919)

MSA   Massachusetts State Archives, Boston

NEW HAMPSHIRE

NHA   *New Hampshire Agriculture: Annual Report of the Board of Agriculture* (Nashua, Concord, and Manchester, 1871–1891)

269

NHF&G   *Report of the Special Commission on the Propagation and Preservation of Fish* (Manchester, 1857); *Report of the Select Commission on Fisheries* (Concord, 1865); *Report of the Commissioner of Fisheries* (Concord, 1866); *Report of the Commission on River Fisheries* (Concord, 1867); *Report of the Commissioners of Inland or River Fisheries* (Concord, 1868); *Report of the Fish Commissioners* (Manchester, Nashua, and Concord, 1869–1880); *Report of the Fish and Game Commissioners* (Concord, 1881–1922)

NHFoC   *Report of the Forestry Commission* (Concord, 1885–1891); *Biennial Report of the New Hampshire Forestry Commission* (Manchester, 1895–1928)

NHRMA   New Hampshire Records Management and Archives, Concord

SPNHF   Society for the Preservation of New Hampshire Forests Papers, Special Collections Department, University of New Hampshire, Durham

SPNHFR   *Annual Report of the Society for the Protection of New Hampshire Forests* (Concord, 1902–1906)

NEW YORK

NYFG&F   *Annual Report of the Commissioners of Fish, Game, and Forests of the State of New York* (Albany, 1895–1900)

VERMONT

VAR   *Annual Report of the Vermont State Board of Agriculture, Manufacturers, and Mining* (Montpelier, 1872–1876); *Annual Report of the Vermont Board of Agriculture* (Montpelier, 1877–1880); *Vermont Agricultural Report* (Montpelier and Burlington, 1881–1908); *Agriculture of Vermont: Annual Report of the Commissioner of Agriculture* (Montpelier, 1909–1913)

VF&G   *Report of the Commissioners Relative to the Restoration of Sea Fish to the Connecticut River and Its Tributaries* (Montpelier, 1866–1870); *Biennial Report of the Fish Commissioners* (Montpelier, 1871–1892); *Biennial Report of the Commissioners of Fisheries and Game* (Montpelier, 1893–1926)

VFoC   *Report of the Forestry Commissioner* (with *VAR*, 1906–1908); *Report of the State Forester on the Progress of Forestry in Vermont* (Burlington, 1909–1912)

VL   *Statutes of the State of Vermont* (Windsor, 1787–1839); *Acts and Resolves Passed by the General Assembly of the State of Vermont* (Burlington and Montpelier, 1840–1890)

VSP   Vermont State Papers, Montpelier

INTRODUCTION

1. *Maine Farmer,* October 30, 1835.

2. *Burlington Free Press,* January 3, 1891.

3. J. Leonard Bates, "Fulfilling American Democracy: The Conservation Movement, 1907 to 1921," *Mississippi Valley Historical Review* 44 (June 1957): 29, 33; Samuel P. Hays, *Conservation and the Gospel of Efficiency: The Progressive Conservation Movement, 1890–1920* (1959; reprint, New York, 1980), p. 1.

4. Donald J. Pisani, "Forests and Conservation, 1865–1890," *Journal of American History* 72 (September 1985): 356; Jim O'Brien, "Environmentalism as a Mass Movement," *Radical America* 17 (March–June 1983): 10; Roderick Nash, *Wilderness and the American Mind* (1967; New Haven, 1982); Max Oelschlaeger, *The Idea of Wilderness from Prehistory to the Age of Ecology* (New Haven, 1991); Philip Shabecoff, *A Fierce Green Fire: The American Environmental Movement* (New York, 1993), p. 46.

5. William Cronon, "Revisiting the Vanishing Frontier: The Legacy of Frederick Jackson Turner," *Western Historical Quarterly* 18 (April 1987): 172.

6. Carolyn Merchant, *Ecological Revolutions: Nature, Gender, and Science in New England* (Chapel Hill, N.C., 1989); Theodore Steinberg, *Nature Incorporated: Industrialization and the Waters of New England* (New York, 1991).

7. William Cronon, "Ecological Prophecies," in *Major Problems in American Environmental History,* ed. Carolyn Merchant (Lexington, Mass., 1993), p. 13.

8. T. D. Seymour Bassett, "Urban Penetration of Rural Vermont, 1840–80" (Ph.D. diss., Harvard University, 1952), pp. 2–3.

9. Hugh M. Raup, "The View from John Sanderson's Farm: A Perspective for the Use of the Land," *Forest History* 10 (April 1966): 10.

10. William Cronon, *Changes in the Land: Indians, Colonists, and the Ecology of New England* (New York, 1983); Merchant, *Ecological Revolutions;* Steinberg, *Nature Incorporated.*

11. Nash, *Wilderness and the American Mind;* Bates, "Fulfilling American Democracy"; Hays, *Conservation and the Gospel of Efficiency;* Stephen Fox, *The American Conservation Movement: John Muir and His Legacy* (Madison, Wis., 1985).

12. Edward C. Kirkland, "Life and Livelihood in the Middle Grants, 1850–1950," *Vermont History* 29 (October 1961): 186.

13. The law was amended in 1869 to apply to ponds over twenty acres. See Lincoln Smith, *The Power Policy of Maine* (Berkeley, Calif., 1951), p. 11. On colonial town regulations, see Yasuhide Kawashima and Ruth Tone,

"Environmental Policy in Early America: A Survey of Colonial Statutes," *Journal of Forest History* 27 (October 1983): 168–179.

14. Donald Worster, *The Wealth of Nature: Environmental History and the Ecological Imagination* (New York, 1993), p. 103.

15. George Perkins Marsh, *Man and Nature* (New York, 1867), p. 35.

16. Donald Worster, *Nature's Economy: A History of Ecological Ideas* (Cambridge, Mass., 1985), pp. 40–45.

17. New York Forest Commission, quoted in *MAG*, 1887, p. 53.

1. THE NORTHEASTERN FRONTIER

1. Genieve Lamson, "Geographic Influences in the Early History of Vermont," in *Proceedings of the Vermont Historical Society for the Years 1921, 1922, and 1923* (Montpelier, 1924), p. 81; Bernard Bailyn with Barbara DeWolfe, *Voyagers to the West: A Passage in the Peopling of America on the Eve of the Revolution* (New York, 1986), p. 8; William D. Williamson, *History of the State of Maine*, vol. 2 (Hallowell, Maine, 1839), p. 550.

2. Norman W. Smith, "A Mature Frontier: The New Hampshire Economy, 1790–1850," *Historical New Hampshire* 24, no. 3 (1969): 3; Randolph A. Roth, *The Democratic Dilemma: Religion, Reform, and the Social Order in the Connecticut River Valley of Vermont, 1791–1850* (New York, 1987), p. 16; Edward N. Torbert, "The Evolution of Land Utilization in Lebanon, New Hampshire," *Geographical Review* 25 (1935): 214.

3. Lewis D. Stilwell, "Migration from Vermont (1776–1860)," *Proceedings of the Vermont Historical Society* 5 (no. 2, 1937): 97.

4. James Walter Goldthwait, "A Town That Has Gone Downhill," *Geographical Review* 17 (October 1927): 532.

5. Stilwell, "Migration from Vermont," p. 75; Frank M. Bryan, "Vermont: The Politics of Ruralism" (Ph.D. diss., University of Connecticut, 1970), pp. 49–50.

6. N. Perkins, *Tour through Vermont* (1789), quoted in Stilwell, "Migration from Vermont," p. 116.

7. Stilwell, "Migration from Vermont," p. 67; Abby Maria Hemenway, *Vermont Historical Gazetteer*, 5 vols. (Burlington, 1868–1891), 1: 321.

8. Hemenway, *Vermont Historical Gazetteer*, 4: 580; Harold Fisher Wilson, *The Hill Country of Northern New England: Its Social and Economic History, 1790–1930* (New York, 1936), pp. 12–25, 124–128, 130.

9. *VAG*, 1883–84, p. 362; Ira Allen, *The Natural and Political History of the State of Vermont* (London, 1798), p. 332; *Report of the Secretary of Agriculture on Southern Appalachian and White Mountain Watersheds* (Wash-

ington, D.C., 1908), p. 25; Helenette Silver, *A History of New Hampshire Game and Furbearers* (Concord, 1957), p. 49.

10. Stilwell, "Migration from Vermont," pp. 67–68.

11. Jamie Eves, "Yankee Immigrants: Ecological Crisis and the Settlement of Maine, 1763–1825" (M.A. thesis, University of Maine, 1988).

12. *Burlington Free Press,* September 20, 1878; *Report on White Mountain Watersheds,* p. 15.

13. "The Merrimack Valley," *Farmer's Monthly Visitor* 12 (June 1852): 183; *NHF&G,* 1877, p. 23.

14. Goldthwait, "Town That Has Gone Downhill," p. 543; *Maine Farmer,* March 6, 1875; Hemenway, *Vermont Historical Gazetteer,* 1: 41.

15. Zadock Thompson, *History of Vermont: Natural, Civil, and Statistical* (Burlington, 1842), pp. 4, 6.

16. Frederick Hall, "Statistical Account of the Town of Middlebury . . . Vermont . . . (1820)," *Massachusetts Historical Collections,* 2d ser., 9 (1832): 124.

17. *VAG,* 1903, pp. 44–45. See Samuel L. Boardman, *The Climate, Soil, Physical Resources, and Agricultural Capabilities of the State of Maine* (Washington, D.C., 1884), p. 37; Charles W. Johnson, *The Nature of Vermont: Introduction and Guide to a New England Environment* (Hanover, N.H., 1980), pp. 61, 64.

18. Bernard Frank and Anthony Netboy, *Water, Land, and People* (New York, 1950), pp. 27, 43; Hugh M. Raup, *Forests in the Here and Now,* ed. Benjamin B. Stout (Missoula, Mont., 1981), p. 60.

19. Hemenway, *Vermont Historical Gazetteer,* 1: 458; *Yankee Farmer* 1 (March 2, 1835): 33.

20. William Cronon, *Changes in the Land: Indians, Colonists, and the Ecology of New England* (New York, 1983), chapter 2; Silver, *New Hampshire Game and Furbearers,* pp. 15–17; David Goodsell Gale, "The History of the Vermont Fish and Game Commission, 1866–1960" (M.A. thesis, University of Vermont, 1963), pp. 3–4.

21. *Burlington Free Press,* November 2, 1865; Thompson, *History of Vermont,* pp. 128–129; Middleton Goldsmith, *An Address on Fish Culture Delivered before the Legislature of Vermont* (Rutland, Vt., 1872), p. 1.

22. Petition of William Brackett (May 22, 1832), box 19, 1830–1834, NHRMA; John M. Weeks, *History of Salisbury, Vermont* (Middlebury, Vt., 1860), p. 3; Johnson, *Nature of Vermont,* p. 123. Flood stories abound in the natural history sections of Hemenway, *Vermont Historical Gazetteer.*

23. John C. Baker, *Sketches of an Excursion through Vermont and among the White Mountains of New Hampshire . . . in 1864 and 1865* (Montreal, 1869), pp. 15–16.

24. Jeremy Belknap, *The History of New-Hampshire*, vol. 3 (Boston, 1813), pp. 50, 53.

25. Hemenway, *Vermont Historical Gazetteer*, 2: 973.

26. Belknap, *History of New-Hampshire*, 3: 51; Hall, *Statistical Account of Middlebury*, pp. 125–127.

27. Weeks, *History of Salisbury*, p. 3.

28. Hemenway, *Vermont Historical Gazetteer*, 3: 756; Allen, *Natural and Political History of Vermont*, pp. 334–335.

29. Belknap, *History of New-Hampshire*, 3: 21, 22, 27.

30. I am indebted to Thomas Dunlap for this insight. On instability in nature, see Raup, *Forests in the Here and Now*, p. 17; Donald Worster, "The Ecology of Order and Chaos," in *The Wealth of Nature: Environmental History and the Ecological Imagination* (New York, 1993), pp. 156–183.

31. Carolyn Merchant, *Ecological Revolutions: Nature, Gender, and Science in New England* (Chapel Hill, N.C., 1989), p. 33; Stephen J. Pyne, *Fire in America: A Cultural History of Wildland and Rural Fire* (Princeton, 1982), pp. 71–83.

32. Weeks, *History of Salisbury*, pp. 71–73, 88; Hemenway, *Vermont Historical Gazetteer*, 1: 89.

33. See Timothy Silver, *A New Face on the Countryside: Indians, Colonists, and Slaves in South Atlantic Forests, 1500–1800* (New York, 1990), pp. 30–31.

34. Silver, *New Hampshire Game and Furbearers*, p. 246; Lyman S. Hayes, *The Connecticut River Valley in Southern Vermont and New Hampshire* (Rutland, Vt., 1929), pp. 51–52; idem, *History of the Town of Rockingham, Vermont* (1898; reprint, Bellows Falls, Vt., 1907), p. 106; A. N. Somers, *History of Lancaster, New Hampshire* (Concord, 1899), p. 291.

35. Somers, *History of Lancaster*, pp. 89, 291; Lamson, "Geographic Influences in the Early History of Vermont," pp. 112–113; John Johnston, *A History of the Towns of Bristol and Bremen in the State of Maine* (Albany, N.Y., 1873), p. 12; Leonard A. Morrison, *The History of Windham in New Hampshire* (Boston, 1883), p. 31; Weeks, *History of Salisbury*, p. 69.

36. John R. Eastman, *History of the Town of Andover, New Hampshire* (Concord, 1910), p. 364.

37. Donald Worster, "History as Natural History: An Essay on Theory and Method," *Pacific Historical Review* 53 (February 1984): 5.

38. Quoted in Robert Malvern, "Of Money Needs and Family News: Brigham Family Letters, 1800–1820," *Vermont History* 41 (Summer 1973): 115–116.

39. Kenneth Lockridge, "Land, Population and the Evolution of New England Society, 1630–1790," *Past and Present* 39 (1968): 70, 76. See Jamie H. Eves, "'The Valley White with Mist': A Cape Cod Colony in Maine,"

Maine Historical Society Quarterly 32 (Fall 1992): 74–107; Alan Taylor, *Liberty Men and Great Proprietors: The Revolutionary Settlement on the Maine Frontier, 1760–1820* (Chapel Hill, N.C., 1990), pp. 6–9.

40. Patricia J. Tracy, "Reconsidering Migration within Colonial New England," *Journal of Social History* 23 (Fall 1989): 105; Hemenway, *Vermont Historical Gazetteer,* 3: 746.

41. Tracy, "Reconsidering Migration," p. 97; John J. Waters, "Family, Inheritance, and Migration in Colonial New England: The Evidence from Guilford, Connecticut," *William and Mary Quarterly* 39 (January 1982): 65; David P. Szatmary, *Shays' Rebellion: The Making of an Agrarian Insurrection* (Amherst, Mass., 1980), p. 7.

42. Richard L. Bushman, "Family Security in the Transition from Farm to City, 1750–1850," *Journal of Family History* 6 (Fall 1981): 246; Allan Kulikoff, "The Transition to Capitalism in Rural America," *William and Mary Quarterly* 46 (January 1989): 141; Szatmary, *Shays' Rebellion,* p. 6; Tamara Plakins Thornton, "Between Generations: Boston Agricultural Reform and the Aging of New England, 1815–1830," *New England Quarterly* 59 (June 1986): 191.

43. Percy Wells Bidwell, "Rural Economy in New England at the Beginning of the Nineteenth Century," *Transactions of the Connecticut Academy of Arts and Sciences* 20 (April 1916): 372; Ernest L. Bogart, *Peacham: The Story of a Vermont Hill Town* (Montpelier, 1948), p. 73.

44. Hemenway, *Vermont Historical Gazetteer,* 1: 395; 3: 319; Richard W. Judd, "Lumbering and the Farming Frontier in Aroostook County, Maine, 1840–1880," *Journal of Forest History* 28 (April 1984): 56–67; Edward C. Cass, "A Town Comes of Age: Pownalborough, Maine, 1720–1785" (Ph.D diss., University of Maine, 1979), p. 73.

45. James T. Lemon, "Agriculture and Society in Early America," *Agricultural History Review* 35, no. 1 (1987): 76.

46. Hayes, *The Connecticut River Valley,* p. 87; Josiah F. Goodhue, *History of the Town of Shoreham, Vermont, from 1761 to the Present Time* (1861; reprint, Shoreham, Vt., 1975), p. 57; Bidwell, "Rural Economy in New England," p. 320; Philip L. White, *Beekmantown, New York: Forest Frontier to Farm Community* (Austin, Texas, 1979), pp. 309–310; Hemenway, *Vermont Historical Gazetteer,* 1: 250; *New England Farmer* 5 (January 1853): 13; *VAG,* 1877, p. 93.

47. *Maine Farmer,* December 4, 1835.

48. Somers, *History of Lancaster,* p. 111; H. C. Woodworth, "A Century of Adjustments in a New Hampshire Back Area," *Agricultural History* 11 (1937): 223.

49. F. Holbrook, "Arboriculture," *Cultivator* 6 (June 1849): 169. See George

Lucius Russell, "The Change from Wheat to Wool in Shoreham, Vermont, 1800–1845: A Quantitative Analysis of the Effects on Land Wealth" (Honors thesis, Harvard University, 1975; copy in University of Vermont Special Collections Department), p. 5; Hemenway, *Vermont Historical Gazetteer,* 3: 883; *VAG,* 1891–92, p. 142.

50. Torbert, "Land Utilization in Lebanon"; Silas H. Jenison, *An Address Delivered at the Annual Fair of the Addison County Agricultural Society . . . 1844* (Middlebury, Vt., 1845), pp. 8–9; Merchant, *Ecological Revolutions,* pp. 150–193; Cronon, *Changes in the Land,* p. 140.

51. Hugh M. Raup, "The View from John Sanderson's Farm: A Perspective for the Use of the Land," *Forest History* 10 (April 1966): 3. I am indebted for this point to Richard Hale, professor emeritus of the Department of Forest Management, University of Maine.

52. Robert P. Wilson, "An Inquiry into the Use the English Inhabitants of Colonial Maine Made of the Fish and Game Resources of that Region" (M.A. thesis, University of Maine, 1953), p. 55; Leonard E. Foote, *A History of Wild Game in Vermont* (Montpelier, 1946), p. 28; Weeks, *History of Salisbury,* pp. 87–88; *Maine Farmer,* February 25, 1864.

53. Hemenway, *Vermont Historical Gazetteer,* 3: 752.

54. Hayes, *Connecticut River Valley,* pp. 89–90; Churchill quoted in Hemenway, *Vermont Historical Gazetteer,* 3: 752.

55. Silver, *New Hampshire Game and Furbearers,* p. 34; C. A. Stephens, *A Busy Year at the Old Squire's* (Norway, Maine, 1922), pp. 10–11, 67, 197; John Langdon Sibley, *History of the Town of Union* (Boston, 1851), pp. 51–54; Alice Verrill Ellis, *The History of Prospect, Maine, 1759–1979* (North Searsport, Maine, 1980), p. 55; *NHA,* 1874, p. 357.

56. Weeks, *History of Salisbury,* pp. 84–89. See Bogart, *Peacham,* p. 314; J. Bailey Moore, *History of the Town of Candia* (Manchester, N.H., 1893), p. 279.

57. Mary M. Grow, "History," in *China, Maine: Bicentennial History,* ed. Marion T. Van Strien (Weeks Mills, Maine, 1975), p. 8; Thompson, *History of Vermont,* p. 50; Silver, *New Hampshire Game and Furbearers,* p. 46.

58. See Laurel Thatcher Ulrich, *A Midwife's Tale: The Life of Martha Ballard, Based on Her Diary, 1785–1812* (New York, 1990), pp. 49–54, 353–359; Mrs. S. W. Foss, "What Herbs Did Our Grandmothers Gather, and Why?" *Granite Monthly* 39 (November 1907): 378–383; *New England Farmer* 2 (April 13, 1850): 128; Moore, *History of the Town of Candia,* p. 44; Belknap, *History of New-Hampshire,* 3: 92–93.

59. *NHF&G,* 1877, p. 24; Myron Gordon and Philip M. Marston, "Early Fishing along the Merrimack," *New England Naturalist* (September 1940): 3; Somers, *History of Lancaster,* pp. 100–101, 315; Charles H. Bell,

History of the Town of Exeter, New Hampshire (Boston, 1888), p. 47; Hayes, *History of the Town of Rockingham,* pp. 47–49.

60. Fred E. Crawford, *The Life and Times of Oramel Crawford, a Vermont Farmer, 1809–1888* (n.p., 1952), p. 132; Lamson, "Geographic Influences in the Early History of Vermont," p. 122; Robert E. Dunbar and George F. Dow, *Nobleboro, Maine: A History* (Nobleboro, 1988), pp. 100–101; Wilson, "Inquiry into the Use of Fish and Game," pp. 72, 86.

61. Eastman, *History of the Town of Andover,* pp. 9, 458.

62. Hemenway, *Vermont Historical Gazetteer,* 3: 319.

63. Silver, *New Hampshire Game and Furbearers,* pp. 42, 72; Richard W. Musgrove, *History of the Town of Bristol,* vol. 1 (Bristol, N.H., 1904), p. 94; Florence J. Perry, "From Colonization and Depredation to Conservation and Education: Progress Report of the Vermont Fish & Game Department," typescript, 1894, p. 4, reference files, Vermont State Archives.

64. Silver, *New Hampshire Game and Furbearers,* p. 45.

65. Hemenway, *Vermont Historical Gazetteer,* 1: 122; Silver, *New Hampshire Game and Furbearers,* pp. 70–72, 203.

66. Thompson, *History of Vermont,* p. 51; Silver, *New Hampshire Game and Furbearers,* pp. 43, 70; Gale, "History of Vermont Fish and Game Commission," p. 13.

67. Middleton Goldsmith, "The Increase and Preservation of Fish and Game," p. 1, appended to George P. Marsh, *Report . . . on the Artificial Propagation of Fish* (Burlington, Vt., 1857); Somers, *History of Lancaster,* p. 311; "Act to Prevent the Destruction of Fish" (November 16, 1869), *VL,* 1869, no. 48, p. 50. I am indebted to Gregory Sanford, Vermont State Archivist, for calling my attention to these laws and suggesting their significance.

68. *VL,* 1876, no. 61, pp. 149–150. "Giant powder" was a nitroglycerin-based blasting powder.

69. Hemenway, *Vermont Historical Gazetteer,* 3: 278; *Maine Farmer,* July 4, 1867; *VAG,* 1875–76, p. 401.

70. Silver, *New Hampshire Game and Furbearers,* p. 47.

71. Stilwell, "Migration from Vermont," p. 154.

72. Russell, "Change from Wheat to Wool in Shoreham," p. 54; Wilson, *Hill Country,* pp. 78–79.

73. Bogart, *Peacham,* pp. 310–311.

74. Based on Michael Williams, *Americans and Their Forests: A Historical Geography* (Cambridge, 1989), p. 119.

75. *Maine Farmer,* December 4, 1835.

76. Holbrook, "Arboriculture"; Russell, "Change from Wheat to Wood in Shoreham," p. 31.

77. *Vermont Watchman and State Journal,* November 5, 1884; William C. Lipke and Philip N. Grime, eds., *Vermont Landscape Images, 1776–1976* (Burlington, 1976), p. 27.
78. Judd, "Lumbering and the Farming Frontier."
79. *Maine Farmer,* April 25, 1867.
80. Johnston, *History of the Towns of Bristol and Bremen,* pp. 42, 327; *Maine Farmer,* August 29, 1874; Somers, *History of Lancaster,* pp. 125–126; Albert G. Comings, *Address before the Connecticut River Valley Society, Lebanon, New Hampshire, September 22, 1853* (Hanover, N.H., 1853), p. 7; Stilwell, "Migration from Vermont," pp. 151–152.
81. Andrea Rebek, "The Selling of Vermont: From Agriculture to Tourism, 1860–1910," *Vermont History* 44 (Winter 1976): 19–20; Lipke and Grime, *Vermont Landscape Images,* p. 27.
82. Hemenway, *Vermont Historical Gazetteer,* 2: 701. See William J. Baker, "English Travelers and the Image of Vermont in Victorian England," *Vermont History* 42 (Summer 1974): 206–207.
83. Comings, *Address before the Connecticut River Valley Society,* p. 6; Cronon, *Changes in the Land,* p. 138.
84. *VAG,* 1887–88, p. 224.
85. *MAG,* 1851, p. 510.
86. Carl Sauer, "The Morphology of Landscape," in *Land and Life: A Selection from the Writings of Carl Ortwin Sauer,* ed. John Leighly (Berkeley, Calif., 1963), p. 343.
87. *MAG,* 1851, p. 511.
88. Belknap, *History of New-Hampshire,* 3: 57.
89. *MAG,* 1851, pp. 510–511.
90. Samuel A. McReynolds, "Rural Life in New England," *American Archivist* 50 (Fall 1987): 534.
91. Baker, *Sketches of an Excursion,* pp. 3–5, 25–26.
92. Lipke and Grime, *Vermont Landscape Images,* p. 24.
93. *MAG,* 1864, p. 95.

2. THE COMMONS IN TRANSITION

1. Bonnie J. McCay and James M. Acheson, "Human Ecology of the Commons," in *The Question of the Commons: The Culture and Ecology of Communal Resources,* ed. McCay and Acheson (Tucson, 1987), p. 3; Garrett Hardin, "The Tragedy of the Commons," *Science* 162 (December 13, 1968): 1243–48.
2. Ibid., p. 7.

3. Daniel W. Bromley, "Property Rights as Authority Systems: The Role of Rules in Resource Management," in *Emerging Issues in Forest Policy*, ed. Peter N. Nemetz (Vancouver, 1992), pp. 453–470.

4. Bonnie J. McCay, "The Culture of the Commoners: Historical Observations on Old and New World Fisheries," in McCay and Acheson, *The Question of the Commons*, pp. 195–196; Yasuhide Kawashima, "Forest Conservation Policy in Early New England," *Historical Journal of Massachusetts* 20 (Winter 1992): 1–15

5. McCay, "Culture of the Commoners," p. 196.

6. Anne Bush MacLear, *Early New England Towns: A Comparative Study of Their Development* (New York, 1908), p. 81.

7. Charles H. Bell, *History of the Town of Exeter, New Hampshire* (Boston, 1888), pp. 129, 131, 134; Frederic P. Wells, *History of Newbury, Vermont* (St. Johnsbury, Vt., 1902), pp. 36, 43.

8. John M. Weeks, *History of Salisbury, Vermont* (Middlebury, Vt., 1860), p. 69; Bell, *History of the Town of Exeter*, pp. 50, 51–52, 137.

9. Michael Zukerman, *Peaceable Kingdoms: New England Towns in the Eighteenth Century* (New York, 1970), pp. 34–35. See *MF&G*, 1872, app. 2; Joseph Dow, *History of the Town of Hampton, New Hampshire* (Salem, N.H., 1893), pp. 30–33; John Langdon Sibley, *History of the Town of Union* (Boston, 1851), pp. 129, 136–137, 421; William D. Williamson, *History of the State of Maine*, vol. 2 (Hallowell, Maine, 1839), pp. 563–564, 571; Weeks, *History of Salisbury, Vermont*, p. 69; Jasper Jacob Stahl, *History of Old Broad Bay and Waldoboro*, vol. 2 (Portland, Maine, 1956), p. 76.

10. David P. Szatmary, *Shays' Rebellion: The Making of an Agrarian Insurrection* (Amherst, Mass., 1980), pp. 7–8; Steven Hahn, "Hunting, Fishing, and Foraging: Common Rights and Class Relations in the Postbellum South," *Radical History Review* 26, no. 10 (1982): 38–39, 43. See Randolph A. Roth, *The Democratic Dilemma: Religion, Reform, and the Social Order in the Connecticut River Valley of Vermont, 1791–1850* (New York, 1987), p. 21; James Hill Fitts, *History of Newfields, New Hampshire* (Concord, 1912), p. 52; Lyman Simpson Hayes, *History of the Town of Rockingham, Vermont* (1898; reprint, Bellows Falls, Vt., 1907), p. 56; Williamson, *History of the State of Maine*, 2: 289, 371, 508.

11. Fred E. Crawford, *The Life and Times of Oramel Crawford, a Vermont Farmer, 1809–1888* (n.p., 1952), pp. 187–188; William Cronon, *Changes in the Land: Indians, Colonists, and the Ecology of New England* (New York, 1983), p. 132.

12. Petition of Joseph P. Martin (February 16, 1839), box 129, envelope 16; Petition of J. P Haygens (January 25, 1844), box 164, envelope 245, MeSA.

13. *VL*, 1787, p. 164; 1828, no. 20, p. 22, and no. 26, p. 25. See David Goodsell Gale, "The History of the Vermont Fish and Game Commission, 1866–1960" (M.A. thesis, University of Vermont, 1963), p. 14.
14. Petition of Joseph Smith (June 1838), box 22, NHRMA. See Petition of Joseph L. Richardson (June 6, 1838), ibid. On fox, see *Index to the Laws of New Hampshire . . . 1679–1883* (Manchester, 1886), p. 195; Zadock Thompson, *History of Vermont, Natural Civil, and Statistical* (Burlington, 1842), p. 35; Abby Maria Hemenway, *Vermont Historical Gazetteer*, 5 vols. (Burlington, 1868–1891), 3: 890; Petition of Jon. Weave [1838], box 22, NHRMA.
15. Edgar Gilbert, *History of Salem, New Hampshire* (Concord, 1907), p. 40.
16. Edward C. Cass, "A Town Comes of Age: Pownalborough, Maine, 1720–1785" (Ph.D. diss., University of Maine, 1979), p. 27. See A. N. Somers, *History of Lancaster, New Hampshire* (Concord, 1899), p. 90.
17. Williamson, *History of the State of Maine*, 2: 289, 371, 508, 514–517, 569, 592, 607, 613–616; Alan Taylor, *Liberty Men and Great Proprietors: The Revolutionary Settlement on the Maine Frontier, 1760–1820* (Chapel Hill, N.C., 1990); Hemenway, *Vermont Historical Gazetteer*, 1: 145–146; John Johnston, *A History of the Towns of Bristol and Bremen in the State of Maine* (Albany, N.Y., 1873), pp. 478–496; James Berry Vickery, *A History of the Town of Unity, Maine* (Manchester, Maine, 1954), pp. 39–41.
18. Florence J. Perry, "From Colonization and Depredation to Conservation and Education: Progress Report of the Vermont Fish & Game Department," typescript, 1894, p. 34, reference files, Vermont State Archives; Leonard E. Foote, *The Vermont Deer Herd: A Study in Productivity* (Montpelier, 1946), p. 10; Ira Allen, *The Natural and Political History of the State of Vermont* (London, 1798), p. 338.
19. *MF&G*, 1872, app. 2, p. 4; *VF&G*, 1873–74, app., p. 54.
20. Petition of the Inhabitants of the Town of Shrewsbury (October 16, 1828), VSP, vol. 60, p. 114.
21. John Whittemore, "The Autobiography of John Whittemore," *Vermont Historical Society Proceedings* 6 (December 1938): 325.
22. William Bacon, "Unenclosed Lands," *Cultivator* 5 (February 1848): 58–59. See *Maine Farmer*, April 21, 1877; Cronon, *Changes in the Land*, pp. 134–137; Ernest L. Bogart, *Peacham: The Story of a Vermont Hill Town* (Montpelier, 1948), p. 307; *MAG*, 1878, p. 160; *VAG*, 1883–84, pp. 98–99; Hayes, *History of the Town of Rockingham*, p. 98.
23. Bacon, "Unenclosed Lands," pp. 58–59. See *Maine Farmer*, April 21, 1877.
24. Moses Greenleaf, *A Survey of the State of Maine* (1829; reprint, Augusta, 1970), pp. 181–182.
25. *Maine Farmer*, February 26 and June 3, 1876; January 27, 1877.
26. Bacon, "Unenclosed Lands," pp. 58–59; Warren Brown, *History of the*

Town of Hampton Falls (Manchester, N.H., 1900), p. 518; *Maine Farmer,* February 26 and June 3, 1876; January 27 and April 21, 1877; Steven Hahn, *The Roots of Southern Populism: Yeoman Farmers and the Transformation of the Georgia Upcountry, 1850–1890* (New York, 1983), pp. 60–63.

27. Clarence A. Day, "A History of the Blueberry Industry in Washington County," typescript, n.d., pp. 1–5, Special Collections Department, University of Maine; J. Bailey Moore, *History of the Town of Candia* (Manchester, N.H., 1893), pp. 279–280.

28. *Maine Industrial Journal,* May 16, 1884; Williamson, *History of the State of Maine,* 2: 550; *MeBA,* 1868, p. 117.

29. Hemenway, *Vermont Historical Gazetteer,* 3: 690.

30. Ibid., p. 1002.

31. Ibid., p. 690; Somers, *History of Lancaster,* p. 102; Crawford, *Oramel Crawford,* p. 188.

32. Somers, *History of Lancaster,* p. 102.

33. Petition of Ruben Gregg (January 1843), box 281, chap. 173, MeSA; Petition of the Inhabitants of the Town of Shrewsbury (October 16, 1828).

34. *Newburyport Herald,* in *New England Farmer* 7 (April 1855): 188.

35. *MeF&G,* 1916, p. 13; *Maine Farmer,* November 4, 1836; "Second Report of the Fish Commissioners," in *MeBA,* 1868, p. 105; Robert E. Dunbar and George F. Dow, *Nobleboro, Maine: A History* (Nobleboro, 1988), p. 53.

36. Petition of David Webster (June 8, 1833), box 19, NHRMA.

37. *Maine Farmer,* March 23, p. 65. See ibid., May 3, 1866; Sibley, *History of the Town of Union,* p. 424; *MeBA,* 1865, pp. 158–159.

38. Petition of Joel Smith; "Act to Prevent the Destruction of Fish in the Town of Lincoln" (February 16, 1824), chap. 110, MSA. See "Act to Prevent the Destruction of . . . Pickerel or Pike . . . in the Towns of Braintree, Canton and Randolph" (January 31, 1823), chap. 54, MSA.

39. S. Dill, in *Maine Farmer,* May 23, 1867.

40. Petition of Phillip Sweetser (May 25, 1828), box 18, NHRMA; untitled (May 31, 1828), ibid.; Petition of Samuel Blackman (October 18, 1821), VSP, 55: 238; Petition of Daniel Warned (October 14, 1826), ibid., p. 186.

41. Untitled (May 31, 1828), box 18, NHRMA; Petition of Turner Marshal (March 3, 1853), box 278, chap. 123, MeSA; Petition of Samuel Blackman (October 18, 1821), VSP, 55: 238; Petition of Daniel Warned (October 14, 1826).

42. Petition of David Gardner (October 13, 1838), VSP, 65: 139. See Petition of Joseph Appleton [ca. November 23–24, 1836], box 21, NHRMA; Petition of John Reed (October 17, 1822), VSP, 56: 191; Petition of Daniel Warned (October 14, 1826); Petition of Turner Marshal (March 3, 1853), box 278, chap. 123, MeSA.

43. Robert E. Shalhope, "Republicanism and Early American Historiography," *William and Mary Quarterly* 39 (April 1984): 335.

44. Roth, *Democratic Dilemma*, pp. 41, 79.

45. Petition of Jairus Hall (October 14, 1833), VSP, 62: 217; Petition of Dorartus Woorster (October 31, 1832), VSP, 63: 27.

46. Untitled (May 31, 1828), box 18, NHRMA. Meetinghouse Pond covers thirty to forty acres.

47. Petition of James Parker (June 1829), box 18, NHRMA.

48. Ibid.

49. Petition of Phillip Sweetser (May 25, 1828).

50. Petition of Jesse Cone (October 13, 1829), VSP, 61: 22. See "Two Brooks" (Bridgewater) [ca. 1839], box 22, NHRMA; Petition of J. A. Varney (May 28, 1839), ibid.; "Petition to Prevent Damages by Fire in Bradford Mill Village" (June 1835), box 21, NHRMA.

51. Petitions of James Parker (June 1829) and Hyman Bent (April 8, 1828), box 18, NHRMA. See "Act to Prevent the Destruction of . . . Pickerel or Pike in . . . Braintree, Canton and Randolph" (January 31, 1823), chap. 54, MSA.

52. Petition of Dorartus Woorster (October 31, 1832).

53. Petition of Joseph Chapman (October 7, 1828), VSP, 60: 87. Chapman's petition was granted.

54. Petition of William Weed (October 10, 1829), VSP, 61: 13.

3. NATURE IN THE NEW AGRARIAN LANDSCAPE

1. *NHA*, 1873, p. 434.

2. W. R. French, *A History of Turner, Maine* (Portland, 1887), pp. 70, 73, 75; Jasper Jacob Stahl, *History of Old Broad Bay and Waldoboro*, vol. 2 (Portland, Maine, 1956), pp. 215, 236–237, 241; Clarence Albert Day, "Pleasant River Papers," typescript, n.d., p. 37, Bangor Public Library; Lura Beam, *A Maine Hamlet* (New York, 1957), p. 58; David P. Szatmary, *Shays' Rebellion: The Making of an Agrarian Insurrection* (Amherst, Mass., 1980), p. 12; Christopher Clark, *The Roots of Rural Capitalism: Western Massachusetts, 1780–1860* (Ithaca, N.Y., 1990), pp. 163–176, 220–224.

3. *MeBA*, 1863, p. 64; Harold Fisher Wilson, *The Hill Country of Northern New England: Its Social and Economic History, 1790–1930* (New York, 1936), pp. 29, 31; Ernest L. Bogart, *Peacham: The Story of a Vermont Hill Town* (Montpelier, 1948), p. 314; *Maine Industrial Journal*, December 10, 1886; *Maine Farmer*, June 8, 1882.

4. Paul W. Gates, "Two Hundred Years of Farming in Gilsum," *Histori-*

cal New Hampshire 33 (Spring 1978): 2; Richard L. Bushman, "Family Security in the Transition from Farm to City, 1750–1850," *Journal of Family History* 6 (Fall 1981): 240; Day, "Pleasant River Papers," p. 37; Beam, *Maine Hamlet,* p. 5; Percy Wells Bidwell, "Rural Economy in New England at the Beginning of the Nineteenth Century," *Transactions of the Connecticut Academy of Arts and Sciences* 20 (April 1916): 365; Collamer M. Abbot, "'Gramp' Abbot's Life: Farming in Central Vermont, 1865– 1913," *Vermont History* 39 (Winter 1971): 34.

5. Bidwell, "Rural Economy in New England," p. 351; Edward N. Torbert, "The Evolution of Land Utilization in Lebanon, New Hampshire," *Geographical Review* 25 (1935): 217; Frank M. Bryan, "Vermont: The Politics of Ruralism" (Ph.D. diss., University of Connecticut, 1970), p. 46; Bogart, *Peacham,* p. 72; *Maine Farmer,* July 18, 1889; *VAG,* 1885–86, p. 159; J. E. Carrigan, *The Agriculture and Forestry of Vermont* (Burlington, 1931), p. 1.

6. *VAG,* 1883–84, p. 366.

7. *VAG,* 1891–92, p. 137. See James Whitelaw, quoted in Edward Miller and Frederic P. Wells, *History of Ryegate, Vermont* (St. Johnsbury, 1913), p. 36; Lewis D. Stilwell, "Migration from Vermont (1776–1860)," *Proceedings of the Vermont Historical Society* 5, no. 2 (1937): 98–99; *NHA,* 1872, p. 352.

8. *NHA,* 1873, p. 418. For another regional perspective, see Steven Hahn, *The Roots of Southern Populism: Yeoman Farmers and the Transformation of the Georgia Upcountry, 1850–1890* (New York, 1983), p. 52.

9. Albert G. Comings, *Address before the Connecticut River Valley Society, Lebanon, New Hampshire* (Hanover, N.H., 1853), p. 11; Wilson, *Hill Country,* p. 46; Carolyn Merchant, *Ecological Revolutions: Nature, Gender, and Science in New England* (Chapel Hill, N.C., 1989), pp. 112, 150, 174–176, 184–188; *NHA,* 1881, p. 294; *New England Farmer* 6 (June 1854): 280; *Maine Farmer,* March 23 and September 21, 1872.

10. *Maine Farmer,* December 14, 1878.

11. *New England Farmer* 7 (March 1855): 118; Robert A. Gross, "Culture and Cultivation: Agriculture and Society in Thoreau's Concord," *Journal of American History* 69 (June 1982): 46–47, 50, 53.

12. *NHA,* 1881, p. 292.

13. *Maine Farmer,* November 4, 1876. See ibid., December 27, 1866; November 23, 1872; April 21, 1877; August 24, 1878; June 8, 1882; *New England Farmer* 6 (April 1854): 167; 5 (January 1853): 13; *VAG,* 1879–80, p. 124; *NHA,* 1889–90, pp. 234, 237; *Granite Monthly* 55 (December 1923): 573; Gross, "Culture and Cultivation," p. 53; Merchant, *Ecological Revolutions,* pp. 122, 127, 204–207.

14. *Maine Farmer,* November 4, 1876.

15. Alan Taylor, *Liberty Men and Great Proprietors: The Revolutionary Settlement on the Maine Frontier, 1760–1820* (Chapel Hill, N.C., 1990), p. 77; *Maine Farmer,* November 4, 1876; February 17, 1877; June 8, 1882.

16. *Maine Farmer,* December 14, 1878; July 4, 1889. See *MeBA,* 1892, p. 119; *Maine Farmer,* January 7, 1864; December 2, 1876; April 26, 1883; July 4, 1889; *Rural Vermonter,* September 20, 1886; *Burlington Free Press,* March 11, 1890; *Journal of the Proceedings of the Maine State Grange, December 21–23, 1897* (Augusta, 1898), p. 7; *MeBA,* 1887, p. 88; *NHA,* 1873, p. 204.

17. H. N. Muller, *From Ferment to Fatigue? 1870–1900: A New Look at the Neglected Winter of Vermont* (Burlington, 1984), p. 2; *NHA,* 1873, p. 437; *MAG,* 1868, p. 157; William L. Taylor, "The Nineteenth Century Hill Town: Images and Reality," *Historical New Hampshire,* pp. 297–299; *Maine Farmer,* October 24, 1874; August 24, 1878; May 14, 1885; *NHA,* 1879, pp. 7–9; *Burlington Free Press,* January 8, 1870.

18. W. L. Eaton, "Agricultural Economy," *Cultivator* 7 (February 1850): 82. See *Maine Farmer,* February 26, 1876; June 26, 1880.

19. Gross, "Culture and Cultivation," p. 54.

20. Carrigan, *Agriculture and Forestry of Vermont,* p. 4; A. B. Valentine, *Report of the Commissioner of Agricultural and Manufacturing Interests of the State of Vermont* (Rutland, 1890), pp. 12–13.

21. Penny E. Hamlet, "Preprogressivism: Farm Activism in Vermont from 1870 to 1900" (Honors thesis, Middlebury College, 1986), p. 18; *VAG,* 1898, p. 131; 1903, pp. 47–49; 1910, pp. 106–108.

22. Bert M. Fernald, *Maine Canning Industry* (Portland, 1902), pp. 4–8; Mary M. Grow, "History," in *China, Maine: Bicentennial History,* ed. Marion T. Van Strien (Weeks Mills, Maine, 1975), p. 222; *MeBA,* 1881, pp. 122–135; *Maine Farmer,* July 10, 1869; James Berry Vickery, *A History of the Town of Unity, Maine* (Manchester, Maine, 1954), p. 142.

23. *Maine Farmer,* March 2, 16, 1882. See ibid., January 24, 1889; Fernald, *Maine Canning Industry,* pp. 4–6; *MeBA,* 1881, pp. 122–133; Grow, "History," p. 222.

24. *MAG,* 1867, sec. 2, pp. 8, 10. See *Maine Farmer,* February 17, 1872; *VAG,* 1909, p. 145; *New England Farmer* 6 (February 1854): 64; *Vermont Family Visitor* 1 (August 1845): 90; *MAG,* 1867, pp. 32–33; Wilson, *Hill Country,* p. 60.

25. *NHA,* 1887–88, pp. 68–69; *VAG,* 1883–84, pp. 362–363; Paul Glenn Munyon, *A Reassessment of New England Agriculture in the Last Thirty Years of the Nineteenth Century: New Hampshire, A Case Study* (New York, 1978), pp. 47, 50; Norman W. Smith, "A Mature Frontier: The New Hampshire Economy, 1790–1850," *Historical New Hampshire* 24, no. 3 (1969): 14–15.

26. Bryan, "Vermont: The Politics of Ruralism," pp. 60–61; Munyon, *Reassessment of New England Agriculture*, p. 42.

27. Wilson, *Hill Country*, p. 26; Muller, *From Ferment to Fatigue?* p. 1; Gates, "Two Hundred Years of Farming in Gilsum," pp. 1, 22.

28. Hal S. Barron, *Those Who Stayed Behind: Rural Society in Nineteenth-Century New England* (New York, 1984). See Bogart, *Peacham*, pp. 311, 350; *MAG*, 1879, pp. 12–13; C. F. Clayton and L. J. Peet, *Land Utilization as a Basis of Rural Economic Organization* (Burlington, Vt., 1933), p. 19; Muller, *From Ferment to Fatigue?* pp. 4–5.

29. Michael M. Bell, "Did New England Go Downhill?" *Geographical Review* 79 (October 1989): 456–457, 460–461, 463. See Muller, *From Ferment to Fatigue?* pp. 10, 16–17; Edwin C. Rozwenc, *Agricultural Policies in Vermont, 1860–1945* (Montpelier, 1981).

30. *New England Farmer* 2 (November 9, 1850): 365; *NHA*, 1873, pp. 194, 434–435, 441, 462; 1874, pp. 370–371; 1889–90, p. 315.

31. Z. E. Jameson, "Vermont as Home," *VAG*, 1872, p. 562. See *VAG*, 1895, p. 125.

32. Muller, *From Ferment to Fatigue?*; *Maine Farmer*, November 11, 1871; November 23, 1872; *VAG*, 1875–76, p. 382; J. Bailey Moore, *History of the Town of Candia* (Manchester, N.H., 1893), pp. 254–255.

33. *VAG*, 1872, p. 545. See *Maine Farmer*, October 24, 1874; May 14, 1885; *VAG*, 1877, p. 89; *NHA*, 1873, p. 203; *Burlington Free Press*, March 31, 1873.

34. Frederic P. Wells, *History of Newbury, Vermont* (St. Johnsbury, 1902), pp. 60–61; Stilwell, "Migration from Vermont," pp. 108–109; J. Q. Bittinger, *History of Haverhill, N.H.* (Haverhill, 1888), p. 361; Grow, "History," pp. 14, 244–245; Mitchell, "Community in Transition," pp. 23, 64–65; Clark, *Roots of Rural Capitalism*, pp. 224–227; Gates, "Two Hundred Years of Farming in Gilsum," pp. 3, 12; Stahl, *History of Old Broad Bay and Waldoboro*, 2: 80, 132; Francis W. Underwood, *Quabbin: The Story of a Small Town, with Outlooks on Puritan Life* (Boston, 1893), pp. 18–19.

35. *MAG*, 1879, p. 11. See Taylor, "Nineteenth Century Hill Town," pp. 287, 297–298, 301; *NHA*, 1889–90, p. 316; *Burlington Free Press*, March 31, 1873; Wilson, *Hill Country*, pp. 45, 146; Clayton and Peet, *Land Utilization*, p. 19.

36. Abby Maria Hemenway, ed., *Vermont Historical Gazetteer*, 5 vols. (Burlington, 1868–1891), 3: 756.

37. Hal S. Barron, "Rediscovering the Majority: The New Rural History of the Nineteenth-Century North," *Historical Methods* 19 (Fall 1986): 143; Clark, *Roots of Rural Capitalism*.

38. Hemenway, *Vermont Historical Gazetteer*, 4: 823.

39. *MeBA,* 1892, p. 121; 1857, pp. 50–51.

40. Reverend L. S. Rowland, "The Social and Intellectual Life of the Farmer," *MAG,* 1880, pp. 110–126.

41. Edwin C. Rozwenc, "The Group Basis of Vermont Farm Politics, 1870–1945," *Vermont History* 25 (October 1957): 270. See *NHA,* 1875, pp. 7–9; 1887–88, pp. 63–64; T. D. Seymour Bassett, "Urban Penetration of Rural Vermont, 1840–1880" (Ph.D. diss., Harvard University, 1952), p. 66.

42. *Our Agricola* 2 (November 2, 1876): 174.

43. *Maine Farmer,* December 4, 1835; *Granite Monthly* 6 (September 1883): 379–381; *NHA,* 1877, p. 131.

44. *NHA,* 1873, p. 191; Wilson, *Hill Country;* Bassett, "Urban Penetration of Rural Vermont," pp. 2–3, 64–66.

45. *Vermont Watchman and State Journal,* April 25, 1877.

46. See, for instance, *Burlington Free Press,* November 12, 1848; *New England Farmer* 3 (April 1852): 185; *VAG,* 1875–76, pp. 381–382; *Vermont Family Visitor* 1 (August 1845): 90.

47. *NHA,* 1880, p. 187. See Silas H. Jenison, *An Address Delivered at the . . . Addison County Fair* (n.p., 1845), p. 10; *VAG,* 1873–74, pp. 610–611; *Maine Farmer,* February 13, 1841; *New England Farmer* 6 (June 1854): 280.

48. *New England Farmer* 3 (March 15, 1851): 100–101; *NHA,* 1880, p. 186; Merchant, *Ecological Revolutions,* p. 149.

49. See *MAG,* 1865, p. 95; *Maine Farmer,* May 13, 1876.

50. Sally McMurry, "Who Read the Agricultural Journals? Evidence from Chenango County, New York, 1839–1865," *Agricultural History* 63 (Fall 1989): 1–3, 18; *Maine Farmer,* February 28, 1867.

51. *Burlington Free Press,* December 28, 1868.

52. *MAG,* 1865, p. 65; *Maine Farmer,* May 13, 1876, February 24, 1877.

53. *VAG,* 1887–88, p. 162. See *Cultivator* 5 (February 1849): 44.

54. *VAG,* 1875–76, p. 454. See *VAG,* 1883–84, p. 206.

55. *Maine Farmer,* December 5 and 19, 1874. See ibid., May 13, 1876; *VAG,* 1883–84, p. 207.

56. *VAG,* 1883–84, p. 14.

57. Donald Worster, "History as Natural History: An Essay on Theory and Method," *Pacific Historical Review* 53 (February 1984): 3. See *VAG,* 1875–76, pp. 394–395; *Cultivator* 5 (February 1849): 44.

58. *VAG,* 1875–76, pp. 455, 466.

59. *New England Farmer* 1 (July 21, 1849): 251.

60. *Cultivator* 6 (July 1849): 208.

61. *Burlington Free Press,* August 31, 1870; *NHA,* 1885–86, pp. 21–22, 24. See *VAG,* 1881–82, p. 352.

62. *Cultivator* 6 (July 1849): 208–209.

63. *MAG,* 1851, p. 513.

64. *Maine Farmer,* October 13, 1864; January 6, 1872.

65. Z. E. Jameson, "Management of Swamp Lands," *VAG,* 1873–74, p. 544.

66. Ibid., pp. 544–545.

67. *American Agriculturist* 16 (June 1857): 131. See also *VAG,* 1881–82, p. 355; Bell, "Did New England Go Downhill?" p. 461.

68. *Patrons' Rural,* December 19, 1884.

69. *New England Farmer,* March 9, 1872.

70. *NHA,* 1879, p. 9. See *Maine Farmer,* January 6, 1872; *Yankee Farmer* 1 (March 30, 1835): 50.

71. *MAG,* 1850, p. 290; *NHA,* 1887–88, p. 67. See Joseph L. Hills, "The Conservation of the Soils in Vermont," in *Report of the Commission on Conservation of Natural Resources of the State of Vermont, 1911–1912* (Rutland, 1912), p. 13.

72. J. W. Seely, "Draining Marshes and Ponds," *Cultivator* 2 (October 1845): 305.

73. *New England Farmer* 5 (November 1853): 510. See *Farmer's Monthly Visitor* 5 (October 31, 1843): 154.

74. *New England Farmer* 5 (November 1853): 510. See ibid., 1 (January 6, 1849): 27; *Burlington Free Press,* January 29, 1855; *Cultivator* 7 (August 1850): 257–258.

75. Jameson, "Management of Swamp Lands," p. 553.

76. C. H. Joyce, *An Address Delivered before the Farmers and Mechanics Club* (n.p., 1870), p. 16. See *MeBA,* 1866, p. 19.

77. *Maine Farmer,* June 1, 1872; September 14, 1899; *NHA,* 1872, pp. 354–355; *Journal of the Proceedings of the Maine State Grange, December 21–23, 1915* (Lewiston, 1915), pp. 117–118; *MeBA,* 1883, p. 111; 1913, p. 147.

78. *MeBA,* 1913, p. 147. See *Atlantic Monthly* 80 (1897): 74–83; *Vermont Watchman and State Journal,* March 14, 1883, August 13, 1884; *Maine Farmer,* August 29, 1874; September 8, 1881; June 10, 1886; July 8, 1897; September 14, 1899; January 25, 1906.

79. David D. Brodeur, "Evolution of the New England Town Common: 1630–1966," *Professional Geographer* 19 (November 1967): 314.

80. *Maine Farmer,* June 1, 1872.

81. *MAG,* 1867, p. 10.

82. *Maine Farmer,* February 1, 1873.

83. Rowland Robinson, quoted in Paul A. Eschholz, "Land of a Thousand Hills: Literary Images of the Vermont Landscape, 1865–1945," in *Vermont Landscape Images, 1776–1976,* ed. William C. Lipke and Philip N. Grime (Burlington, 1976), p. 16.

84. *Maine Farmer,* October 10, 1868.

85. Ibid., February 25, 1864; July 13, 1865.

86. *MeBA,* 1866, pp. 18–19; 1913, p. 15; *Maine Farmer,* September 14, 1899.

87. *MeBA,* 1869, p. 69.

88. Jay E. Cantor, "The Landscape of Change: Views of Rural New England, 1790–1865," *Magazine Antiques* 109 (April 1976): 776–777; *MeBA,* 1892, p. 173; Hemenway, *Vermont Historical Gazetteer,* 3: 311.

89. Lipke and Grime, *Vermont Landscape Images,* p. 10.

90. Ibid.; *Maine Farmer,* February 25, 1864; July 13, 1865.

91. Churchill and Zadock Thompson, quoted in Hemenway, *Vermont Historical Gazetteer,* 3: 765–767. See *Farmer's Monthly Visitor* 4 (September 1842): 141; *Maine Farmer,* March 21, 1868.

92. *Farmer's Monthly Visitor* 6 (October 31, 1844): 158. See ibid., 6 (October 31, 1844): 156–157.

93. *Cultivator* 2 (October 1845): 309.

94. *VAG,* 1912, p. 21.

95. *Vermont Watchman and State Journal,* June 18, 1879. See *NHA,* 1871, p. 347; *Cultivator* 7 (October 1850): 341; Donald Worster, *Nature's Economy: A History of Ecological Ideas* (Cambridge, Mass., 1985), p. 11.

96. *Cultivator* 7 (October 1850): 341. See ibid., 2 (October 1845): 309; *NHA,* 1871, p. 346.

97. *Vermont Watchman and State Journal,* September 17, 1884. See *NHA,* 1881, p. 278.

98. *MAG,* 1865, p. 95.

99. *Vermont Watchman and State Journal,* November 27, 1878. See ibid., September 4, 1878; June 4 and September 17, 1884; *VAG,* 1872, pp. 323–324; *MAG,* 1865, pp. 102–103; *Cultivator* 5 (June 1848): 195.

100. *VAG,* 1872, p. 324; *MAG,* 1865, p. 104.

101. *NHA,* 1872, p. 324; *MAG,* 1865, p. 104.

102. Audubon quoted in *MAG,* 1865, p. 98.

103. *Cultivator* 7 (October 1850): 341.

104. *Vermont Watchman and State Journal,* September 17, 1884. See *Maine Farmer,* June 1, 1839; *MAG,* 1865, p. 100.

105. *Vermont Watchman and State Journal,* September 17, 1884; January 15, 1879.

106. *MAG,* 1865, p. 99–100; *Vermont Watchman and State Journal,* January 15, 1879.

107. Edward A. Samuels, *Our Northern and Eastern Birds* (New York, 1883), pp. 96–97.

108. Fairbanks quoted in *Vermont Watchman and State Journal,* May 14, 1879.

109. Edward Howe Forbush, *Birds of Massachusetts and Other New England States* (Norwood, Mass., 1927), p. 278. See Arthur Cleveland Bent, *Life Histories of North American Woodpeckers* (Washington, D.C., 1939), pp. 126–135.

110. Robin W. Doughty, *Feathers, Fashions, and Bird Preservation: A Study in*

NOTES TO PAGES 83–88

Natural Protection (Berkeley, Calif., 1975), pp. 31, 152. On New England, see Edward Howe Forbush, *A History of the Game Birds, Wild-Fowl and Shore Birds of Massachusetts and Adjacent States* (Norwood, Mass., 1912), pp. 497–498.

111. Oliver H. Orr Jr., *Saving American Birds: T. Gilbert Pearson and the Founding of the Audubon Movement* (Gainesville, Fla., 1992); *Burlington Free Press,* February 9, 1887.

112. *MF&G,* 1908, p. 8.

113. *MF&G,* 1907, pp. 44, 47–50.

114. *MF&G,* 1903, pp. 141, 143.

115. *Rural Vermonter,* June 11, 1886.

116. See Doughty, *Feathers, Fashions, and Bird Preservation,* p. 59, for the founding principles of the first Audubon Society.

117. *NHA,* 1873, pp. 309–310. See *NHA,* 1883, pp. 222–233.

118. *VAG,* 1909, p. 106.

119. *VAG,* 1881–82, p. 359.

120. *Maine Farmer,* January 11, 1879.

121. Bidwell, "Rural Economy in New England," p. 335.

122. *Cultivator* 2 (December 1845), p. 385; Bidwell, "Rural Economy in New England," p. 335.

123. *Rural Vermonter,* April 29, May 6, 1887.

124. *New England Farmer* 2 (March 2, 1850): 76.

125. *Burlington Free Press,* August 15, 1868; May 8, 1869; *NHA,* 1884, p. 80; *Cultivator* 4 (August 1848): 252; *New England Farmer* 1 (December 9, 1848): 5.

126. *MAG,* 1864, pp. 208–213.

127. *NHA,* 1872, p. 367; *New England Farmer* 1 (March 31, 1849): 130; *Massachusetts Ploughman,* in *Burlington Free Press,* December 17, 1877; *MAG,* 1882, p. 277; *Maine Farmer,* January 20, 1872.

128. *Farmer's Monthly Visitor* 4 (September 30, 1842): 127; *MAG,* 1851, p. 512; 1875, p. 144; 1884, pp. 131, 142; 1887, p. 62; *NHA,* 1877, p. 131; *New England Farmer,* January 20, 1872; *Cultivator* 6 (June 1849): 171; *VAG,* 1908, p. 90.

129. *Rural Vermonter,* April 22, 1887.

130. *NHA,* 1889–90, p. 284. See *NHA,* 1884, p. 88; *Maine Farmer,* July 21, 1871.

131. *NHA,* 1884, p. 88.

132. *Burlington Free Press,* March 12, 1870; *MAG,* 1884, pp. 142–144.

133. Hiram A. Cutting, *The Forests of Vermont* (Montpelier, 1886), p. 20; *NHA,* 1889–90, p. 283; *Maine Farmer,* December 25, 1862.

134. *Maine Farmer,* January 11, 1879; February 14, 1889; *MAG,* 1884, p. 130; *Cultivator* 4 (August 1848): 253; *NHA,* 1877, p. 132.

289

135. *New England Farmer,* June 17, 1871. See *MAG,* 1851, pp. 513–514.
136. *Rural Vermonter,* April 22, 1887; *NHA,* 1890–91, p. 169.
137. Thomas R. Cox, Robert S. Maxwell, Phillip Drennon Thomas, and Joseph J. Malone, *This Well-Wooded Land: Americans and Their Forests from Colonial Times to the Present* (Lincoln, Neb., 1985), p. 146.
138. *VAG,* 1873–74, pp. 443, 501; *MAG,* 1887, p. 63; *NHA,* 1890–91, p. 162; *New England Farmer* 1 (December 9, 1848): 1–2; *Cultivator* 2 (December 1845), p. 385; *Maine Farmer,* January 28 and April 14, 1864.
139. *Vermont Watchman and State Journal,* April 25, 1877; *Maine Farmer,* May 12, 1881.
140. *Farmer's Monthly Visitor* 6 (April 30, 1844): 59; *MeBA,* 1859, p. 40.
141. *Burlington Free Press,* May 7, 16, 1849; *VAG,* 1873–74, p. 624; *Maine Farmer,* May 8 and October 2, 1835; February 25, 1864; July 13, 1865; February 8, 1873.
142. Lipke and Grime, *Vermont Landscape Images,* p. 10.

4. COMMON STEWARDSHIP AND PRIVATE FORESTS

1. *MeBA,* 1869, p. 82.
2. Ralph Widner, ed., *Forests and Forestry in the American States* (Washington, D.C, 1968); Philip Ayers, "Forest Problems in New Hampshire," *Forestry Quarterly,* July 1903, box 2, no. 34, SPNHF.
3. Charles S. Sargent, quoted in *MAG,* 1887, p. 52. See Donald Pisani, "Forests and Conservation, 1865–1890," *Journal of American History* 72 (September 1985): 340–358.
4. Samuel P. Hays, *Conservation and the Gospel of Efficiency: The Progressive Conservation Movement, 1890–1920* (1959; reprint, New York, 1969), pp. 127, 141–146; Steven Fox, *The American Conservation Movement: John Muir and His Legacy* (Madison, Wis., 1985), pp. 107–147.
5. Francis LeRoy Harvey, "Prof. Harvey's Paper," in *Forestry Convention* (Bangor, 1888), pamphlet, Bangor Public Library, Maine.
6. *Maine Farmer,* January 27, 1872; *VAG,* 1885–86, pp. 157–158; *New England Farmer* 1 (December 9, 1848): 5; (March 17, 1849): 100; *MAG,* 1854, pp. 103–104; A. N. Somers, *History of Lancaster, New Hampshire* (Concord, 1899), pp. 11, 111; Lyman Simpson Hayes, *History of the Town of Rockingham, Vermont* (1898; reprint, Bellows Falls, Vt., 1907), p. 92; Warren Brown, *History of the Town of Hampton Falls, New Hampshire* (Manchester, 1900), p. 518; Thomas R. Cox, Robert S. Maxwell, Phillip Drennon Thomas, and Joseph J. Malone, *This Well-Wooded Land: Americans and Their Forests from Colonial Times to the Present* (Lincoln, Neb.,

1985), chap. 3; Michael Williams, *Americans and Their Forests* (New York, 1989), pp. 55–80.

7. *Vermont Family Visitor* 1 (October 1845): 142; *Cultivator* 4 (August 1848): 253; *Burlington Free Press*, March 16, 1864; *Maine Farmer*, January 27, 1872; December 20, 1873.

8. *VAG*, 1873–74, p. 444; 1881–82, p. 356; *Burlington Free Press*, February 23, 1883; *New England Farmer* 3 (January 4, 1851): 9–10; Pisani, "Forests and Conservation," p. 344; Stephen Pyne, *Fire in America: A Cultural History of Wildland and Rural Fire* (Princeton, 1982), pp. 39, 54, 56; *NHA*, 1872, p. 386; *MAG*, 1882, pp. 273, 278.

9. *NHA*, 1873, p. 440. See *NHFoC*, 1887, p. 7.

10. *VAG*, 1881–82, pp. 256–257; *Maine Farmer*, January 11, 1879.

11. *VAG*, 1891–92, pp. 122–123. See *Timberman*, September 24, 1892, "Maine Forests and Forestry," U.S. Forest Service Clipping File, Forest History Society, Durham, N.C. (hereafter cited as USFS); *MAG*, 1882, p. 274.

12. *NHA*, 1873, p. 445. See Samuel H. Boardman, *The Climate, Soil, Physical Resources, and Agricultural Capabilities of the State of Maine* (Washington, D.C., 1884), p. 29; Lt. Col. Edward Burr, *The Influence of Forests on Stream Flow in the Merrimac River Basin [of] New Hampshire and Massachusetts*, 1910, 62d Cong., 1st sess., HD no. 9 (Washington, D.C., 1911), pp. 9, 15–16; *Rural Vermonter*, July 29, 1887.

13. *New England Farmer*, January 5, 1901; William Chapin, "Forestry and Maple Sugar Making," *VAG*, 1887–88, p. 322. See Alfred K. Chittenden, *Forest Conditions of Northern New Hampshire* (Washington, D.C., 1905), pp. 20–21, box 7, no. 5, SPNHF; *Burlington Free Press*, November 7, 1884; September 21, 1891.

14. J. G. Jack, "Notes on Forest Conditions in Vermont," typescript, ca. 1901, pp. 1–2, "Vermont," USFS.

15. Ibid., pp. 6, 12–13, 22; *VAG*, 1900, p. 62; A. F. Hawes, "Short-Sighted Lumbering in Vermont," in *Report of the Commission on Conservation of Natural Resources of the State of Vermont, 1911–1912* (Rutland, 1912), p. 15; *NHA*, 1883, p. 76; *Vermont Watchman and State Journal*, March 14, 1883; *Burlington Free Press*, September 21, 1891.

16. Harvey, "Prof. Harvey's Paper."

17. *MeBA*, 1869, p. 67.

18. *Maine Farmer*, January 11, 1879. See William C. Lipke and Philip N. Grime, eds., *Vermont Landscape Images, 1776–1976* (Burlington, 1976), p. 10.

19. *New England Farmer*, June 17, 1871; *Vermont Watchman and State Journal*, May 10, 1882.

20. George Perkins Marsh, in *Cultivator* 4 (September 1848): 283.

21. *Burlington Free Press,* July 30, 1883.

22. Pisani, "Forests and Conservation," pp. 352–353; *Burlington Free Press,* February 28, 1857; March 16, 1864.

23. *MAG,* 1875, p. 251; Abby Maria Hemenway, *Vermont Historical Gazetteer,* 5 vols. (Burlington, 1868–1891), 3: 755.

24. *NHA,* 1872, p. 381. See *VAG,* 1881–82, p. 362; Roderick Nash, *Wilderness and the American Mind* (1967; reprint, New Haven, 1982), pp. 23–43; John R. Stilgoe, *Common Landscape of America, 1580 to 1845* (New Haven, 1982), pp. 10–11; *New England Farmer,* June 17, 1871.

25. *MeBA,* 1869, pp. 73–77; Noah Webster and George Perkins Marsh, in *MAG,* 1875, p. 252; George Perkins Marsh, *Man and Nature* (New York, 1867), pp. 140–155, 197–209.

26. C. H. Hitchcock, *The Geology of New Hampshire* (Concord, 1874), p. 321; *NHFoC,* 1885, pp. 15–19. See George Perkins Marsh, *Report . . . on the Artificial Propagation of Fish* (Burlington, Vt., 1857); *Burlington Free Press,* April 13, 1875; November 7, 1884; *Maine Farmer,* October 10 and 24, 1868; November 8, 1879; *New England Farmer* 1 (September 1, 1848): 302; *MAG,* 1875, p. 146; *Rural Vermonter,* October 15, 1886; Jamie H. Eves, "'Shrunk to a Comparative Rivulet': Deforestation, Stream Flow, and Rural Milling in 19th-Century Maine," *Technology and Culture* 33 (January 1992): 38–65.

27. *NHFoC,* 1885, pp. 21, 23; Hitchcock, *Geology of New Hampshire,* pp. 123–124; *Vermont Watchman and State Journal,* June 10, 1885.

28. Ward Shepard, *Forests and Floods* (Washington, D.C., 1928), pp. 5–7, 11. See Gordon B. Dodds, "The Stream-Flow Controversy: A Conservation Turning Point," *Journal of American History* 56 (June 1969): 60; *NHA,* 1883, pp. 73–74; *Maine Farmer,* January 6 and June 21, 1872; *MAG,* 1887, pp. 51–53; Cox et al., *Well-Wooded Land,* p. 149; and especially *New England Farmer,* October 19, 1872.

29. *Maine Farmer,* January 24, 1889. See *Amherst Record,* January 25, 1901, "New England Forests & Forestry," USFS; *NHA,* 1883, p. 82; *Vermont Watchman and State Journal,* November 22, 1882; *Burlington Free Press,* February 23, 1883.

30. *Vermont Watchman and State Journal,* November 5, 1884. See *Boston Evening Transcript,* May 25, 1915, "Massachusetts Forests & Forestry," USFS; Cox et al., *Well-Wooded Land,* p. 169.

31. *NHFoC,* 1915–16, p. 86.

32. *NHFoC,* 1885, p. 9.

33. *NHFoC,* 1900, pp. 3–4, 20.

34. *Westborough Chronicle,* April 27, 1901; *Boston Evening Transcript,* January 10, 1902, "Massachusetts Forestry Association," USFS; *Boston Evening*

Transcript, February 16 and March 25, 1903, "Massachusetts State Forester," USFS.

35. *Montpelier Watchman,* October 23, 1901, "Vermont Forests and Forestry," USFS.

36. *Vermont Watchman and State Journal,* November 22, 1882; January 3, 1883; November 5, 1884; *Burlington Free Press,* July 30, 1883; September 19 and November 7, 1884; April 28, 1885; *VAG,* 1906, pp. 45–46; 1907, pp. 17–19; Robin W. Winks, *Frederick Billings: A Life* (New York, 1991), pp. 295–297; Perry Merrill, ed., *A Half Century of Forestry, 1920–1970* (Montpelier, 1959), pp. 8–9.

37. *VAG,* 1908, p. 89; 1910, pp. 94, 211; *NHFoC,* 1900, pp. 4–5; 1909–10, p. 91; 1915–16, p. 59; *Maine Farmer,* May 11, 1872; *Boston Herald,* July 20, 1897, "Massachusetts Forests & Forestry," USFS.

38. *VAG,* 1910, p. 14. For typical gifts, see ibid., pp. 228–231. For New Hampshire, *NHFoC,* 1900, pp. 4–5; 1911–12, pp. 76–77.

39. *NHFoC,* 1915–16, pp. 4, 86.

40. *MAG,* 1882, pp. 276–278; *MF&G,* 1907, pp. 50–51; *VFoC,* 1910, pp. 43–48; *NHA,* 1883, p. 80; *NHFoC,* 1911–12, pp. 24–25.

41. Henry S. Graves, *Public Regulation of Private Forests* (Concord, N.H., 1919), p. 11.

42. *NHA,* 1883, p. 64; *Bangor Commercial,* October 17, 1901; *Waterville Mail,* January 10, 1903, "Maine Forests and Forestry," USFS; *VFoC,* 1912, p. 53.

43. *VFoC,* 1912, p. 7. See *Granite Monthly* 59 (January 1927): 11–12; *VAG,* 1900, pp. 62–65.

44. *NHFoC,* 1900, pp. 8–9.

45. Chittenden, *Forest Conditions of Northern New Hampshire,* pp. 77, 91.

46. Ibid., pp. 14–15.

47. *Boston Globe,* March 1, 1903, "New Hampshire Forests and Forestry," USFS. See *NHFoC,* 1913–14, p. 41; Gerald R. Ogden and Leslie S. Clark, *Public Action in Forestry: The Society for the Protection of New Hampshire Forests* (Concord, n.d. [ca. 1979]), p. 92, box 25, no. 2, SPNHF.

48. *Report of the Secretary of Agriculture on Southern Appalachian and White Mountain Watersheds* (Washington, D.C., 1908), p. 28; Chittenden, *Forest Conditions of Northern New Hampshire,* p. 78; *SPNHFR,* 1905–06, p. 59.

49. *Boston Herald,* March 9, 1902, in Joseph T. Walker scrapbook (1901–1905), box 37, no. 1, SPNHF; *Boston Herald,* March 9, 1902, "New Hampshire Forests and Forestry," USFS; Jack, "Notes on Forest Conditions in Vermont," p. 20; Helenette Silver, *A History of New Hampshire Game and Furbearers* (Concord, 1957), pp. 64–65.

50. *People and Patriot,* February 21, 1902; *Boston Herald,* March 9, 1902, Walker scrapbook; *SPNHFR,* 1901–02, p. 24.

51. *SPNHFR,* 1901–02, pp. 18, 22, 23.

52. Ibid., pp. 1, 18–32. See Jack, "Notes on Forest Conditions in Vermont," p. 50.

53. *Lowell Currier,* July 10, 1901, "New Hampshire Forests and Forestry," USFS; Chittenden, *Forest Conditions of Northern New Hampshire,* p. 77.

54. Joseph B. Walker, *The White Mountain Region: An Address Delivered before the American Forestry Association* (Concord, N.H., 1895), box 31, no. 22, SPNHF.

55. Joseph B. Walker, *An Address upon the Forests of New Hampshire* (Manchester, 1872), box 31, no. 19; idem, *Our New Hampshire Forests: An Address* (Concord, 1891), box 31, no. 21; idem, *White Mountain Region.*

56. Chittenden, *Forest Conditions of Northern New Hampshire,* pp. 33–34, 38, 62; *SPNHFR,* 1903, p. 7; *New England Farmer,* May 6, 1905, Walker scrapbook.

57. Walker, *White Mountain Region;* Ogden and Clark, *Public Action in Forestry,* p. 93; *Concord Patriot,* July 20, 1897, "New Hampshire Forests and Forestry," USFS.

58. New Hampshire Land Company, *The American Timber Supply: Statement of the Property in Timber Lands Belonging to the New Hampshire Land Company* (Boston, 1880), pp. 6, 13, 14, Special Collections Department, University of New Hampshire.

59. John E. Johnson, *The Boa Constrictor of the White Mountains, or the Worst "Trust" in the World* (North Woodstock, N.H., 1900), box 19, no. 7, SPNHF.

60. "An Impending Peril to New England," *New England Homestead,* November 24, 1900, Walker scrapbook.

61. *Lowell Courier,* July 10, 1901; *Boston Post,* January 4, 1901; *Brattleboro Reformer,* January 11, 1901; *Eastern Argus,* January 11, 1901, "New Hampshire Forests and Forestry," USFS.

62. *SPNHFR,* 1901–02, p. 4; *New England Homestead,* January 19, 1901, Walker scrapbook; Ogden and Clark, *Public Action in Forestry,* p. 93.

63. Chittenden, *Forest Conditions of Northern New Hampshire,* pp. 32–33; Ayers, "Forest Problems in New Hampshire," p. 5; *SPNHFR,* 1901–02, p. 20; 1910, pp. 11–12.

64. *Boston Globe,* March 1, 1903, "New Hampshire Forests and Forestry," USFS.

65. "Great Value of Forests," unidentified clipping, August 24, 1901, Walker scrapbook.

66. *Boston Globe,* February 26, 1903, "Massachusetts Forestry Association," USFS; *SPNHFR,* 1903, pp. 7–8.

67. *Portsmouth Times,* November 16, 1901, "New Hampshire Forests and

Forestry," USFS; Chittenden, *Forest Conditions of Northern New Hampshire,* p. 10.

68. *Among the Clouds* 26 (August 23, 1902): 4; 29 (July 1905): 1; 29 (July 21, 1905): 1.

69. *SPNHFR,* 1901–02, pp. 12–15.

70. Allen Chamberlain, "Save the Timber Lands!" *Boston Transcript,* February 20, 1900. See *Mirror and Farmer,* December 13, 1900; *Boston Herald,* March 9, 1902, "New Hampshire Forests and Forestry," USFS.

71. *SPNHFR,* 1901–02, p. 15; "The Work in Forestry of the New Hampshire Woman's Clubs," pp. 2–3 (ca. 1918), box 32, no. 14, SPNHF.

72. *White Mountain Echo* 26 (July 25, 1903): 6. See John Reiger, *American Sportsmen and the Origins of Conservation* (New York, 1975); Thomas R. Cox, "Americans and Their Forests: Romanticism, Progress, and Science in the Late Nineteenth Century," *Journal of Forest History* 29 (October 1985): 156–159.

73. *Among the Clouds* 26 (August 23, 1902): 4; 28 (September 8, 1904): 4; 29 (July 21, 1905): 1; (July 29, 1905): 1; *White Mountain Echo* 25 (August 9, 1902): 6.

74. *Boston Transcript,* June 21, 1903, Walker scrapbook. See Chamberlain, "Save the Timber Lands!"; "Resolutions and Petitions, Appalachian and White Mountain National Forests," box 61, American Forestry Association Papers, Forest History Society, Durham, N.C. (hereafter cited as AFA); *SPNHFR,* 1901–02, p. 19; 1903, p. 11; Charles D. Smith, "The Mountain Lover Mourns: Origins of the Movement for a White Mountain National Forest, 1880–1903," *New England Quarterly* 33 (March 1960): 37–56.

75. *Portsmouth Times,* November 16, 1901, "New Hampshire Forests and Forestry," USFS. See *Concord Monitor,* February 9, 1904; *Nashua Press,* March 5, 1901, "New Hampshire Forests and Forestry," USFS.

76. Smith, "Mountain Lover Mourns," p. 41; *SPNHFR,* 1901–02, pp. 7, 27; SPNHF, *The White Mountain Forest and How It Is to Be Made Useful* (Concord, n.d. [ca. 1913]), box 32, no. 2; T. Jefferson Coolidge, in *SPNHFR,* 1903, p. 12; "Resolutions," box 61, AFA; Richard Hale, personal correspondence with the author, February 1995; *Boston Transcript,* March 8, 1889, "New Hampshire Forests and Forestry," USFS; W. R. Brown, "Briefs of Minutes and Annual Reports, 1901–1951, Inclusive," pp. 4–5, box 24, no. 5, SPNHF; *Congressional Record,* House, March 1, 1909, pp. 3523–24; *Among the Clouds* 27 (July 15, 1903): 1; *White Mountain Echo* 2 (September 1899): 11.

77. Ogden and Clark, *Public Action in Forestry,* p. 93.

78. Ayres, quoted in ibid., pp. 93–94; Sherman Adams, *The Weeks Act: 75th Anniversary Appraisal* (New York, 1986), pp. 11–12.

79. *New York Post,* August 20, 1901, "New Hampshire Forests and Forestry," USFS.

80. *New York Post,* August 20, 1901; *Boston Traveler,* December 31, 1902, "New Hampshire Forests and Forestry," USFS. On cooperative private-public forestry, see Carl A. Schenck, *The Birth of Forestry in America: Biltmore Forest School, 1898–1913* (Santa Cruz, 1974); Thomas R. Cox, "The Stewardship of Private Forests," *Journal of Forest History* 25 (October 1981): 188–196.

81. *Boston Transcript,* July 17, 1901, October 14, 1904, Walker scrapbook.

82. Ogden and Clark, *Public Action in Forestry,* p. 94.

83. Adams, *The Weeks Act,* p. 12.

84. *Boston Transcript,* June 21, 1903, Walker scrapbook; Brown, "Briefs of Minutes and Annual Reports."

85. *New York Times,* July 30, 1903, Walker scrapbook.

86. *Woonsocket Reporter,* September 8, 1902, "New Hampshire Forests and Forestry," USFS; *Manchester Union,* October 6, 1903; *Concord Monitor,* February 5, 1904, Walker scrapbook; *SPNHFR,* 1903, pp. 9–10; Philip Ayres, *Forest Problems in New Hampshire* (Concord, n.d. [ca. 1903]), p. 6; George Ward Cook, *Remarks Made before the American Forestry Association* (Haverhill, Mass., n.d.); "Resolutions," box 61, AFA.

87. Brown, "Briefs of Minutes and Annual Reports"; Chittenden, *Forest Conditions of Northern New Hampshire,* p. 11; *SPNHFR,* 1905–06, p. 5; *Congressional Record,* House, March 1, 1909, pp. 3514–35.

88. Appalachian Mountain Club, *Bulletin* 1 (May 1908): 8; Dodds, "Stream-Flow Controversy," p. 61.

89. *Maine Farmer,* December 20, 1873; *MAG,* 1887, p. 56; Burr, *Influence of Forests on Stream Flow,* pp. 8–9.

90. Burr, *Influence of Forests on Stream Flow,* pp. 10, 27; *NHFoC,* 1885, p. 20; Harold K. Steen, *The U.S. Forest Service: A History* (Seattle, 1976), pp. 123–129; Dodds, "Stream-Flow Controversy," p. 62, 64.

91. Charles G. Washburn, *The Life of John W. Weeks* (Boston, 1928), pp. 5–6, 39, 80 (letter to Pinchot on p. 75); *Congressional Record,* House, March 1, 1909, pp. 3514–35.

92. "Weeks Act, 1911," in *Encyclopedia of American Forest and Conservation History,* ed. Richard C. Davis (New York, 1983), p. 685.

93. *SPNHFR,* 1913–14, p. 49.

94. Widner, *Forests and Forestry,* p. 123; Richard W. Judd, *Aroostook: A Century of Logging in Northern Maine* (Orono, 1989), pp. 201–221.

95. Smith, "Mountain Lover Mourns," p. 38; *VAG,* 1895, pp. 83–85.

96. *MeBA,* 1869, pp. 77–78.

97. "Commissioner Ring Protests in Behalf of Maine Forests," unidentified clipping, March 25, 1908, p. 132, Edgar E. Ring scrapbook, Special Col-

lections Department, University of Maine; Sylvester Baxter, "The Redevelopment of an Old State," *Review of Reviews* 33 (January 1906): 55–62.

98. *Maine Farmer,* May 18, 1905; *Board of Trade Journal* 12 (May 1899): 9; 8 (December 1895): 230; *Maine Sportsman* 6 (July 1899): 5; 8 (November 1900): 204; 14 (March 1907): 134; *Maine Woods,* November 2, 1906; July 26 and November 8, 1907; January 13, 1909; January 20, 1910.

99. *Maine Woods,* January 4, 1907; March 20, 1908; *Bangor Commercial,* October 17, 1901.

100. Judd, *Aroostook,* p. 211; *MeFoC,* 1891, p. 1.

101. George F. Talbot, in *MeFoC,* 1891, p. 54.

102. *Maine Industrial Journal,* November 4, 1892; *MeFoC,* 1894, pp. 7, 11.

103. Austin Cary, "On the Growth of Spruce," *MeFoC,* 1894, pp. 21, 27 (quotation on p. 16); David C. Smith, *A History of Lumbering in Maine* (Orono, 1972), pp. 344–349.

104. *MeFoC,* 1896, p. 12.

105. Austin Cary, "Report," ibid., pp. 92–93, 183–184; *Northeastern Lumberman,* April 18, 1896, "Maine Forests and Forestry," USFS.

106. Cary, "Report," pp. 90, 93.

107. *Northeastern Lumberman,* April 18, 1896, "Maine Forests and Forestry," USFS.

108. Cary, "Report," pp. 186–187 (quotations on pp. 138–139).

109. Ibid., pp. 80–81, 101, 105.

110. Ibid., pp. 114–115.

111. *Bangor News,* June 28(?) and July 18, 1901, Ring scrapbook (unpaginated section).

112. *Bangor News,* June 28(?), 1901.

113. *MeFoC,* 1902, pp. 5, 6, 8, 59. See *New York Tribune,* August 31, 1902; *Bangor News,* December 5, 1902; November 16, 1903; *Portland Advertiser,* February 10, 1903, all in "Maine Forests and Forestry," USFS; Ralph Hosmer, "A Study of the Maine Spruce," *MeFoC,* 1902, p. 5. On Hosmer's subsequent career, see Thomas R. Cox, "The Birth of Hawaiian Forestry: The Web of Influences," *Pacific Historical Review* 61 (May 1992): 169–192.

114. *Pearson's Magazine,* April 1904, p. 14; unidentified clipping, *Bangor News*(?), 1905, p. 22; *Bangor Commercial,* June 18, 1903, p. 30, all in Ring scrapbook; *Boston Journal,* January 30, 1903, "Maine Forests and Forestry," USFS; *SPNHFR,* 1905–06, p. 26; Christopher S. Beach, "The Pulpwood Province and the Paper State: Corporate Reconstruction, Underdevelopment, and Law in New Brunswick and Maine, 1890–1930" (Ph.D. diss., University of Maine, 1991), pp. 66–67.

115. *Bangor News*(?), 1905, p. 22, Ring scrapbook; *Bangor News,* November 16, 1903, "Maine Forests and Forestry," USFS.

116. *Maine Farmer,* February 14 and 21, March 28, 1907; *Star,* September 21, 1901; *Messenger,* September 24, 1901; *Enterprise,* September 5, 1901, *New York Tribune,* August 31, 1902, all in "Maine Forests and Forestry," USFS; *Boston Journal,* May 25, 1907, p. 54, Ring scrapbook; *MeBILS,* 1899, pp. 53–60; Mark McPheters, in *Bangor Commercial,* March 8, 1902. On women's clubs, see unidentified clipping, *Bangor News*(?), 1904, p. 8, Ring scrapbook.

117. *Bangor Commercial,* May 18, 1908, p. 58, Ring scrapbook; *Maine Farmer,* February 14, 1907; Frank Putnam, "Maine: A Study in Land-Grabbing, Tax Dodging, and Isolation," *New England Magazine* 36 (July 1907): 515–540; Liberty B. Dennett, "Maine's Wildlands and Wildlanders," *Pine Tree Magazine* 6 (January 1907): 539–548; 7 (February 1907): 78–87; (March 1907): 183–193; (April 1907): 273–280; (May 1907): 359–367; (June 1907): 456–463; (July 1907): 551–557; 8 (August 1907): 53–61.

118. *Bangor Commercial,* May 14 and 18, 1908, p. 58, Ring scrapbook; Maine Legislature, *Legislative Documents,* Senate, no. 1 (Augusta, 1909); *Forest and Stream,* in *Maine Woods,* July 22, 1908.

119. *Bangor Commercial,* March 16, 1907; unidentified clipping, *Bangor News*(?), 1904, p. 8; *Boston Globe,* March 17, 1907, pp. 56, 143, all in Ring scrapbook.

120. Philip T. Coolidge, *History of the Maine Woods* (Bangor, 1963), pp. 499–503.

121. Dennett, in *Maine Farmer,* March 21, 1889; *Journal of the Proceedings of the Maine State Grange, December 19–21, 1905* (Lewiston, 1905), p. 22. See *Aroostook Times,* February 24, 1905; *Maine Farmer,* January 18, March 1, December 6, 1906; Dennett, "Maine's Wildlands and Wildlanders," pp. 540, 542; *Bangor Commercial,* March 20, 1903; *MeBILS, 1906,* p. 186; Putnam, "Maine," pp. 530–531.

122. *Waterville Sentinel* (ca. 1906), p. 50, Ring scrapbook; Judd, *Aroostook,* p. 213; *Maine Farmer,* January 26, 1905; *Maine Woods,* March 22, 1907, and especially *Machias Union,* January 10, 1905.

123. "More Money Is Wanted," unidentified clipping, ca. 1907, p. 67; "Land Owners Met," unidentified clipping, ca. 1908, p. 81; "For Protection of Our Forests," unidentified clipping, October 1908, p. 109, Ring scrapbook.

124. Unidentified clipping, March 20, 1909, p. 110; "Hon. C. E. Oaks' [*sic*] Address," undated clipping, p. 7; Edgar E. Ring, "Game, Fishing and Forestry," unidentified clipping, p. 5; unidentified clipping, November 18, 1908, p. 123; "Maine Forests and Forest Fires," unidentified clipping, 1905, p. 23, all in Ring scrapbook; *Bangor Whig and Courier,* September 22, 1899; *Bangor Commercial,* March 20, 1903.

125. *Bangor Commercial,* December 19, 1906, p. 50, "Alarming Menace to Maine Timberlands," unidentified clipping, ca. 1905, p. 36, Ring scrapbook. On early multiple-use concepts, see David A. Clary, *Timber and the Forest Service* (Lawrence, Kans., 1986), p. 42.

126. Austin Cary, in Judd, *Aroostook,* p. 215; *Bangor Commercial,* January 27 and 30, February 19, and March 23, 1909; *Eastern Argus,* March 5, 1909; Maine Legislature, *Legislative Documents,* Senate, no. 138 (Augusta, 1915); *Paper Trade Journal* 60 (June 10, 1915): 28.

127. *Waterville Sentinel,* ca. 1906, p. 50, Ring scrapbook. See *Maine Farmer,* January 26, 1905, and, for a critical appraisal, William R. Pattangall, *Maine's Hall of Fame* (Lewiston, 1924), pp. 223–227.

128. William T. Haines, *Inaugural Address* (Augusta, Maine, 1913), p. 23.

129. Judd, *Aroostook,* pp. 215–216; Austin Wilkins, *Ten Million Acres of Timber* (Woolwich, Maine, 1978), pp. 39–47; *Bangor Commercial,* October 1910, p. 52, Ring scrapbook; *Maine Woods,* December 2, 1909.

130. Adams, *The Weeks Act,* p. 14.

131. Donald Worster, *The Wealth of Nature: Environmental History and the Ecological Imagination* (New York, 1993), p. 104.

5. CONFLICTING RIGHTS IN FISHERIES

1. Petition of the Inhabitants of Gouldsborough (January 7, 1840), box 133, env. 36, MeSA.

2. On the informal constraints implicit in common-pool resource regimes, see Elinor Ostrom, *Governing the Commons: The Evolution of Institutions for Collective Action* (New York, 1990), pp. 35–36, 88–89; and Arthur F. McEvoy, *The Fisherman's Problem: Ecology and Law in the California Fisheries, 1850–1980* (New York, 1986), pp. 95–98.

3. Middleton Goldsmith, "The Increase and Preservation of Fish and Game," p. 1, appended to George Perkins Marsh, *Report . . . on the Artificial Propagation of Fish* (Burlington, Vt., 1857); *MF&G,* 1875, pp. 20–21.

4. *Maine Farmer,* March 6, 1875. See *MF&G,* 1884, pp. 39–40; *NHF&G,* 1894, p. 96.

5. Petition of Paul Hammond [1855], box 308, chap. 81, MeSA. See *NHF&G,* 1857, p. 8; Charles H. Stevenson, "The Shad Fisheries of the Atlantic Coast of the United States," in U.S. Commissioner of Fish and Fisheries, *Report of the Commissioner for the Year Ending 1898,* part 24 (Washington, D.C., 1899), p. 104.

6. Petition of Ulrich Reed (May 5, 1850), box 256, chap. 156, MeSA.

7. Remonstrance of John B. Smith (February 16, 1837), box 158, chap. 100, MSA. See McEvoy, *Fisherman's Problem*, pp. 6, 72–73.

8. A. N. Somers, *History of Lancaster, New Hampshire* (Concord, 1899), pp. 100–101.

9. Petition of Benjamin H. Medes (July 15, 1846), box 181, chap. 15, MeSA. See Petition of David Chaney (May 16, 1850) and "Act to Regulate the Salmon, Shad, and Alewive Fisheries in the Kennebec River" (1850), box 256, chap. 156, MeSA.

10. Petitions of Ulrich Reed and David Chaney; remonstrances of William Crawford (May 1, 1850) and Prince H. Look (June 4, 1850), box 256, chap. 156, MeSA.

11. Ruth Bogin, "Petitioning and the New Moral Economy of Post-Revolutionary America," *William and Mary Quarterly*, 3rd ser., 45 (July 1988): 392.

12. Petition of the Inhabitants of Harpswell (January 25, 1843), box 157, env. 11, MeSA.

13. Petition of Asa Turner (January 11, 1844), box 197, chap. 79; Petition of Joshua W. Norton (February 10, 1845), box 174, env. 2, MeSA.

14. Petitions of Henry Wilson (December 12, 1835) and John Carver (February 10, 1836), box 110, env. 27, MeSA.

15. Petition of Asa Turner (January 11, 1844); "Act to Regulate the Herring Fisheries in the Town of Jonesport" (March 21, 1844), box 240, chap. 152; Petition of Selectmen of Friendship (February 11, 1845), box 178, chap. 11, MeSA.

16. "Act to Prevent the Destruction of Fish in the Eastern Penobscot River" (July 16, 1846); petitions of Alonso Perry (July 9, 1846) and Andrew S. Soper [1846], box 214, chap. 108, MeSA.

17. Petition of Committees of Towns of Nobleboro and Newcastle (January 20, 1845), box 174, env. 16; Remonstrance of David Haggett (July 12, 1848); Petition of Hiram Palmer (July 13, 1848), box 232, chap. 96, MeSA.

18. Petition of Hiram Palmer; Petition of Asa Densmore (July 12, 1848), box 232, chap. 96, MeSA.

19. Bogin, "Petitioning and the New Moral Economy," p. 394.

20. Petition of John Gliddin (June 14, 1848), box 232, chap. 96; remonstrances of William Howe (January 1845) and Job Hussey [1845], box 174, env. 16, MeSA.

21. Morton J. Horwitz, *The Transformation of American Law, 1780–1860* (Cambridge, Mass., 1977), p. 31. See Remonstrance of Samuel Glidden (February 8, 1845), box 174, env. 16; "Communication of Town of Warren" (February 6, 1837); Petition of the Inhabitants of the Town of Warren (February 16, 1837), box 110, env. 9, MeSA.

22. Petition of Jonathan Morgan (May 26, 1852), box 225, env. 16; Petition of Jonathan Morgan (January 10, 1853), box 231, env. 10, MeSA.

23. Remonstrance of the Portland Steam Co. (February 15, 1853), box 231, env. 10, MeSA.

24. "Act to Regulate the Taking of Alewives in the Stream Leading from Gray's Pond" (May 5, 1848); Petition of Jacob Snow (May 5, 1848), box 230, chap. 74, MeSA.

25. Petition of Matthew Fowler (November 15, 1836), box 147, chap. 164, MeSA. See "Act . . . to Regulate the . . . Fishery in the River St. Croix" (1839), box 165, chap. 51, MeSA.

26. John T. Cumbler, "The Early Making of an Environmental Consciousness: Fish, Fisheries Commissions, and the Connecticut River," *Environmental History Review* 15 (Winter 1991): 80; Martha Leeman, "A History of Woolwich, Maine" (M.A. thesis, University of Maine, 1948), p. 84; Remonstrance of Samuel Reed (February 10, 1836), box 132, chap. 182; Petition of Benjamin F. Tallman (January 11, 1836), box 222, chap. 103, MeSA.

27. Remonstrance of David How [*sic*] (February 18, 1845), box 174, chap. 103; "Act to Construct Fishways and Remove Obstructions in Ducktrap Stream" and Petition of James Thomas (June 12, 1847), box 222, chap. 103; Petition of Joseph Miller (December 31, 1844), box 174, env. 12, MeSA.

28. Petition of Joseph Miller; "Act to Construct Fishways and Remove Obstructions in Ducktrap Stream"; Petition of James Thomas; depositions of Martin W. Tower and Asa Spaulding (July 1847), box 222, chap. 103, MeSA.

29. Deposition of John Patten (n.d.); Petition of the Town of Surry (January 16, 1837), box 109, env. 16, MeSA.

30. Remonstrance of David How; Remonstrance of David P. Andrews (July 1847), box 222, chap. 103, MeSA.

31. Petition of the Selectmen of Prospect (July 28, 1849), box 210, env. 31, MeSA.

32. Petition of Simeon B. Perry (December 8, 1835), box 134, chap. 220, MeSA.

33. Subcommittee report accompanying Petition of the Selectmen of Prospect.

34. Remonstrance of Samuel Thatcher Jr. (February 17, 1837), box 195, env. 5; "Communication of Benjamin Shaw, Fish Warden, Relative to Fisheries on Penobscot River" (n.d.); Benjamin Shaw to Hon. R. Nickerson and Brother G. T. Sweat, July 7, 1845, box 195, env. 5, MeSA.

35. Petitions of Lemuel Messer (February 9, 1838) and Joseph Treat (February 9, 1838), box 158, chap. 100, MeSA.

36. Remonstrance of Sewall Heath [ca. February 1853], box 231, env. 9, MeSA.
37. Remonstrance of John B. Smith (February 16, 1837).
38. Petition of the Inhabitants of the Town of Warren (February 16, 1837).
39. Remonstrance of John B. Smith; "Act . . . for the Preservation of Salmon, Shad and Alewives in the Penobscot River" and petitions (January 1836), box 134, chap. 220, MeSA.
40. Remonstrance of Sewall Heath; remonstrances of James Davis (February 29, 1844) and Adams Treat (January 13, 1844), box 164, env. 35; Petition of S. A. Sanders (January 30, 1838), box 158, chap. 100, MeSA.
41. *Bangor Democrat,* January 28, 1839.
42. Petition of James Austin (January 8, 1839), box 132, env. 19, MeSA.
43. "Act . . . for the Preservation of Salmon, Shad and Alewives in the Penobscot River" and petitions (January 1836); Petition of John Brown (December 29, 1838), box 132, env. 18; "Act for the Preservation of Fish in the Saint Croix River"; Petition of Matthias Vickery (June 20, 1849), box 242, chap. 95, MeSA. See also remonstrances of E. B. Pierce (January 23, 1844) and Jeremiah G. Lowell (February 5, 1844), box 164, env. 35, MeSA.
44. Petition of Orrin Sow[?] (February 14, 1845), box 174, env. 4; Petition of Ware Eddy (November 30, 1843), box 164, env. 35, MeSA.
45. Petition of the Town of Penobscot (December 27, 1838), box 126, env. 11; petitions of Isaac Ames (February 4, 1839) and Nathaniel Beverage (December 26, 1838), box 127, env. 3, MeSA.
46. Petitions of Ware Eddy (November 30, 1843), Adams Treat (January 13, 1844), and William Kendall (January 24, 1844), box 164, env. 35, MeSA.
47. "Report of the Joint Select Committee, Appointed to Take into Consideration the Expediency of Repealing All Fish Laws" (March 6, 1839), p. 6, box 170, chap. 16, MeSA.
48. "Report on an Act to Regulate the Taking of Fish" (1840), box 130, env. 10, MeSA; "Report of the Joint Select Committee," pp. 3–6.
49. "Report of the Joint Select Committee," p. 5; "Report on an Act to Regulate the Taking of Fish."
50. Ostrom, *Governing the Commons,* pp. 173–177; McEvoy, *Fisherman's Problem,* p. 99.
51. Petition of the Inhabitants of Old Town [ca. 1843], box 155, env. 40; "Act for the Preservation of Salmon, Shad, and Alewives in Penobscot River" (1843), box 192, chap. 82; draft of "Bill Concerning Fish-Ways" (January 31, 1843), box 159, env. 27; "Act to Prevent the Destruction of Fish in the Eastern Penobscot River"; petitions of Alonso Perry (July 9, 1846) and Andrew S. Soper [1846].

52. *MF&G,* 1884, p. 41. See "Report of the Committee on Fisheries" (1855), chap. 401, MSA.

53. "Act . . . to Regulate the Fishery in Taunton Great River" (February 20, 1832); Petition of Edward Simmons (1832), chap. 44, MSA.

54. Ostrom, *Governing the Commons,* pp. 94–95; "Act Regulating the Taking of Fish in the Town of Bridgewater" (February 15, 1825); Petition of the Selectmen of Bridgewater; "Memorial of the Inhabitants of Middleboro" [1824], chap. 76; "Act to Regulate the Fishery in Taunton Great River" (March 24, 1843); Remonstrance of Jonathan N. Fairbanks (1843), chap. 73, MSA.

55. "Act to Regulate the Fishery in the Taunton Great River"; petitions of Gamaliel Rounsevitte [1843] and Joseph A. Hall [1843], chap. 73, MSA.

56. "Resolve Concerning the Fisheries on Taunton Great River" (March 17, 1854), chap. 22, MSA.

57. "Report of the Committee on Fisheries."

58. Ibid.

59. "Act to Regulate the Fisheries in Taunton Great River and the Newmasket River" (May 19, 1855); "Report of the Committee on Fisheries."

60. Benjamin Shaw to Hon. R. Nickerson and Brother G. T. Sweat, July 7, 1845.

61. Ibid. On the Allagash diversion see Richard W. Judd, *Aroostook: A Century of Logging in Northern Maine* (Orono, 1989), pp. 167–168.

62. *Maine Farmer,* December 27, 1866.

63. "Act for the Preservation of Fish in the Saint Croix River"; Petition of Matthias Vickery (June 20, 1849); Petition of Albert Kean (February 14, 1852), box 218, env. 7, MeSA.

64. Petition of B. G. Ricker (January 22, 1840), box 143, env. 12, MeSA.

65. "Communication of Town of Warren" (February 6, 1837); Petition of the Inhabitants of the Town of Warren (February 16, 1837).

66. *MF&G,* 1884, pp. 44–45; *New England Farmer,* March 27, 1869.

67. McEvoy, *Fisherman's Problem,* p. 101, discussing the U.S. Fish Commission, created in 1871.

6. THE POLITICS OF INTERSTATE FISHERIES

1. Robert B. Roosevelt, "Centennial Meeting," in *Transactions of the American Fish Culturists' Association, 1877* (New York, 1877), pp. 11, 13.

2. Ibid., pp. 16, 17.

3. Ibid., p. 16; *MF&G,* 1872, pp. 5, 6.

4. *Maine Farmer,* March 23, 1865; July 19, 1866; *Our Agricola* 2 (December

7, 1876): 193; "Act . . . for the Preservation of Fish in the Penobscot Waters" (1839), box 158, chap. 100, MeSA; *MeBA*, 1865, p. 156.

5. *NHF&G*, 1878, p. 49; *MeF&G*, 1874, p. 5.

6. *Forest and Stream* 4 (July 29, 75): 389.

7. Seth Green, *Home Fishing and Home Waters: A Practical Treatise on Fish Culture* (New York, 1888), pp. 11, 14, 23–24.

8. *MAG*, 1878, p. 35. On farming and pisciculture, see *New England Farmer* 1 (May 12, 1849): 166–167; *Proceedings of the American Fish Culturists' Association, 1873* (Albany, N.Y., 1873), p. 6; *MAG*, 1868, p. 155.

9. *Yankee Farmer* 1 (March 30, 1835): 50. See *Forest and Stream* 4 (July 29, 1875): 405; *MF&G*, 1876, p. 58; 1878, p. 11; *MAG*, 1851, p. 514; *NHF&G*, 1878, p. 52; *VF&G*, 1866, p. 23; *Burlington Free Press*, December 28, 1868.

10. *NHF&G*, 1878, p. 52. See *Burlington Free Press*, March 16, 1867; December 28, 1868; *Maine Farmer*, July 3, 1869.

11. *NHF&G*, 1865, pp. 4–6; *Burlington Free Press*, March 20, 1865; Louis Agassiz, "Fish Breeding," in *MAG*, 1869, p. 130.

12. T. Garlick, "The Beginning of Fish Culture in America," in *Transactions of the American Fish Culturists' Association, 1883* (New York, 1883), p. 47; E. D. Potter, "The Origins of Fish Culture in the United States," in *Transactions of the American Fish Culturists' Association, 1890* (Put-In-Bay, Ohio, 1890), p. 42.

13. E. C. Kellogg, "Experiments in Artificial Fish-Breeding," in George Perkins Marsh, *Report . . . on the Artificial Propagation of Fish* (Burlington, Vt., 1857). See G[eorge] Brown Goode, "Epochs in the History of Fish Culture," in *Transactions of the American Fish Culturists' Association, 1881* (New York, 1881): 43.

14. *Maine Farmer*, April 23, 1863; *Eastern Argus*, March 3, 1863.

15. *Maine Farmer*, June 7, 1866; December 18, 1862; April 23, 1863; June 30, 1864; *Eastern Argus*, March 3, 1863.

16. *Maine Farmer*, March 19, 1870; January 20, 1872. See *Farmer's Monthly Visitor* 6 (October 31, 1844): 156–157.

17. *Maine Farmer*, June 30, 1864; March 23, 1865; July 5 and December 27, 1866; *MF&G*, 1873, p. 14; *NHF&G*, 1868, p. 4; *American Agriculturist* 28 (December 1869): 453; *New England Farmer*, March 27, 1869.

18. *New England Farmer*, March 27, 1869; *Burlington Free Press*, April 9, 1870.

19. *MF&G*, 1878, p. 21; *VF&G*, 1866, pp. 18–19; *NHF&G*, 1885, pp. 10–11. See John T. Cumbler, "The Early Making of an Environmental Consciousness: Fish, Fisheries Commissions, and the Connecticut River," *Environmental History Review* 15 (Winter 1991): 78.

20. *NHF&G*, 1857, p. 3; "Act for the Preservation of Fish in the Merrimack River" and Petition of Ambrose Lawrence (1856), chap. 289, MSA.

21. Goode, "Epochs in the History of Fish Culture," p. 44; *Transactions of the American Fish Culturists' Association, 1872* (New York, 1872), p. 33.

22. Marsh, *Report; NHF&G*, 1857, p. 4.

23. "Report of the Joint Special Committee in Relation to the Fish-Ways on the Merrimack River" (1856), chap. 289, MSA.

24. Ibid.

25. "Act for the Preservation of Fish in the Merrimack River."

26. *NHF&G*, 1857, p. 12; Theodore Lyman, "Sketch of the Progress of Fish-Culture in New England," in *MF&G*, 1876, p. 50.

27. *NHF&G*, 1866, pp. 4, 8–9; *Burlington Free Press*, March 20, 1865; *NHF&G*, 1885, p. 11; untitled report [1865], chap. 45, MSA.

28. *NHF&G*, 1865, pp. 4–6; *Burlington Free Press*, March 20, 1865. See Cumbler, "Early Making of an Environmental Consciousness," p. 81.

29. *NHF&G*, 1880, pp. 33–34. See *NHF&G*, 1865, pp. 3–6.

30. Theodore Lyman and Alfred Reed, "Obstructions to the Passage of Fish," December 1, 1865, pp. 18–21, 51–55, chap. 238; "Resolve Concerning the Obstructions to the Fish in the Connecticut and Merrimack Rivers" (May 3, 1865), chap. 45, MSA.

31. "Act Concerning the Obstructions to the Passage of Fish in the Connecticut and Merrimac Rivers" (May 22, 1866), chap. 238. Included in the legislative document are the reports of the Massachusetts Fish Commissioners and the joint resolutions from Vermont and New Hampshire.

32. Goode, "Epochs in the History of Fish Culture"; *Burlington Free Press*, August 21, 1889; *VAG*, 1875–76, p. 415; *MeF&G*, 1898, p. 11; 1900, p. 7; *Bath Sentinel*, May 6, 1867.

33. *Maine Farmer*, December 10, 1870; November 23, 1882; Ezekiel Holmes, "Dr. Holmes' Report on the Fishes of Maine," in *Second Annual Report upon the Natural History and Geology of the State of Maine* (Augusta, 1862–63); Samuel L. Boardman, "General View of the Agriculture and Industry of the County of Kennebec," in *MeBA*, 1865, p. 156.

34. Boardman, "General View," p. 160.

35. Samuel L. Boardman, "Aquaeculture," *Maine Farmer*, March 23, 1865; idem, "General View," p. 159.

36. *MeF&G*, 1872, p. 6. See *Maine Farmer*, July 18, 1868.

37. *MeF&G*, 1874, pp. 3–4; 1884, p. 17.

38. Stevenson, "Shad Fisheries of the Atlantic Coast," pp. 105, 107, 110, 112; *MF&G*, 1899, pp. 12–13.

39. *VF&G*, 1877–78, pp. 4–5; 1872, p. 9; Seth Green, "The Trials and Tribulations . . . of a Practical Fish-Culturist," *Forest and Stream* 2 (March 12, 1874): 68; *NHF&G*, 1868, p. 5.

40. Green, "Trials and Tribulations," p. 19; *MF&G*, 1874, p. 18.

41. Fred Mather, "The Influence of Railroads on Fish Culture," in *Transactions of the American Fisheries Society, 1895* (New York, 1896), p. 19; *NHF&G*, 1877, p. 33. See idem, "Fish Culture," *Forest and Stream* 1 (August 14, 1873): 10.

42. *VF&G*, 1872, p. 9. See Lyman, "Sketch of the Progress of Fish-Culture," p. 60.

43. *NHF&G*, 1885, p. 12; *MeF&G*, 1871, pp. 5–11; 1872, p. 5; 1874, p. 11; *MF&G*, 1884, p. 46; *Maine Farmer*, December 2, 1871; December 7, 1872; November 22, 1873; December 31, 1885; Goode, "Epochs in the History of Fish Culture," p. 45.

44. *VF&G*, 1873–74, apps.; 1875–76, p. 4; *NHF&G*, 1866, pp. 4–5, 7.

45. Marsh, *Report*, p. 59; *VF&G*, 1866, p. 6.

46. *MF&G*, 1883, pp. 6–7.

47. "Act in Regard to the Mill Dams on Mill River" (April 24, 1873); "Hearing in Relation to . . . Dams over Mill River" (February 1873), pp. 29–30, chap. 230, MSA.

48. "Hearing in Relation to . . . Dams," pp. 2, 4, 7, 11. See Petition of Charles L. Livering [1873], chap. 230, MSA.

49. *Maine Farmer*, October 24, 1867; Theodore Steinberg, *Nature Incorporated: Industrialization and the Waters of New England* (New York, 1991), p. 105.

50. "Hearing in Relation to . . . Dams," pp. 6, 7, 14, 15, 16.

51. Ibid., p. 11. Alewife runs on the Taunton River gradually increased after 1875. See *MF&G*, 1917, p. 112.

52. Lyman, "Sketch of the Progress of Fish-Culture," pp. 56–57; *NHF&G*, 1870, p. 6; 1871, pp. 5–6; 1876, p. 12; *NHA*, 1871, pp. 218–219.

53. *NHF&G*, 1877, pp. 28–31; 1878, pp. 3–4. See *NHF&G*, 1878, p. 57; *VF&G*, 1877–78, p. 11; *MF&G*, 1878, p. 19.

54. *NHF&G*, 1880, p. 3. See *MF&G*, 1878, pp. 7–10, 19, 21; 1887, p. 13; *NHF&G*, 1878, p. 8; 1880, p. 15.

55. *Transactions of the American Fish Culturists' Association, 1877*, p. 31; *MF&G*, 1873, pp. 5, 9–10; 1876, p. 54; 1885, pp. 11–13; *NHF&G*, 1870, p. 6.

56. *MF&G*, 1882, p. 13; 1877 report in *MF&G*, 1881, p. 16. See *MF&G*, 1881, pp. 41–43; 1884, pp. 15–17; 1885, pp. 11–13.

57. *MF&G*, 1893–1896; Myron Gordon and Philip M. Marston, "Early Fishing along the Merrimack," *New England Naturalist*, September 1940, p. 6.

58. Lyman, "Sketch of the Progress of Fish-Culture," pp. 56–57, 60; *MF&G*, 1876, p. 60; 1878, p. 21; 1891, pp. 37–38; *VF&G*, 1877–78, pp. 7–9.

59. Lyman, "Sketch of the Progress of Fish-Culture," pp. 56–57; Stevenson,

"Shad Fisheries of the Atlantic Coast," pp. 253–254; *MF&G*, 1878, p. 21; *VAG*, 1875–76, p. 403; *VF&G*, 1875–76, p. 14; 1877–78, pp. 5–7.

60. *VF&G*, 1877–78, p. 9. See *MF&G*, 1878, p. 10; New Hampshire commissioners in *VF&G*, 1877–78, p. 9.

61. Connecticut commissioners in *MF&G*, 1886, p. 31. See *VF&G*, 1877–78, pp. 5–8; *MF&G*, 1879, p. 9.

62. *VF&G*, 1877–78, pp. 6, 11; *MF&G*, 1878, p. 21; Lyman, "Sketch of the Progress of Fish-Culture," pp. 56–57.

63. *MF&G*, 1878, pp. 20–26; 1880, pp. 14, 15; 1881, pp. 6–7; 1886, p. 28; 1889, p. 13.

64. Stevenson, "Shad Fisheries of the Atlantic Coast," pp. 253, 255–257; *MF&G*, 1886, pp. 26, 28–29, 35; 1889, p. 13; 1895, pp. 6–7; *VF&G*, 1894, pp. 101–102.

65. *Maine Farmer*, July 3, 1835; January 13, 1837.

66. Boardman, "General View," pp. 152, 156; *MeF&G*, 1880, p. 25; 1884, p. 8; *MeBA*, 1867, p. 118.

67. *Maine Farmer*, October 18 and July 19, 1866; January 31, 1867; June 19, 1869; April 23, 1870.

68. *MeF&G*, 1869, p. 3. See *Maine Farmer*, July 3, 1869; July 2, 1870; *MeF&G*, 1870, p. 24.

69. *MeF&G*, 1874, pp. 7–10, 20–21; 1876, p. 12; 1879, pp. 19–20; 1880, pp. 25, 29.

70. *MeF&G*, 1879, p. 20; 1880, p. 29; 1884, p. 10.

71. John E. Godfrey, "Annals of Bangor," in *History of Penobscot County, Maine*, ed. Henry A. Ford (Cleveland, 1882), p. 703; Richard S. Davies, "History of the Penobscot River: Its Use and Abuse" (M.A. thesis, University of Maine, 1972), p. 49; *Maine Woods*, April 14, 1905; *MeBA*, 1868, pp. 92–95; *MeF&G*, 1870, p. 13; 1882, p. 9; 1884, p. 9.

72. *MeF&G*, 1869, pp. 14–15. See *MeF&G*, 1870, pp. 13–14; 1872, p. 4; 1877, p.3; 1878, p. 7; 1879, pp. 7–10, 23; 1880, pp. 4, 8–9.

73. *MeF&G*, 1887–88, p. 14; Davies, "History of the Penobscot River," p. 47.

74. *MeF&G*, 1887–88, p. 13.

75. *MeF&G*, 1889–90, p. 8; 1891–92, pp. 5–7.

76. *MeF&G*, 1891–92, p. 5. See *Maine Woods*, July 19, September 6 and 27, 1907; *MeF&G*, 1919, p. 15; 1920, pp. 6–7; 1922, pp. 9–10; 1924, p. 7; *Lewiston Journal*, July 18, 1928.

77. *MF&G*, 1903, p. 53; 1918, pp. 163–164, 166–169; 1921, pp. 82–83; 1923, p. 20; Gordon and Marston, "Early Fishing along the Merrimack," p. 10; *MeF&G*, 1884, p. 8; 1891–92, pp. 5, 7.

78. *VF&G*, 1867, pp. 6, 12; 1894, pp. 103–107; *MF&G*, 1872, app. 2, p. 246; *NHF&G*, 1877, p. 32; *Forest and Stream* 2 (April 23, 1874): 165; Fred

Mather, "Poisoning and Obstructing the Waters," in *Transactions of the American Fish Culturists' Association, 1875* (Rochester, N.Y., 1875), pp. 14–18; *MeBA,* 1867, p. 142; *MeF&G,* 1882, p. 7; 1884, pp. 12–13; Stuart E. DeRoche, *Fishery Management in the Androscoggin River* (Augusta, Maine, 1967), p. 10.

79. *NHF&G,* 1890, p. 9; 1892, p. 79.
80. *Burlington Free Press,* October 25, 1892.
81. *VF&G,* 1894, pp. 85–87; 1896, pp. 22–23; 1902, p. 20; *NHF&G,* 1889, pp. 4–5; *MF&G,* 1901, p. 38; 1902, pp. 47–48; 1904, p. 126; 1909, p. 43.
82. *MF&G,* 1912–1914, pp. 86–91; 1919, p. 93.
83. *NHF&G,* 1894, p. 97; *MF&G,* 1902, p. 46; 1903, p. 71; 1919, p. 110; *VF&G,* 1908, p. 10.
84. *VF&G,* 1908, p. 10.
85. *MF&G,* 1888, pp. 20–22; 1912–1914, p. 10.
86. *NHF&G,* 1894, p. 97.
87. *VAG,* 1878, p. 138; *Maine Farmer,* January 4, 1879; September 8 and December 2, 1881; February 19, 1885.
88. *MF&G,* 1902, p. 48.
89. *MF&G,* 1903, p. 54; 1902, pp. 49–50.
90. *Transactions of the American Fisheries Society, 1890* (New York, 1890), pp. 79–83.
91. *Maine Industrial Journal,* January 31, 1896; *MeF&G,* 1882, p. 10.
92. A. N. Chaney, "Food Fish and Fish Food," in *Transactions of the American Fish Culturists' Association, 1883,* p. 28. See *NHF&G,* 1878, p. 53; 1889, p. 41; *MF&G,* 1872, pp. 5, 28; 1878, p. 28; 1885, p. 12.
93. *MF&G,* 1908, p. 25.

7. FORGING A CONSERVATION ETHIC

1. *NHF&G,* 1872, p. 3.
2. *VF&G,* 1866, p. 22.
3. *Burlington Free Press,* April 23, 1870.
4. J. Leonard Bates, "Fulfilling American Democracy: The Conservation Movement, 1907 to 1921," *Mississippi Valley Historical Review* 44 (June 1957): 38.
5. David Goodsell Gale, "The History of the Vermont Fish and Game Commission, 1866–1960" (M.A. thesis, University of Vermont, 1963), p. 55; *Burlington Free Press,* April 17, 1871; *Maine Farmer,* January 4, 1879.
6. *VL,* 1867, no. 44, pp. 54–55. See *NHF&G,* 1883, p. 17.
7. *Burlington Free Press,* April 23, 1870; *Maine Farmer,* March 6, 1875. See *NHF&G,* 1868, p. 5; 1878, p. 22.

8. *VF&G,* 1867, p. 23. See *NHF&G,* 1896, p. 6; *NHA,* 1875, p. 216.

9. Middleton Goldsmith, "Dr. Goldsmith's Second Report," in *VF&G,* 1873–74, p. 55. See Dwight Curtis, "Vermont Fish and Game Department: Management of Fisheries in the 19th Century," typescript, 1984, p. 9, Special Collections Department, University of Vermont; *VF&G,* 1887–88, p. 4; 1896, pp. 127–128.

10. *Vermont Watchman and State Journal,* January 10, 1883. See James A. Tober, *Who Owns the Wildlife? The Political Economy of Conservation in Nineteenth-Century America* (Westport, Conn., 1981), p. 219.

11. *VF&G,* 1873–74, pp. 57–58.

12. *MF&G,* 1892, p. 29.

13. *NHF&G,* 1878, p. 23. See Florence J. Perry, "From Colonization and Depredation to Conservation and Education: Progress Report of the Vermont Fish & Game Department," typescript, 1894, p. 12, reference files, Vermont State Archives; *VL,* 1876, chap. 60, pp. 148–149.

14. *VF&G,* 1898, p. 31. See *Burlington Free Press,* April 23, 1870; May 10, 1894; *MF&G,* 1891, pp. 33–34; *VL,* 1888, no. 128, p. 135.

15. *Vermont Watchman and State Journal,* November 22, 1882. See *VF&G,* 1887–88, p. 12.

16. *VF&G,* 1875–76, p. 7; 1896, p. 11; *NHF&G,* 1884, p. 34.

17. *VF&G,* 1881–82, pp. 14–17. See *VF&G,* 1873–74, pp. 43, 50–51; 1910, p. 21; 1912, pp. 4–6.

18. *Vermont Watchman and State Journal,* May 16, 1877.

19. *NHF&G,* 1889, p. 43; Richard R. Wescott, "Early Conservation Programs and the Development of the Vacation Industry in Maine, 1865–1900," *Maine Historical Society Quarterly* 27 (Summer 1987): 2–13; *Maine Farmer,* January 6, 1876; January 4, 1879; *New England Farmer,* March 27, 1869; *NHF&G,* 1866, p. 15; 1877, p. 23; 1889, p. 42; *NHA,* 1872, pp. 473–474.

20. *Burlington Free Press,* March 20, 1875; *VAG,* 1875–76, p. 415; *MF&G,* 1879, p. 17; 1882, p. 19; 1886, p. 8; *NHF&G,* 1880, p. 32; *VF&G,* 1869, pp. 8–9.

21. Boardman in *Maine Farmer,* August 4, 1864; March 23, 1865. See *Burlington Free Press,* April 13, 1875.

22. *Vermont Watchman and State Journal,* January 10, 1883; *Burlington Free Press,* December 30, 1884.

23. George Perkins Marsh, *Report . . . on the Artificial Propagation of Fish* (Burlington, Vt., 1857), pp. 7–8, 11. See Goldsmith, "Second Report," p. 58; idem, *An Address on Fish Culture* (Rutland, Vt., 1872), pp. 14–15.

24. *Maine Farmer,* March 23, 1865.

25. A. N. Somers, *History of Lancaster, New Hampshire* (Concord, 1899), p. 102.

26. *VF&G,* 1887–88, p. 4.

27. *Burlington Free Press,* March 20, 1865; *NYCFG&F,* 1895, p. 13.

28. *NHF&G,* 1880, pp. 40–41; *VF&G,* 1881–82, pp. 14–17.

29. *Burlington Free Press,* April 13, 1875; Abby Maria Hemenway, *Vermont Historical Gazetteer,* vol. 1 (Burlington, 1868), p. 89. A. C. Hamlin, "On the Salmon of Maine," in U.S. Commissioner of Fish and Fisheries, *Report of the Commissioner for 1872 and 1873,* part 2 (Washington, D.C., 1874), p. 338, thought that the range of this "miniature shark" in Maine was "very limited" before introductions beginning around 1700.

30. *Burlington Free Press,* December 7, 1891. See *Maine Farmer,* March 23, 1865; May 3, 1866; *Farmer's Monthly Visitor* 6 (October 31, 1844): 157; *NHF&G,* 1876, pp. 8–9.

31. Seth Green, in *Transactions of the American Fish Culturists' Association, 1878* (New York, 1878), p. 12; Fred Mather, "Fish Culture," *Forest and Stream* 1 (August 14, 1873): 11; Theodore Lyman, in *Burlington Free Press,* February 26, 1869.

32. E. Lewis Sturtevant to commissioners, December 23, 1875, in *MF&G,* 1876, p. 46.

33. *VF&G,* 1866, p. 21; 1900, pp. 66–67.

34. *Burlington Free Press,* April 9, 1870; *VF&G,* 1873–74, p. 6.

35. *NHF&G,* 1872, p. 3; 1876, p. 6. On the Adirondacks see Philip G. Terrie, "Observations on Fish and Fishing," typescript report for the Adirondack Museum, 1972, especially pp. 3, 12–15, courtesy of Philip Terrie.

36. *MF&G,* 1891, pp. 52–53; *Burlington Free Press,* April 28, 1887.

37. W. C. Prime, in *Patrons' Rural,* November 27, 1885.

38. Seth Green, "Propagation of Fish," in *Transactions of the American Fish Culturists' Association, 1876* (Rutland, Vt., 1876), p. 11. See *NHF&G,* 1879, p. 16; 1884, p. 4; 1889, pp. 16–17; *MF&G,* 1880, pp. 14–15; 1881, pp. 10–11; 1891, p. 53.

39. *NYCFG&F,* 1896, pp. 176–180. See Perry, "From Colonization and Depredation," p. 19. Terrie, "Observations on Fish and Fishing," p. 20, suggests that today there is very little public desire to return the lakes to their original conditions.

40. *Maine Farmer,* May 23, 1867; *NHF&G,* 1866, p. 14; 1867, p. 572; 1870, pp. 7–8; 1894, p. 95; *MF&G,* 1881, p. 13; *Maine Farmer,* July 5, 1866; *Burlington Free Press,* November 14, 1891.

41. *NHF&G,* 1881–82, p. 5; 1885, p. 7; 1889, p. 17; *MF&G,* 1879, pp. 12–13; *VF&G,* 1912, p. 9; John W. Titcomb, "Vermont's Fish and Game Interests," *The Vermonter* 2 (July 1897): 212.

42. Somers, *History of Lancaster,* p. 100.

43. Sylvester Judd, *History of Hadley* (Springfield, Mass., 1905), p. 307.

44. Ibid., pp. 307–308.

45. *Vermont Watchman and State Journal,* October 30, 1878.

46. William Stark, in Leonard A. Morrison, *The History of Windham in New Hampshire* (Boston, 1883), p. 114.

47. "Report to the Legislature of Massachusetts, May 1857," p. 2, appended to Marsh, *Report*. See *MF&G*, 1871, p. 4.

48. *NHF&G*, 1878, p. 13.

49. *MF&G*, 1878, p. 9. See *MF&G*, 1879, p. 16; *NHF&G*, 1880, p. 15; 1914, p. 6; *VF&G*, 1881–82, pp. 19, 20.

50. *NHF&G*, 1871, p. 4.

51. Elinor Ostrom, *Governing the Commons: The Evolution of Institutions for Collective Action* (New York, 1990), pp. 177–178; *VF&G*, 1873–74, p. 59; 1875–76, pp. 6–7.

52. *New England Farmer*, March 27, 1869. See Theodore Steinberg, *Nature Incorporated: Industrialization and the Waters of New England* (New York, 1991), pp. 195–196.

53. George E. Burnham, "Amoskeag's Old Fishing Rocks," *Manchester Historic Association Collections* 4 (1908): 60; Lyman S. Hayes, *The Connecticut River Valley in Southern Vermont and New Hampshire* (Rutland, Vt., 1929), p. 552; S. Blodgett, "'Namaooskeag' Falls, and the Amoskeag Manufacturing Company," *Farmer's Monthly Visitor* 12 (October 1852): 291.

54. "Act to Incorporate the East Falmouth Herring River Company in Falmouth, March 12, 1863," in *MF&G*, 1872, p. 240. See *NHF&G*, 1867, app., p. 573; 1869, p. 10.

55. Steven Hahn, "Hunting, Fishing, and Foraging: Common Rights and Class Relations in the Postbellum South," *Radical History Review* 26, no. 10 (1982): 39. See *VF&G*, 1875–76, pp. 12–13.

56. Seth Green, "Fish Culture," appended to *NHF&G*, 1889, p. 41. See *VF&G*, 1872, p. 15; *MF&G*, 1876, p. 62.

57. Marsh, *Report*, p. 20; "Report to the Legislature of Massachusetts, May 1857," p. 4, appended to ibid.

58. Middleton Goldsmith, "A Communication about Fisheries and Their Present Relations to Law," pp. 1, 2, appended to *VF&G*, 1857.

59. Middleton Goldsmith, "The Increase and Preservation of Fish and Game," p. 6, appended to Marsh, *Report*; *MF&G*, 1872, p. 258.

60. *VF&G*, 1875–76, pp. 12–13.

61. Goldsmith, "Second Report," p. 57.

62. Goldsmith, "Communication about Fisheries," pp. 2–3, 4, 5.

63. *VF&G*, 1867, pp. 13, 25. See "Report to the Legislature of Massachusetts, May 1857," pp. 3–5, appended to Marsh, *Report*.

64. Steinberg, *Nature Incorporated*, p. 196; Daniel W. Bromley, "Property Rights as Authority Systems: The Role of Rules in Resource Management," in *Emerging Issues in Forest Policy*, ed. Peter N. Nemetz (Vancouver, 1992), p. 457; *MF&G*, 1876.

65. Hahn, "Hunting, Fishing, and Foraging," p. 52; *MF&G*, 1912–1914, p. 11.

66. *VL*, 1848, no. 44, p. 30; 1867, no. 45, pp. 55–56.

67. Middleton Goldsmith, "Public Policy in the Manner of Managing Fisheries," pp. 19–20, appended to *VF&G*, 1873–74. See *VF&G*, 1873–74, pp. 20–21.

68. *VF&G*, 1877–78, pp. 14, 19. See *VF&G*, 1887–88, p. 14.

69. Curtis, "Vermont Fish and Game Department," p. 9.

70. *VF&G*, 1895, pp. 119–120. See *VF&G*, 1898, pp. 30–31, 94–95.

71. *MF&G*, 1908, p. 24.

72. Gale, "History of Vermont Fish and Game Commission," p. 197.

73. *MF&G*, 1912–1914, p. 11.

74. *New England Farmer* 7 (April 1855): 188; Perry, "From Colonization and Depredation," p. 11; *NHF&G*, 1871, p. 3; 1877, p. 5.

75. *MF&G*, 1876, p. 45.

76. George H. Perkins, "The Relation of Natural History to Agriculture," in *VAG*, 1883–84, p. 208.

77. *MF&G*, 1907, p. 48.

78. Donald J. Pisani, "Forests and Conservation, 1865–1890," *Journal of American History* 72 (September 1985): 357.

79. Marsh, *Report*, pp. 12–15.

80. *Maine Farmer*, July 12, 1866.

81. *VF&G*, 1902, p. 20; *MF&G*, 1895, p. 16.

82. Frank J. Carleton, "Why Forest Preservation Should Interest Fishermen," in *VF&G*, 1900, pp. 98–105.

83. *MF&G*, 1896, p. 17. See *MF&G*, 1903, pp. 140–141.

84. For similar political strategies in the early U.S. Forest Service, see David Clary, *Timber and the Forest Service* (Lawrence, Kans., 1986), p. 40.

8. THE ROMANTIC LANDSCAPES OF TOURISM

1. *Maine Farmer*, February 9, 1899.

2. John Reiger, *American Sportsmen and the Origins of Conservation* (New York, 1975), p. 60.

3. John F. Sears, *Sacred Places: American Tourist Attractions in the Nineteenth Century* (New York, 1989), pp. 3–5; William C. Lipke, "Changing Images of the Vermont Landscape," in *Vermont Landscape Images, 1776–1976*, ed. William C. Lipke and Philip N. Grime (Burlington, 1976), p. 36; *Maine Farmer*, July 2, 1870.

4. Sears, *Sacred Places*, p. 4.

5. T. D. Seymour Bassett, "Documenting Recreation and Tourism in New

England," *American Archivist* 50 (Fall 1987): 554; Leroy T. Carleton, *Maine as a Vacation State* (Portland, 1902), p. 10; Richard R. Wescott, "Early Conservation Programs and the Development of the Vacation Industry in Maine, 1865–1900," *Maine Historical Society Quarterly* 27 (Summer 1987): 2–13; Richard W. Judd, "Reshaping Maine's Landscape: Rural Culture, Tourism, and Conservation, 1890–1929," *Journal of Forest History* 32 (October 1988): 180–190; *New York Times,* March 18, 1928, part 10, p. 10; *Maine Woods,* March 31, 1905.

6. *The Nation* 65 (August 19, 1897): 145–146; Maine Legislature, *Legislative Record, 1909,* p. 349; Nelson Dingley Jr., "The State of Maine," *New England Magazine* 4 (July 1891): 569.

7. J. H. Huntington, "Scenery of Coos County," in C. H. Hitchcock, *The Geology of New Hampshire* (Concord, 1874), pp. 636–637.

8. *NHFoC,* 1885, p. 11; 1928, pp. 122–123; Hitchcock, *Geology of New Hampshire,* pp. 73–87; *NHF&G,* 1880, p. 39.

9. Louise B. Roomet, "Vermont as a Resort Area in the Nineteenth Century," *Vermont History* 44 (Winter 1976): 5. See T. D. Seymour Bassett, "Urban Penetration of Rural Vermont, 1840–80" (Ph.D. diss., Harvard University, 1952), p. 324; Andrea Rebek, "The Selling of Vermont: From Agriculture to Tourism, 1860–1910," *Vermont History* 44 (Winter 1976): 17, 20.

10. Rebek, "Selling of Vermont," pp. 22–23.

11. *Maine Industrial Journal,* June 30, 1882. See "General Description by Counties," *VAG,* 1891–92, pp. 128, 131–132; *New York Times,* March 21, 1920, part 2, p. 2; *MeBLIS,* 1887, p. 239; 1898, p. 36; *Board of Trade Journal* 2 (October 1889): 185; *Maine Sportsman* 3 (September 1895): 11; *Maine Industrial Journal,* August 15, 1884; July 1916.

12. *Board of Trade Journal* 1 (June 1888): 79; 15 (July 1902): 77; 15 (April 1903): 369; *Maine Central* 7 (February 1899): 34; Carleton, *Maine as a Vacation State,* p. 14; *Maine Sportsman* 1 (May 1894): 9.

13. Robert H. Babcock, "The Rise and Fall of Portland's Waterfront, 1850–1920," *Maine Historical Society Quarterly* 22 (Fall 1982): 79–85; *Board of Trade Journal* 1 (January 1889): 271; 4 (October 1891): 166; 21 (July 1908): 137; 25 (October 1912): 310; 26 (February 1914): 450; *Maine Central* 4 (May 1897): 214.

14. Roomet, "Vermont as a Resort Area," p. 10.

15. *Board of Trade Journal* 1 (December 1888): 239. Lipke and Grime, *Vermont Landscape Images,* p. 11; *Maine Central* 7 (February 1899): 24.

16. *Board of Trade Journal* 8 (January 1896): 264, 265; 23 (August 1910): 167; 1 (August 1888): 119; 4 (September 1891): 143; (October 1891): 172; 10 (May 1897): 9; 23 (June 1910): 52; *MeF&G,* 1919, pp. 5–6. On Roosevelt

see *Maine Woods,* July 22, 1908; *Maine Central* 2 (September 1895): 6; C. A. Stephens, *A Busy Year at the Old Squire's* (Norway, Maine, 1922), p. 95.

17. *New York Times,* March 21, 1920, part 2, p. 2; *Maine Sportsman* 1 (September 1893): 3; Day Allen Willey, "A National Breathing Spot," *Outing* 52 (July 1908): 405–412; *Maine Central* 4 (July 1897): 282; Robert Herrick, "The State of Maine—'Down East,'" *The Nation* 115 (August 23, 1922): 183. See Alfred Elden, "Maine Fishermen at Grips with Death," *New York Times,* September 13, 1925, part 4, p. 8; *Granite Monthly* 42 (August 1910): 253; *Hill-Top* 3 (August 9, 1896): 2.

18. William Henry Bishop, "Hunting an Abandoned Farm in Upper New England," *Century Magazine* 26 (1894): 31.

19. Willey, "National Breathing Spot," p. 409; *Board of Trade Journal* 8 (December 1895): 230; 10 (August 1897): 107; 19 (June 1906): 58–59; *Maine Sportsman* 1 (May 1894): 11; Martha K. Norkunas, *The Politics of Public Memory: Tourism, History, and Ethnicity in Monterey, California* (Albany, N.Y., 1993), p. 93.

20. Newman Smyth, "The Lake Country of New England," *Scribner's Magazine* 8 (October 1890): 493; Norkunas, *Politics of Public Memory,* p. 76. See also *Maine Central* 1 (May 1894): 4; *MeBA,* 1892, p. 166.

21. Bishop, "Hunting an Abandoned Farm," pp. 30–43; idem, "The Abandoned Farm Found," *Century Magazine* 40 (1901): 884–892; Minnie L. Randall, "One of New Hampshire's Abandoned Farms," *Granite Monthly* 35 (July 1903): 44–46.

22. Bishop, "Abandoned Farm Found," p. 889.

23. *Board of Trade Journal* 9 (October 1896): 167; *NHA,* 1890–91, pp. 163–164.

24. George W. Perry, "A Convenient and Profitable Home Market," in Vermont State Horticultural Society, *Fifth Annual Report, 1908* (Bellows Falls, Vt., n.d.), pp. 85–86. See also *Board of Trade Journal* 12 (August 1899): 134; Harold Fisher Wilson, *The Hill Country of Northern New England: Its Social and Economic History, 1790–1930* (New York, 1936), p. 278.

25. Perry, "Convenient and Profitable Home Market," p. 87; *Hill-Top* 26 (July 30, 1921): 6; *MeF&G,* 1900, pp. 14–15. See *Board of Trade Journal* 4 (August 1891): 135; 5 (September 1892): 134; 12 (November 1899): 198; *MeF&G,* 1898, p. 14; Maine Legislature, *Legislative Record, 1909,* p. 350.

26. Paul W. Gates, "Two Hundred Years of Farming in Gilsum," *Historical New Hampshire* 23 (Spring 1978): 17; *VAG,* 1896, p. 109; *Maine Farmer,* July 8 and 22, 1897; *NHA,* 1881, pp. 294–296; *NHF&G,* 1884, pp. 39, 42; *Granite Monthly* 28 (June 1900): 347–349.

27. *The Nation* 65 (August 19, 1897): 145; Bishop, "Abandoned Farm Found,"

p. 890; Wilson, *Hill Country,* pp. 196–197, 293–294; Rebek, "Selling of Vermont," pp. 24–25; *Maine Farmer,* February 9, 1899. See *Board of Trade Journal* 19 (November 1906): 356; *Rural Vermonter,* October 7, 1887.

28. Paul A. Eschholz, "The Land of a Thousand Hills: Literary Images of the Vermont Landscape, 1865–1945," in Lipke and Grime, *Vermont Landscape Images,* p. 13; George S. Wasson, "The Rusticators at the Cove," in *Cap'n Simeon's Store* (Boston, 1903), pp. 155–166.

29. Reiger, *American Sportsmen,* p. 35; Maine Legislature, *Legislative Record, 1909,* p. 349; *Maine Sportsman* 3 (February 1896): 12; *NHA,* 1881, p. 308; Helenette Silver, *A History of New Hampshire Game and Furbearers* (Concord, 1957), p. 96; *Maine Woods,* February 10, 1905; Carleton, *Maine as a Vacation State,* pp. 17–18. See *Maine Central* 4 (November 1896): 32; *Maine Farmer,* March 10, 1877.

30. *MeF&G,* 1877, p. 17; 1875, p. 23; 1874, p. 22; 1876, p. 15; 1878, pp. 17–18; 1880, p. 5; *Maine Farmer,* August 4, 1864.

31. *NHF&G,* 1896, p. 6; *MeF&G,* 1881, pp. 7, 9, 18; *Burlington Free Press,* January 17, 1881; Reiger, *American Sportsmen,* pp. 38–39; Arthur F. Stone, *The Vermont of Today,* vol. 2 (New York, 1929), pp. 714–715; *Charter and By-Laws of the Vermont Association for the Protection and Preservation of Fish and Game* (Bennington, 1876); David Goodsell Gale, "The History of the Vermont Fish and Game Commission, 1866–1960" (M.A. thesis, University of Vermont, 1963), pp. 3, 38–39, 40, 55; Florence J. Perry, "From Colonization and Depredation to Conservation and Education: Progress Report of the Vermont Fish & Game Department," typescript, 1894, p. 16, reference files, Vermont State Archives; Silver, *New Hampshire Game and Furbearers,* p. 407; *Maine Farmer,* March 6, 1875; *NHF&G,* 1914, p. 11; *Maine Industrial Journal,* July 17, 1885.

32. *MeF&G,* 1904, p. 74. See *VF&G,* 1900, p. 74; 1904, pp. 10–11.

33. James A. Tober, *Who Owns the Wildlife? The Political Economy of Conservation in the Nineteenth Century* (Westport, Conn., 1981), p. 181; *MeF&G,* 1889–90, p. 4; 1908, p. 37.

34. *Maine Industrial Journal,* November 21, 1890; April 20, 1891; *Maine Woods,* November 15, 1907; *MeF&G,* 1898, p. 15.

35. *Maine Industrial Journal,* May 8, 1891.

36. *Maine Industrial Journal,* April 24, 1891. See *MeF&G,* 1898, p. 15; 1900, p. 13.

37. *Maine Woods,* February 17 and 24, 1905. See ibid., October 7, 1908. On hatcheries see *MEF&G,* 1898–1908; *Maine Woods,* November 15, 1907; February 21, 1908. On subsequent debates over plug fishing, see Maine Legislature, *Legislative Record, 1925,* p. 542; *1927,* pp. 626–628; *1931,* p. 760; *1933,* p. 154.

38. Tober, *Who Owns the Wildlife?* pp. 119–128. See Edward Howe Forbush, *A History of the Game Birds, Wild-Fowl, and Shore Birds of Massachusetts and Adjacent States* (Boston, 1912), p. 33.

39. *MF&G*, 1887, p. 30; *NHF&G*, 1880, p. 43; 1902, p. 4; 1914, p. 21; 1918, p. 7; *MF&G*, 1899, p. 20; 1901, p. 75; 1904, pp. 127, 139–140; 1909, p. 73; Perry, "From Colonization and Depredation," pp. 8, 59; *VF&G*, 1910, p. 14; Forbush, *History of the Game Birds*, pp. 370–373.

40. Sappiel Soccalexis, in "Caribou Notes"; "Father's Articles and About Game," p. 17, notebook; *New York Sun*, 1899; all in box 618, Fanny Hardy Eckstorm Papers, Special Collections Department, University of Maine; *MeF&G*, 1900, pp. 19–21; 1904, pp. 20–24; 1907, p. 20; 1919, p. 11; *Maine Woods*, September 30, 1902; December 23, 1904; Silver, *New Hampshire Game and Furbearers*, pp. 228–229; *Maine Farmer*, November 19, 1870; March 23, 1872, April 5, 1888; *Maine Industrial Journal*, March 20, 1896.

41. Leonard E. Foote, *The Vermont Deer Herd: A Study in Productivity* (Montpelier, 1946), pp. 7–12; Gale, "History of Vermont Fish and Game Commission," p. 12; Peter Giroux, "The Vermont Deer Herd: A History of Control," typescript, 1970, p. 1, Vermont State Library; Perry, "From Colonization and Depredation," pp. 3, 33, 35; Silver, *New Hampshire Game and Furbearers*, pp. 81–84, 205–206; *MF&G*, 1887, p. 31. See *MF&G*, 1891, pp. 48–49.

42. *NYCFG&F*, 1895, p. 166; Foote, *Vermont Deer Herd*, p. 65, 67, 73; Silver, *New Hampshire Game and Furbearers*, pp. 133, 201; Randall, "One of New Hampshire's Abandoned Farms," pp. 44–46; P. L. Buttrick, "Forest Growth on Abandoned Agricultural Land," *Scientific Monthly* 5 (July 1917): 82–87; James Walter Goldthwait, "A Town That Has Gone Downhill," *Geographical Review* 17 (October 1927): 542; Roland M. Harper, "Changes in the Forest Area of New England in Three Centuries," *Journal of Forestry* 16 (April 1918): 444.

43. *VF&G*, 1894, pp. 58–59; 1898, pp. 69, 76; *NHF&G*, 1892, p. 98; 1894, p. 92; Foote, *Vermont Deer Herd*, p. 13; Giroux, "Vermont Deer Herd," pp. 2–3; Silver, *New Hampshire Game and Furbearers*, pp. 83–84.

44. *VAG*, 1891–92, p. 157; 1912, pp. 3–5; *NHF&G*, 1902, p. 5; *MeF&G*, 1904, pp. 13, 70–71; 1916, p. 21; *Maine Sportsman* 14 (December 1906): 63–69; (March 1907): 134; *Maine Woods*, October 7, 1904; March 15, 1907.

45. *Maine Woods*, September 30, 1902.

46. *MF&G*, 1891, p. 51; *Boston Transcript*, in *Maine Sportsman* 2 (November 1894): 7; *Maine Farmer*, December 31, 1885. See ibid., January 19, 1888; *MeF&G*, 1900, p. 24; 1880, p. 3.

47. *Maine Farmer*, February 2, 1905. See ibid., January 9, 1890; February 23, 1905; May 30, 1907. According to an "informal poll" taken by the *Maine*

Woods (February 10, 1905), only 6 percent of Oxford County farmers favored total repeal of game laws.

48. Thomas R. Dunlap, *Saving America's Wildlife* (Princeton, 1988), p. 8.

49. *VF&G,* 1873–74, app., p. 53; *Maine Farmer,* January 19, 1905.

50. Jock Darling, in "On Dogging Deer," box 618, no. 10, Eckstorm Collection. See Abby Maria Hemenway, *Vermont Historical Gazetteer,* vol. 2 (Burlington, 1871), p. 613; *NYCFG&F,* 1895, pp. 223–224.

51. *NYCFG&F,* 1895, pp. 107, 216. See ibid., pp. 166–178, 107, 209–209, 214, 216–228; *Burlington Free Press,* May 10, 1869; November 29, 1883; April 19, 1886; Tober, *Who Owns the Wildlife?* pp. 194–199.

52. Manly Hardy, "Reply to 'Special'" (1891), in "Father's Articles and About Game"; Reiger, *American Sportsmen;* Dunlap, *Saving America's Wildlife,* pp. 37–38; Lisa Mighetto, *Wild Animals and American Environmental Ethics* (Tucson, 1991), pp. 27–41; Tober, *Who Owns the Wildlife?* pp. 43–51; *MeF&G,* 1891–92, p. 13; *MF&G,* 1891, p. 50; *Maine Sportsman* 1 (October 1893): 4. See Wilbur Day, *Wilbur Day (1864–1924), Hunter, Guide, and Poacher: An Autobiography,* ed. Edward D. Ives (Orono, Maine, 1985), p. 56; *New York Times,* November 4, 1889; *Maine Industrial Journal,* January 30, 1885; January 25, 1889.

53. *Maine Farmer,* February 20, 1902; Hardy, "Reply to 'Special'"; *Maine Farmer,* March 12, 1903. See Hardy, "Those Ninety Deer," in "Father's Articles and About Game"; *Machias Union,* January 3, 1905; *Maine Industrial Journal,* January 18, 1884; February 17, 1888; February 6, 1891; *Ellsworth American,* February 1, 1883; *Maine Farmer,* February 23, 1899; April 16 and October 1, 1903; Tober, *Who Owns the Wildlife?* p. 217; Maine Legislature, *Legislative Record, 1909,* p. 348; *Portland News,* January 10, 1928; *Maine Sportsman* 14 (December 1906): 62; *Maine Central* 4 (October 1896): 3; *Maine Woods,* December 21, 1906.

54. *Maine Industrial Journal,* February 17, 1888; *Maine Sportsman* 4 (June 1897): 3. See *MF&G,* 1900, p. 46; 1909, p. 77; *VF&G,* 1902, pp. 23–25; 1904, p. 141; 1910, p. 16; *NHF&G,* 1878, pp. 22–23; 1883, p. 30; 1891, p. 62; *MeF&G,* 1883, p. 18; 1886, p. 8; *Vermont Watchman and State Journal,* November 22, 1882; October 29, 1884; "Wardens," box 618, file 10, Eckstorm Collection; *Maine Industrial Journal,* November 19, 1886; January 11, 1888; January 25, 1889; Edward D. Ives, *George Magoon and the Down East Game War: History, Folklore, and the Law* (Urbana, Ill., 1988).

55. *Maine Farmer,* February 9, 1899; January 29, February 12 and 26, 1903. See ibid., December 8, 1898; August 8, 1901; February 4, 1904; Tober, *Who Owns the Wildlife?* pp. 55, 219.

56. Silver, *New Hampshire Game and Furbearers,* pp. 102–104; *Maine Farmer,* February 9, 1899.

57. *Maine Farmer,* July 26, August 2 and 25, 1900; C. H. Abbott, in *Maine Farmer,* January 24, 1900. See ibid., October 25, 1900; January 15 and December 3, 1903; January 28 and March 17, 1904.

58. Grand Master Obidiah Gardner, in *Journal of the Proceedings of the Maine State Grange, December 15–17, 1903* (Lewiston, 1903), pp. 23, 24; *Maine Farmer,* October 15, 1903. See ibid., July 26, 1900; January 29, February 26, and December 17, 1903.

59. *Maine Farmer,* May 17 and July 26, 1900. See ibid., October 15, 1903; January 28, 1904; *Waterville Mail,* February 8, 1900, in U.S. Forest Service Clipping File, "Maine Forests and Forestry," Forest History Society, Durham, N.C.

60. *Maine Farmer,* January 18, 1900; August 8, 1901, January 29, February 26, and April 9, 1903; July 7, 1904; January 19, 1905; *Maine Woods,* March 3, 1905; *Board of Trade Journal* 8 (March 1896): 330; *Maine Industrial Journal,* April 9, 1896; Carleton, *Maine as a Vacation State;* MeF&G, 1900, pp. 29–30; 1904, p. 15. See *Maine Farmer,* February 26, 1903; *Journal of the Proceedings of the Maine State Grange, December 19–21, 1905* (Lewiston, 1905), p. 25.

61. *New York Times,* December 20, 1913; *Maine Farmer,* January 19, 1905. See MeF&G, 1904, p. 15; 1908, p. 60; *Maine Woods,* February 10 and March 3, 1905; February 24, 1910.

62. "Decisive Test," Greenfield, Mass., *Gazette,* in *Maine Farmer,* April 11, 1907; "Deer Must Be Exterminated," in MF&G, 1916, p. 59. See VF&G, 1910, p. 28; MF&G, 1909, p. 71; Giroux, "Vermont Deer Herd," p. 3; Perry, "From Colonization and Depredation," pp. 37–38; NHF&G, 1906, pp. 171–172.

63. MF&G, 1907, p. 8. See NHF&G, 1914, p. 22; 1916, p. 8; 1922, p. 9; MF&G, 1910, p. 177; 1912–1914, p. 76; Giroux, "Vermont Deer Herd," p. 3; VF&G, 1912, p. 7.

64. *Maine Farmer,* October 25, 1900; January 13 and June 23, 1910; MeF&G, 1900, pp. 14–15, 1914, pp. 5, 21; Maine Legislature, *Legislative Record, 1909,* p. 350; *1917,* pp. 1031–32; VAG, 1891–92, p. 158; VF&G, 1900, p. 76; NHF&G, 1914, p. 7; *Maine Woods,* April 21, 1910.

65. NHF&G, 1918, p. 6; 1904, p. 126; 1906, pp. 171–172; MeF&G, 1902, p. 16, 1904, pp. 25–26, 57; *Maine Woods,* October 26, 1906. See VF&G, 1908, pp. 6–7; NHF&G, 1910, p. 3; MeF&G, 1919, p. 8; Perry, "From Colonization and Depredation," p. 21; Gale, "History of Vermont Fish and Game Commission," p. 190; Silver, *New Hampshire Game and Fur-bearers,* p. 92; Tober, *Who Owns the Wildlife?* pp. 207–210.

66. VF&G, 1894, pp. 39–40; 1902, p. 22; Perry, "From Colonization and Depredation," pp. 15, 20; Gale, "History of Vermont Fish and Game Commission," pp. 57–58; MeF&G, 1904, p. 57; 1914, p. 5; 1919, pp. 7–10.

67. Nathan Lowrey, "A Historical Perspective on the Northern Maine Guide," *Maine Historical Society Quarterly* 26 (Summer 1986): 2–21; *MeF&G*, 1898, p. 25; *Maine Sportsman* 4 (October 1896): 16; (November 1896): 56; (January 1897): 6; (February 1897): 3; 5 (September 1897): 9; (August 1898): 6; *MeF&G*, 1898, p. 36; 1900, pp. 44, 64.

68. Dunlap, *Saving America's Wildlife;* Reiger, *American Sportsmen,* pp. 80–81; Gale, "History of Vermont Fish and Game Commission," pp. 75–79, 126.

69. Tober, *Who Owns the Wildlife?* pp. 139, 184.

70. *New Northeast* 1 (July 1894): 4, 6.

71. C. Vey Holman, "The Advantages of Maine for Electrochemical Industries," *Transactions of the American Electrochemical Society* 19 (1911): 2–3; Lincoln Smith, *The Power Policy of Maine* (Berkeley, 1951), pp. 15–24; *Maine Sportsman* 1 (October 1893): 8; Maine Legislature, *Legislative Record, 1907,* p. 476.

72. *Maine Woods,* March 1, 1907; *Maine Central* 4 (October 1896): 10; Arthur L. Golder, "The Rangeley Lakes," *New England Magazine* 22 (July 1900): 565; *Board of Trade Journal* 10 (July 1897): 76.

73. Maine Legislature, *Legislative Record, 1907,* p. 484. See ibid., pp. 476, 480; *Maine Woods,* March 8 and 15, 1907; Maine Legislature, *Legislative Record, 1907,* pp. 473, 486; *Lewiston Journal,* February 9, 15, and 21, March 8, 1907; Committee on Interior Waters, "Report on . . . Union Water Power Company" (1907), box 924, MeSA; *Waterville Sentinel,* March 5, 1907. See Theodore Steinberg, *Nature Incorporated: Industrialization and the Waters of New England,* (New York, 1991).

74. David Richards, "An Eden out of a Country Farm: Purity and Progress in the Landscapes of the Poland Spring Resort," *Maine History* 34 (Fall 1994): 136–153; *Hill-Top* 3 (September 6, 1896): 1–2; *Board of Trade Journal* 19 (June 1906): 85; 21 (June 1908): 75; *Lewiston Journal,* February 23, 1921.

75. The *Waterville Sentinel* (July 1, 1908) claimed that Fernald's election was assured by "the shrewd business ability of the men who have made a fortune from a boiling spring in a state containing half a million just like theirs." See ibid., January 18, 1907; July 1, 2, and 17, 1908; *Maine Woods,* July 29, 1908; January 7, 1909.

76. *Lewiston Journal,* February 9, 1907. See ibid., February 23, 1921; *Waterville Sentinel,* February 27, 1907.

77. *Waterville Sentinel,* February 5 and 25, March 1, 2, and 5, 1907; *Lewiston Journal,* February 21, 1907; Maine Legislature, *Legislative Record, 1907,* p. 482.

78. *Maine Farmer,* February 14, 1907; *Lewiston Journal,* February 9, 1907. Even the bill's proponents admitted that rural Franklin and Oxford counties opposed the draw-down. See *Lewiston Journal,* March 7, 1907;

Maine Woods, March 8, 1907; Maine Legislature, *Legislative Record, 1907,* p. 478.

79. *Maine Woods,* March 15, 1907; *Lewiston Journal,* February 21, 1907. On monopoly in Maine's staple industries, see Richard W. Judd, Edwin A. Churchill, and Joel W. Eastman, eds., *Maine: The Pine Tree State from Prehistory to the Present* (Orono, 1995), pp. 391–419.

80. Maine Legislature, *Legislative Record, 1907,* pp. 380–381. See ibid., pp. 483, 487; *Lewiston Journal,* February 9 and 14, 1907; *Maine Sportsman* 14 (February 1907): 115; *Waterville Sentinel,* February 28, 1907.

81. *Lewiston Journal,* February 14, 1907. See ibid., March 7, 1907.

82. *Eastern Argus,* January 27, 1909. See *Lewiston Journal,* February 9 and 14, 1907.

83. *Lewiston Journal,* March 4, 1907.

84. Quoted in *Board of Trade Journal* 26 (February 1914): 457–458.

85. Stephen Fox, *The American Conservation Movement: John Muir and His Legacy* (Madison, Wis., 1985), pp. 106–107, 100.

86. F. C. Barker, in Committee on Interior Waters, "Report on . . . Union Water Power Company." See Barker in *Waterville Sentinel,* March 6, 1907.

87. Arthur G. Staples, "Evolution of Maine Waterpowers," *Sprague's Journal of Maine History* 12 (July–September 1924): 196; *Lewiston Journal,* March 22, 1921.

9. TRADITION AND SCIENCE IN THE COASTAL FISHERIES

1. Elinor Ostrom, *Governing the Commons: The Evolution of Institutions for Collective Action* (New York, 1990), p. 175. See Raoul Andersen, "Extended Jurisdiction and Fisherman Access to Resources," in *Modernization and Marine Fisheries Policy,* ed. John R. Maiolo and Michael K. Orback (Ann Arbor, 1982), p. 21.

2. Edward A. Ackerman, *New England's Fishing Industry* (Chicago, 1941), p. 43; Arthur F. McEvoy, *The Fisherman's Problem: Ecology and Law in the California Fisheries, 1850–1980* (New York, 1986), pp. 9–11; idem, "Toward an Interactive Theory of Nature and Culture: Ecology, Production, and Cognition in the California Fishing Industry," *Environmental Review* 11 (Winter 1987): 289–305; Garrett Hardin, "The Tragedy of the Commons," *Science* 162 (December 13, 1968): 1243–48; Richard A. Cooley, *Politics and Conservation: The Decline of the Alaska Salmon* (New York, 1963), p. 58; Margaret E. Dewar, *Industry in Trouble: The Federal Government and the New England Fisheries* (Philadelphia, 1983), pp. 20, 134–135; James M. Acheson, "The Lobster Fiefs: Economic and Ecological

Effects of Territoriality in the Maine Lobster Industry," *Human Ecology* 3, no. 3 (1975): 183–184; Francis T. Christy Jr. and Anthony Scott, *The Common Wealth in Ocean Fisheries: Some Problems of Growth and Economic Allocation* (Baltimore, 1965), p. 9.

3. Cooley, *Politics and Conservation,* p. 200. See Bonnie J. McCay and James M. Acheson, "Human Ecology of the Commons," in *The Question of the Commons: The Culture and Ecology of Communal Resources,* ed. McCay and Acheson (Tucson, 1987), p. 9.

4. Samuel P. Hays, *Conservation and the Gospel of Efficiency: The Progressive Conservation Movement, 1890–1920* (1959; reprint, New York, 1980), pp. 1–2, 23–27; Clayton R. Koppes, "Efficiency/Equity/Esthetics: Towards a Reinterpretation of American Conservation," *Environmental Review* 11 (Summer 1987): 129–130; McEvoy, "Toward an Interactive Theory," p. 295.

5. Elizabeth Ann R. Bird, "The Social Construction of Nature: Theoretical Approaches to the History of Environmental Problems," *Environmental Review* 11 (Winter 1987): 255; Dewar, *Industry in Trouble,* pp. 174–180; Lee G. Anderson, *The Economics of Fisheries Management* (Baltimore, 1977), pp. 151–186.

6. McEvoy, *Fisherman's Problem,* p. 99.

7. Bonnie J. McCay, "The Culture of the Commoners," in McCay and Acheson, *Question of the Commons,* p. 206. See Andersen, "Extended Jurisdiction," p. 18; and, generally, McCay and Acheson, *Question of the Commons.*

8. Orvar Lofgren, "From Peasant Fishing to Industrial Trawling," in Maiolo and Orback, *Modernization and Marine Fisheries Policy,* pp. 159–161; William H. Bishop, *Fish and Men in the Maine Islands* (New York, 1885), pp. 45–46, 50.

9. Ray Morris, "Maine Coast Philosophy," *Atlantic Monthly* 132 (July 1923): 35–36; *MeBLIS,* 1887, p. 114; George Brown Goode, *The Fisheries and Fishery Industries of the United States,* vol. 2 (Washington, D.C., 1887), pp. 25, 85; David Thelen, *Paths of Resistance: Tradition and Dignity in Industrializing Missouri* (New York, 1986), pp. 12–15. See *Maine Industrial Journal,* July 25, 1884; December 2, 1887; July 18, 1890; Alfred Elden, "Old Folk Inhabit Maine's Lonely Isles," *New York Times,* August 1, 1926, part. 4, p. 14; Bishop, *Fish and Men,* pp. 35, 50; Harold A. Davis, *An International Community on the St. Croix (1604–1930)* (1950; reprint, Orono, Maine, 1974), pp. 172–173; Ansley Hall, "The Herring Industry of the Passamaquoddy Region, Maine," in U.S. Commissioner of Fish and Fisheries, *Report of the Commissioner for the Year Ending 1895,* part 22 (Washington, D.C., 1896), pp. 452–453; Goode, *Fisheries and Fishery*

Industries, pp. 15, 19; Wayne M. O'Leary, "The Maine Sea Fisheries, 1830–1890: The Rise and Fall of a Native Industry" (Ph.D diss., University of Maine, 1981), p. 5.

10. Davis, *International Community,* pp. 85, 173, 236; Dewar, *Industry in Trouble,* p. 18; Goode, *Fisheries and Fishery Industries,* pp. 25, 85; *MF&G,* 1872, pp. 18–19; 1904, p. 43; 1910, p. 10.

11. Spencer F. Baird, "Conclusions as to Decrease of Cod-Fisheries on the New England Coast," in *MF&G,* 1875, p. 39. Baird summered in Treat's home town of Eastport in 1869. See William Healey Dall, *Spencer Fullerton Baird: A Biography* (Philadelphia, 1915), pp. 385, 419.

12. Spencer F. Baird to E. M. Stilwell, in *MF&G,* 1874, pp. 42–44; Baird, "Conclusions as to Decrease of Cod-Fisheries," p. 38. On the opinions of other scientists, see Dall, *Spencer Fullerton Baird,* p. 426.

13. *MF&G,* 1884, pp. 51, 46–47.

14. *MF&G,* 1884, p. 48; Committee on the Fisheries, "Report on Petition of T. D. Eliot" (April 14, 1870) (unpassed legislation), MSA; *MF&G,* 1872, pp. 26–27, 33; "Report of the Minority of the Committee on Fisheries and Game in the Matter of the Petition of Edward H. Burgess" (March 15, 1893), pp. 1–2, HR no. 139 (unpassed legislation), MSA. See McCay, "Culture of the Commoners," p. 204, for the same controversy on the New Jersey coast.

15. "Petition of Lilburne Hiller et al.," in *MF&G,* 1891, p. 62.

16. Committee on the Fisheries, "Report on Petition of T. D. Eliot"; petitions of Hon. T. D. Eliot (January 13, 1870), J. Howland Jr. (January 28, 1870), Gerard C. Tobey (February 11, 1870) (unpassed legislation), MSA.

17. Joseph D. Proctor, "The Resolutions of the Board of Trade of Gloucester," February 15, 1870. See remonstrances of J. C. Smith (February 1, 1870), Addison Gott (January 25, 1870), Edward D. Mandew (February 23, 1870), Pacific Guano Company (January 28, 1870), Isaac Rich (February 10, 1870), Cape Cod Railway (February 9, 1870) (unpassed legislation), MSA.

18. Committee on the Fisheries, "Report on Petition of T. D. Eliot." See *MF&G,* 1872, p. 17.

19. *MF&G,* 1872, pp. 17, 32–33.

20. *MF&G,* 1876, pp. 67–68.

21. *MF&G,* 1872, p. 40.

22. Remonstrance of A. F. Crowell (n.d.); "Petition of Lilburne Hiller et al.," in *MF&G,* 1891, p. 65. See *MF&G,* 1872, p. 39; "Act . . . for the Protection of Fisheries in the Headwaters of Buzzard's Bay" (May 29, 1874); Petition of Mr. Mason (March 24, 1874), chap. 282, MSA; "Report of the Minority of the Committee on Fisheries and Game in the Matter of the Petition of Edward H. Burgess," HR no. 139, March 15, 1893;

petitions from John W. Delano (February 12, 1890), Gerard Tobey (February 5, 1890), J. F. Phinney (February 24, 1890), citizens of the Town of Bourne [ca. 1890], chap. 229, MSA; *New Bedford Standard,* April 1, 1870 (regarding sports fishers). See Remonstrance of John F. Mason (April 21, 1874), chap. 282; Remonstrance of George D. Hiller (February 29, 1886), chap. 192; "Act Relating to the Fisheries in Buzzard's Bay" (March 23, 1891); "Office of the Selectmen" (March 21, 1891) (Fairhaven warrant), chap. 327, MSA; *MF&G,* 1894, pp. 33–34.

23. Petition of Edward H. Burgess (February 2, 1893), chap. 205; Petition of John S. Nicholson (January 31, 1901), chap. 184, MSA; Committee on the Fisheries, "Report on Petition of T. D. Eliot."

24. "Report of the Minority of the Committee on Fisheries and Game in the Matter of the Petition of Edward H. Burgess," HR no. 139, March 15, 1893 (unpassed legislation).

25. Charles H. Stevenson, "The Shad Fisheries of the Atlantic Coast of the United States," in U.S. Commissioner of Fish and Fisheries, *Report of the Commissioner for the Year Ending 1898,* part 24 (Washington, D.C., 1899), p. 261.

26. *MF&G,* 1890, p. 19, 51–64; 1892, pp. 16–17, 35–39; See *MF&G,* 1890, pp. 18–19; 1889, pp. 31–32; 1895, pp. 14, 34.

27. Carl J. Sinderman, *Statistics of Northwestern Atlantic Herring Stocks of Concern to the United States* (Highlands, N.J., 1979), p. 37; New England Fishery Management Council, *Environmental Impact Statement, Fishery Management Plan for the Atlantic Herring Fishery of the Northwest Atlantic* (Washington, D.C., 1978), unpaginated.

28. *Maine Industrial Journal,* June 26, 1891; Goode, *Fisheries and Fishery Industries,* pp. 1–12, 18–19, 36, 39; Francis H. Shaw, "The History of the William Underwood Company" (Ph.D. diss., Harvard University, 1954), p. 52; O'Leary, "Maine Sea Fisheries," pp. 12–14; Davis, *International Community,* p. 236; *MeBLIS,* 1887, p. 114; Maine Legislature, *Legislative Record, 1905,* pp. 592, 595; Hall, "Herring Industry of the Passamaquoddy Region," p. 443.

29. *Maine Industrial Journal,* May 13 and July 1, 1898; February 3, 1888; March 24, August 4 and 18, 1899; May 17, 1901; Hall, "Herring Industry of the Passamaquoddy Region," p. 466; *Board of Trade Journal* 12 (May 1899): 9; 14 (December 1901): 238; *MeSSF,* 1897, pp. 12, 23; 1898, pp. 11–13; 1900, pp. 8–9; F. C. Weber, *The Maine Sardine Industry* (Washington, D.C., 1921), pp. 4, 18; Shaw, "History of the William Underwood Company," pp. 6–7; John Toft, "Report on the Sardine Industry at Eastport, Maine," typescript, n.d., p. 75, Fogler Library, University of Maine; Davis, *International Community,* pp. 241, 244–245; *Ellsworth American,* February 11, 1903; Luther Maddocks, "Looking Backward: Memories from the Life

of Luther Maddocks," typescript, ca. 1920, p. 57, Fogler Library; Toft, "Sardine Industry at Eastport," p. 4.

30. H. F. Moore, "Observations on the Herring and Herring Fisheries of the Northeast Coast," in U.S. Commissioner of Fish and Fisheries, *Report of Commissioner for Year Ending 1895*, p. 389. See *MeSSF,* 1917–18, p. 22; Weber, *Maine Sardine Industry,* p. 7; *Maine Industrial Journal,* December 2, 1887; July 18, 1890; Toft, "Sardine Industry at Eastport," pp. 7–10; *Eastport Sentinel,* February 1, 1933.

31. *Eastport Sentinel,* February 22, 1933; Clarence Day, "Roque Bluffs: A Narrative," typescript, n.d., p. 60, Bangor Public Library, Maine. See Moore, "Observations on Herring," pp. 418–422; Maine Legislature, *Legislative Record, 1905,* p. 597.

32. Maine Legislature, *Legislative Record, 1905,* p. 591; *MeSSF,* 1909–10, pp. 14–15; 1911–12, pp. 15–16; 1913–14, p. 14; Moore, "Observations on Herring," pp. 418–422; 505–506; "Petition of Joshua W. Norton," February 10, 1845, box 174, env. 2; "Petition of Asa Turner," January 11, 1844, box 197, chap. 79, MeSA; Maddocks, "Looking Backward," p. 45.

33. *Maine Industrial Journal,* December 2, 1887.

34. Toft, "Sardine Industry at Eastport," pp. 10–11, 18; *Ellsworth American,* February 11, 1903; *Board of Trade Journal* 14 (December 1901): 238; Maine Legislature, *Legislative Record, 1905,* p. 596; *MeSSF,* 1917–18, p. 22.

35. Maine Legislature, *Legislative Record, 1905,* pp. 592, 593, 600; *MeSSF,* 1896, p. 13; Maddocks, "Looking Backward," pp. 108–109. See *MeSSF,* 1913–14, p. 14.

36. *MeSSF,* 1898, p. 10. See *MeSSF,* 1897, p. 13; 1900, p. 12; 1903–04, p. 13; 1909–10, pp. 9, 15, 17; 1917–18, pp. 7, 10; *Maine Industrial Journal,* March 1, 1889; Maine Legislature, *Legislative Record, 1925,* pp. 593–594, 408; *Machias Union,* February 21, 1905.

37. *Maine Industrial Journal,* November 24, 1899; Hall, "Herring Industry of the Passamaquoddy Region," p. 450; Maine Legislature, *Legislative Record, 1905,* p. 579. See *Machias Union,* February 21 and March 21, 1905; McCay, "Culture of the Commoners," p. 207.

38. Maine Legislature, *Legislative Record, 1905,* p. 607. See *Machias Union,* March 28, 1905.

39. *Machias Union,* April 4, 1905.

40. *Eastport Sentinel,* February 15 and 22, March 22, 1911; *MeSSF,* 1911–12, pp. 15, 25.

41. Leslie W. Scattergood and S. N. Tibbo, *The Herring Fishery of the Northwest Atlantic* (Ottawa, Ont., 1959), p. 10; Wallace C. Dunham and Elizabeth F. McGrath, *Trends in the Landings of Fish and Shellfish in Maine, 1928–1976* (Orono, 1980), pp. 4, 12; Stonington (Maine) Lobster

Cooperative, "A Plan for Reviving Maine's Finfish Industry," typescript, May 30, 1975, pp. 10–11, Maine State Library, Augusta.

42. *MeSSF,* 1909–10, p. 9; 1928, p. 18. See Maine Legislature, *Legislative Record, 1911,* pp. 553–554.

43. *MF&G,* 1894, p. 29; 1884, p. 20; 1889, p. 39. For an overview of lobster fishing in Maine, see Kenneth R. Martin and Nathan R. Lipfert, *Lobstering and the Maine Coast* (Bath, 1985), pp. 9–29; John N. Cobb, "The Lobster Fishery of Maine," *Bulletin of the U.S. Fish Commission* 16 (1889): 250–252; Goode, *Fisheries and Fishery Industries,* p. 24; S. M. Chase, "Lobsterman's Island," *Scribner's Magazine* 46 (July 1909): 1–11.

44. Richard Rathbun, in Goode, *The Fisheries and Fishery Industries of the United States,* pp. 781, 783–784; *MF&G,* 1889, p. 39; "Act for the Protection of Traps, Trawls, and Seines" (March 11, 1882), chap. 53, MSA.

45. Robert L. Dow, *The Story of the Maine Lobster* (Augusta, 1949), pp. 5–6; *MeSSF,* 1903–04, p. 40; Martin and Lipfert, *Lobstering and the Maine Coast,* pp. 31–33; Cobb, "Lobster Fishery," p. 256.

46. I am grateful to Nathan R. Lipfert for a chronology of Maine's lobster legislation. On rising concern in the 1870s, see Martin and Lipfert, *Lobstering and the Maine Coast,* p. 43. See also *Maine Industrial Journal,* December 17, 1886; *MeSSF,* 1917–18, p. 18; *Republican Journal* (Belfast, Maine), February 8 and 15, 1883; Cobb, "Lobster Fishery," p. 258; Edward H. Myers, "The Law of the Lobster," *New England Galaxy* 4 (Spring 1963): 16.

47. Cobb, "Lobster Fishery," pp. 246, 253; *Maine Industrial Journal,* December 17, 1886; February 18, 1887; February 1, 1889; November 1901, p. 18; *MeSSF,* 1891–92, pp. 22–25; 1903–04, pp. 37, 39; 1905–06, p. 29; *Republican Journal,* February 8, 1883; Martin and Lipfert, *Lobstering and the Maine Coast,* p. 16; petitions of Charles Stanwood (January 20, 1874) and Dudley B. Davis (February 7, 1874), chap. 110, MSA; *MF&G,* 1874, pp. 46–48; 1889, p. 39.

48. *Maine Industrial Journal,* November 25, 1887; *MF&G,* 1886, pp. 15–16; 1888, p. 28; 1889, p. 39; 1891, p. 15; 1894, pp. 29–30; 1907, p. 19; *MeSSF,* 1917–18, pp. 29–30; *Maine Sportsman* 1 (July 1894): 14.

49. *MF&G,* 1884, pp. 19–20; 1889, p. 34; 1891, p. 46; 1892, pp. 15–16; 1893, p. 21; "Act for the Better Protection of Lobsters" (February 12, 1884), chap. 212; "Act Providing for the Enforcement of an Act for the Protection of Lobsters" (May 22, 1885), chap. 256; "Act for the Protection of Lobsters" (May 26, 1887), chap. 314; "Act for the Further Protection . . . of Lobsters" (March 13, 1889), chap. 109; "Act for the Better Protection of Lobsters" (May 14, 1890), chap. 293, MSA.

50. *Maine Industrial Journal,* February 20, 1891; Governor Carl E. Milliken,

Annual Address (Augusta, Maine, 1917), p. 13; *Board of Trade Journal* 20 (October 1907): 284–285; *MeSSF,* 1902, p. 21; 1903–04, p. 33; 1905–06, p. 19; 1917–18, p. 30; Hugh M. Smith, *Report of the Special Commission for the Investigation of the Lobster and Soft-Shell Clam* (Washington, D.C., 1905), p. 142; *MeBLIS,* 1887, p. 112.

51. *MF&G,* 1894, p. 44; *MeSSF,* 1893–94, p. 35. See *MeSSF,* 1907–08, p. 18.

52. *MF&G,* 1886, p. 17; 1887, pp. 20–21, 24; 1891, pp. 14, 47; 1894, pp. 29–30, 45; 1895, p. 35, 37; remonstrances of Thomas Holway (January 29, 1889), Alonzo B. Veeder (January 28, 1888); Petition of James A. Mayhew (January 27, 1889) (unpassed legislation); "Act Relative to the Taking of Lobsters" (June 16, 1892), chap. 403, MSA.

53. M. Levi, in Ostrom, *Governing the Commons,* p. 94; George F. Freeman (South Duxbury) in *MF&G,* 1901, p. 48; *MF&G,* 1899, p. 15; "Report . . . on the Petition of Charles F. Davis for Legislation to Prevent the Extermination of Lobsters," HR no. 50, March 14, 1905; Petition of Henry H. Kimball, Secretary of Massachusetts Fish and Game Protective Association (March 14, 1905) (unpassed legislation), MSA. See *MF&G,* 1903, p. 95; 1904, pp. 50–51.

54. Petition of C. E. Davis (January 29, 1904); "Report . . . on the Petition of C. E. Davis for Legislation Relative to the Protection of Lobsters," April 7, 1907, HR no. 7 (unpassed legislation), MSA.

55. Francis H. Herrick, *Natural History of the American Lobster* (Washington, D.C., 1911).

56. George W. Field, "Biological Basis of Legislation Governing the Lobster Industry," *Science,* n.s., 15 (April 18, 1902): 612–616.

57. *MF&G,* 1907, pp. 17–21.

58. *MF&G,* 1908, pp. 25, 26; 1909, pp. 22–23, 25; "Report . . . on Petition of T. L. Davis Relative to Length of Lobsters," April 7, 1904, HR no. 12; "Report . . . on Petition of William J. Dunn . . . to Make the Legal Length at Which Lobsters May Be Sold Nine Inches," March 26, 1907, HR no. 25 (unpassed legislation), MSA.

59. P. Harvey Middleton, "Saving the American Lobster," *Scientific American* 101 (October 16, 1909): 277–278; *MeSSF,* 1896, pp. 20–21; 1903–04, p. 10; 1907–08, p. 19; 1911–12, pp. 17–18.

60. McCay, "Culture of the Commoners," p. 207; *MF&G,* 1918, pp. 18–19; 1919, p. 157; "Report . . . as Relates to the Better Protection of the Lobster," April 27, 1904, HR no. 20; Petition of James H. Bagnall (April 18, 1904) (unpassed legislation), MSA.

61. *MF&G,* 1894, p. 45; 1918, p. 248; 1919, p. 157.

62. *MF&G,* 1919, pp. 157–158.

63. *MF&G,* 1919, p. 157.

64. Maine Legislature, *Legislative Record, 1905,* pp. 695, 1055. See *Machias*

Union, March 14, 1905; *Board of Trade Journal* 29 (January 1917): 223; Governor William T. Haines, *Annual Address* (Augusta, Maine, 1913), p. 8.

65. Maine Legislature, *Legislative Record, 1917,* p. 1055; *1919,* p. 1146.

66. Maine Legislature, *Legislative Record, 1917,* pp. 1188–89. See *1919,* p. 1146.

67. W. A. Eastman to Horatio Crie, June 14, 1932, box 3, Maine Sea and Shore Fisheries Commission Correspondence, Department of Marine Resources, MeSA (hereafter cited as SSF). See Elmer Donnell to Crie, July 1, 1932, box 3, SSF; Maine Legislature, *Legislative Record, 1917,* pp. 1049, 1050–51, 1052, 1055, 1057, 1092, 1181, 1192, 1195; *1921,* p. 577.

68. Eastman to Crie, June 14, 1932; Acheson, "Lobster Fiefs"; idem, "Territories of the Lobstermen," *Natural History* 81 (April 1972): 60–69.

69. C. S. Beale to Horatio Crie, June 19, 1932, box 2; Fred F. Craine to Crie, August 28, 1930, box 3, SSF; Maine Legislature, *Legislative Record, 1933,* pp. 447, 452; *MeSSF,* 1932–33, p. 5; Martin and Lipfert, *Lobstering and the Maine Coast,* p. 77. See Ostrom, *Governing the Commons,* p. 99.

70. R. T. Henderson to Horatio Crie, June 2, 1932, box 4, SSF.

71. C. S. Beale to Horatio Crie, August 27, 1933, box 2, SSF; Maine Legislature, *Legislative Record, 1933,* p. 447; Vernon L. Gould to Crie, February 16, 1931, box 3; C. S. Beale to Crie, September 19, 1931, box 2; M. D. Gatt to Crie [ca. November 1931], box 3; Fred F. Crane to Crie, December 29, 1931, box 3; Crie to Senator Frederick Hale, January 13, 1932, box 4; C. S. Beale to Crie, October 19, 1932, box 2; Alvin Beal to Crie, August 18, 1933, box 2; Crie, ms. for proposed article, typescript, n.d., box 3, SSF; *Eastport Sentinel,* January 4, 1933; Llewellyn E. Crowley to Crie, February 4, 1931, box 3; Henry H. Y. Brownwell to Crie, July 1, 1931, box 2; Crie to W. T. Gardner, January 4, 1932, box 3; Esten L. Beal to Crie, February 8, 1932, box 2; Alton Dobbin to Franklin D. Roosevelt, March 17, 1933, box 3; George O. Beal to Crie, May 2, 1933, box 2, SSF; Maine Legislature, *Legislative Record, 1933,* p. 468.

72. *Eastport Sentinel,* January 4, 1933.

73. Ibid.; Maine Legislature, *Legislative Record, 1933* (special session), pp. 196–197; Horatio Crie to Howard Burdick, December 18, 1933, box 2; C. E. Pennard to Crie, June 11, 1934, box 2, SSF.

74. C. S. Beale to Crie, March 11, 1933, box 2. See F. M. Jasper to Horatio Crie, December 31, 1932, with clipping, box 4; Will Grindle to Crie, November 24, 1933, box 3; Llewellyn Crowley to Crie, December 1, 1933, box 3; Alton F. Dobbin to Crie, December 13, 1933, box 3; Clarence Goldthwaite to Crie, December 22, 1933, box 3, SSF; "The Fisherman's View of Proposed Legislation," typescript, February 23, 1933, vertical file, "Lobsters," Maine Legislative and Law Library, Augusta.

75. Horatio Crie to Llewellyn Crowley, December 16, 1933, box 3, SSF;

Maine Legislature, *Legislative Record, 1933* (special session), pp. 152, 197, 199.

76. Ralph E. Townsend, "Some Economic Issues in the Management of Maine's Shellfish Resources" (Ph.D diss., University of Wisconsin, 1983), p. 58; James M. Acheson, Robert Boyer, and Peter Daniels, "The Political Use of Scientific Information in the Maine Lobster Fishery," typescript, n.d., p. 13, courtesy of James Acheson; Robert L. Dow, "Changes in the Abundance of the Maine Lobster Resource with Sea Temperature Fluctuations and Increases in Fishing Effort," typescript, 1971, Fogler Library; idem, "Some Nonbiological Problems of Lobster Culture," typescript, 1974, Department of Maine Resources, Augusta.

77. Cooley, *Politics and Conservation,* pp. 29–33, 93–97; McEvoy, *Fisherman's Problem,* pp. 93–96, 99.

78. Cooley, *Politics and Conservation,* p. 98.

79. McCay and Acheson, *Question of the Commons;* Andersen, "Extended Jurisdiction."

CONCLUSION

1. Stephen Fox, *The American Conservation Movement: John Muir and His Legacy* (Madison, Wis., 1985), p. 110.

2. C. A. Stephens, *My Folks in Maine* (Norway, Maine, 1934), pp. 36–37.

3. Richard W. Judd, Edwin A. Churchill, and Joel Eastman, eds., *Maine: The Pine Tree State from Prehistory to the Present* (Orono, 1995), pp. 310–341.

4. John R. Stilgoe, *Common Landscape of America, 1580 to 1845* (New Haven, 1982), p. 3.

5. Lura Beam, *A Maine Hamlet* (New York, 1957), p. 25.

6. Elinor Ostrom, *Governing the Commons: The Evolution of Institutions for Collective Action* (New York, 1990), pp. 58–102.

Abbot, C. H., 217–218
Acheson, James M., 257
Ackerman, Edward A., 229
Ackley, H. A., 149–150
Adams, Sherman, 120
Adirondack Mountains, 180, 181, 214
Agassiz, Louis, 149
Agriculture. *See* Farming
Alewives, 50, 128–130, 185, 234, 236
Allagash River, 144
Allen, Ira, 17, 21
American commons, 8, 120, 264, 265
American Fish Culturists'
  Association, 146, 171
American Sportsman, 214
Ammonoosuc River, 20, 101
Amoskeag Falls (N.H.), 183
Andover (N.H.), 22, 30–31
Androscoggin River, 122–123, 126
Angling. *See* Fishing, elite
  perspectives on
Atkins, Charles G., 155, 159
Atwood, N. E., 236
Audubon, John James, 81
Augusta dam, 165
Ayres, Philip, 107, 114

Baird, Spencer F., 156, 233–234, 244,
  247
Baker, John C., 37
Bangor, 133–135, 166
Barker, Fred C., 228
Barrett, Charles, 155, 180
Barron, Hal S., 65
Barstow, Gov. John L., 97
Bass: black, 180–181; striped, 234, 236
Bates, J. Leonard, 2–3, 10, 174
Battell, Joseph, 2, 97
Beal, C. S., 259
Beam, Lura, 264–265
Beaver, 22

Belknap, Jeremy, 20, 21, 36
Bell, Michael M., 65
Bellows, Henry A., 155, 159
Bellows Falls (Vt.), 125
Berkshire Hills, 17
Berlin Mills Company, 99, 106–107,
  108, 114
Bidwell, Percy Wells, 24
Billings, Frederick, 97
Birds, protection of, 79–85
Bishop, William Henry, 201–203, 205
*Boa Constrictor of the White
  Mountains,* 102–103
Boardman, Samuel L., 156–157, 177,
  178
Bogin, Ruth, 127, 130
Bogs. *See* Wetlands
Boone and Crockett Club, 214
Boothbay Harbor, 253
Bounty laws, 43–44
Brackett, E. A., 160
Brackett, J. W., 219–220
Brassua Lake (Maine), 223
Bridgewater (Mass.), 142
Brigham, Uriah, 23
Bromley, Daniel W., 40–41
Brown, Orton B., 107
Brown Company. *See* Berlin Mills
  Company
Buzzards Bay, 234–240

Camel's Hump (Vt.), 97
Canada. *See* Maritime Provinces
Cape Cod, 234, 238, 247, 248
Cardigan, Lake (N.H.), 182
Caribou, 49, 210
Carleton, Frank H., 193–194
Carleton, Leroy, 216–217, 218, 219
Carp, 182
Cary, Austin, 108, 114–116, 118–119
Chesuncook Lake (Maine), 223

Churchill, Samuel, 24
Clark, Christopher, 67
Colonial Revival, 201–203
Comings, Albert G., 35–36
Commercial farming, 60–64, 66–67, 72
Common property management, 7–8, 9, 40–43, 50–56, 123–124, 126–130, 145, 229–231, 233, 236, 239, 254, 257–258, 260, 262, 265. *See also* American commons
Connecticut River, 18, 125, 132, 151, 158–159, 163–165, 185
Conservation: historians' perspectives on, 4, 6, 229–230, 261–262, 263–264; moral basis for, 9, 239, 245, 250; scientific, 9, 265; vs. preservation, 27, 222, 226. *See also* Farm reform; Fish conservation; Fish laws; Fishways; Forest conservation; Forestry; Landscape reform; Pisciculture
Cooke, Jay, Jr., 208
Cooley, Richard A., 229–230, 261
Coos County (N.H.), 17
Cox, Thomas R., 88, 106
Craig's Pond (Maine), 159
Crawford, Abel, 199
Crawford, Ethan Allen, 199
Crie, Horatio D., 256, 257, 258
Cronon, William, 4, 5–6
Crows, 81
Cumbler, John T., 132
Cushing (Maine), 128

Dairy farming, 63–64
Damariscotta (Maine), 50
Damariscotta River, 129–130
Dams: controversy over, 130–139, 142, 160–161, 223–228; Lawrence dam and fishway, 151, 153–154, 159–160, 161–163, 166–167; Lowell dam, 151; South Hadley dam and fishway, 151, 156, 158–160, 163, 164, 165; Augusta dam, 165. *See also specific rivers*
Darling, Jock, 214
Daughters of New Hampshire, 105–106
Davis, Charles E., 250–252
Davis, Gov. Daniel F., 165

Deer, 31, 45, 210–219; recovery of, 210–211; damage to crops, 211, 218–220; dogging (hounding), 213–214; jacking, 214. *See also* Hunting
Deforestation, 91–93, 101, 103, 112
Dennett, Liberty B., 117, 118
Derryfield (Manchester) (N.H.), 183
Diamond Match Company, 100–101
Dill, S., 51
Dogfish, 250–252
Double-gauge law (lobster fishery), 252–253, 256, 259–260
Doughty, Robin W., 83
Ducktrap Stream (Maine), 132–133

Eastern River (Maine), 128–129
Eastport (Maine), 247–248
Enfield (Maine), 135
Environmental history. *See* Conservation, historians' perspectives on
Essex Company. *See* Lawrence dam and fishway

Fairbanks, Henry, 82
Farm abandonment, 64–67, 76–77, 86–87
Farm clearing. *See* Pioneering
Farming: prospects in northern New England, 16–18; sheep, 32; commercial, 60–64, 66–67, 72; mixed, 60–64, 66; dairy, 63–64
Farm journals, 69, 70
Farm reform, 8–9, 73–79; debates over, 62–64; and fish conservation, 147. *See also* Landscape reform
Farmscape. *See* Landscape reform
Fellows, Joseph, 30–31
Fences, 45–46
Fernald, Gov. Bert M., 224
Fernow, Bernhard, 99
Field, George W., 252, 253, 256
Field and Stream, 214
Fish: distribution, 19; private property in, 184–189
Fish and game clubs, 207–208
Fish commissions, 9–10, 124, 145, 147, 151; founding of, 155–156
Fish conservation, 49–56, 178–182, 190; moral basis for, 123, 125,

126–127, 131, 136–137, 147;
democratic basis for, 142–144, 145,
172, 175–182, 190; tourism and,
169–170, 206–208; scientific basis
for, 172, 229–230, 233–234, 239,
240, 244, 247, 252, 253, 256,
259–262; resistance to, 174–175,
176; educational efforts in, 189,
209. *See also* Fish laws; Pisciculture
Fish culture. *See* Pisciculture
Fisheries, depletion of, 124–125, 146,
233–234, 237, 246
Fishing: pioneering and, 30, 125, 132,
137, 144; ethics of, 52–56;
commercial, 124–125, 128–129, 183,
184, 234; recreational, 169–170,
177–178, 182–183, 190; elite
perspectives on, 170, 178, 181, 182,
207–209; forage, 171, 178–179,
182–184, 206–209; ice, 206–207
Fish laws, 133–139, 140, 141, 144–145,
170–171, 174–176, 184. *See also* Fish
conservation
Fish propagation. *See* Pisciculture
Fish stocking. *See* Fish conservation;
Pisciculture
Fish transplanting. *See* Fish
conservation
Fish wardens, 142, 144
Fishways, 135–136, 142, 155, 157–168;
Lawrence dam and fishway, 151,
153–154, 159–160, 161–163, 166–167;
South Hadley dam and fishway,
151, 156, 158–160, 163, 164, 165
Fletcher, W. W., 159
Fly-casting. *See* Fishing, elite
perspectives on
Foraging, 28–31, 34, 42, 44, 124;
forage fishing, 171, 178–179,
182–184, 206–209
Forbush, Edward Howe, 83
Forest: distribution of, 19; destruction
of, 91–93, 101, 103, 112; role in
balance of nature, 93–96, 104–105;
climate and, 95; state, 98, 119;
tourism and, 101–102, 106, 112, 117,
118–119; fisheries and, 192–194. *See
also* Forest conservation
Forest commissions, 96–99, 112
Forest conservation: moral basis for,
87–88, 90, 93–96, 99, 107, 109–111;

popular views on, 90–91, 108, 111,
115, 116–117, 120; reforestation, 92,
210–211; New Hampshire, 99–111;
Maine, 111–120. *See also* Forestry
Forest fire, 98, 99, 116, 118, 119–120
Forestland taxation, 117–118, 119
Forestry: woodlot, 85–89; private,
98–99, sustained-yield, 107–108,
111, 114–116, 117; Maine vs. New
Hampshire, 111–112, 119–120. *See
also* Forest conservation
Foster, Nathan W., 155, 160
Fox, bounties on, 43
Fox, Stephen R., 263
Friendship (Maine), 128

Game laws. *See* Wildlife conservation
Game wardens, 220
Garfield, Harrison, 38
Garlick, Theodatus, 149–150
Gates, Paul W., 65
Goldsmith, Middleton, 185–187, 188
Goode, George Brown, 232
Gouldsborough (Maine), 123
Granby (Vt.), 93
Grand Lake Stream (Maine), 182
Grange, 68, 105, 113, 117, 118, 218,
219, 220
Graves, Henry S., 98
Great Depression, 257–260
Great Northern Paper Company, 99,
116
Great Pond Ordinance, 7, 118, 175, 186
Green, Seth, 148–149, 156, 158–159,
163, 180, 181
Green Mountains, 17, 64–65
Greenleaf, Moses, 46
Grime, Philip N., 78–79
Gross, Robert A., 63
Guides, hunting and fishing, 220

Hager, Albert D., 155, 180
Hahn, Steven, 43, 185
Haines, Gov. William T., 119
Hale, Edward Everett, 104
Hall, Frederick, 20–21
Hardhack, 38
Hardin, Garrett, 40–41
Hardy, Manly, 214, 215
Harpswell (Maine), 127
Hays, Samuel P., 3, 10, 91, 227, 230, 262

Herrick, Francis H., 252, 256, 259
Herring, 128, 240–247
Holmes, Ezekiel, 156
Holyoke Water Power Company. *See* South Hadley dam and fishway
Horwitz, Morton J., 131
Hosmer, Ralph, 116
Hough, Franklin B., 96
Hubbardton (Vt.), 24, 67
Hunting, 29–30, 45, 197, 211–212; ethics of, 47, 49; democratic basis for, 214–215; elite perspectives on, 214; forage, 214–215; licenses, 220

Ice-fishing, 206–207
International Paper Company, 99, 118
Ives, Edward D., 216

Jack, J. G., 92, 93
Jameson, Z. E., 65–66, 73–74, 75, 76
Johnson, John E., 102–103, 107, 110
Jonesport, Maine, 128
Judd, Sylvester, 182–183

Keene (N.H.), 101
Kellogg, E. C., 150, 153
Kennebec River, 1, 46, 114, 137, 156–157, 165, 166–167
Kineo House (Maine), 202
Kirkland, Edward C., 6

Lancaster (N.H.), 22
Landscape, perceptions of, 1, 2, 10, 35–39, 202–204, 205, 206, 218–219, 224–225, 227
Landscape reform, 73–79, 87–89, 204–205, 227
Lawrence, Ambrose, 151
Lawrence dam and fishway, 151, 153–154, 159–160, 161–163, 166–167
Lawrence, Mrs. Edward M., 227
Leavitt, O. H., 197–198
Lipke, William C., 78–79
Lobsterers' associations, 254
Lobsters, 127–128, 247–260; depletion of, 248–250; licenses for, 253; Massachusetts, 248–255; propagation of, 253; Maine, 254–260
Lobster wardens, 253–254, 257
Longfellow Hills (Maine), 17

Lowell dam, 151
Lumbering, 34. *See also* Forest, destruction of; Forest conservation
Lyman, Theodore, 154–155, 180

Machias River, 15, 144
MacLear, Anne Bush, 42
Magalloway Lake (Maine), 226, 228
Maine Board of Agriculture, 89, 156
Maine Central Railroad, 200
Maine Farmer, 150, 156
Maine Federation of Women's Clubs, 116–117
Maine Forestry Association, 118
Maine Forestry District, 119
Maine Lumbermen and Landowners Association, 118
Manchester (N.H.). *See* Derryfield
Maritime Provinces, 248, 254–255, 257, 258
Marlborough (N.H), 51
Marsh, George Perkins, 8, 94–95, 102, 153, 177, 184, 185, 192
Mason, Ellen M., 104
Massachusetts Board of Agriculture, 86, 149
Massachusetts Forestry Association, 97
Massachusetts Society for Promoting Agriculture, 85
Mather, Fred, 158–159, 180
McCay, Bonnie J., 231
McEvoy, Arthur F., 145, 229, 261
McMurry, Sally A., 69
Meetinghouse Pond (N.H.), 51, 52–53
Megantic Fish and Game Corporation, 223
Menhadens, 234, 236, 245
Merchant, Carolyn, 4, 5–6, 21, 69, 72
Merrimack River, 4, 18, 106, 109, 125, 151, 185
Middleboro (Mass.), 142
Mill River (Mass.), 160–161
Mississippi River, 193
Monhegan Island (Maine), 201
Monopoly, 130, 225, 237, 238, 241, 245, 260, 261, 262, 264
Moose, 31, 210
Morgan, Jonathan, 131
Mount Katahdin, 17
Mount Washington, 106, 199
Muller, H. N., 66

Multiple use, 198, 199, 204, 216–217, 222, 228
Musquatamisus Pond (N.H.), 53, 54–55

Nash, Roderick, 3, 6, 227
National Forest Reservation Commission. *See* White Mountain National Forest
Natural history, 69–73, 151, 191–192
Newburyport (Mass.), 162
Newcastle (Maine), 129, 130
New England Commission of River Fisheries, 156
New England Homestead, 103
Newfound Lake (N.H.), 182
New Hampshire Federation of Women's Clubs, 104, 105, 106
New Hampshire Forestry Commission, 107–108
New Hampshire Land Company, 102–103
Nickerson, A. R., 244
Nobleboro (Maine), 129, 130
Norkunas, Martha K., 202
North Andover (Mass.), 162
Northern New England: as a bioregion, 5; topography, 16–18

Oak, Charles E., 114, 116
O'Brien, Jim, 3
Oelschlaeger, Max, 3
Oquossoc Angling Association, 209, 223
Orland River. *See* Eastern River
Ornithology, 80, 82–83, 84
Ostrom, Elinor, 229, 257, 265
Otter Creek (Vt.), 20–21
Outdoor recreation. *See* Tourism
Outmigration. *See* Farm abandonment

Packard, Cyrus A., 113, 114
Panther, bounties on, 43
Paper industry, 99, 100, 106–107, 108, 112, 166
Passamaquoddy Bay, 240
Pasturing, 45–46
Patrons of Husbandry. *See* Grange
Pemigewasset River, 162
Penobscot Bay, 139
Penobscot River, 46, 133–139, 143

Perch, 177
Perkins, George H., 191
Perry, George W., 204
Petersham (Mass.), 28–29
Pheasants, 210
Phelps, Edward J., 97
Pickerel, 50, 53, 178, 179–180
Pinchot, Gifford, 8–9, 88, 99, 119
Pioneering, 15–16, 28; motivations for, 23–24; capital for, 24–25; impact on landscape, 25–28, 31–35, 59; fishing and, 30, 125, 132, 137, 144. *See also* Foraging
Pisani, Donald J., 3, 95, 192
Pisciculture, 146–148, 156–157, 158–159, 171–172; farmers and, 148–149, 150–151, 157, 169, 172, 173–174, 185, 187, 190–191, 207. *See also* Fish conservation
Poaching, 165–166, 168–169, 176
Poland Spring Hotel (Maine), 204, 224
Pollution, river, 154, 166–167, 192
Portland, 200
Pottle, David C., 150
Pownal (Vt.), 52
Presidential Range (N.H.), 105, 107, 115
Presumpscot River, 131
Prime, W. C., 181
Pulp and paper industry. *See* Paper industry
Putnam, Frank, 117

Quackenbos, John D., 104–105
Quail, 210

Randall, Minnie L., 203
Rangeley Lakes, 208–209, 222–228
Raquette Lake (N.Y.), 180
Raup, Hugh M., 5, 28–29
Reed, Alfred, 154–155
Reforestation, 92, 210–211
Reiger, John F., 106, 197, 206, 221
Republicanism, 10, 23–24, 31, 52, 123, 124, 143, 145, 245–247, 254–255, 261–262, 264
Ricker, Edward P., 224–227
Ring, Edgar E., 116, 117, 119–120
Robins, 80–81
Robinson, Henry C., 155

Robinson, Rowland, 77
Rollins, Frank W., 104, 107
Romanticism, 8–9, 71, 91, 197–198, 265
Roosevelt, Robert B., 146, 156
Roosevelt, Theodore, 117, 201, 214
Roth, Randolph A., 52
Rowland, Rev. L.S., 67–68
Rozwenc, Edwin C., 68
Rural beautification. *See* Landscape reform
Russell, F. W., 155

St. Croix River, 137, 150
St. George River, 50
Salmon, 151, 159, 163, 164, 165, 169, 178, 182
Samuels, Edward A., 82
Sanborn, Winborn A., 155
Sardine canning, 240–241, 243
Sargent, Charles S., 91
Sauer, Carl O., 35, 36
Sawmills, 99–101, 131–133, 135–139, 167, 170
Schoodic Lake (Maine), 182
Scup, 234, 236
Sears, John F., 199
Sebago Lake (Maine), 182, 223
Seine fishing, 236, 239, 244, 246, 260
Settlement. *See* Pioneering
Seymour, Horatio, 156
Shabecoff, Philip, 3
Shad, 151, 157–159, 162–163, 164, 182
Shaw, Benjamin, 143–144, 145
Sheep farming, 32
Smith, John B., 135, 136
Smyth, Gov. Frederick, 155
Society for the Preservation of New Hampshire Forests (SPNHF), 104, 112, 117
Soils: composition of, 18–19; conservation of, 69; distribution of, 73–74
South Hadley (Mass.), 182–183; dam and fishway, 151, 156, 158–160, 163, 164, 165
Sport-fishing. *See* Fishing, recreational
Staples, Arthur G., 228
Stark, William, 183
State forest commissions. *See* Forest commissions
State forests, 98, 119

Steinberg, Theodore, 4, 5–6, 161, 187
Stephens, C. A., 264
Stilgoe, John R., 264
Stilwell, Elias M., 212, 233
Surry (Maine), 245
Sustained-yield forestry, 107–108, 111, 114–116, 117
Swamps. *See* Wetlands
Szatmary, David P., 42–43

Talbot, George F., 113
Taunton River, 141–143, 160–161
Tautog, 234, 236
Taylor, Alan, 45, 63
Territoriality (lobster fishery), 247, 253, 257–258, 260
Thelen, David P., 233
Thornton, Tamara Plakins, 24
Timberland taxation, 117–118, 119
Titcomb, Frank W., 189, 193
Tober, James A., 209, 221–222
Todd, Rev. John, 32–33
Tourism: forest conservation and, 101–102, 106, 112, 117, 118–119; fish conservation and, 169–170, 206–208; rural resistance to, 173, 205, 206; wildlife conservation and, 197; expansion of, 198–206; water conservation and, 208–220, 223–224; lobster conservation and, 255–256
Tracy, Patricia J., 24
Tragedy of the commons, 40–41, 186, 229–230
Treat, Upham S., 150, 233, 247–248
Trespass, 29–30, 44–47, 118, 186, 216–217. *See also* Foraging
Trout, 51, 169, 170, 174, 177, 178, 192
Turner, Frederick Jackson, 15

Union Water Power Company, 223, 224, 226
U.S. Army Corps of Engineers, 109–110
U.S. Bureau of Fisheries, 156, 189, 193, 252, 261, 262
U.S. Division of Forestry. *See* U.S. Forest Service
U.S. Fish and Fisheries Commission. *See* U.S. Bureau of Fisheries
U.S. Forest Service, 92, 99, 105, 110, 116, 118

Vermont Board of Agriculture, 191
Vermont Fish and Game League, 189

Walker, Joseph B., 101–102
Walker, Joseph T., 104
Waquoit Bay (Mass.), 237
Wardens: fish, 142, 144; game, 220;
    lobster, 253–254, 257
Water power, conservation of, 222–228
Watershed, 109–111, 228; deforestation
    and, 95–96
Weeks, John M., 86
Weeks, John W., 110
Weir fishing, 125–127, 129–130,
    234–240, 245, 246, 260
Wetlands, 73–74, 75–76
White, Wallace, 226
White Mountain National Forest,
    105–111, 120
White Mountains, 17, 20, 64–65;
    forest conservation in, 99–111

Widner, Ralph R., 90, 111
Wildlands, See Timberland taxation
Wildlife conservation, 209–222;
    resistance to, 197, 209–210,
    213–222; tourism and, 197
Wilson, Harold Fisher, 65, 205
Winslow (Maine), 1
Wolf, bounties on, 43
Woodlot forestry, 85–89
Woods Hole (Mass.), 253
Woodstock (N.H.), 103, 110
Woolwich (Maine), 132
Worster, Donald, 8, 9, 71, 120,
    263–264

Yellow-bellied sapsucker, 81–83

Zukerman, Michael, 42